FRIENDS
OF ACPL

Children's Understanding of Television

Research on Attention and Comprehension

Children's Understanding of Television

Research on Attention and Comprehension

Edited by

JENNINGS BRYANT
Department of Communication
University of Evansville
Evansville, Indiana

DANIEL R. ANDERSON
Department of Psychology
University of Massachusetts
Amherst, Massachusetts

ACADEMIC PRESS 1983
A Subsidiary of Harcourt Brace Jovanovich, Publishers
New York   London
Paris   San Diego   San Francisco   São Paulo   Sydney   Tokyo   Toronto

ACADEMIC PRESS, INC.
111 Fifth Avenue, New York, New York 10003

United Kingdom Edition published by
ACADEMIC PRESS, INC. (LONDON) LTD.
24/28 Oval Road, London NW1 7DX

Library of Congress Cataloging in Publication Data
Main entry under title:

Children's understanding of television.

    Includes bibliographical references and index.
    1. Television and children--United States.
2. Attention in children. 3. Comprehension in children.
I. Bryant, Jennings. II. Anderson, Daniel R.
HQ784.T4C54 1983 305.2'3   82-16280
ISBN 0-12-138160-9

PRINTED IN THE UNITED STATES OF AMERICA

83 84 85 86   9 8 7 6 5 4 3 2 1

Contents

chapter **3**

Effects of Static and Dynamic Complexity
on Children's Attention
and Recall of Televised Instruction   69
JAMES H. WATT, JR., and ALICIA J. WELCH

chapter **4**

Children Learning to Watch Television   103
ROBERT KRULL

chapter **5**

Interpretation and Inference in
Children's Television Viewing   125
W. ANDREW COLLINS

Contents

chapter **6**

How Is Children's Learning from Television Distinctive?
Exploiting the Medium Methodologically   151
LAURENE K. MERINGOFF, MARTHA M. VIBBERT, CYNTHIA A. CHAR,
DAVID E. FERNIE, GAIL S. BANKER, and HOWARD GARDNER

chapter **7**

Television Watching and Mental Effort:
A Social Psychological View   181
GAVRIEL SALOMON

chapter **8**

No Shortcuts to Judging Reality   199
AIMÉE DORR

chapter **9**

Entertainment Features
in Children's Educational Television:
Effects on Attention and Information Acquisition   221
JENNINGS BRYANT, DOLF ZILLMANN, and DAN BROWN

List of Contributors

Numbers in parentheses indicate the pages on which the authors' contributions begin.

DANIEL R. ANDERSON (1, 331), Department of Psychology, University of Massachusetts, Amherst, Massachusetts 01003

JAMES A. ANDERSON[1] (297), Department of Communication, The University of Utah, Salt Lake City, Utah 84112

GAIL S. BANKER (151), Harvard Project Zero, Graduate School of Education, Harvard University, Cambridge, Massachusetts 02138

DAN BROWN (221), Department of Communication, University of Evansville, Evansville, Indiana 47702

JENNINGS BRYANT (221, 331), Department of Communication, University of Evansville, Evansville, Indiana 47702

CYNTHIA A. CHAR[2] (151), Harvard Project Zero, Graduate School of Education, Harvard University, Cambridge, Massachusetts 02138

W. ANDREW COLLINS (125), Institute of Child Development, University of Minnesota, Minneapolis, Minnesota 55455

[1]*Present address:* Department of Telecommunications, Radio–TV Center, Indiana University, Bloomington, Indiana 47405.

[2]*Present address:* Center for Children and Technology, Bank Street College of Education, New York, New York 10025.

xi

AIMÉE DORR (199), School of Education, University of California, Los Angeles, Los Angeles, California 90024

DAVID E. FERNIE (151), Harvard Project Zero, Graduate School of Education, Harvard University, Cambridge, Massachusetts 02138

HOWARD GARDNER (151), Harvard Project Zero, Graduate School of Education, Harvard University, Cambridge, Massachusetts 02138

ALETHA C. HUSTON (35), Center for Research on the Influence of Television on Children, Department of Human Development, University of Kansas, Lawrence, Kansas 66045

ROBERT KRULL (103), Communication Research Laboratory, Rensselaer Polytechnic Institute, Troy, New York 12181

ELIZABETH PUGZLES LORCH (1), Department of Psychology, University of Kentucky, Lexington, Kentucky 40506

LAURENE K. MERINGOFF (151), Harvard Project Zero, Graduate School of Education, Harvard University, Cambridge, Massachusetts 02138

KEITH W. MIELKE (241), Children's Television Workshop, New York, New York 10023

GAVRIEL SALOMON (181), School of Education, The Hebrew University of Jerusalem, Jerusalem 91905, Israel

DOROTHY G. SINGER (265), Family Television Research and Consultation Center, Department of Psychology, Yale University, New Haven, Connecticut 06520

JEROME L. SINGER (265), Family Television Research and Consultation Center, Department of Psychology, Yale University, New Haven, Connecticut 06520

MARTHA M. VIBBERT (151), Harvard Project Zero, Graduate School of Education, Harvard University, Cambridge, Massachusetts 02138

JAMES H. WATT, JR. (69), Department of Communication Sciences, University of Connecticut, Storrs, Connecticut 06268

ALICIA J. WELCH (69), Department of Communication Sciences, University of Connecticut, Storrs, Connecticut 06268

JOHN C. WRIGHT (35), Center for Research on the Influence of Television on Children, Department of Human Development, University of Kansas, Lawrence, Kansas 66045

DOLF ZILLMANN (221), Institute for Communication Research, Indiana University, Bloomington, Indiana 47405

Preface

Television is unquestionably *the* medium of mass communication in the present era. Concern over its pervasiveness and influence is repeatedly expressed in political, educational, artistic, and scientific circles. In the past, most of the concern has addressed the effects of television viewing on social behavior, particularly aggression, which led to numerous social scientific investigations of the effects of television. The results of these studies contributed to a general consensus that television indeed has a measurable impact on social behavior, although the form and extent of that impact are still debated. Besides demonstrating the potentially adverse impact of television, as in the studies of the effects of televised violence on antisocial behavior, the research on television effects also showed that watching television can increase prosocial behavior and that it can be an effective teaching instrument. The general conclusion must be that viewers learn from television and that this learning influences their behavior.

In the 1970s and 1980s public and research interest in television has been increasingly directed at the *act of television viewing* itself. This interest has taken several forms: the desire to increase the effectiveness of television for education and commercial applications; social concern about the apparent passivity and amount of time spent viewing television; and the belief that an elucidation of the fundamental psychological processes underlying television viewing is essential for any full understanding of its impact. As a result, researchers in psychology and communication have begun to study systematically children's attention to and comprehension of television. This research has been published in widely scattered book chapters and in psychology, communication, education, and human development journals. Yet no compilation or synthesis has been available.

This book brings together for the first time most of the major contributors to research on the *fundamental nature of children's television viewing*. Some of the contributors are more concerned with children's *attention* to television; others explore more directly children's *comprehension* of the content and format features of the medium; whereas some contributors are primarily concerned with *application* of these findings either to produce effective educational television programs or to mediate potentially harmful effects of viewing television. Yet, to the editors' surprise, the state of the art has advanced to such a degree that none of the research programs represented can presently be categorized as focusing strictly on "attention" or "comprehension." We have evolved to the point where the findings, protocols, or perspectives of most of the programs represented have begun to have an effect on the research of other scholars in the field. Such seems to be the natural process of forming a healthy, maturing area of inquiry.

The editors sincerely hope that this book will facilitate the process of integration that seems to have begun. We have frequently been told by our contributors, reviewers, editors, and others that the "time is right" for such a book. If so, and we think it is, we are pleased to have been in the right place, with the right idea, at the right time.

Each chapter of this volume presents the assumptions, methodologies, theories, and major research findings of a particular research program or tradition. As can be seen from an examination of the table of contents, the first four chapters are directed toward the examination of attention; Chapters 5 through 9 are oriented toward comprehension; and Chapters 10 through 13 deal with research application or intervention. The unifying feature is that each of the contributors is concerned to some extent with the process of television viewing per se. In the final chapter the editors attempt to draw on each of these reports to synthesize and provide a "state-of-the-art" report, as well as to suggest areas where clarification, integration, and/or future research are needed.

We hope that this book will be as useful and exciting for the scholars, educators, and students for whom it was written as it was for the editors. We have found its formation to have been a most gratifying and educational process.

chapter **1**

Looking at Television:
Action or Reaction?[1]

DANIEL R. ANDERSON
ELIZABETH PUGZLES LORCH

Visual Attention to Television

Television is popularly considered to be a visual medium despite its audiovisual nature. Theoretical discussions of its structure and "syntax" concentrate on visual factors such as editing, camera technique, and lighting to the relative exclusion of sound (e.g., Metz, 1974). The act of using television is even called "watching television." An account of the determinants and importance of visual attention to television is thus a necessary step toward a full understanding of television's use and impact.

In this chapter we justify the use of visual orientation, as opposed to visual fixation as a measure of visual attention. We then suggest that there has been a dominant, although usually implicit, theory of television viewing that underlies most popular and professional discussions of visual attention to television. This theory sees visual attention, es-

[1]This chapter was written while the first author held a Research Scientist Development Award from the National Institute of Mental Health. Much of the research discussed here was supported by grants from the National Science Foundation, the National Institute of Mental Health, the W. T. Grant Foundation, and research contracts from the Children's Television Workshop which in turn received the funds from the United States Office of Education.

1

pecially that of the young viewer, as primarily *reactive* and controlled by the television set. Based on our own research, we present an alternative: Visual attention is actively under the control of the viewer, even the young viewer, and is in the service of the viewer's efforts to understand the television program and to deploy attention efficiently between the television and other aspects of the viewing environment. We review the research (primarily our own) as it bears on these two alternatives, and finally we suggest issues requiring future research.

Visual Orientation versus Visual Fixation

Visual attention to television has been studied both as visual orientation (eyes directed toward the screen) and as visual fixation (precise location on the screen toward which eyes are directed, given visual orientation). In this chapter we treat visual attention as equivalent to visual orientation in part because studies of eye movements and visual fixations examine television viewing only under highly constrained laboratory conditions. The viewer in a typical eye-movement investigation is required to keep his or her head motionless while viewing a 17-inch television screen 3 feet away (Flagg, 1978), thus subtending a horizontal visual angle of about 21.7°. In a field study of children's television viewing at home, on the other hand, we have found that nearly all children's preferred viewing location (as pointed out by parents) is at a distance from the television such that the screen subtends a visual angle considerably less than that used in the eye-movement laboratory. Figure 1.1 summarizes data from 80 5-year-old viewers (Anderson, 1981). It is apparent that these children's preferred viewing positions generally place them so that the television screen subtends a visual angle close to that of parafoveal vision (generally estimated as 10° horizontally; Ditchburn, 1973). Although we have not yet analyzed the data from older children and adults, it appears to us from our videotapes of home television viewing that they view television at even smaller visual angles than 5-year-olds.[2] Since the optimal field of view for rapid picture identification is 11.5° (Saida & Ikeda, 1979), only in the most extreme cases do young children sit so close to the screen that successive eye-movements might be necessary for identification of scenes.

Besides being more ecologically relevant, an advantage of using visual orientation as a measure of visual attention is that it is tech-

---

[2]The study involves placing time-lapse video cameras in homes and videotaping family television viewing over a 10-day period.

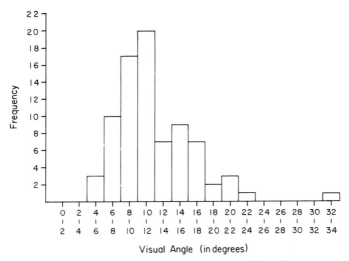

Figure 1.1. *Distribution of horizontal visual angle subtended by television screen at the preferred viewing position of 80 5-year-olds (M = 11.9°; SD = 4.6°).*

nologically easier to measure than eye fixations. Visual orientation to the television screen is readily recorded by an observer pushing a button when a viewer orients toward the screen and by releasing it when the viewer looks away. The button may be connected to a chart recorder, computer, or other data recording device that can record continuously in "real" time. Interobserver reliabilities are invariably high (e.g., Anderson & Levin, 1976). Eye fixation research, nevertheless, does have heuristic value and is useful in developing some educational and advertising television productions, but it remains unclear whether factors affecting eye-movements under laboratory conditions similarly influence visual attention in a more natural environment.

The Theories

The Popular Thesis: Visual Attention as Reactive

Until recently there has been no formally developed theory of visual attention to television. There is, nevertheless, an implicit theory that underlies nearly all professional and popular conceptions of the nature of television viewing. According to this theory, visual attention to television is fundamentally reactive and passively controlled by superficial nonmeaningful characteristics of the medium. In general, the youngest viewers are seen as the most reactive and passively controlled by it.

A plausible development of the reactive theory of television viewing can be illustrated using a modified schematic of social learning theory (Bandura, 1977), which is diagrammed in Figure 1.2. The reactive theory states that television elicits and maintains attention by virtue of certain salient formal features which include visual complexity, movement, cuts, pans, zooms, and some auditory features, such as sound effects. Attention may be further maintained by past reinforcement for attending, a high level of arousal, and the like. Once attention has been captured, more or less automatic comprehension and retention processes occur: "Models presented in televised form are so effective in capturing attention that viewers learn much of what they see without requiring any special incentives to do so [Bandura, 1977, p. 25]." Two important features of the reactive theory are that the direction of influence is from the television to the viewer and that the influence of viewer intentions, plans, strategies, and experience are minimized.

The theory needs a mechanism for television's ability to get and maintain attention. Jerome Singer (1980), who comes closest to explicitly developing the reactive theory of television viewing, proposes that television's "powerful appeal" occurs because the "constant movement and pattern of change that characterize the screen produces a continuous series of orienting reflexes in us, and it is hard to habituate to the set . . . [p. 46]." According to Singer, the television "plays on our orienting response and the inherent pleasure we get from manageable doses of novelty, neatly packaged in a small box [p. 48]." He considers children to be especially susceptible since they are less in control of their own behavior than are adults. Comprehension processes follow automatically and rotely from attention to television. The information retained is considered to be at a relatively low level since the "pressures of attention to novel stimulation can actually interfere

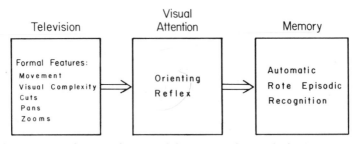

Figure 1.2. *A schematic diagram of the reactive theory of television viewing.*

with our ability to store [p. 38]." Television viewing, as a "passive" cognitive activity, "will yield considerable recognition memory without efficient retrieval [p. 42]."

Singer (1980) states notions that underlie nearly all popular conceptions of television viewing. Harvey Lesser (1977) promotes a similar idea: " . . . the child can be extremely attentive to a television program in an involuntary manner. For instance, he may watch primarily because of the newness and attractiveness of what is presented rather than because of any effort at deliberate attention. . . . This acceptance of an involuntary form of attention by the young child may perhaps be the basis for his extended viewing of television . . . [p. 61]." Lesser suggests that more voluntary, strategic forms of attention characterize the viewing of older children and adults. Lesser, as well as Bandura and Singer, generally subscribes to the proposition that the child is an active, cognitive, and social being. Television is seen as providing such an exceptionally powerful influence that the child becomes reactive in its presence.

Probably the most influential popular book on children's television viewing is the *Plug-In Drug* by journalist Marie Winn (1977). She takes the reactive view, repeatedly suggesting that children's attention is "controlled" by compelling formal features, including tight framing of television scenes, "contours that are evermoving," rapid scene changes, and overt movement. The reactive concept is also taken up by Jerry Mander (1978), an advertiser, in his book *Four Arguments for the Elimination of Television*. Mander again emphasizes television's "control" over attention: "We become affixed to the changing images, but as it is impossible to do anything about them as they enter us, we merely give ourselves over to them . . . [p. 204]." Like Singer (1980), Mander suggests that, as attention is controlled by the changing scenes, cognition is passive: "no cognition, no discernment, no notations upon the experience one is having" such that "the viewer is little more than a vessel of reception [p. 204]."

The reactive theory of television viewing has been popularly adopted, despite a paucity of evidence and a failure to consider alternatives. Pingree and Hawkins (1981) note that such an uncritical adoption of a theory of television viewing has profound consequences for theories of television's impact on conceptions of social reality (e.g., Gerbner & Gross, 1980). We argue that the unsupported acceptance of the reactive theory has also shaped notions of the cognitive effects of television on children (e.g., Singer, 1980), strategies for educational and entertainment television production (e.g., G. Lesser, 1974; H. Lesser, 1977), the use of television in educational settings (e.g., Postman, 1979), and conceptions of the potential use for and impact of new communications technologies (e.g., Swerdlow, 1981). To the degree to which social, educational, and communications policy and practice are guided by theory (if only implicitly), the reactive theory of television viewing may have already had a substantial impact.

The Antithesis: Visual Attention as Active

When we began our program of research, the reactive theory of television viewing implicitly guided our own initial efforts to identify those formal attributes of television programs which we and most other people thought "glued" children's attention to the television screen (Anderson & Levin, 1976; Levin & Anderson, 1976). A series of unexpected findings, however, forced us to a fundamentally different perspective on young children's television viewing. Rather than being a reaction to the screen, we have come to see television viewing as an active cognitive transaction between the young viewer, the television, and the viewing environment. We here offer a theoretical account of that transaction as it applies to visual attention to television.

The spirit of our theoretical effort is in keeping with recent cognitive theory directed at explaining the comprehension of connected discourse (e.g., Collins, Chapter 5; Graesser, 1981; Kintsch & Van Dijk, 1978; Mandler, 1979; Schank & Abelson, 1977; Stein & Trabasso, in press.) A basic notion is that ongoing cognitive processing of television is to a great extent schema driven. A schema is a mental structure composed of abstract knowledge reflecting prototypical properties of the individual's experiences. The schema is assumed to be acquired and modified by induction from previous and ongoing experience. It functions by guiding the comprehender in constructing expectations as to what information will occur (Stein & Trabasso, in press). We assume that the viewer, through experience with television as well as through general world experience, develops expectations about the temporal and conceptual flow of normal television programs. Importantly, we assume that visual attention to television is to a great extent driven by these expectational schemata. Fluctuations of attention to a program reflect the viewer's moment-to-moment understanding of the television content ("bottom-up" processing) as well as schematic strategies of processing television in the context of available alternative activities ("top-down" processing).

We suggest four premises for a theory of visual attention to television. These premises have been largely developed inductively through our studies of children's television viewing and have been initially presented in earlier papers (Alwitt, Anderson, Lorch, & Levin, 1980; Anderson, 1979; Anderson & Lorch, 1979; Anderson, Lorch, Field, & Sanders, 1981; Anderson, Lorch, Smith, Bradford, & Levin, 1981; Lorch, Anderson, & Levin, 1979). The premises represent an initial attempt to account for the onset, maintenance, and termination of "looks" at the television as well as the maintenance of nonlooking "pauses." The theory is diagrammed schematically in Figure 1.3.

PREMISE 1: ALTERNATIVE ACTIVITIES

Visual attention to television depends on the degree to which the viewing environment supports available alternative activities. This premise is hardly exciting but requires explicit statement. Many discussions of television viewing put the television itself as the sole determiner of attention, but it is apparent to us that the attractions and demands of alternative activities will affect the patterning of attention as such activities are carried on simultaneously with viewing. Indeed, a major characteristic of television, as distinct from cinema, is the radically different viewing environment. Time-sharing television viewing with other activities is apparently quite common (Robinson, 1981) and must be considered to be part of the viewer's attentional strategy.

PREMISE 2: MAINTENANCE OF VISUAL ATTENTION

Visual attention is maintained in part by the viewer's ability and need to answer "questions" posed by his comprehension schemata. If sufficient information is available such that there are no gaps in the viewer's understanding of the program, then attention is terminated. Such a circumstance might arise if, for example, the plot is utterly predictable, or if the viewer has seen the same program before. The other extreme leading to termination of attention would occur if the material were sufficiently unfamiliar or difficult such that the viewer is unable to apply a comprehension schema to the program. A young child viewing a talk show on nuclear disarmament strategies might be able to instantiate an elementary, perhaps overly predictable schema such as "adults talking" but be unable to comprehend the content of the conversation. Since the young viewer could pose no "questions," attention would be terminated. This concept of the schema maintaining attention by providing "slots" to be filled with expected information (taken from Schank & Abelson, 1977), bears considerable similarity to the notion of the inverted U-curve relating stimulus complexity and attention in research with animals and infants (e.g., Berlyne, 1960; Kagan, 1971).

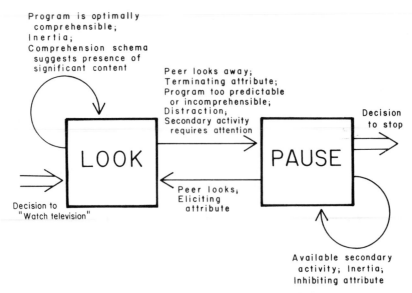

Figure 1.3. *A schematic diagram of the active theory of television viewing.*

A corollary feature of Premise 2 is that the viewer should be sensitive to content boundaries. When one program ends and another begins, other things being equal, attention will be terminated. This follows insofar as the comprehension schema should be fulfilled (all "slots" filled) by the end of the program, or barring this, the comprehension schema becomes irrelevant to the new program. This sensitivity to content boundaries stands in dynamic opposition to the attentional inertia of Premise 4 described later.

PREMISE 3: ELICITATION OF VISUAL ATTENTION

In periods of visual inattention, during which attention may be directed to an alternative activity, the viewer uses informative cues to guide visual attention back to the television screen. These cues are primarily auditory from the program itself but can also consist of other factors such as fellow viewers' attention to the television. We tentatively suggest that the viewer has a tendency not to process the audio at a semantic, conceptual level during these periods of visual inattention. Rather, he or she tends to monitor the audio for cues which indicate the presence of content relevant to the current schema.[3] The degree of

---

[3]Collins (1979) and G. Lesser (1974) have also remarked on the possibility that the inattentive television viewer monitors the audio for informative cues.

semantic processing of the audio, however, may vary with the demands of the alternative activity (cf. Kahneman, 1973).

Visual attention and inattention are maintained not only by ongoing cognitive involvement with specific program content (or nonviewing activity) but also by a nonstrategic attentional phenomenon called "attentional inertia" (Anderson, Alwitt, Lorch, & Levin, 1979). Attentional inertia maintains cognitive involvement across breaks in comprehension and changes of content. Attentional inertia also maintains nonviewing "pauses." Such a mechanism has been suggested by Hochberg and Brooks (1978) as being essential for the viewer to maintain continuity of perception over complex shot sequences.

IMPLICATIONS OF THE ACTIVE THEORY

The theory tries to account for the onsets and offsets of visual attention as a function of individual characteristics of the viewer, the form and content of the television program, and the nature of the viewing environment. Insofar as visual attention is guided by schematic comprehension, the active theory puts control of viewing directly with the viewer rather than with the television set. The viewer does not simply respond reflexively to inherently meaningless salient features of the medium. Rather, based on his or her experience with the medium, familiarity with the specific program, level of cognitive development, and general world knowledge, the viewer applies viewing strategies more or less appropriate to the program and viewing environment. Variations in visual attention to the television are thus seen as having a rational basis and represent an ongoing interaction between the unfolding conceptual content of the program and the viewer's understanding of that content.

Schema theorists generally point out that a person can apply alternative schemes, if available, depending on intentions, goals, and perceived demands of the setting (e.g., Graesser, Higginbotham, Robertson, & Smith, 1978; Pichert & Anderson, 1977; Schank & Abelson, 1977). It is similarly presumed here that, in principle, a viewer may apply different strategies of viewing depending on his or her reasons for watching television. Patterns of attention might differ depending on, for example, whether viewing is a primary or a secondary activity or whether the viewer is deliberately looking for specific information (e.g., the weather) as compared to seeking entertainment.

Since schemata applied to television viewing depend on experience, knowledge, and cognitive development, there are numerous implications for the analysis of children's viewing. A significant implication, we believe, is that if a child can effectively apply no schema, that is, finds the program largely incomprehensible, the child will for the most part not watch television if alternative activities are available (Premise 2). Thus, early viewing schemata, we hypothesize, include as a central component the direction of attention to comprehensible programming. Since an infant presumably enters the world with no television viewing schemata, per se, there should be a progressive development of viewing behavior, reflecting the child's increasing understanding of the world, cognitive growth, and experience with television. As viewing schemata develop, they include strategies controlling the maintenance and onset of visual attention to the television.

The theory provides a general structure within which considerable future development is required in order to make predictions about attention to television in specific situations. There is, nevertheless, considerable empirical support for the theory. In the next section we review supporting evidence, primarily from our own research with young children. Although most of the discussion applies to pre-schoolers, we believe that the theory is equally applicable to adults.

The Evidence

Qualitative Description of Young Children's Television Viewing

Many popular and professional discussions of children's television viewing include qualitative, anecdotal descriptions of children staring intently at the television, invulnerable to distraction. These anecdotes virtually never derive from systematic observation and may describe only exceptional circumstances. We here add our own qualitative observations, fully aware of their subjective nature. These observations are based, nevertheless, on watching literally hundreds of children watch television, both in laboratory and home situations.

When a preschool child watches a program such as Sesame Street in our laboratory (comfortably furnished, stocked with a variety of toys), the child does not simply sit quietly and stare at the television. The child plays with toys, converses with a parent or other child (if present), occasionally comments on the program, and the like. The child frequently looks at and away from the television, averaging about 150 looks at and away from the screen per hour (Alwitt et al., 1980; Anderson & Levin, 1976), the vast bulk of which are under 15 seconds in length.

It is our impression that toy play during viewing is often imaginative and constructive, and, although frequently interrupted by visual attention to the television, is continued when the child ceases looking, as if the interruption never occurred. This is not to say that play would not be different if the television was off (see Gadberry, 1974), but, nevertheless, the child appears to competently control his or her own behavior. In an experimental analysis, we could find no evidence that the quality of toy play in the laboratory differed following a viewing session, as compared to a parent reading stories (Anderson, Levin, & Lorch, 1977).

Our qualitative impressions of the young child's viewing in a laboratory setting is corroborated by descriptions of viewing at home (Bechtel, Achepohl, & Akers, 1972; Murray, 1972). In our own extensive videotapes of family viewing at home, we see a wide variety of viewing styles both within and between viewers. We speculate that style of viewing is a function of age, viewing environment, relevance of the program to the viewer, and viewer intention. As an example, a 5-year-old girl rather intently viewed a favorite program on Saturday morning but never looked at an evening hockey game. In the first case, we suggest, the child's intent was to be entertained by the television and in the second case to play with her father (who *was* trying to watch the hockey game). Nevertheless, in both cases, the child was rated by her parents as "watching television."

Impressionistic observations, while a starting point, are hardly conclusive of the active nature of television viewing. The popular writing of Mander (1978), Postman (1979), and Winn (1977), among many others, is replete with anecdotes of young children seemingly mesmerized by television. We only rarely see such rapt viewing by children in the laboratory or in homes, because even the intently viewing young child frequently gets up and leaves the viewing room. Until systematic analyses of home television viewing are published, we can conclude only that anecdotal qualitative accounts of children's viewing are conflicting.

Visual Attention to Television as a Function of Age

If attention to television by young children is reflexively controlled by dynamic formal features, infants and toddlers would seem to be the most vulnerable to such control. This follows insofar as such young children are seen as being more "stimulus bound" (e.g., Wartella &

Ettema, 1974) and less under self-control. If, as Singer (1980) suggests, the orienting reaction is the basis for television viewing, we would expect high levels of attention to television in infants and toddlers as soon as the orienting reflex is well established, or after about 3 months of age (Appleton, Clifton, & Goldberg, 1975). In fact, Hollenbeck and Slaby (1979) report that 6-month old infants do pay some visual attention to television at home when kept near the television in a playpen without toys (49% attention measured over 16 minutes; "chance" attention would be about 4%). Under less restrictive viewing circumstances, however, attention to television by infants and toddlers appears to be infrequent.

Anderson and Levin (1976) report a fourfold increase in visual attention to *Sesame Street* in the laboratory from 12 to 48 months of age. This increase with age was due partly to increases in the lengths of looks at the television but was primarily due to a dramatic increase in the frequency of looking at the television at 30 months of age. This finding was paralleled by parents' reports of a dramatic increase in home television viewing at 30 months. Carew (1980) recently substantiated this finding in a home observational study: She reported little attention to the television by toddlers until nearly a threefold increase in visual attention to television occurs between 24 and 30 months of age. Similarly, Schramm, Lyle, and Parker (1961) found that parents reported 2.8 years as the average age at which their children began to make regular use of television. The evidence thus converges on a large increase in television viewing at 2½ years of age.

Qualitatively, we noticed in our laboratory research that under age 2 ½ years children's attention appeared to be far more sporadic. The children rarely sat physically oriented toward the television. Older children, on the other hand, appeared to have the concept of "watching television" as something to do: They would take a position in the room oriented toward the television set (Anderson & Levin, 1976), playing with toys, but looking up frequently. In the present context, we suggest that by age 2½ years children have finally developed a viewing schema. The increase in viewing at age 2½ is consistent with theories of cognitive development which assert that between 2 and 3 years of age there is a major transition from sensorimotor representation and knowledge to higher level preoperational or "iconic" representation which is more symbolic and less immediate in nature (e.g., Bruner, 1964; Piaget, 1952). This cognitive growth finally enables the child to develop and apply comprehension schemas to television, leading to the observed sharp increase in television viewing. We do not see how the reactive theory can account for this early developmental trend.

Beyond 2½ years, visual attention to television increases throughout the preschool years (Alwitt et al., 1980; Anderson & Levin, 1976; Anderson, Lorch, Field, & Sanders, 1981) and may level off during the school-age years (Calvert, Huston, Watkins, & Wright, 1982). We suggest this increase reflects cognitive development, increased world knowledge, and understanding of the cinematic codes and format structures of television. To the normally developing child, more and more of television becomes understandable (cf. Collins, 1979) and thus becomes more potentially informative and entertaining.

The Relationship between Visual Attention and Comprehension

The reactive theory holds that understanding of television by young children proceeds rotely once attention has been reflexively captured by "electronic gimmicks." Although attention does not guarantee any memory or comprehension (thus many popular accounts of a child staring at the television blankly), attention is necessary for any memory and comprehension that does occur (e.g., Bandura, 1977).

Singer (1980) and his colleagues (Singer & Singer, 1981; Tower, Singer, Singer, & Biggs, 1979) suggest an interesting variation on this theme. If television is rapidly paced and thus reflexively maintains attention, it may not allow the child any opportunity for reflection and mental reorganization. Such memory as occurs is superficial and not reflected in recall. Thus Singer (1980) would seem to predict, at least in some cases, that the greater the attention to television, the poorer the comprehension.[4] In either case, however, the reactive theory asserts that the causal relationship is from attention to comprehension.

The active theory makes a substantially different assertion. Since the distribution of visual attention throughout the program is guided by the

---

[4]Singer (1980) and Singer and Singer (1981) cite one of their studies (Tower et al., 1979) as evidence that rapid television pacing interferes with comprehension. They showed preschoolers either Mister Rogers' Neighborhood or Sesame Street, followed by comprehension questions. They reported that, although there were no differences in overall comprehension performance, children who watched Mister Rogers' Neighborhood better answered factual questions whereas children who watched Sesame Street better answered inferential questions. In a variety of newspaper interviews and magazine articles, they attributed the lesser performance of the Sesame Street viewers on factual questions to the program's more rapid pacing which reflexively holds attention.

There are problems with this reasoning. First, there are numerous differences between the two programs other than pacing; any of these differences might produce differences in comprehension. Second, Tower et al. (1979) acknowledged that there was no evidence that the comprehension questions were equivalently difficult. Third, the two programs' goals are substantially different. The children may well have learned what each program's producers intended; the pacing of the programs may have been entirely irrelevant.

viewer's ongoing comprehension processes, the primary causal relationship is from comprehension to attention. These contrasting assertions about the relationship of attention and comprehension provide a
fundamental distinction between the reactive and active theories.

As a test of the relationship between attention and comprehension,
we created a situation in which children attended differentially to the
same program, after which we tested comprehension (Lorch et al.,
1979). One group of 5-year-old children viewed a Sesame Street program with a selection of attractive toys available in the room (toys
group), whereas another group viewed the program without toys available (no toys group). Continuous records of visual attention were obtained and cued recall of information from the program was tested.

The logic of the experiment is straightforward: If raising attention
increases comprehension (or decreases it), there should be a difference
between the toys and no toys groups reflecting the differing attention
paid to the television. As we expected, the presence or absence of toys
had a large effect on visual attention (which incidentally, provides
evidence for Premise 1). Visual attention in the toys group averaged
44%, and in the no toys group it averaged 87%. In contrast, however,
the two groups did not differ in recall.

The results do not mean that comprehension and visual attention are
unrelated. Although raising visual attention did not change comprehension, there was a significant correlation between the comprehension score for a particular question, and the average percentage
of attention during the exact time the information needed to answer the
question was presented. Recently, Pezdek and Hartman (1981) completed a study, part of which repeated the procedure of Lorch et al.
(1979). Their findings were completely in accord with ours. In addition, they found that comprehension of bits which were primarily visual in nature (little or no supportive audio) was reduced in the toys
group, suggesting the importance of audio cues in guiding visual
attention.

At the time we did this experiment, we implicitly adhered to the
reactive theory. The results produced a revolution in our assumptions
about children's television viewing. Doubling attention produced no
increase in comprehension, but comprehension and attention were
nevertheless related, suggesting that the causal relation was from comprehension to attention. We were led to the conclusion that the 5-year-
olds in the toys group were attending quite strategically, distributing
their attention between toy play and viewing so that they looked at
what for them were the most informative parts of the program. This
strategy was so effective that the children could gain no more from

increased attention. We were startled enough by the results to search for alternatives to the reactive theory. Sometimes, when our own comprehension schemata are sufficiently violated, we are moved to adopt new ones. We developed a new respect for children and also a hypothesis of comprehension-guided television viewing, a hypothesis that needed further verification.

There was a major uncertainty about the Lorch et al. (1979) findings: Our interpretation of the children's behavior as strategic depended on the positive correlations between visual attention at critical information points and comprehension of those points. It is possible that attention was reactively elicited at those times due to production devices inserted by Sesame Street producers who themselves may implicitly adopt the reactive theory of television viewing (cf. G. Lesser, 1974). Unfortunately for our interpretation, a content analysis of Sesame Street revealed that that was indeed the case (Bryant, Hezel, & Zillmann, 1979). The correlation between attention and comprehension could be consistent with the reactive theory.

If our hypothesis is correct that the young child's television viewing involves a strategy to attend to those parts of the program which are understandable, then any a priori index of understandability should be predictive of attention. We expected that television dialogue would be more understandable to perschoolers when the referent of the dialogue was immediately and concretely present than when it was spatially or temporally removed (e.g., Brown, 1976; de Villiers & de Villiers, 1978). Therefore, we also expected visual attention to be greater when the referent of the dialogue was visually or auditorily present ("immediate dialogue") than when it was not ("nonimmediate dialogue") (see Rice, 1979). We (Anderson, Lorch, Field, & Sanders, 1981) rated all points in 15 1-hour Sesame Street shows as belonging to one of three mutually exclusive categories: immediate dialogue, nonimmediate dialogue, and dialogue absent. One of the 15 shows was viewed by each of 150 5-year-olds and 149 3-year-olds (this data set is referred to later in this chapter as the "15-shows data"). At both ages, children attended more to immediate dialogue than to nonimmediate dialogue, as we predicted.

These results support the hypothesis that more comprehensible programming leads to higher attention. These findings are also in accord with a similar study reported by Krull and Husson (1979) after our work was in progress. However, since there was no control over variations in formal features which might have accompanied variations in dialogue type, we could not rule out the possibility that formal features were somehow correlated with dialogue type and so were actually determining attention. In a further study (Anderson, Lorch, Field, & Sanders, 1981, Study 2), we eliminated this possibility by experimentally manipulating program comprehensibility while holding formal features constant.

In order to accomplish this goal, we reduced the comprehensibility of *Sesame Street* by three different techniques. First, scenes within *Sesame Street* bits were rearranged, making the sequence of actions logically inconsistent and difficult to comprehend (a technique suggested from Collins, Wellman, Keniston, & Westby, 1978). Editing to rearrange scenes was done professionally, using preexisting edit points. Thus, the randomly edited segments were indistinguishable from the originals in terms of formal attributes. Second, professionally dubbed Greek language *Sesame Street* bits were used. The voices in these versions were similar in quality to the English language originals. Third, using a special editing procedure, the original dialogue was dubbed in backward, utterance by utterance, such that each utterance occupied the same video frames, but ran backward. Thus, original voice qualities, intonations, and approximate lip synchronization were retained, but the dialogue was semantically unintelligible. Both foreign language and backward dialogue segments were visually identical to the originals.

With toys available in the viewing room, 16 2-, 2.5-, and 5-year-old children viewed one of two 1-hour *Sesame Street* videotapes. Visual attention was continuously recorded. Each tape was composed of normal, randomly edited, foreign language, and backward dialogue segments. The two tapes were mirror images of one another, such that normal segments on one tape appeared in a distorted version on the other, and vice versa. This arrangement allowed for both within subjects comparisons across segment types and between subjects comparisons of attention to analogous segments. Since in each type of distortion, the formal features were retained in their original form, the comparison of attention to normal and distorted segments provides a strong test of the reactive versus active theories of television viewing. If young children pay attention to television because formal features elicit attention, there should be no differences between normal and distorted segments. If, on the other hand, young children's attention is guided by comprehension schemata (especially a scheme which includes seeking out comprehensible parts of the program), then attention to the distorted segments should be reduced. The results indicated that normal segments received higher attention than randomly edited segments, and much greater attention than foreign dialogue or backward dialogue segments. The reductions in attention due to the dialogue manipulations were somewhat less in the younger children but were significant at each age.

After the attention data were collected, 20 adult observers (10 for each tape) rated the comprehensibility of the segments. As reflected in the patterns of preschool visual attention, the adults rated normal segments as more comprehensible than randomly edited segments, which in turn were rated as more comprehensible than foreign dialogue or backward dialogue segments. These adult comprehensibility ratings correlated significantly with the children's visual attention.

The results of these studies combined with those of Krull and Husson (1979), Lorch et al. (1979), and Pezdek and Hartman (1981), strongly support the premise that preschoolers' comprehension of a program guides their visual attention. The results also contradict widely held beliefs in the psycholinguistic literature that young children watching television are insensitive to the comprehensibility of the dialogue (e.g., Snow, Arlman-Rupp, Hassing, Jobse, Joosten, & Vorster, 1976).[5]

In sum, five studies support the major premise of the active theory which states that visual attention is guided by the ongoing process of comprehension. Krull and Husson (1979) and Anderson, Lorch, Field, and Sanders (1981, Study 1) showed that attention was greater to immediate than nonimmediate dialogue; Lorch et al. (1979) and Pezdek and Hartman (1981) showed that raising attention does not by itself increase comprehension; and Anderson, Lorch, Field, and Sanders, (1981, Study 2) showed that reducing comprehensibility while holding the structure of formal features constant, reduced attention. Young children's visual attention to television is influenced by their understanding of program content, and the importance of comprehensible dialogue in maintaining visual attention is apparent.

Cues for Attention

FORMAL ATTRIBUTES

Several studies have been directed at analyzing the relationship between attributes of television programming and visual attention (Alwitt et al., 1980; Anderson & Levin, 1976; Bernstein, 1978; Calvert et al., 1982; Wartella & Ettema, 1974; Welch & Watt, 1982), and one study examined the relationship between visual attention and peer viewing behavior (Anderson, Lorch, Smith, Bradford, & Levin, 1981). We believe that most of the findings of these studies can be interpreted as

[5]We thank Mabel Rice for alerting us to this point.

supporting the notion that viewers pay attention according to comprehension schemata.

A key consideration in analyzing the relationship between visual
attention and attributes of programs is whether or not the viewer is
looking at the television at the time the attribute occurs. One aspect of
this consideration is the fact that visual attributes cannot influence
attention if the viewer is not looking at the television, whereas auditory
attributes can potentially influence visual attention in either case. Another aspect is theoretical: We hypothesize in Premises 2 and 3 that
different factors influence look onsets and look offsets. Look offsets
should be somewhat idiosyncratically tied to program content whereas
look onsets should be more stereotypically tied to auditory cues which
signal important content. [Other theoretical discussions of attention to
television (e.g., Krull & Husson, 1979) consider attention as a continuous variable and do not distinguish between onset and offset.] Most
studies have either examined the temporal overlap of attributes and
attention (Anderson & Levin, 1976; Calvert et al., 1982) or have used
correlational multivariate analyses predicting average levels of attention over blocks of time (Bernstein, 1978; Krull & Husson, 1979; Welch
& Watt, 1982). Only one study has examined attributes as a function of
looking and not looking.

In this study (Alwitt et al., 1980), we obtained continuous records of
the visual attention of 60 3-, 4-, and 5-year-old children as they
watched 3 hours of heterogeneous children's programming (1 hour per
session). Snacks and attractive toys were available during viewing. The
onsets and offsets of 37 visual and auditory attributes of the television
programs were rated. The analyses took into account whether or not the
child was looking at the television and whether the attribute had just
begun, was continuing, or had just ended. The analyses compared the
probability of a look being elicited or maintained by an attribute, given
the child either was or was not looking, to the probability of a look
being elicited or maintained in the absence of the attribute. (The analyses are described in detail in Alwitt et al., 1980, and in Anderson et al.,
1979.)

Several aspects of the results are worth noting here. There were
many more effective attributes during periods of inattention than for
periods of attention. Of the 14 audio attributes, 8 elicited attention from
the inattentive viewer (auditory change, sound effects, laughter, wom-
en's voices, children's voices, peculiar voices, and instrumental music); 3 inhibited attention (men's voices, individual singing, and slow
music); 2 had mixed effects (the onsets of lively music or rhyming
elicited attention, but their continuation beyond 3 seconds inhibited

attention); and 2 were nonsignificant (group singing and applause). If the child was looking at the television, both video and audio attributes were potentially effective. We found 6 visual attributes maintained attention (black man, black boy, white woman, active stationary behavior, cuts, and motion); 6 visual attributes terminated attention (animals, eye contact with the audience, still photos, long camera pans, long zooms, and maintained still camera); 8 visual attributes were nonsignificant (black woman, white boy, white girl, black girl, puppets, animation, inactivity, and script); 3 auditory attributes maintained attention (children's voices, rhyming, and sound effects); 3 auditory attributes terminated attention (men's voices, individual singing, and slow music); and 5 were nonsignificant (auditory change, peculiar voices, instrumental music, group singing, and lively music).

We have argued (Alwitt et al., 1980) that these findings are better subsumed by the active rather than reactive theories of television viewing. The production features which supposedly have the power to maintain the attention of young children were, with one exception, not particularly effective: Cuts weakly maintained whereas pans and zooms terminated attention. Motion, on the other hand, did have a strong maintaining relationship. Although auditory aspects of television are not usually discussed by adherents of the reactive theory, several auditory attributes are candidates: Auditory change and sound effects elicit attention, and sound effects also maintain attention. Thus it could be argued that our own analyses show that motion, auditory change, and sound effects are positively related to attention and thus provide support for the reactive theory. Although there are no conclusive arguments against this interpretation, we believe that the weight of evidence supports the interpretations of Premises 2 and 3: The viewer strategically uses attributes as cues for paying full attention. Sound effects and auditory changes indicate that some *change* in the program has occurred; a good stretegy could be to look up at the program at such likely change points, thus accounting for the eliciting effects. The maintaining effects of motion and sound effects, on the other hand, could well be due to their correlation with a certain type of content which is eminently comprehensible and entertaining to preschool children, namely, concrete immediate visual action. This latter interpretation is reinforced by the analyses of attribute effects as a function of age. Levin and Anderson (1976) show that for 1-year-olds (whose viewing should be most subject to primitive orienting reflexes) motion, sound effects, and auditory change have no relationship to attention to television. Auditory change shows a positive relation at 24 months and older, whereas sound effects and motion show positive effects at 30 months and older. These age effects would not be predicted by the reactive theory but are consistent with the active theory's premises that these attributes are effective by virtue of their association with understandable content. Alwitt *et al.* (1980) make analogous arguments for other attributes and other age effects.

THE INFLUENCE OF PEERS' BEHAVIORS

If young children use attributes of television as cues to guide their attention to comprehensible aspects of programs, it could well be that they also use cues provided by the social environment. Using the 15-shows data set, we examined the degree to which 3- and 5-year-olds' viewing behavior was related to the television program and also to the behavior of a coviewing peer (Anderson, Lorch, Smith, Bradford, & Levin, 1981). Children viewed singly, in groups of two, or in groups of three. One parent was always present. During the viewing session distractor slides were rear-projected onto a one-way mirror a few feet from the television screen. A new slide was shown every 8 seconds, with each slide change signalled by a distinct "beep." An observer (one for each child) took continuous recordings of the onset and offset of three behaviors: visual attention to the television, visual attention to the slides, and overt involvement with the television program. Involvement was defined as any overt expression of interest in the program other than visual attention (e.g., talking about the program, laughing, pointing, and so on).

We were interested, however, in whether the children's behavior showed synchronization indicating that they use each other's behaviors as cues for their own viewing. To illustrate the analyses of synchronization, consider two children, Child A and Child B, viewing together. Child A looks at the television; if Child B is not already looking at it at this time, Child B has the opportunity to initiate a look. If Child B is already looking at the television when Child A looks, then Child B has no opportunity to initiate a look. The analysis for look initiation calculated for each pair of children the proportion of times, given the opoprtunity, that a child looked at the television within a 3-second interval of the other child's look initiation. We did not distinguish *which* child initiated the look; the proportion of "following," given the opportunity, was calculated for the pair as a whole.

It is necessary to realize that two children might "follow" not only because they were influencing each other's behavior but also because they were both responding to some aspect of the television program. Therefore, proportions of following for pairs viewing together were compared with proportions of following for all possible pairs of children of the same age and group size who watched the same program, but not together. The degree of following in these "separate" pairs indicates the common influence of the program. Four dependent variables were thus analyzed: television look initiation, television look termination, slide distractor look initiation, and involvement initiation.

The proportions of following for each dependent measure, by pair type (together or separate) and age, are presented in Table 1.1. Comparisons of together and separate pairs indicated that, at both ages, peers influenced each other's behaviors above and beyond the common influence of the television program. When one child looked at the television, looked away from it, looked at the distractor, or initiated overt involvement, the other child tended to do the same. Our conclusion is that the children monitor each other's attentional and other behaviors as cues to their own behavior.

Another aspect of these data merits comment. Regardless of viewing condition, the children were more coherent with respect to one another in their look onsets than in their look offsets. This highly robust finding is consistent with Premise 3 of the active theory, that is, look onsets are cued by relatively stereotyped characteristics of the medium which the children have learned are predictive of significant content. Insofar as looks are maintained by relatively idiosyncratic comprehension of content as suggested by Premise 2, the substantially reduced coherence in look offsets is also expected by the active theory.

ATTENTIONAL INERTIA

Thus far, we have characterized visual attention to television as active, selective, and strategically guided by learned comprehension schemata. Premise 4, on the other hand, suggests a principle of "attentional inertia" in television viewing (Anderson et al., 1979) which would seem to be inconsistent with this perspective. The longer a view-

Table 1.1
Proportion of Synchronous Behaviors by Age and Pair Type

Measure	3-year-olds		5-year-olds	
	Separate	Together	Separate	Together
Television look initiation	.342	.431	.478	.552
Television look termination	.195	.311	.151	.227
Distractor look initiation	.124	.248	.144	.245
Television involvement initiation	.022	.067	.037	.121

er continuously maintains a look at television the more likely it is that he or she will continue to do so. The functions increase rapidly until a look at the television has been continuously maintained for about 15 seconds after which they increase only slowly. There are also virtually no age differences in the shape of the function. The shape of the function is not a result of averaging artifacts insofar as individual functions accurately reflect the shape of the group function (Anderson et al., 1979). The function characterizes visual attention to television in viewers as young as 12 months as well as that of adults; Figure 1.4 (solid lines) shows the functions obtained for six college students, each of whom watched 4½ hours of self-selected prime-time television.[6]

The question arises as to whether attentional inertia is specific to television viewing. Significantly, the inertia pattern characterizes the nonlooking pauses during which the viewer engages in some alternative activity. The longer it has been since the viewer last looked at the television, the less probable it is that he or she will look back (Anderson et al., 1979). This function is expressed as the dotted lines for the data from the six college students shown in Figure 1.4. Similar functions hold for children.

We have further examined the nature of attentional inertia in television viewing. One analysis examines the degree to which the phenomenon represents involvement with the particular content of a program. It could be that if the content is not involving (e.g., incomprehensible to young children), a look is ended early; whereas if the content is involving, the look is maintained longer. An alternative hypothesis is that attentional inertia represents a general nonspecific arousal such that attention is more likely to be maintained, following a period of continuous attention, regardless of the specific content. The question is whether or not attentional inertia in television viewing is content specific.

Consider the program Sesame Street. It is produced in magazine format consisting of approximately 40 discrete bits. Each bit is distinct from its preceding and succeeding bits in a number of ways: characters, formats, content, and concepts. As an example, a film bit about buffaloes may be succeeded by an animated bit about the number two. Now consider a look in progress at the end of a bit. If attentional inertia indicates involvement with specific content, there should be no relationship between the time a look is in progress prior to the bit boundary

---

[6]Krull and Husson (1979) note that there is a substantial correlation between average levels of attention from one 30-second interval to the next. They label this autocorrelation "attentional inertia." Since their data combine look onsets and offsets into a general percentage of attention per 30-second interval, it is not clear whether their autocorrelation is a measure of the same phenomenon.

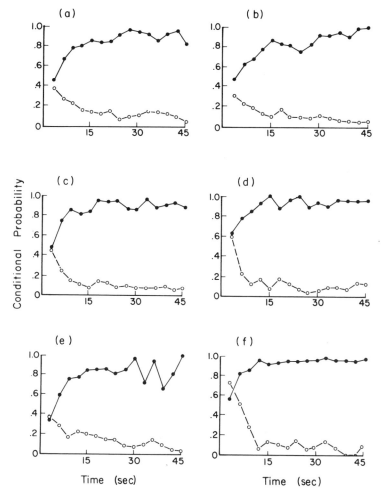

Figure 1.4. *Inertia curves plotted for six college students. Solid lines are for visual attention to television; dotted lines are for nonviewing pauses.*

and the time it remains in progress after the bit boundary. If, on the other hand, attentional inertia involves nonspecific arousal, then the longer a look is in progress prior to a bit boundary, the longer it should remain in progress after the bit boundary, regardless of the change in specific content. This inertial effect should be detected despite the fact that bit boundaries have a terminating effect on looks in progress (Alwitt *et al.*, 1980; Miskiewicz, 1980). Figure 1.5 shows average look length following the bit boundary plotted as a function of look length

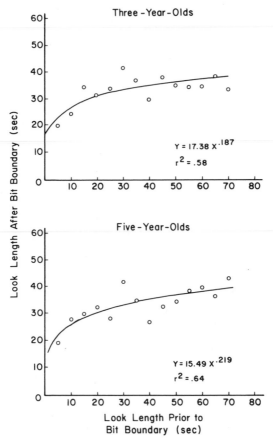

Figure 1.5. *Average time a look remains in progress after a bit boundary as a function of time the look is in progress prior to the bit boundary.*

prior to the bit boundary for the 15-shows data set. Despite variability introduced by the disruptive effects of the content boundary, the results indicate that attentional inertia is not content specific: Average look length after a bit boundary increases as a function of look length prior to the bit boundary. Attentional inertia serves to "drive" looks across content boundaries so that attention is maintained well into the next segment. Combined, the results suggest that the viewer is indeed sensitive to content changes, but that if attention is continuously maintained for some time prior to the content change, there is a tendency to maintain attention across that content change.

Since attentional inertia to television is observed in children as young as a year of age, and, since it is not bound to specific content, we believe that it is not a voluntary, strategic aspect of attention. Nor do we believe that this reliable aspect of attention evolved in the 30 years since children began watching television. Rather, we have begun to see attentional inertia as being the conceptual opposite of habituation. Since habituation is the attentional response to a repetitive, meaningless, static stimulus, then attentional inertia may be the attentional response to a somewhat unpredictable, meaningful, dynamic stimulus. Attentional inertia, we believe, provides the means by which attention is maintained to a source of information even across breaks in the continuity of that information. Rather than the television-viewing child being a victim of attentional inertia, we see it as an essential weapon in the child's cognitive arsenal. Attentional inertia allows the child to keep processing a stimulus even when it is currently not understandable. Attentional inertia thus sometimes produces a dynamic tension with program comprehensibility: Although in general the young child stops paying attention when the program becomes incomprehensible, attentional inertia serves to maintain attention further than it might otherwise go. As such, attentional inertia may be part of the means by which the child comes to process a stimulus that is poorly understood. This enforced, nonstrategic, attention may thus occasionally provide the child the means by which he or she ventures into unknown cognitive territory, occasionally leading to new cognitive discoveries.

Summary of the Evidence

Table 1.2 summarizes the empirically derived factors leading to the initiation, maintenance, and termination of looks, as well as maintenance of pauses. Each of these factors (attribute effects, program comprehensibility, peer viewing behavior, distraction, inertia, and age) has

Table 1.2
Factors Affecting Visual Attention

Look maintained	Look terminated
Age (looks longer with age)	Distraction
Inertia	Peer looks away from television
Program comprehensibility	Program incomprehensible
Maintaining attributes (e.g., motion)	Program boundary
	Terminating attribute (e.g., long zoom)
Look elicited	**Pause maintained**
Age (pauses interrupted more frequently with age)	Inertia
	Available alternative activity
Eliciting attribute (e.g., child voice)	Inhibiting attribute (e.g., male voice)
Peer looks at television	

effects generally consistent with the active theory of television viewing. Several effects, such as the influence of motion, may also be consistent with the reactive theory, but most of the factors appear to be beyond the scope of the reactive theory either to predict or explain. In addition to findings from our laboratory, the active theory is supported by the work of Pezdek and Hartman (1981) and Krull and Husson (1979) described earlier. Krull and Husson (1979) also report "cycles of anticipation" in visual attention by school-age children viewing *The Electric Company*. These cycles apparently correspond roughly to bit boundaries and were interpreted as indicating the children's knowledge of the overall format of the program. The cycles were not found in preschoolers' viewing of *Sesame Street*. Insofar as the "cycles of anticipation" prove to be reliable phenomena, Krull and Husson's interpretation is consistent with Premises 2 and 3 of the active theory: Children should be responsive to the format structure of a television program, within the limits of their cognitive development. It may be that preschool children tend to deal with television in units considerably smaller than whole programs (a notion consistent with comprehension studies; e.g., Collins, 1979), and thus fail to show evidence of such cycles.

Other findings, such as relationships of attention to measures of production dynamics (e.g., scene "entropy" as discussed by Welch & Watt, 1982) are difficult to interpret as uniquely supporting either the active or reactive theories, since factors such as the comprehensibility of the content may be intimately related to the structure of the formal features used to convey that content. There is as yet no evidence that visual attention to television is determined by formal features separately from content (but see Bryant, Zillmann, & Brown, Chapter 9).

Status of the Active Theory

The premises of an active theory of television viewing which we have offered here constitute only the merest beginning for a full theoretical and empirical accounting of visual attention to television. A number of issues that should be explored further include:

1. The role of auditory attention—does a viewer indeed tend to listen with less understanding when not looking at the screen? Anderson *et al.* (1979) reviewed the meager evidence concerning auditory attention to television. Since then, little has been added to our understanding other than a number of findings which indicate the importance of audio in determining visual attention to television (Aisbett & Holman, 1981; Anderson, Lorch, Field, & Sanders, 1981; Calvert *et al.*, 1982; Krull & Husson, 1979; Pezdek & Hartman, 1981).

2. Methods should be developed for characterizing the real-time structure of a television narrative. The active theory asserts that visual attention should reflect both format and content features of the television program. Perhaps variations on techniques developed by Newtson (1976) for segmenting visual action sequences could be combined with techniques of text narrative analysis (e.g., Kintsch & Van Dijk, 1978; Mandler & Johnson, 1977; Omanson, in press; Stein & Glenn, 1979). When within-segment content boundaries can be identified in real time, relationships of attention to content fluctuations can be examined.

3. The influence of the television-viewing environment should be further explored. One approach is the observation of television viewing at home such as that of Bechtel et al. (1972) and our own efforts. Another approach might be to experimentally manipulate television-viewing environments such as the toy versus no toy or peer presence experiments. A further approach might be to manipulate the perceived demands of the viewing situation. Graesser et al. (1978), for example, found that readers comprehended a newspaper differently when they expected to be tested on the content as compared to reading it for entertainment. Salomon (see Chapter 7) has made the argument that processing of television differs from text in part because of the differences in context in which the media are encountered, particularly by children.

4. Research that experimentally varies supposedly attention-getting production features while holding comprehensibility constant should be attempted. Production devices such as quick cutting, unusual camera angles, and dramatic lighting are the very hallmark of professional television and are widely believed to be essential in children's educational programming (e.g., G. Lesser, 1974). We have remarked on viewers' uses of many of these devices as "markers" of interesting content, but a question remains as to whether they have intrinsic value in raising attention to and comprehension of a program as a whole (see Bryant et al. Chapter 9). If they do, the premises of the active theory must be significantly modified to account for such an effect. Such a modification may constitute a synthesis between the active and reactive theories.

Toward a Synthesis

We have presented the outlines of a theory of visual attention to television which has as its central premise the cognitively active nature of television viewing. But this central premise is contrary to the deeply

held beliefs of many lay and research people that television viewing is
fundamentally reactive and passive. These beliefs, despite the weight
of evidence to the contrary, must have some foundation. Several investigators have offered hypotheses that may point toward an eventual
synthesis and resolution of the active and reactive theories.

Salomon (see Chapter 7) argued that television viewing may, for the
experienced viewer, be a highly overlearned cognitive activity such
that it consumes little in the way of mental resources. For the adult and
older child, viewing becomes virtually automatic. Furthermore, since
typical commerical (American) programming provides little that is cognitively challenging, the viewer tends to ascribe the perceived cognitive demands of viewing as being low. In combination, the viewer
expends little mental energy on viewing (especially relative to reading),
making no attempt to think deeply about the program. Salomon thus
might see the young viewer as cognitively active in television viewing
since the young child may still be learning how to decode the cinematic
"syntax" of television montage, but the older viewer adopts a viewing
strategy that excludes deep processing of content. Since our theory was
derived from research with young children, a potential resolution exists: Contrary to popular opinion, cognitive activity may be greatest in
young viewers, declining with cognitive development and viewing experience. Future research should employ online measures of cognitive
processing demand (e.g., Posner, 1978) in order to fully examine this
possibility. A subsidiary point should be made here. Despite the belief
that reading is an activity that necessarily consumes mental resources
and is thus more cognitively demanding than television viewing (Salomon, 1979; Singer, 1980), there is little evidence in support. Many
recent studies have shown that a practised reader actually has great
difficulty avoiding reading text even when a task such as the Stroop test
demands it. Reading is often an "automatic" activity (La Berge & Samuels, 1974).

A second potential synthesis of the active and reactive theories
might come from the recent theoretical and empirical efforts of Wright
and Huston (1981) and Calvert et al. (1982). They advanced a theory of
television viewing that shares some concepts in common with the present theory. Of particular interest in the present context is their notion
that salient formal features such as motion may serve to enhance learning through a kind of emphasis (perhaps similar to underlining in
texts). Calvert et al. (1982) show that those children whose attention is
most influenced by formal features (such as motion) also show the
greatest comprehension. They do not, however, offer a mechanism to
explain such an effect. One explanation, which is consistent with the

active theory, is that content conveyed through motion is explicit, concrete, and visual. Comprehension of such content should benefit from visual attention, and so the individual differences in attention and comprehension could be a consequence of different levels of skill in watching television. A more reactive explanation, however, is that the formal feature indeed elicits an orienting reflex and that the orienting reflex momentarily increases the viewer's information processing activity. This interpretation is consistent with all recent research and theory on the function of the orienting reflex (e.g., Ohman, 1979; Pribram, 1979; Siddle & Spinks, 1979; Sokolov, 1969), Singer's (1980) assertions notwithstanding. If this interpretation of the Calvert et al. (1982) findings can be supported, (and the chapter by Bryant, et al., Chapter 9, provides support) a synthesis of the active and reactive theories of television viewing may be possible. Such a synthesis would recognize the rational strategic viewing described by the active theory but would add to the automatic process of attentional inertia that of the attentional enhancing role of the orienting reflex. Ultimately, a theory of television viewing must specify and elaborate on the complex interplay of strategic and automatic cognitive processes.[7]

Conclusions

We have presented a theory of attention to television as actively guided by the viewer's efforts to understand the television program. This theory takes a considerably more optimistic perspective than the reactive theory on the potential for television as an educational tool. It implies that production techniques should be oriented toward conveying content as part of the means to attracting attention. It also implies that the new video technologies should be well received insofar as these technologies offer greater choice of content and direct interaction.

The theory does not imply that any given television content is either "good" or "bad," and in no way contradicts findings indicating that some kinds of programming can lead to antisocial behavior. The theory does suggest, however, that the viewer does not passively incorporate any and all content in a uniform manner. Rather, the viewer applies his

---

[7]Krull and Husson (1979) present a "viewing mini-theory" that incorporates both active and reactive components. The theory is intended to account for variations in attention as a function of program set complexity (changes in settings over time). The theory invokes expectancy, satiation, and interest in viewing as intervening variables. Their theorizing is unique insofar as they try to account for attention as a consequence of overall program pacing dynamics.

or her own experience and understanding to that content. Efforts to account for the impact of television should consider what the viewer brings to the television at least as much as it brings to the viewer.

Acknowledgments

We would like to thank Catherine Fischer, Cindy Burger, Robin Smith, and Diane Field for their assistance and comments.

References

Aisbett, K. M., & Holman, J. *The role of auditory attributes of form on attention to television.* Paper presented at the Society for Research in Child Development Biennial Meeting, Boston, 1981.

Alwitt, L. F., Anderson, D. R., Lorch, E. P., & Levin, S. R. Preschool children's visual attention to attributes of television. *Human Communication Research,* 1980, *7,* 52–67.

Anderson, D. R. *Active and passive processes in children's television viewing.* Paper presented at the annual meeting of the American Psychological Association, New York, 1979.

Anderson, D. R. *A descriptive analysis of viewing distance and visual angles of television viewing at home.* Unpublished data, 1981.

Anderson, D. R., Alwitt, L. F., Lorch, E. P., & Levin, S. R. Watching children watch television. In G. Hale & M. Lewis (Eds.), *Attention and cognitive development.* New York: Plenum, 1979.

Anderson, D. R., & Levin, S. R. Young children's attention to *Sesame Street. Child Development,* 1976, *47,* 806–811.

Anderson, D. R., Levin, S. R., & Lorch, E. P. The effects of TV program pacing on the behavior of preschool children. *AV Communication Review,* 1977, *25,* 159–166.

Anderson, D. R., & Lorch, E. P. *A theory of the active nature of young children's television viewing.* Paper presented at the Society for Research in Child Development Biennial Meeting, San Francisco, 1979.

Anderson, D. R., Lorch, E. P., Field, D. E., & Sanders, J. The effects of TV program comprehensibility on preschool children's visual attention to television. *Child Development,* 1981, *52,* 151–157.

Anderson, D. R., Lorch, E. P., Smith, R., Bradford, R., & Levin, S. R. The effects of peer presence on preschool children's television viewing behavior. *Developmental Psychology,* 1981, *17,* 446–453.

Appleton, T., Clifton, R., & Goldberg, S. The development of behavioral competence in infancy. In F. D. Horowitz (Ed.), *Review of child development research.* Chicago: University of Chicago Press, 1975.

Bandura, A. *Social learning theory.* Englewood Cliffs, N.J.: Prentice-Hall, 1977.

Bechtel, R. B., Achelpohl, C., & Akers, R. Correlates between observed behavior and questionnaire responses on television viewing. In E. A. Rubinstein, G. A. Comstock, & J. P. Murray (Eds.), *Television and social behavior* (Vol. 4), *Television in day-to-day life: Patterns of use.* Washington, D.C.: U.S. Government Printing Office, 1972.

Berlyne, D. E. *Conflict, arousal and curiosity*. New York: McGraw-Hill, 1960.

Bernstein, L. J. *Design attributes of Sesame Street and the visual attention of preschool children*. Unpublished doctoral dissertation, Columbia University, 1978.

Brown, I., Jr. Role of referent concreteness in the acquisition of passive sentence comprehension through abstract modeling. *Journal of Experimental Child Psychology*, 1976, *22*, 185–199.

Bruner, J. The course of cognitive growth. *American Psychologist*, 1964, *19*, 1–15.

Bryant, J., Hezel, R., & Zillmann, D. Humor in children's educational television. *Communication Education*, 1979, *28*, 49–59.

Calvert, S. L., Huston, A. C., Watkins, B. A., & Wright, J. C. The relation between selective attention to television forms and children's comprehension of content. *Child Development*, 1982, *53*, 601–610.

Carew, J. V. Experience and the development of intelligence in young children at home and in day care. *Monographs of the Society for Research in Child Development*, 1980, *45*(187), 1–89.

Collins, W. A. Children's comprehension of television content. In E. Wartella (Ed.), *Children communicating: Media and development of thought, speech, understanding*. Beverly Hills, Calif.: Sage, 1979.

Collins, W. A., Wellman, H., Keniston, A., & Westby, S. Age-related aspects of comprehension and inference from a televised dramatic narrative. *Child Development*, 1978, *49*, 389–399.

de Villiers, J. G., & de Villiers, P. A. *Language acquisition*. Cambridge, Mass.: Harvard University Press, 1978.

Ditchburn, R. W. *Eye-movements and visual perception*. London: Oxford University Press, 1973.

Flagg, B. N. Children and television: Effects of stimulus repetition on eye activity. In J. W. Senders, D. F. Fisher, & R. A. Monty (Eds.), *Eye movements and the higher psychological functions*. Hillsdale, N.J.: Erlbaum, 1978.

Gadberry, S. Television as a babysitter: A field comparison of preschoolers' behavior during playtime and during television viewing. *Child Development*, 1974, *45*, 1132–1136.

Gerbner, G., & Gross, L. The violent face of television and its lessons. In E. Palmer & A. Dorr (Eds.), *Children and the faces of television: Teaching, violence, selling*. New York: Academic Press, 1980.

Graesser, A. C. *Prose comprehension beyond the word*. New York: Springer-Verlag, 1981.

Graesser, A. C., Higginbotham, M. W., Robertson, S. P., & Smith, W. R. A natural inquiry into the National Enquirer: Self-induced versus task-induced reading comprehension. *Discourse Processes*, 1978, *1*, 355–372.

Hochberg, J., & Brooks, V. Film cutting and visual momentum. In J. W. Senders, P. F. Fisher, & R. A. Monty (Eds.), *Eye movements and the higher psychological functions*. Hillsdale, N.J.: Erlbaum, 1978.

Hollenbeck, A. R., & Slaby, R. G. Infant visual responses to television. *Child Development*, 1979, *50*, 41–45.

Kagan, J. *Change and continuity in infancy*. New York: Wiley, 1971.

Kahneman, D. *Attention and effort*. Englewood Cliffs, N.J.: Prentice-Hall, 1973.

Kintsch, W., and Van Dijk, T. A. Toward a model of text comprehension and production. *Psychological Review*, 1978, *85*, 363–394.

Krull, R., & Husson, W. Children's attention: The case of TV viewing. In E. Wartella (Ed.), *Children communicating: Media and development of thought, speech, understanding*. Beverly Hills, Calif.: Sage, 1979.

La Berge, D., & Samuels, J. Automatic processes in reading. *Cognitive Psychology*, 1974, 6, 293–323.

Lesser, G. S. *Children and television: Lessons from Sesame Street.* New York: Random House, 1974.

Lesser, H. *Television and the preschool child.* New York: Academic Press, 1977.

Levin, S., & Anderson, D. The development of attention. *Journal of Communication*, 1976, 26(2), 126–135.

Lorch, E. P., Anderson, D. R., & Levin, S. R. The relationship of visual attention to children's comprehension of television. *Child Development*, 1979, 50, 722–727.

Mander, J. *Four arguments for the elimination of television.* New York: Morrow, 1978.

Mandler, J. M. Categorical and schematic organization in memory. In C. R. Puff (Ed.), *Memory organization and structure.* New York: Academic Press, 1979.

Mandler, J. M., & Johnson, N. S. Remembrance of things parsed: Story structure and recall. *Cognitive Psychology*, 1977, 9, 111–151.

Metz, C. *Language and cinema.* The Hague: Mouton, 1974.

Miskiewicz, R. *Inertial effects in television viewing.* Unpublished Master's thesis, University of Massachusetts, 1980.

Murray, J. P. Television in inner-city homes: Viewing behavior of young boys. In E. A. Rubinstein, G. A. Comstock, & J. P. Murray (Eds.), *Television and social behavior* (Vol. 4), *Television in day-to-day life: Patterns of use.* Washington, D.C.: U.S. Government Printing Office, 1972.

Newtson, D. Foundations of attribution: The perception of ongoing behavior. In J. Harvey, W. Ickes, & R. Kidd (Eds.), *New directions in attribution research.* Hillsdale, N.J.: Erlbaum, 1976.

Ohman, A. The orienting response, attention, and learning: An information processing perspective. In H. D. Kimmel, E. H. van Olst, & J. F. Orlebeke (Eds.), *The orienting reflex in humans,* Hillsdale, N.J.: Erlbaum, 1979.

Omanson, R. C. An analysis of narratives: Identifying central, supportive and distracting content. *Discourse Processes*, in press.

Pezdek, K., & Hartman, E. F. *Children's television viewing: Attention and memory for auditorally versus visually presented information.* Unpublished manuscript, 1981. (Available from K. Pezdek, Claremont Graduate School, Claremont, Calif.)

Piaget, J. *The origins of intelligence in children.* New York: International Universities Press, 1952.

Pichert, J. W., & Anderson, R. C. Taking different perspectives on a story. *Journal of Educational Psychology*, 1977, 69, 309–315.

Pingree, S., & Hawkins, R. P. What children do with television: Implications for communication research. In B. Dervin & M. Voight (Eds.), *Progress in communication sciences* (Vol. 3). Norwood, N.J.: Ablex, 1981.

Posner, M. I. *Chronometric exploration of mind.* Hillsdale, N.J.: Erlbaum, 1978.

Postman, N. *Teaching as a conserving activity.* New York: Delacorte, 1979.

Pribram, K. J. The orienting reaction: Key to brain re-presentational mechanisms. In H. D. Kimmel, E. H. van Olst, & J. F. Orlebeke (Eds.), *The orienting reflex in humans.* Hillsdale, N.J.: Erlbaum, 1979.

Rice, M. *Television as a medium of verbal communication.* Paper presented at American Psychological Association Annual Meeting, New York, September 1979.

Robinson, J. P. Television and leisure time. *Journal of Communication*, 1981, 31, 120–130.

Saida, S., & Ikeda, M. Useful visual field size for pattern perception. *Perception & Psychophysics*, 1979, 25, 119–125.

Salomon, G. *Interaction of media, cognition, and learning*. San Francisco: Jossey-Bass, 1979.

Schank, R., & Abelson, R. *Scripts, plans, goals, and understanding*. Hillsdale, N.J.: Erlbaum, 1977.

Schramm, W., Lyle, J., & Parker, E. B. *Television in the lives of our children*. Stanford, Calif.: Stanford University Press, 1961.

Siddle, D. A. T., & Spinks, J. A. Orienting response and information-processing: Some theoretical and empirical problems. In H. D. Kimmel, E. H. Van Olst, & J. F. Orlebeke (Eds.), *The orienting reflex in humans*. Hillsdale, N.J.: Erlbaum, 1979.

Singer, J. L. The power and limitations of television: A cognitive–affective analysis. In P. H. Tannenbaum & R. Abeles (Eds.), *The entertainment functions of television*. Hillsdale, N.J.: Erlbaum, 1980.

Singer, J. L., & Singer, D. G. *Television, imagination and aggression: A study of preschoolers*. Hillsdale, N.J.: Erlbaum, 1981.

Snow, C. E., Arlman-Rupp, A., Hassing, Y., Jobse, J., Joosten, J., & Vorster, J. Mothers' speech in three social classes. *Journal of Psycholinguistic Research*, 1976, *5*, 1–20.

Sokolov, E. N. The modelling properties of the nervous system. In M. Cole & I. Maltzman (Eds.), *A handbook of contemporary Soviet psychology*. New York: Basic Books, 1969.

Stein, N. L., & Glenn, C. G. An analysis of story comprehension in elementary school children. In R. Freedle (Ed.), *Multidisciplinary approaches to discourse comprehension*. Norwood, N.J.: Ablex, 1979.

Stein, N. L., & Trabasso, T. What's in a story: Critical issues in comprehension and instruction. In R. Glaser (Ed.), *Advances in the psychology of instruction* (Vol. 2). Hillsdale, N.J.: Erlbaum, in press.

Swerdlow, J. A question of impact. *Wilson Quarterly*, 1981, *5*, 86–99.

Tower, R. B., Singer, D. G., Singer, J. L., & Biggs, A. Differential effects of television programming on preschoolers' cognition, imagination, and social play. *American Journal of Orthopsychiatry*, 1979, *49*, 265–281.

Wartella, E., & Ettema, J. S. A cognitive developmental study of children's attention to television commercials. *Communication Research*, 1974, *1*, 69–88.

Welch, A., & Watt, J. H. Visual complexity and young children's learning from television. *Human Communication Research*, 1982, *8*, 133–145.

Winn, M. *The plug-in drug*. New York: Viking, 1977.

Wright, J. C., & Huston, A. C. The forms of television: Nature and development of television literacy in children. In H. Gardner & H. Kelly (Eds.), *Children and the worlds of television*. San Francisco: Jossey-Bass, 1981.

chapter 2

Children's Processing of Television: The Informative Functions of Formal Features[1]

ALETHA C. HUSTON
JOHN C. WRIGHT

Television is distinguished from other communications media by its forms, not its content. When new media first appear, they mimic the forms of already existing media. Early television programs often seemed like radio programs with pictures, just as early films contained relatively static scenes that were reminiscent of theater. As time passes, the new and unique possibilities of a medium are developed so that it comes to have its own codes and modes of representing information. In the case of television, many adults are hardly aware of those codes because they have appeared gradually and are highly familiar.

Consider the young child, however, who grows up in a world where television is an integral and important part of the home environment. How does that child come to decode the visual and auditory sensations arising from the talking box with a screen in it? What is it about television that attracts even very young viewers to watch or listen? How does the child learn the codes of television and become increasingly sophisticated in understanding its content? Does the child who grows up in

[1]The preparation of this chapter and much of the research reported in it was supported by a grant from the Spencer Foundation. Many members of the Center for Research on the Influence of Television on Children (CRITC) have contributed to the ideas presented here.

the television world learn different modes of thinking, processing, and representing information than one who is socialized without television? Are these modes used outside the television context as well as within it? Some of these questions were raised by McLuhan (1964) nearly 20 years ago, but researchers and theorists have only recently given them serious consideration.

In the first few decades of television, most research was focused on content—violence, stereotypes, advertising, prosocial behavior, and so on. Like the television producers, researchers of the new medium adapted their questions from those asked about movies, radio, and books. Only recently have psychological investigators begun to consider the unique qualities of television as a medium. In this chapter, we describe our efforts to understand how children learn to process the forms and codes of television.

What Are Television Forms?

Television consists of a stream of visual and auditory images that are packaged in particular ways. Although television is similar to film in many respects, the two media are not identical. Television producers often attempt to create a sense of naturalness and spontaneity and to avoid the appearance of arty, contrived, or slick packages that are the hallmark of many films. Nevertheless, their product consists of visual images generated by several cameras with the capacity to change perspectives, zoom and pan, and by electronic techniques which can produce all manner of unusual visual events that do not occur in the real world. The visual images are accompanied by a sound track containing music, sound effects, laughing, and other auditory events. Of course, television usually contains speech in the form of dialogue and narration, as well. At a more molar level, producers make choices about pacing, variation, and levels of action. All of these program attributes— action, pace, visual techniques, verbal and nonverbal auditory events— are *formal features,* and they can be defined independently from the content of a television program. That is, they are program attributes that result from production and editing techniques, and they are applicable to many types of content.

The distinction between form and content revolves around the degree to which an attribute can be used across different themes and messages. The distinction can be made clearly in most instances, although there are some ambiguous cases. For example, the presence or absence of dialogue is a formal feature of a program; the meaning of the words spoken is the content. Frequent shifts from scene to scene define the formal feature, rapid pace; the particular people or places in those scenes are the content. Although formal features are in principle independent of content, there are widespread production conventions associating certain features with particular categories of content. For example, violent action–adventure programs often contain loud, fast music and sound effects as well as rapid movement on the screen (Huston, Wright, Wartella, Rice, Watkins, Campbell, & Potts, 1981). Flat lighting, fuzzy images, and soft, dreamy music are used in commercials for feminine products. In fact, as we shall explain later in more detail, one aspect of media literacy is learning these conventions, so that formal features can be used as signals of the content likely to come next. Nevertheless, many of them are arbitrary and nonuniversal. For example, in American television, animation is used almost exclusively with content intended for young children, and animated programs are quite likely to be both violent and humorous (Huston et al., 1981). But there is nothing inherent in animation that restricts it to such content. Cartoons produced in many other countries are not violent or noisy. Furthermore, animation could be used to present a variety of adult content ranging from political parody to instruction about organic chemistry. Many other production conventions are the result of habit or custom rather than some inherent quality of the content, and many are not shared across cultures or even across different types of television programming.

The Structure of Formal Features in Children's Programs

We began our investigations by attempting a detailed description of the forms used on contemporary American television for children (see Huston et al., 1981). Some 25 features were coded for two samples of programs (Ns = 64 and 73) representing all available network and PBS children's programming for one week in the fall and one week in the winter. Programs fell in three categories that differed in target age group and/or program intent: Saturday morning, daytime educational, and prime-time children's programs. The target audience for Saturday morning and daytime educational programs is primarily young children; whereas prime-time children's programs are targeted for adolescent and family viewing as well. Daytime educational programs differ from the other two groups, because they are designed primarily for the education and development of children rather than primarily for entertainment. After-school children's programming contains a mixture of Saturday morning reruns, prime-time reruns, and educational programs.

Not surprisingly, many of the Saturday morning programs were animated, and most were intended to be humorous. These commercially produced programs for young children were characterized by rapid action (physical movement of characters), rapid pace (changes of scene and character), and variation of setting. Such molar features were accompanied by auditory and visual techniques including sound effects, loud music, visual special effects, and rapid cuts. This package of features combines rapid pace, physical motion, unusual and unexpected perceptual events, and intense auditory stimulation—attributes that we describe as *perceptually salient*. These features occurred frequently in cartoons, but they also distinguished live Saturday morning programs from other program categories. Commercial programs for young children appear to be based on an image of the child viewer as one whose attention must be captured and held by constant action, change, and noise, as well as slapstick violence.

A second cluster of features, which we have labeled reflection, characterized daytime educational programming for children. It consists of long zooms, singing, and moderate levels of physical activity. Each of these features appears well suited to rehearse, repeat, or elaborate on content themes, hence the label *reflection*. Zooms and moderate action present information in a visual form easily understood by children; singing contains rhythm, rhyme, and repetition—verbal forms that are readily encoded and recalled. These forms are often used to summarize and recapitulate content—as if to make sure the child understands and remembers. Although educational daytime programs also employed visual special effects, sound effects, and rapid pace, these features were used less extensively than in Saturday morning programs.

The third cluster of features consists of character dialogue or speech. When critics and researchers describe television as a visual medium, they often ignore the obvious fact that it also relies heavily on verbal communication. We classified speech simply as adult, child, or nonhuman dialogue. Adult dialogue was most frequent on prime-time programs, and child dialogue occurred most often on daytime educational programs. A small subsample of programs was subjected to a more refined analysis of language properties by Mabel Rice (1979). Programs varied considerably on dimensions that are likely to influence children's understanding of the content presented. For example, the educational programs contained techniques for drawing attention to speech or making dialogue comprehensible such as focusing, stressed single

words, and reference to immediately present events. Commercial programs contained frequent references to content that was not present,
nonliteral word meanings, and other attributes that might make language somewhat difficult for children to understand (Rice, Huston, &
Wright, 1982).

How Formal Features Influence Cognitive Processes

The analysis of television forms was a necessary first step in the
main task of attempting to understand their influence on children's
attention and comprehension of television content. Following our own
proposed developmental sequence, we turned first to the perceptually
salient features that distinguish Saturday morning children's television
so clearly. The theory and pertinent data are described later. As we
proceeded, however, we became increasingly interested in the role that
television forms serve in structuring and giving meaning to the sensory
images emerging from the television screen. Some hypotheses and evidence about these "informative" functions of formal features are presented in the sections that follow.

Perceptual Salience

At one level, formal features can be described as sensory events
which can be analyzed for perceptual qualities along basic dimensions
of intensity, movement, contrast, change, novelty, and incongruity
(Berlyne, 1960). We have used these dimensions to define *perceptual
salience* of formal features. Salience, by this definition, is an attribute
of the stimulus, not of the person doing the perceiving. This usage
differs from the more common tendency in the perception literature to
define as salient whatever attracts attention. Because we are attempting
to learn what properties of television programs influence attention, it
would be circular to define salience as that which determines attention.
Therefore, salience is defined independently by sensory qualities of the
stimuli. Such qualities are basic to human perceptual activity and are
similar to dimensions of visual stimuli that have been identified by
scholars of artistic analysis and visual literacy (e.g., Dondis, 1973). To
some degree, they probably represent unlearned or primitive mechanisms in the human perceptual apparatus (Cohen & Salapatek, 1975).
The television formal features which have been identified as salient
include physical activity of characters, rapid pace, variability of scenes,
visual special effects, loud music, sound effects, and peculiar or non-

human voices. Each of these represents several of the "collative" dimensions outlined by Berlyne (1960). Human speech, physical inactivity, and background music generally lack perceptual salience, whereas other formal features are intermediate in salience (e.g., moderate action, zooms) because they are characterized by only one or two collative properties.

Our research program began with the hypothesis that perceptual salience of formal features would elicit and maintain attention to television, particularly for very young viewers. Although salient stimuli can produce momentary attention at any age (as in the example of a fire alarm or bright flash of light), there is probably a developmental progression of increasing familiarity and habituation to the sensory qualities which define salience in this model. Developmental changes in the importance of perceptual salience have been postulated by a number of theorists, and there is a body of experimental data to support such a hypothesis (Gibson, 1969).

In the theoretical model guiding our work, the child is viewed as moving gradually from *exploration to search* as a primary mode of information getting (Wright & Vlietstra, 1975). Exploration involves responding to immediate, salient, discrete parts of the stimulus environment. It is discontinuous and impulsive. Exploration is most likely when an individual is unfamiliar with the situation. With increasing exposure, a person's attention gradually habituates to salient stimuli (i.e., to those with high levels of movement, intensity, incongruity, and the like). Application of this model to television experience leads to the hypotheses that among the youngest and least experienced viewers, attention is guided largely by the perceptually salient auditory and visual forms of the medium.

Exploration gives way in familiar contexts to perceptual search, a kind of information-getting activity that is instrumental rather than consummatory and that is guided by internally generated goals rather than by external sensory events. In the case of television viewing, the shift from exploration to search enables the child to ignore many of the perceptually salient cues and to select for attention those features that are informative, interesting, or pertinent to her reasons for viewing. Some of the stimuli that attract attention may be perceptually salient, but attention to them is based on their informativeness or relevance to the viewer's goals rather than on their perceptual qualities.

In general, the theory predicts a shift with age from primary reliance on exploration to greater use of search strategies. This prediction is based partly on the fact that children gain familiarity with an increasingly wide range of stimulus situations as they get older, and partly on developmental changes in metacognitive ability to select relevant and informative portions, to integrate events over time, to engage in goal-directed activities, while suppressing the more automated responses to the immediate perceptual environment. Therefore, we have predicted a decline with age in children's responsiveness to perceptual salience on television.

The theory also posits familiarization as a microgenetic process that can occur at any age in a new stimulus context (Wright, 1977). Even an adult may go through a "gee whiz" experience of absorbing disconnected bits of information when entering a new setting. A person seeing a film by Godard or Altman may process each bit as it comes with attention primarily to the most salient components. An experienced viewer of such avant-garde techniques more readily finds symbols, connections, and underlying meanings. For that reason, experience with television probably contributes to the shift from attentional focus on perceptually salient features to concern with feature informativeness. The experience is necessary but not sufficient—basic cognitive developmental change is equally critical to this transition.

From our analysis of children's television programs, it appears that producers also believe in the potency of perceptual salience for attracting young viewers and in the increasing importance of alternative program attributes as children grow older. Saturday morning television is characterized by extreme levels of every salient formal feature in our scoring system, sometimes summarized by the popular term *hype*. Nonsalient features occur more often in educational programs and in those aimed at older children and families (Huston et al., 1981)

Empirical Findings. One means of evaluating these hypotheses was an analysis of national viewership for the two samples of programs which had been coded in our investigation of the taxonomy of formal features. The feature scores were used to predict the number of viewers of different ages in New York, Chicago, and Los Angeles according to national audience ratings during the same weeks we recorded these programs. Scheduling, format, and the like accounted for much of the variance in viewing audience. Nevertheless, with those variables partialled out, programs with high levels of action were most appealing to young preschool children (2- and 3-year-olds). Those with rapid pace appealed most to children from about 4 to 9 years of age (Wright,

Huston-Stein, Potts, Thissen, Rice, Watkins, Calvert, Greer, & Zapata, 1980). Nonsalient features, such as human dialogue characterized the more popular programs among older viewers, aged 8 to adult.

Another type of evidence comes from laboratory investigations in which children's visual attention to television has been observed directly. Studies by several different investigators have yielded findings supporting the contention that salient formal features elicit and maintain children's attention to television. Although slightly different systems of coding television production features have been used in different studies, several consistent patterns have emerged (Alwitt, Anderson, Lorch, & Levin, 1980; Anderson, Alwitt, Lorch, & Levin, 1979; Anderson & Levin, 1976; Bernstein, 1978; Calvert, Huston, Watkins, & Wright, 1982; Greer, Potts, Wright, & Huston, 1982; Huston-Stein, Fox, Greer, Watkins, & Whitaker, 1981; Potts, 1980; Rubinstein, Liebert, Neale, & Poulos, 1974; Susman, 1978; Wartella & Ettema, 1974; Wright, Calvert, Huston-Stein, & Watkins, 1980).

First, nonverbal auditory features such as lively or loud music, sound effects, peculiar voices, nonspeech vocalizations, and auditory changes recruit and maintain children's attention. Second, salient visual features such as special effects and pans maintain attention, but other visual features do not. In fact, long zooms consistently lose attention. Third, high levels of physical activity hold attention. In our analyses, we have separated "moderate action" (movement through space at the pace of a walk) from "rapid action" (movement through space faster than a walk). Both hold attention, but moderate action appears to be used more effectively to convey plot information, whereas rapid action is more often used purely for its sensory excitement. Our analyses also indicate that physical action and its associated features are consistently more important correlates of preschoolers' attention than violent content (Huston-Stein et al., 1981; Potts, 1980; Wright, Huston-Stein, Potts, Thisser, Rice, Watkins, Calvert, Greer, & Zapata, 1980).

Rapid pace was also defined originally as a salient feature because it entails frequent changes of scene and characters. However, rapidly paced programs do not generally maintain higher levels of attention than slow-paced programs. Anderson, Levin, & Lorch (1977) found no differences in attention to high- and low-paced versions of Sesame Street. In a recently completed study in our laboratory, children's attention to a large number of high- and low-paced programs was compared; there were no differences in attention as a function of pace (Wright & Huston, 1982). Furthermore, an internal analysis in two of our earlier studies indicated that scene and character changes elicited attention from children who were not viewing, but often lost attention from those who were looking (Wright, Calvert, Huston-Stein, & Watkins, 1980). Anderson *et al.* (1979) similarly found that scene and bit changes elicited attention briefly but that they were also the occasion for termination of viewing. Rapid pace may produce more shifts in attention than slow pace but apparently does not enhance the overall amount of attention devoted to the program.

Some nonsalient features, such as dialogue by child characters, maintain children's attention (Alwitt *et al.*, 1980; Anderson & Levin, 1976; Calvert *et al.*, 1982; Rubinstein *et al.*, 1974; Wright, Calvert, Huston-Stein, & Watkins, 1980). Speech by adults receives more mixed reactions; in particular male adult speech sometimes loses attention (Alwitt *et al.*, 1980; Calvert *et al.*, 1982). The fact that children attend to nonsalient features does not necessarily diminish the importance of salience, but it does indicate the need to identify other determinants of attention, even at fairly young ages.

Developmental Differences. Although the available data support the hypothesis that salient formal features influence children's attention, the evidence for developmental change is weaker. In the age range from about 4 to 10, there are relatively small age differences in patterns of attention, primarily because older as well as younger children attend to salient features of television. In three studies comparing preschool children (4–6 years) with those in middle childhood (8–10 years), there were some instances in which younger children attended to salient features more than older ones, but the magnitudes of the age differences were small (Calvert *et al.*, 1982; Wartella & Ettema, 1974; Wright, Calvert, Huston-Stein & Watkins, 1980). In our recently collected data using 16 different television programs and 160 children, there were virtually no age differences in the degree to which salient features maintained attention within the programs.

One interpretation of our failure to find large developmental differences might be that we have not sampled children early enough to locate the critical period for familiarization with television. This interpretation is contradicted, however, by Anderson and Levin's (1976) finding that, from ages 1 to 4, children become increasingly responsive to salient features such as animation and auditory change when viewing *Sesame Street* (see Anderson & Lorch, Chapter 1, this volume for a more complete discussion). Furthermore, it is not the case that 4–6-year-old children are unresponsive to salience; rather, even 8–10-year-olds continue to respond to it. It seems reasonable to explore other functions beyond the sensory level that may be served by perceptually salient features. For that reason, we present next an extended analysis

of the ways in which formal features may influence children's understanding of what they see and hear on television.

Perceptual salience may not only elicit and maintain attention, but it
may also influence comprehension by serving as an aid in *selection* of
content. Producers often use salient features to highlight certain components of the program for the viewers. Letters on the screen in *The
Electric Company* oscillate, move, and change from one bright color to
another while the background people or objects remain still and quiet.
A drum roll or loud crash of music can announce a critical event in a
story. Similar phenomena occur in stage productions in which one
dancer or singer is spotlighted while the others stay fairly stationary in
lower lighting. One study in our laboratory (Calvert et al., 1982) demonstrated that content accompanied by salient nonverbal auditory features, such as vocalizations and sound effects or by physical activity of
characters was recalled better than content presented with nonsalient
verbal or nonverbal features. Obviously, the type of content that is
emphasized by salience depends on producers' decisions about how
salient features are to be used. Such features can highlight a message,
story line, or violent action, or they can distract from the major
intended message if they accompany incidental or irrelevant content.
For example, a still speaker accompanied by cavorting animated
clowns in the background may not be understood very well unless his
speech is well coordinated with their actions.

The selective function of salient features may be particularly important for young children because they have difficulty in discriminating
"relevant" or central content from incidental content in a story or other
television program. Both basic research on memory and numerous
studies of children's comprehension of television show that the ratio of
central to incidental information recalled increases from the preschool
years into adolescence (e.g., Collins, 1970; Hale, Miller, & Stevenson,
1968; Hawkins, 1973). One reason for this change appears to be developmental improvement in the ability to select relevant and important
information for further processing. Although salient perceptual events
may influence selection of information at all age levels, older children
presumably have a larger variety of cognitive bases for selection, so
they should be less exclusively reliant on perceptual salience than are
young children. This hypothesis is supported in the study by Calvert et
al. (1982). Younger children's comprehension was considerably better
when content was accompanied by salient features than when it was
not. Older children's comprehension was less closely associated with

feature salience, but again, the developmental differences were relatively small, because even the older children understood content associated with salient features better than content that was presented without such features.

Informative Functions of Formal Features

In the developmental model described earlier, the shift away from
salience was accompanied by an increasing ability to search for informative content. We proposed, therefore, that older children should
attend more than younger children to informative formal features, that
is, to features that are used to convey the critical information necessary
for understanding the central messages or plot of the program. It became clear as we pursued this analysis that the informativeness of a
feature could not be defined independently of the viewer or of the
context in which it occurred. It is true that some features, such as
dialogue or those we have defined as the reflection cluster, are often
intended to carry central information, but they may or may not be
informative depending on what the viewer seeks or understands.
Therefore, rather than describing particular features as more or less
informative, we discuss later some of the ways in which a variety of
formal features may be used by the child to make sense of the stream of
visual and auditory images flowing from the television screen and to
make judgments about how interesting and attention-worthy they are.

Children's uses of features for these purposes probably depend more
heavily on learning and experience than do responses to perceptual
qualities. Learning about the functions of form on television is one
aspect of media literacy. The literate viewer knows form codes on at
least three levels of specificity: (a) those that are unique to a particular
program series or perhaps to a genre of programs; (b) those that are
specific to the television medium; and (c) those that draw on codes that
are generic to the culture beyond the medium. Although mastery of
each level is almost certainly influenced by cognitive developmental
changes, the first two should depend more directly than the third on
experience with the specific programs or with television generally.

Form cannot exist without content, but neither is it identical to
content. Our approach to understanding the functions of form in relation to content is parallel to that used by psycholinguists to analyze
syntax and semantics. The two constructs can be separated for purposes of analysis but must be resynthesized because they do not function independently when human beings use language in real life contexts. In the following discussion, the informative functions of formal

features are arranged roughly from those that are primarily syntactic, containing little reference to content, to those which are integrally related to content understanding.

At one level of analysis, formal features constitute the grammar and syntax of television. Visual or auditory techniques are used to mark breaks in content, changes in scene, connections between distant events, and as bit and program boundary organizers. They are analogous to punctuation, capitalization, paragraphing, and chapter headings in print. We call this the *segmental marker* function of formal features. Some animated programs contain an audiovisual bit such as a whirling logo or a shimmering color bar between major scenes. At a more subtle level, fades and dissolves signal changes of time or place; zooms in from a distance mark the beginning of a story sequence and zooms out to a panorama often mark the end of a story or bit. Visual special effects can mark an instant replay or a sudden shift in time, (although American sports viewers have become so media literate that instant replays no longer need to be marked at all). A person's face gradually becoming fuzzy signifies a dream, fantasy, or altered state of consciousness.

Some of the syntactic conventions are program-specific as in the case of the swirling bat that marks a scene change in *Batman* or a musical theme associated with the end of each episode. Program–commercial separators can also be unique for a program or a network (e.g., "STOP—The Captain will be back"). Many feature marker functions are, however, general across television programs and sometimes films as well (e.g., a dissolve showing a major scene change). Still other syntactical functions of features draw on cultural knowledge outside the medium. The most obvious one is language. Language is used to organize, segment, and otherwise structure television content, but its form is basically similar to that which occurs in the child's real-world experience. That is, the language codes used on television are like their real-world counterparts. When the announcer says, "We'll return after these messages," children can decode the meaning of this remark using the same linguistic processing strategies and constraints that they draw upon in the presence of live speakers. Certain phrases may be beyond the child's understanding (e.g., "part of a balanced breakfast"), but the linguistic forms and meanings are not unique to television.

Research evidence on children's understanding of markers is sparse. The issue received considerable attention in policy discussions of children's advertising. Some early studies suggested that young children had difficulty discriminating programs from commercials, at least partly because they did not understand the subtle formal feature cues that marked transitions from one type of content to another (National Science Foundation, 1977). For that reason, the regulatory codes currently in use prescribe that a "separator" be inserted between children's programs and commercials. These separators are 3–5-second audiovisual bits designed to be sufficiently obvious that children will understand that content is changing. In the one empirical investigation of separators, however, young children did not understand the intended function of the markers. Instead, they seemed to interpret the "separators" as bridging devices indicating continuity of content across the transition (Palmer & McDowell, 1979).

There are age differences in children's attentional responses to transitions on television which suggest increasing ability to detect subtle feature cues marking changes between program and commercial or between parts of a program. In the age range from about 5 to 10, several studies report that older children's attention drops during commercials (as compared to programs), whereas younger children continue attending during commercials at approximately the same level that they attended to the program (National Science Foundation, 1977; Zuckerman, Ziegler, & Stevenson, 1978). In two studies conducted in our laboratory, older children's attention dropped following minor scene and character changes, but younger children did not show that pattern (Wright, Calvert, Huston-Stein, & Watkins, 1980). In a more recent study, patterns of attention to 16 high- and low-paced programs were compared. Pace was defined by the frequency of scene and character changes. Although there were no overall differences in the amount of attention to the two types of programs, older children had longer durations per look during low-paced than during high-paced programs. During programs with longer scenes, their looks continued longer, once started, than during programs with shorter scenes. Younger children had a slightly reversed pattern (Wright & Huston, 1982). All of these studies suggest that older children detect the subtle feature cues marking transitions more readily than younger children do and that their attention patterns are more consistently guided by such transitions.

SIGNIFYING OR SUGGESTING CONTENT

Televised formal features come to signify or suggest classes of content to the knowledgeable viewer, and they often carry connotative or contextual meanings about content messages. The first function, signifying classes of content, has been emphasized in Anderson's work (see

Chapter 1). For example, animation suggests content appropriate for children, whereas an adult on screen without scenery suggests adult content. A staged appearance and music suggest fictional as opposed to real content, whereas background noise and unfilled silence suggest real world events. Peculiar voices or a laugh track signal humor; a human speaker without sound effects and loud music suggests serious content. In specific programs, theme songs can signal the entrance of a particular character or a stylized story script (e.g., *Sesame Street's* "Sneaking Up on You" music; Lesser, 1974).

The planners of *Sesame Street* and *The Electric Company* have deliberately created "recurrent formats," forms which can alert the viewer that particular classes of content are about to appear (Palmer, 1978). For example, the musical theme, "Which of These Things Is Not Like the Others?" regularly precedes a classification problem. The baker with his pies is always associated with a number and counting. Palmer argues cogently that such formats can promote the child's understanding of content because they help to create a mental set or to call forth the appropriate schema to be used for processing the content of a segment. The child who knows the meaning of the theme song is ready to think about similarities and differences between stimuli rather than trying to decode a letter or expecting a social message from Ernie and Bert.

Forms also convey and reinforce the connotative meanings of content. In fact, many production conventions are designed to meld form and content to maximize the communication of meaning or to enhance the emotional impact of a sequence. Some of these conventions are specifically matched with stereotyped content such as the slide whistle when Wile E. Coyote falls down the chasm in a *Road Runner* cartoon. Some are more general to the medium. For example, in American television, animation with its associated salient feature package, signals violence, often combined with humor. Even in live shows, violence is associated with rapid action, high noise levels, and frequent change of scene as well as with the relative absence of child dialogue and long zooms (Huston et al., 1981). Many of these associations are based on arbitrary production conventions that can be learned from watching television, but others draw on culturally shared images learned in real-world experience. One example of the latter, the set of formal features used to convey sex-typed connotations, has been explored in a recent series of studies.

In the initial study, commercials aimed at boys, girls, or both sexes were coded for formal features. (The intended audience was defined operationally by the gender of the children shown in the commercial.) Background music, fades and dissolves, and female narrators were used more often in feminine commercials than in neutral or masculine advertisements. By contrast, high levels of activity, variation in scenes, rapid cuts, loud music, and sound effects appeared more often in masculine toy commercials than in neutral or feminine ads (Welch, Huston-Stein, Wright, & Plehal, 1979). These formal features are consistent with culturally shared images of femininity as soft, dreamy, and gentle, and of masculinity as active, abrupt, noisy, and forceful, although techniques specific to television were employed.

The next question: To what extent and at what ages do children understand such connotative meanings of television forms? To probe children's understanding of the formal features independently of content, three sets of stimuli were presented to children from first through sixth grade: (a) real commercials for sex-neutral products that varied on sex-typed forms; (b) pseudo commercials (made for the study) with abstract, meaningless content; and (c) verbal descriptions of formal features (e.g., "a lot of different places" for rapid scene changes). On all three types of stimuli, children recognized the sex-typed formal features. For the real commercials, however, they responded to the formal features only when they were instructed to ignore content and concentrate on the techniques used in the commercial (e.g., "Pay attention to the kind of music," or "Think about the picture"; Greer, Huston, Wright, Welch, & Ross, 1981). This pattern exactly parallels findings concerning children's understanding of sex-typed language forms. During the elementary school years, they come to recognize the subtle formal language cues, but their dominant tendency is to make judgments on the basis of content (Edelsky, 1977). In both cases, children in middle childhood know the connotative meanings of sex-typed formal cues, but that knowledge exists at a relatively low level of awareness.

PROVIDING MODES OF MENTAL REPRESENTATION

Formal features are the means by which the television producer encodes information for communication. The content of television is presented in visual pictorial or visual symbolic images and in auditory forms, both verbal and nonverbal. These forms may be adopted or adapted by the viewer as his or her own modes of mentally representing the information received. Several investigators have compared children's understanding of the visual and verbal information in television programs, but discussions of this issue sometimes confound the visual–auditory distinction with the distinction between iconic and symbolic modes of representation (Bruner, 1966; Glass, Holyoak, & Santa, 1979). Iconic or analog modes of representation are isomorphic or analogous to the object being represented, such as a picture, an onomatopoetic word, or a sound effect simulating a real world happening. Symbolic modes of representation involve symbols that are arbitrarily assigned to their referents. Most language, visual symbols such as a swastika, or music with particular connotations are symbolic. Obviously, each form of representation can occur in visual or auditory modalities. In most television programs, the major content information appears to be carried by visual analogs and verbal symbolic representations, but the sensory modality needs to be unconfounded from the type of representation in order to understand how each set of variables influences children's cognitive processing.

There is no theoretical reason to predict superiority of the visual or auditory sensory modality, but one would expect iconic modes of representation to be processed more easily than symbolic modes, particularly by children below the ages of 7 and 8. The results of some recent investigations support the hypothesis that children understand and recall televised information that is presented visually (usually with moderate to high rates of character action) better than content that is presented primarily through dialogue or other verbal forms (Calvert et al., 1982; Hayes & Birnbaum, 1980; Watkins, Calvert, Huston-Stein, & Wright, 1980). Information that is presented simultaneously in both visual and verbal modes, however, is generally better understood than content presented in either form alone, suggesting an interaction between modes of representation and/or sensory modalities (Calvert et al., 1982; Friedlander, Wetstone, & Scott, 1974).

Multiple forms on television may also aid in learning symbolic modes of representation, particularly language. The conventional wisdom among students of language development says that children do not learn language from television (e.g., Clark & Clark, 1977). There is, however, very little evidence on the subject. If verbal forms of encoding information are paired with simpler analogs, particularly visual ones, children may learn word meanings and other language skills from television despite the absence of opportunities for productive language and interactive encounter with the medium (Rice & Wartella, 1981).

Television forms can also represent cognitive skills, or mental operations, such as visual analysis, perspective taking, and spatial manipulations. Visual presentations can serve two distinct functions at different levels of competence of the mental skill in question: They can provide through visual means the successive outcomes of the mental operations for children who do not possess those operations, and they can suggest or cue the use of those operations for children who already possess the mental skill. Salomon (1979) calls these representational functions *supplanting* and *eliciting*, respectively. One example is found in his study of children's understanding of part–whole relationships. In a cut from a wide shot to a close-up shot, children with poor skill in visual analysis did not understand the part–whole relationship between the detail of the tight shot and the larger scene in the wide shot. More skilled children did. However, when a long zoom was used to make the transition from the wide shot to the tight shot, the less skilled children understood the relationship. Salomon interprets the long zoom as a visual analog of the mental skill, which served to model the skill, carry out the operation, and provide a representation that could eventually be internalized and used. More skilled children use the cut to close-up as a cue to make use of the part–whole logic they already possess. In fact, the zoom was not only unnecessary for them, but it tended to confuse them or to interfere with their performance.

The function of television forms as representations of logical operations is also illustrated in a pair of studies designed to teach Piagetian number conservation to children who lacked it and to evaluate the generalization of matched television and live training to both televised and live modes of testing. The televised training segments provided visual analogs of various spatial displacements, pairing of elements, and reversibility of operations. The televised training was successful in both studies, but, in the first (Wright & Butt, 1979), where the child was accompanied by a silent adult during training, the improvement attributable to training occurred only in a posttest where the task materials were displayed on television, not on a posttest where the child saw real objects. In the second study (Wright & Raeissi, 1981) where an adult coviewer interacted with the child during viewing, the training by television was as effective as live training in both televised and live posttests. Television alone provided a supplanting function in the first study, as indicated by the children's continuing dependence on the televised format to carry out the logical operations modeled. It appears in the second study that an interactive adult coviewer facilitated acquisition of the mental skill at a deeper, logic-based level that became independent of the supplanting function of the visual cues provided by the televised presentation.

Television forms may also serve an eliciting function for children's language. In one study conducted in our laboratory (Rice, 1979; Rice et al., 1982), children's spontaneous conversations were observed as they watched four different television programs that varied in the amount of dialogue and in the level of salient formal features. All programs were simple cartoons that were probably quite familiar and comprehensible to the children. During the one cartoon without dialogue, children had much higher rates of conversation generally, and conversation about the content of the program, in particular, than during the three cartoons that had some dialogue. The most obvious interpretation of these findings—that children listen when there is dialogue and talk when there is not—does not completely account for the results. The second highest rate of talking occurred during a show with very high rates of dialogue, although the children's conversation was more often irrelevant to the television show. Whether similar effects would occur for programs that were less familiar and repetitive is not known, but it appears that the absence of dialogue in a program that is familiar and easy to understand elicits conversation and linguistic processing of the television content from children as they view.

Summary

The formal features of television are an integral part of the communication aimed at and received by the child. In this section, we discussed a variety of ways in which features may influence the child's cognitive processing of televised information. We began by examining perceptual salience of many television forms as an influence on attention. Children in the preschool and elementary school years attend differentially to salient features of television, and there is relatively little evidence for a decline with age in such responsiveness. Salient features may enhance children's comprehension of content by emphasizing or spotlighting plot elements or themes. Appropriate use of salient features in production could help the child select relevant and important content for further processing. Formal features may also serve informative functions regardless of their perceptual salience. The forms of television constitute the syntax or grammar by which the flow of visual and auditory images is parsed. Forms serve as markers of transitions from program to commercial or from scene to scene, and they act as organizers just as punctuation, spaces between words, and paragraphs organize printed information. Formal features also signal the type of content being transmitted—whether it is fiction or reality, whether it is aimed at children or adults, and the like. They carry connotative meanings about the content. Is it masculine or feminine? Is it violent or nonviolent? Is it fiction or nonfiction? Finally, formal features can serve as modes of representing information. The visual and auditory techniques of television are the producer's method of encoding messages; they may also serve as the child's mode of encoding or representing the information. Hence, some forms may be understood better than others, depending on how well they fit the child's capacities for representation. Conversely, television forms may serve to teach the child new or expanded modes of mental representation and information processing. Although some of these proposed informative functions of formal features are supported by empirical data, study of them is just beginning and needs considerable expansion before many definitive statements about developmental patterns can be made.

The Process of Learning from Television

We turn now from television forms per se, to a more general analysis of the processes involved in learning from television. First, it is proposed that most of what children acquire from television occurs through incidental rather than intentional learning. In this context the importance of the child's motives and goals for viewing television needs to be emphasized. We then proceed to an analysis of the cognitive processes that children use to deal with television. In both theory and research, attention and comprehension are the two major categories of processing discussed. Operationally, attention is typically measured by the child's visual orientation to the television set, and comprehension is generally measured by some form of recall. It is obvious, however, that these operations tap two facets of an ongoing sequence of cognitive activities that should be conceptualized in relation to one another. We propose that attention and comprehension are interactive and suggest a variety of ways in which formal features of television may influence different aspects of that interaction. Finally, we attempt some synthesis of cognitive processes with goals and motives, discussing how television forms may contribute to both.

Some Basic Premises

In an effort to dispel the stereotype of the mental zombie in front of the boob tube, we psychologists sometimes talk as if the child viewer approached each new program as an intellectual challenge to be mastered. In fact, young children most often seek entertainment, humor, or fun from television. They less often approach it with an intention to learn, although their enjoyment may be partially dependent on their ability to apprehend some of its messages. Therefore, two premises guide the following discussion.

First, a full understanding of how children process television must include a careful analysis of the motives, goals, and satisfactions achieved as well as analysis of the cognitive operations employed. Research on "needs and gratifications" involved in watching television has been carried out almost entirely by communications scholars, and much of the literature provides rather general information about the reasons for watching television rather than the reasons for selecting particular programs or attending at particular moments (Comstock, Chaffee, Katzman, McCombs, & Roberts, 1978).

One important contributor to children's enjoyment or preference for certain programs is humor. Both commercial and educational programs use humor extensively (Bryant, Hezel, & Zillmann, 1979; Huston *et al.*, 1981), and children often say they like a program because it is funny. Most of the favorite programs of elementary school-aged children are situation comedies (Lyle & Hoffman, 1972) or high action slapstick comedies such as *The Dukes of Hazard*. Children also sometimes enjoy the fear-provoking elements of horror programs, the excitement of tense drama, or arousing suspense (Lyle & Hoffman, 1972; Zillman, Hay, & Bryant, 1975). The need for information, such as what the weather will be like tomorrow, can also constitute a goal toward which viewing selections and attention are directed. An additional goal, frequent among children, is a need to know about the programs most liked and discussed by the peer group, perceived as necessary for acceptance and inclusion. We know less about how motives and goals guide children's television viewing than we do about their cognitive processing of televised information. An adequate model to describe children's use of television requires a balance between the two.

The second major premise is that, because most television viewing occurs in a context of relaxed entertainment-seeking, it is most reasonable to discuss the cognitive processing involved as incidental rather than intentional learning. An incidental learning model is especially appropriate for very young children. At the preoperational level of cognitive development, the formal distinction between intentional and incidental learning appears to have little meaning—it is all incidental by adult standards. For instance, research on metacognitive processes in memory demonstrates that preschool children do not remember material any better when instructed to remember than they do without such instructions. It appears that the metacognitive ability to guide and plan one's processing so that memory is improved under intentional learning conditions (as compared to incidental learning conditions) develops during middle childhood (Flavell, 1977). That this pattern applies to complex television narratives was demonstrated when children were instructed to watch a television program carefully because they would later be asked questions about it. Eighth-grade children's recall benefited from such instructions, but second graders' did not (Collins, 1982).

Even children who are old enough to use processes of metamemory may not invoke them when watching television. When learning is incidental, the child may use less than her full cognitive capacity for processing. Salomon (1981) has recently proposed that television often elicits relatively little mental effort, and hence little mental elaboration, efforts at encoding, comparison with existing schemas, deliberate attempts to select important information, or rehearsal of information. He found that American children in late childhood perceived television as demanding less mental effort than print, expended less effort on a televised presentation than on a book, and consequently learned less from television than from a comparable printed communication. Those who considered themselves most skilled at understanding television (i.e., considered it least demanding) learned least, presumably because they did not invest as much effort in mental processing. Interestingly, a similar study with Israeli children supported earlier findings by Cohen and Salomon (1979) that Israeli children take television more seriously and learn more from it than do American children. Israeli children learned as much from a television presentation as they did from reading comparable material (Salomon, Chapter 7, this volume). Hence, the difference in amount learned is not inherent in the medium, but results in part from the expectations or motivations with which the medium is approached.

Relation between Attention and Comprehension

Given the general premises just outlined, we proceed now to a more detailed discussion of the major components of cognitive processing: attention and comprehension. The search for determinants of children's attention to television is based at least partially on an implicit assumption that attention influences comprehension. That assumption has been challenged recently by Anderson and his associates (Anderson, Lorch, Field, & Sanders, 1981; Lorch, Anderson, & Levin, 1979), who have argued that ongoing attention is determined primarily by the comprehensibility of the content. Still a third plausible hypothesis is that, beyond a minimal level, attention is unrelated to comprehension However, available data indicate a correlation between visual attention to a televised stimulus and recall of the content, although the strength of the relation varies considerably. In a laboratory modeling task, with variable distractors, children's attention was highly related to comprehension (Yussen, 1974). In several studies of television stimuli, children's attention was correlated with recall of advertisements (Zuckerman et al., 1978), prosocial theses (Watkins, 1979), and educational content (Zillmann, Williams, Bryant, Boynton, & Wolf, 1980).

A few investigators have attempted to assess *selective* attention to particular aspects of the program rather than total duration of looking. In one approach, used by Lorch et al. (1979), children's attention was assessed at the moment each item of crucial information was presented. Such selective attention was positively related to comprehension. In another approach, carried out in our laboratory (Calvert et al., 1982), patterns of differential visual attention to selected formal features were examined as predictors of comprehension of a prosocial story. In general, attention during child dialogue, nonspeech vocalizations, and sound effects predicted comprehension; inattention to adult narration and long zooms were also related to comprehension. These findings suggest that attentional patterns which enable the child to select informative and comprehensible content may be more important than overall duration of "eyes on the screen."

Positive correlational findings are consistent with both hypotheses: that attention influences comprehension or that comprehensibility influences attention. Anderson and his associates cogently argue support for the latter causal direction on the basis of experiments showing: (a) that experimentally increasing the amount of time spent looking at the screen did not increase comprehension (Lorch et al., 1979); and (b) reducing the comprehensibility of content by using backward or foreign speech decreased preschoolers' visual attention. A third manipulation intended to reduce comprehensibility involved scrambling the scenes within a segment; it produced little or no reduction in attention, particularly for children at the older end of the 3–5 year age range (Anderson et al., 1981).

How can these findings be integrated? First, attention is a logically necessary, though not sufficient, condition for comprehension (or any further cognitive processing) to occur. If we failed to find that momentary visual attention predicted comprehension of specific information, we would conclude that our methods were faulty. The child must have been listening or using other cues from the program if he recalls information presented when he was not looking.

Second, the experimental studies just described provide persuasive evidence that comprehensibility and incomprehensibility of content *can* influence attention. It is likely that the relationship between comprehensibility and attention corresponds to a ∩-shaped curve rather than being linear (Lorch et al., 1979; Rice et al., 1982). That is, content which is very simple or very difficult to comprehend probably maintains attention less well than content in an intermediate range of difficulty for the child.

Comprehension, however, is not an all-or-none phenomenon. The same content can be processed at different levels, and the same program may contain differentially accessible messages. For example, *Sesame Street* is often criticized for its adult-level puns, satire, or parodies that preschool children do not fully understand (e.g., "Monster-piece Theatre, hosted by Alistair Cookie"). Such verbal humor is deliberately included to make the program appealing to parents, but there is also a great deal of content that young children can process. Our 9-year-old loves to watch *Benny Hill*, even though many of the jokes are well beyond her understanding. She knows she does not understand all of the content but finds enough of interest to maintain her attention and enjoyment. In both examples, much of the content being processed is probably in nonverbal visual or auditory form. The sight gags are funny even if one does not understand the verbal asides. Hence, comprehensibility of content depends partly on the *forms* in which information is presented and, particularly for young children, is not limited to the linguistically presented information.

Although some level of comprehension may be a necessary condition for continuing attention, we would propose that it is usually not sufficient. That is, the child must be able to process the televised message at some level, or attention will probably drop off rather quickly, but comprehensibility alone is not enough to insure sustained attention. In one study, 3- and 4-year-olds spent more time looking at *Sesame Street* than at *Mister Rogers' Neighborhood* when the two programs were placed in direct competition (Wright & Shirley, 1974). Other analyses of content indicate that *Mister Rogers' Neighborhood* has patterns of language use, concrete presentation, and slow pace which should make it readily comprehensible to young children (Rice, 1979; Tower, Singer, Singer, & Biggs, 1979). More direct evidence comes from our recently collected data in which high- and low-paced programs with high continuity (stories) or low continuity (magazine shows) were compared. Recall of the temporal sequence of events was the index of comprehension. Both high continuity and low pace promoted comprehension. High continuity was also associated with attention, but low pace was not. That is, the program attributes that demonstrably contributed to comprehensibility did not consistently promote attention (Wright & Huston, 1982).

The studies demonstrating the influence of comprehensibility have so far used only bits from *Sesame Street*, which contains not only perceptually salient, but highly entertaining features, humorous content, and the like. Although the possible confounding of form with comprehensibility was controlled in the latest of these studies (Anderson et al., 1981, Study 2), the levels of various feature clusters have not been systematically varied. A full design to test the relative influence on attention of a variety of determinants, such as comprehensibility, salience, humor, or warmth and intimacy of a style like that of *Mister Rogers' Neighborhood* would require independent factorial variations of each.

We have now proposed two statements about the limiting conditions for the relation between attention and comprehension: (a) attention at the moment information is presented is a necessary, but not sufficient, condition for comprehension; and (b) some level of comprehension is a necessary, but probably not sufficient, condition for attention to continue. The central issue is whether increases in attention brought about by variables *other* than perceived comprehensibility (e.g., salience, humor, markers suggesting interesting content) can improve children's comprehension of televised material. Obviously, the question is relevant only for that range of material that is intermediate in difficulty for the child. If the content is extremely simple, then comprehension may reach asymptote very quickly, and further attention cannot produce additional knowledge. At the opposite extreme, if the content is beyond the child's capacities to process, attention will not produce comprehension.

In the middle range, however, will increases in attention brought about by formal features, humor, or attractive characters contribute to the child's comprehension of the message? If formal features suggest that the content will be interesting, funny, or designed for children, or that the content is similar to something the child has previously enjoyed, then the child may attend *and* expend some mental effort on processing the content. An anecdote may illustrate this process. A 5-year-old son of our colleague was sitting in the room while his mother watched the national news. He was busy drawing and was completely disinterested in the news. Then, an animated parody portraying Ronald and Nancy Reagan at breakfast with a ghost named David Stockman was shown. About 5 seconds after it started, the young boy looked up, started to look away, looked again, and continued to view until the animation ended. The formal features drew his attention, and he probably made some effort to understand the content. In fact, he probably did make some sense out of it, though his understanding may have been different from an adult's. If tbe content is within the child's range of understanding, then features that draw his attention will probably enhance comprehension, particularly if they are used in some of the informative ways discussed earlier. Features that turn off attention may lead a child to ignore comprehensible content. At the same time, even the most attentive child will not understand content that is beyond his present capacities for processing.

A Sampling Model of Attention

Sensory appeal, comprehensibility, entertainment value, and all other potential determinants of attention share the classic paradox of attentional processes, namely: How can one determine if a televised segment will be attention-worthy without first attending to it? Clearly the solution must involve sampling small bits by attending briefly from time to time, evaluating the appeal of that small sample, and making a decision about whether to continue attending on the evidence contained in the sample. Such decisions in effect amout to predictions about what the remainder of the bit, scene, or program will be like. For example, judgments about comprehensibility are in fact decisions about perceived or expected comprehensibility, not achieved comprehension, for attentional decisions must precede in time the achievement of comprehension of any given bit of information. Presumably, the child makes a judgment about the likely comprehensibility of the upcoming material on the basis of previous experience, either with the immediately preceding material or with similar material on other occasions. Judgments about the likely entertainment value, humor, or dramatic interest similarly involve predictions based on the child's general knowledge of media form and content cues as well as previous experience in processing the particular program material being viewed.

We propose that attentional sampling is not continuous, but occurs mostly at identifiable nodes in the program, such as at scene- and bit-change boundaries. There are enough auditory features associated with the visual events indicating a scene, bit, or program change, that even the child who is not looking is likely to attend during at least the first few seconds of such segments and to make a decision about whether to continue looking. This hypothesis is supported by the data discussed earlier showing that scene and bit changes recruit attention for those who are not looking *and* lose attention among those who are looking. The effect does not imply that such segment changes are either higher or lower in attention worthiness than other moments in the program, only that many viewers make an attentional decision based on a sample of viewing at or near a scene change, and that *some* of them will change their minds about the attention-worthiness of the segment at that point—more will do so then than at other, unmarked moments in the program.

If the initial decision is *not* to attend, there are three classes of events, two of them tied to the program itself, that could elicit a brief look, and thereby make a new sample available for a new attentional decision—to continue or not. The first category of such recruiting events are those very salient, mostly auditory events that can demand at least a brief look. Sirens, screams, crashes, and the like, if they are intense and reasonably infrequent, can override whatever a person is doing and gain attention. A second category of events, again largely auditory, are those that are perhaps slightly less salient but convey a particular quality of appealing content or signal a change in content, for example a change from adult to children's voices, sustained audience laughter, a familiar musical theme, applause, a change of music, and the like. A third cause for rerecruitment of attention is a set of properties of the viewing environment and the child, not of the program. If the child's alternative activity satiates, habituates, or comes to a stopping point, a return of attention to television is prompted.

Most of the successive judgments involved in an attentional decision probably occur fairly rapidly after the child's attention to the initial sample has been recruited. For example, one can make fairly rapid decisions about whether the content looks appropriate to one's interests, whether humor is present, whether it is completely incomprehensible, or whether it is hopelessly simple and boring. The longer the content, scene, or bit continues, the lower the likelihood that additional samples are going to lead to a different attentional decision than the initial one. This prediction is consistent with data presented by Anderson *et al.* (1979) showing that the probability of changes in attention (from looking to not looking or from not looking to looking) declines over time in a negatively accelerating pattern.

Criteria for Attentional and Processing Decisions

Assuming that attentional decisions are discrete events that occur at specifiable moments in a program, a more detailed look at how such decisions are reached is our next concern. The variables affecting these decisions and attentional choice points are grouped under two rubrics: cognitive processing and motivational judgments. One might think of a child asking herself or himself a series of questions such as "Can I understand this? Is this intended for me? What type of program is this? Do I recognize it?" (cognitive processing judgments) and "Do I like it? Is it a sensory thrill or pleasure? Is it funny? Does it fit my goals for viewing?" (motivational judgments). Obviously, we are not suggesting an articulated decision-making process of which the child is aware, but a hypothetical set of steps through which the child passes. The initial decisions are probably made on the basis of a quick assessment of program features and content. Subsequent decisions are probably based increasingly on the additional information which becomes available as a result of initial attempts to process the form and content.

A preliminary analysis of some of the steps in the attentional decision process, together with the role played by television forms at each step, is presented in Table 2.1. The entries are very roughly ordered from immediate to subsequent judgments and from shallower to deeper processing. Deeper levels are ordinarily reached by those whose attention and involvement have been maintained by passing earlier criteria. At each level, features affect both processing and motivation, and these, in turn affect each other. Initially features can recruit attention and provide enjoyment at a perceptual level. Features such as animation can quickly signal the type of content, suggest its general level of difficulty, and identify the kind of program or specific program series. Initial cognitive processing consists of recognizing markers and such content cues as familiar voices, faces, and settings. Recognition then makes possible a reference to past viewing of the program series and recall of past viewing satisfactions or gratifications, as well as comprehension, which can be applied to the present program and can prompt a decision regarding continued attention and processing.

Next the program's general level of difficulty, its comprehensibility, and its intended audience may be inferred (assuming it is not already familiar) from formal cues, such as presence of narration or laugh track, comprehensibility of speech, and the like, and a decision can be made about whether it fits the child's goal or preferences for viewing. If attention continues, decisions begin to be based on the outcomes of initial efforts to process the content. The child may decide quickly that the content is incomprehensible if it is marked by unambiguous cues, such as being in a foreign language, and cease to attend. However, if cues to comprehensibility are more ambiguous or less clearly marked, then attention may continue for a period of trial-and-error processing. This masking of comprehensibility may be why the scrambling of scenes within a bit did not lose attention in one of the studies by Anderson et al. (1981)—the children were not aware of the difficulties for comprehension and continued trying to understand it.

Clearly deeper processing occurs when the media-wise viewer can decode formal features carrying contextual and connotative meanings and can evaluate the interest level implied thereby. Where features

Table 2.1
Levels of Processing Television, Criteria of Involvement, and Roles of Formal Features

Roles played by formal features	Cognitive processing	Motivational criteria
Features as perceptually salient events	Initial orienting and attending	Is it perceptually thrilling, exciting, funny, novel, etc.?
Features as signals of content type, markers of particular programs, indicators of program's difficulty and intended audience, conveyors of connotative meanings.	Do I recognize it? Is it comprehensible? Is it for me or people like me? Can it be assimilated to my existing television schemes and scripts? Is it real–fictional; masculine–feminine; story–magazine format?	Is this one I liked before? Does it fit my goals and reasons for viewing right now? Will it be funny, affectively involving, full of suspense? Will favorite characters appear? Does its reality level, gender type, etc., appeal to me?
Features as representations of cognitive operations, key content, selective emphasis. Features that segment and structure the flow of content, provide cues for logical and temporal integration.	Can I encode it? Verbally? Iconically? What parts are central–incidental? Is logical–temporal integration needed? Am I getting it? What inferences are needed? How much mental effort will be required to follow it further?	Would this be fun to share? Is it memorable? Is it obvious or uncertain how it will come out? Can I anticipate what will happen next? Will the satisfaction be worth the mental effort required?
	Implications for subsequent viewing	
Program–series identifiers, standard introduction, music, set, characters, logo, etc.	What features are reliable indicators of all other episodes of this program–series?	Do I want to watch this program again?

serve to supplant or elicit cognitive operations, serve as modes of representation, and mark critical content with selective emphasis, the child can base decisions on outcomes of her efforts to encode verbally or visually and to integrate program events. Evaluation decisions may include judgments about whether the program would be interesting to share with others as well as whether the content appeals to the individual's tastes.

Some aspects of deeper cognitive processing depends upon features to structure the flow of content as regards temporal and causal sequences. Cognitively the child may monitor his own processing to decide if he is getting the message contained in the program, what inferences will be needed to make sense of it at a minimally satisfying level of comprehension, and how much mental effort will be needed to achieve that integrated comprehension. Motivationally the child will decide, at least implicitly, whether that effort is worth making. Part of that decision will involve judgment as to whether there are surprises, interesting plot events, or affectively appealing content to be revealed later if the child continues to work at comprehension.

Finally, information can be stored in memory that will have implications for subsequent viewing. Features that will serve as series identifiers for future reference may be noted as those situational, characterological, and contextual aspects of the production that will be most readily discriminated in the future. The general level of satisfaction and gratification achieved can then be associated with the distinctive features by which the program will henceforth be recognized, so as to facilitate future viewing (or avoidance) of the program series.

The consequences of decisions to continue or discontinue attending at any step are assymetrical. Initially, children must be able to use knowledge of feature cues and television story schemes to identify properties of the whole from a small sample. They must also evaluate their own level of comprehension accurately, a skill that cannot be automatically assumed (Patterson & Kister, 1980). The accuracy of their expectations will also depend, of course, on whether the forms presented early in a segment follow the marker conventions they have learned to use and whether the content of the initial portion stands as a representative example of the content to follow. When the child's sample-based anticipations are accurate, the process is straightforward. When the predictions of comprehensibility, appeal, and other aspects of attention-worthiness prove to be in error, then a decision to attend will soon be reversed, whereas a decision *not* to attend may endure for the remainder of the segment, or until a salient auditory event occurs, despite the fact that the bit might have been both comprehensible and interesting.

The main points in this analysis have been (a) there is probably a continual interplay of cognitive and motivational decisions that determine whether processing continues and at what level; and (b) formal features serve multiple marking, signaling, and encoding functions at several levels to make processing more effective for tbe viewer.

Summary and Conclusions

We have tried to synthesize two basic analyses of how television is structured and how children come to process and understand it. Previous studies of the forms of television (as distinct from its content) have shown how discriminable categories of formal production features are clustered in children's programs. Any feature can be used to inform, depending on the context and how the child viewer uses the feature, but certain features have much more perceptual salience or sensory impact than others. Such salient features may be appealing for their face value as perceptually entertaining or humorous events, but they may also serve to highlight informative content for selective attention and processing.

Accordingly, our first analysis concerns the functions of formal features in guiding selective attention, parsing and segmenting the stream of content, signifying contextual meanings, marking critical events, and representing content and the mental operations required to encode it. Contrary to previous expectations, it appears that children attend to salient features across a wide age range, but most of the other roles of formal features are dependent upon the development of cognitive and linguistic skills and the accumulation of experience with the medium.

The second part of this chapter is oriented toward a general analysis of the cognitive and motivational processes involved in learning from television. Specifically the interaction of attention and comprehension are analysed in relation to televised formal features. Divergent literature on this subject can be integrated by analyzing the process of viewing as incidental, rather than intentional learning. Such an analysis requires the inclusion of children's purposes, goals, and satisfactions in viewing along with their varying levels of processing as joint determinants of attention and comprehension. Multiple determinants of selective attention, motivation and involvement, effort required and expended, and level of comprehension achieved are identified.

A model of processing over time is proposed in which brief moments of attention occur at critical points in a program (bit or scene boundaries) that are marked by formal features. Samples of form and content attended to are evaluated for their interest, appeal, comprehensibility, and relevance. If the sample attended to passes these tests, attention continues and leads to deeper processing and more extensive evaluation of attention-worthiness. The longer a child attends, the more information is available on which to base the next decision about whether to continue and the less likely is a change in decision. When a child stops attending, salient features, features marking a segmental boundary, or a stopping place in alternative activity may precipitate the rerecruitment of attention, resulting in a new sample from which a new decision on continued attention can be made.

Because the vast majority of attentional and processing decisions are made on the basis of fragments attended to, the marking, signaling, and encoding functions of readily recognizable formal features play important roles. Television literacy develops not only as a consequence of growing cognitive skills, linguistic competence, and world knowledge, but also as a consequence of learning the forms and formats that constitute the medium's critical features. The literate viewer then uses such features and bits of associated content in two ways. One is to evaluate a bit of programming for its interest, appeal, comprehensibility, memorability, and relevance to the viewer's goals. The other is to interpret its messages, that is, to index its structure, complexity, processing requirements, and sometimes its meaning. Learning to learn from television consists at least in part of acquisition of these feature-using skills.

References

Alwitt, L. F., Anderson, D. R., Lorch, E. P., & Levin, S. R. Preschool children's visual attention to attributes of television. *Human Communication Research*, 1980, *7*, 52–67.

Anderson, D. R., Alwitt, L. F., Lorch, E. P., & Levin, S. R. Watching children watch television. In G. Hale & M. Lewis (Eds.), *Attention and the development of cognitive skills*. New York: Plenum, 1979.

Anderson, D. R., & Levin, S. R. Young children's attention to *Sesame Street*. *Child Development*, 1976, *47*, 806–811.

Anderson, D. R., Levin, S. R., & Lorch, E. P. The effects of TV program pacing on the behavior of preschool children. *AV Communication Review*, 1977, *25*, 159–166.

Anderson, D. R., Lorch, E. P., Field, D. E., & Sanders, J. The effects of TV program comprehensibility on preschool children's visual attention to television. *Child Development*, 1981, *52*, 151–157.

Berlyne, D. E. *Conflict, arousal and curiosity*. New York: McGraw-Hill, 1960.

Bernstein, L. J. *Design attributes of* Sesame Street *and the visual attention of preschool children.* Unpublished doctoral dissertation, Columbia University, 1978.

Bruner, J. S. On cognitive growth: I and II. In J. S. Bruner, R. R. Olver, & P. M. Greenfield (Eds.), *Studies in cognitive growth.* New York: Wiley, 1966.

Bryant, J., Hezel, R., & Zillmann, D. Humor in children's educational television. *Communication Education,* 1979, *28,* 49–59.

Calvert, S. L., Huston, A. C., Watkins, B. A., & Wright, J. C. The effects of selective attention to television forms on children's comprehension of content. *Child Development,* 1982, *53,* 601–610.

Clark, H., & Clark, E. *Psychology of language.* New York: Harper & Row, 1977.

Cohen, A. A., & Salomon, G. Children's literate television viewing: Surprises and possible explanations. *Journal of Communication,* 1979, *29*(3), 156–163.

Cohen, L. B., & Salapatek, P. *Infant perception: From sensation to cognition.* New York: Academic Press, 1975.

Collins, W. A. Learning of media content: A developmental study. *Child Development,* 1970, *41,* 1133–1142.

Collins, W. A. Cognitive processing aspects of television viewing. In D. Pearl, L. Bouthilet, & J. Lazar (Eds.), *Television and Behavior: Ten years of scientific progress and implications for the eighties.* Washington, D.C.: U.S. Government Printing Office, 1982.

Comstock, G., Chaffee, S., Katzman, N., McCombs, M., & Roberts, D. *Television and human behavior.* New York: Columbia University Press, 1978.

Dondis, D. A. *A primer of visual literacy.* Cambridge, Mass.: MIT Press, 1973.

Edelsky, C. Acquisition of an aspect of communicative competence: Learning what it means to talk like a lady. In S. Ervin-Tripp, & C. Mitchell-Kernan (Eds.), *Child Discourse.* New York: Academic Press, 1977.

Flavell, J. H. *Cognitive Development.* Englewood Cliffs, N.J.: Prentice-Hall, 1977.

Friedlander, B. Z., Wetstone, H. S., & Scott, C. S. Suburban preschool children's comprehension of an age-appropriate information television program. *Child Development,* 1974, *45,* 561–565.

Gibson, E. J. *Principles of perceptual learning and development.* Englewood Cliffs, N.J.: Prentice-Hall, 1969.

Glass, A. L., Holyoak, K. J., & Santa, J. L. *Cognition.* Reading, Mass.: Addison–Wesley, 1979.

Greer, D., Huston, A. C., Wright, J. C., Welch, R. L., & Ross, R. P. *Children's comprehension of television forms with masculine and feminine connotations.* Paper presented at the Society for Research in Child Development Biennial Meeting, Boston, April 1981.

Greer, D., Potts, R., Wright, J. C., & Huston, A. C. The effects of television commercial form and commercial placement on children's attention and social behavior. *Child Development,* 1982, *53,* 611–619.

Hale, G. A., Miller, L. K., & Stevenson, H. W. Incidental learning of film content: A developmental study. *Child Development,* 1968, *39,* 69–77.

Hawkins, R. P. Learning of peripheral content in films: A developmental study. *Child Development,* 1973, *44,* 28–33.

Hayes, D. S., & Birnbaum, D. W. Preschoolers' retention of televised events: Is a picture worth a thousand words? *Developmental Psychology,* 1980, *16,* 410–416.

Huston, A. C., Wright, J. C., Wartella, E., Rice, M. L., Watkins, B. A., Campbell, T., & Potts, R. Communicating more than content: Formal features of children's television programs. *Journal of Communication,* 1981, *31*(3), 32–48.

Huston-Stein, A., Fox, S., Greer, D., Watkins, B. A., & Whitaker, J. The effects of action and violence in television programs on the social behavior and imaginative play of preschool children. *Journal of Genetic Psychology*, 1981, *138*, 183–191.

Lesser, G. S. *Children and television: Lessons from Sesame Street*. New York: Random House, 1974.

Lorch, E. P., Anderson, D. R., & Levin, S. R. The relationship of visual attention to children's comprehension of television. *Child Development*, 1979, *50*, 722–727.

Lyle, J., & Hoffman, H. Children's use of television and other media. In E. A. Rubinstein, G. A. Comstock, & J. P. Murray (Eds.). *Television and social behavior* (Vol. 4). *Television in day-to-day life: Patterns of use*. Washington, D.C.: U.S. Government Printing Office, 1972.

McLuhan, H. M. *Understanding media: The extensions of man*. New York: McGraw–Hill, 1964.

National Science Foundation. *Research on the effects of television advertising on children*. Washington, D.C.: U.S. Government Printing Office, 1977.

Palmer, E. L. *A pedagogical analysis of recurrent formats on Sesame Street and The Electric Company*. Paper presented at the International Conference on Children's Educational Television, Amsterdam, June 1978.

Palmer, E. L., & McDowell, C. N. Program/commercial separators in children's television programming. *Journal of Communication*, 1979, *29*, 197–201.

Patterson, C. J., & Kister, M. C. The development of listener skills for referential communication. In W. P. Dickson (Ed.), *Children's oral communication skills*. New York: Academic Press, 1980.

Potts, R. *Effects of television form and content on children's social behavior*. Unpublished Master's thesis, University of Kansas, 1980.

Rice, M. *Television as a medium of verbal communication*. Paper presented at the American Psychological Association Annual Meeting, New York, September 1979.

Rice, M. L., Huston, A. C., & Wright, J. C. The forms and codes of television: Effects on children's attention, comprehension, and social behavior. In D. Pearl, L. Bouthilet, & J. Lazar (Eds.), *Television and behavior: Ten years of scientific progress and implications for the eighties*. Washington, D.C.: U.S. Government Printing Office, 1982.

Rice, M. L., & Wartella, E. Television as a medium of communication: Implications for how to regard the child viewer. *Journal of Broadcasting*, 1981, *25*, 365–372.

Rubinstein, E. A., Liebert, R. M., Neale, J. M., & Poulos, R. W. *Assessing television's influence on children's prosocial behavior*. Stony Brook, N.Y.: Brookdale International Institute, 1974.

Salomon, G. *Interaction of media, cognition, and learning*. San Francisco: Jossey-Bass, 1979.

Salomon, G. Introducing AIME: The assessment of children's mental involvement with television. In H. Kelly & H. Gardner (Eds.). *New directions for child development: Viewing children through television*. No. 13. San Francisco: Jossey-Bass, 1981.

Susman, E. J. Visual and verbal attributes of television and selective attention in preschool children. *Developmental Psychology*, 1978, *14*, 565–566.

Tower, R. B., Singer, D. G., Singer, J. L., & Biggs, A. Differential effects of television programming on preschoolers' cognition, imagination, and social play. *American Journal of Orthopsychiatry*, 1979, *49*, 265–281.

Wartella, E., & Ettema, J. S. A cognitive developmental study of children's attention to television commercials. *Communication Research*, 1974, *1*, 69–88.

Watkins, B. *Children's attention to and comprehension of prosocial television: The effects of plot, structure, verbal labeling, and program form*. Unpublished doctoral dissertation, University of Kansas, 1979,

Watkins, B., Calvert, S., Huston-Stein, A., & Wright, J. C. Children's recall of television material: Effects of presentation mode and adult labeling. *Developmental Psychology*, 1980, *16*, 672–674.

Welch, R. L., Huston-Stein, A., Wright, J. C., & Plehal, R. Subtle sex-role cues in children's commercials. *Journal of Communication*, 1979, *29*(3), 202–209.

Wright, J. C. *On familiarity and habituation: The situational microgenetics of information getting*. Paper presented at the Society for Research in Child Development Biennial Meeting, New Orleans, March 1977.

Wright, J. C., & Butt, J. *Televised training of preschoolers in number conservation*. Unpublished manuscript, Center for Research on the Influence of Television on Children, University of Kansas, 1979.

Wright, J. C., Calvert, S. L., Huston-Stein, A., & Watkins, B. A. *Children's selective attention to television forms: Effects of salient and informative production features as functions of age and viewing experience*. Paper presented at the Meeting of the International Communication Association, Acapulco, Mexico, 1980.

Wright, J. C., & Huston, A. C. The forms of television: Nature and development of television literacy in children. In H. Kelly & H. Gardner (Eds.), *New directions for child development: Viewing children through television*. No. 13. San Francisco: Jossey-Bass, 1981.

Wright, J. C., & Huston, A. C. *The information processing demands of television and "media literacy" in young viewers*. Paper presented at the Annual Meeting of the American Educational Research Association, New York, March 1982.

Wright, J. C., Huston-Stein, A., Potts, R., Thissen, D., Rice, M., Watkins, B. A., Calvert, S., Greer, D., & Zapata, L. *Formal features of children's TV programs as predictors of viewership by age and sex: A tale of three cities*. Paper presented at the Meeting of the Southwestern Society for Research in Human Development, Lawrence, Kansas, March 1980.

Wright, J. C., & Raeissi, P. *Television as a means of educating young children in logical concepts*. Fourth Annual Report to the Spencer Foundation. Center for Research on the Influence of Television on Children, University of Kansas, October 1981.

Wright, J. C., & Shirley, K. Matching communication pace with children's cognitive styles. In D. D. Hearn (Ed.), *Values, feelings and morals: Part I: Research and perspectives*. Washington, D.C.: American Association of Elementary–Kindergarten–Nursery Educators, 1974.

Wright, J. C., & Vlietstra, A. G. The development of selective attention: From perceptual exploration to logical search. In H. W. Reese (Ed.), *Advances in child development and behavior* (Vol. 10). New York: Academic Press, 1975.

Yussen, S. R. Determinants of visual attention and recall in observational learning by preschoolers and second graders. *Developmental Psychology*, 1974, *10*, 93–100.

Zillmann, D., Hay, T. A., & Bryant, J. The effect of suspense and its resolution on the appreciation of dramatic presentations. *Journal of Research in Personality*, 1975, *9*, 307–323.

Zillmann, D., Williams, B. R., Bryant, J., Boynton, K. R., & Wolf, M. A. Acquisition of information from educational television programs as a function of differently paced humorous inserts. *Journal of Educational Psychology*, 1980, *72*, 170–180.

Zuckerman, P., Ziegler, M., & Stevenson, H. W. Children's viewing of television and recognition memory of commercials. *Child Development*, 1978, *49*, 96–104.

chapter 3

Effects of Static and Dynamic Complexity on Children's Attention and Recall of Televised Instruction

JAMES H. WATT, JR.
ALICIA J. WELCH

This chapter is divided into three major parts. The first is a general discussion of the concept of television form complexity and a review of some of the research relating form complexity to visual attention and learning. The second section presents a formal definition of a very general set of audio and visual form complexity variables for television. The final section presents an application of the defined complexity variables to two children's programs and draws some conclusions about the general relationship of different types of form complexity to children's learning from television.

Prior Research into Form Complexity

The idea that form may affect the responses of receivers of the communication is not radical. It has received extensive discussion both from the point of view of aesthetics (cf. Arnheim, 1971; Berlyne, 1971; Moles, 1968) and from the point of view of learning from communications (cf. Anderson Levin, 1976; Lesser, 1974; Welch & Watt, 1982). We are primarily concerned with learning from communications, athough matters of aesthetics are implicitly involved in the process, particularly in gaining and holding the learner's attention.

There have been a number of studies that have attempted to relate the form of television programming to its effectiveness in attracting viewers and/or communicating desired content. However, the manner of conceptualizing form in these studies has varied. An early approach utilized categories based on television production techniques. For example, Crane and MacLean (1962) used a set of such categories to describe styles of educational programming. Hazard, Moriarty, and Timmons (1964) related viewer ratings of programs to production style categories of program form (cf. Watt, 1979). Lichty and Ripley (1970) proposed a set of program attributes which were primarily formal in nature and were labeled with very general terms in common use in the television industry, such as "pace," "variety," and "climax."

One theme which seems to run through a number of the concepts of program form is *change* or *difference*. For example, Anderson and Levin (1976) measured attributes such as moving through space, and change to a familiar scene to predict viewer visual attention to *Sesame Street* segments. Others (cf. Huston, Wright, Wartella, Rice, Watkins, Campbell, & Potts, 1981) have used such production techniques as pan and zoom as variables, which also imply change in the visual field. Similar use of the concepts of difference and change has been made with regard to elements on the auditory channel. Anderson and Levin, for example, used the attributes of auditory changes and peculiar voices. In terms of differences, the former attribute is self-explanatory, whereas the latter presumably refers to voices that are different from "normal" voices.

Watt and Krull (1974) developed a set of measures of program form based on information theory (Shannon & Weaver, 1949). They chose information theory as a basis for their concepts because it provided a theoretical bridge between program characteristics and viewer response. Program characteristics defined in terms of information level imply the levels of the information processing required of the viewer. This theoretical linkage is conspicuously missing in program form variables that rely essentially on operational definitions of program production techniques. It is intuitively plausible that a program which contains more sensory information may make demands on a viewer that affect learning; it is much less clear why a zoom, for instance, should have this effect.

Mathematical information theory also provides a useful means of relating the general concept of difference or change to information content. Berlyne (1957; Berlyne, Craw, Salapatek, & Lewis, 1963) presented the idea that the information level could be considered synonymous with the complexity of a stimulus. Thus, a stimulus which simultaneously exhibits differences in elements (e.g., a line drawing of many different objects) or which changes rapidly over time (e.g., a series of still photographs flashed sequentially on the screen) will be found to score high in entropy (the measure of information). This entropy score can be considered a measure of the complexity of the stimulus. From the receiver's point of view, drawings or photographs with many different objects are harder to process perceptually and cognitively, and the viewer would experience them as being more "complex" and more difficult to understand in a fixed time period. Likewise, the rapid presentation of stimuli over time would also result in processing difficulty, and the stimulus would be perceived as being complex.

A Simple Flow of Effects Model

A number of the formal attributes of television programming that have been used by different researchers to predict viewer responses to programming actually have been form complexity variables, whether explicitly defined as such or not. Before discussing form complexity more rigorously, let us present a general model relating program form complexity to visual attention and learning of program content, the two viewer responses of interest here.

Figure 3.1 summarizes the process. Form complexity (which is actually a number of variables) may influence visual attention in a number of ways—attracting, maintaining, or decreasing it. Visual attention in turn may affect learning of the presented material, insofar as it is an indicator of cognitive orientation toward the material being presented. Furthermore, it may be crucial for the learning of material presented on the visual track.

Form complexity, however, can have an effect on learning beyond that produced by visual attention. Even with identical levels of attention, differences in the complexity of the televised material may produce different levels of learning, due to perceptual and cognitive processing demands made by the program on the viewer. Imagine a person shown a 10-minute film run at 10 times normal speed, then given a recall test on the film's content. The same film is then presented at

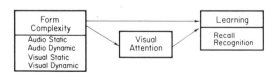

Figure 3.1. *General flow of effects.*

normal speed and another recall test is given. The only difference between the two conditions is the dynamic, or over-time, complexity of the presentation. Even though visual attention might be identical in both cases, learning undoubtedly would be different. With this general flow-of-effects model in mind, we will review some prior research into the relationships described.

Visual Complexity and Attention

Of all the relationships examined in this chapter, that between visual complexity and visual attention rests on the strongest base of research. Alwitt, Anderson, Lorch, and Levin (1980) found that a number of visual factors derived from a cross section of children's programs influenced the visual attention of preschoolers (cf. Anderson & Levin, 1976). Many of these visual factors, however, depressed attention once the effects of concomitant auditory attributes were controlled. Alwitt et al. (1980) found that stationary activity maintained visual attention, but that movement first elicited and then inhibited visual attention. Watt and Krull (1977) found a slight positive relationship between their measures of form complexity (based on information theory) and visual attention, again, among Sesame Street viewers. Welch and Watt (1982) found static visual complexity to be negatively related to visual attention, whereas dynamic visual complexity was positively related. Krull and Husson (1979; 1980) found that visual attention both predicted and was predicted by a number of visual form complexity variables in their time series analyses of data involving school-aged viewers of The Electric Company, but, interestingly, they also found that the visual attention of younger viewers of Sesame Street was not influenced by the complexity variables.

The very tentative conclusions that one might draw from these results are that the inclusion of various visual attention-grabbing production techniques produce somewhat inconsistent effects, but, more importantly, that they are not terribly consequential for preschool viewers. The major exceptions are some kinds of movement or activity that elicit visual attention probably via peripheral vision, and, in some cases, sustain it over time.

Auditory Complexity and Visual Attention

The fact that most of the impact of visual factors found by Alwitt et al. (1980) could be accounted for by concomitant auditory factors indicates that the auditory channel is probably more influential in terms of its impact on visual attention, particularly among visually inattentive viewers. It is therefore interesting that audio features have received less attention in the research literature to date.

Alwitt et al. (1980) found that most of their auditory factors at minimum elicited visual attention, while certain of these, especially ones involving unusual sounds and children's voices, also maintained it. Wartella and Ettema (1974) studied the effects of both visual and auditory stimulus complexity on preschoolers' visual attention to commercials. They found that the auditory factor explained variations in visual attention much more successfully than did the visual factor, especially among the youngest viewers. In contrast, Krull and Husson (1979; 1980) found no significant impact on the visual attention behavior of Sesame Street viewers for verbal interaction complexity, an audio feature.

A theoretical explanation for relationships between both visual and auditory complexity and visual attention is that of an individual "optimal level of stimulation" (Berlyne, 1971). Presumably, both very low and very high levels of sensory stimuli are aversive to the individual. Persons will seek to increase stimulation if they are on the low side of the optimum, and they will seek to avoid stimulation if they are on the high side. The operation of this principle in a television-viewing situation must take into account the level of stimulation being provided by the environment, in addition to that of the television program. For instance, if the environment is boring, a viewer might attend to a more stimulating television program, but if the environment is too stimulating, television might be used to reduce stimulation. Thus the interaction of the complexity of programming and the complexity of the viewer's environment may help determine attention levels. Individual need for stimulation is also important, as the optimal point will vary from individual to individual and should also vary according to age. Seen from this viewpoint, attention to programming is a collaboration between the needs of the viewer, who is active in selecting which material to attend to, and the producers, who must provide programming that fulfills a range of viewer needs for stimulation. Visual and auditory complexity will enhance attention levels only to the degree to which they provide desirable levels of stimulation for the viewer.

Visual Attention and Learning

Moving to the next link in the general model presented in Figure 3.1, we will examine the impact of visual attention on learning. There is a small body of accumulating research literature that addresses this relationship. When examining the visual attention–learning relationship, one of the first conclusions one arrives at is that the former is not necessarily sufficient to produce the latter. The vast sums spent on television advertising notwithstanding, viewing does not ensure learning or recall. There are too many individual differences in viewers' abilities, needs, and predispositions for audiences to be passively and uniformly influenced by any stimulus. As a case in point, the discouraging results of some of the studies accessing the learning effectiveness of *Sesame Street* (e.g., Sprigle, 1972; Minton, 1975) stand in contrast to the popularity of (and thus apparent attention to) the program. Likewise, Hofman and Flook (1980) recently concluded that viewing a television program designed to teach shape recognition had no impact on the learning of these skills among preschoolers, although practice (via the pretest) did have an effect. Thus, visual attention does not inevitably lead to comprehension. At best, we can hope to determine what conditions of television viewing do help to produce some learning.

In their study of *Sesame Street* viewers, Watt and Krull (1977) measured visual attention and verbal recall and found the two to be slightly but significantly positively related. In a study involving older children (grades 2 to 4) viewing commercials, Zuckerman, Ziegler, and Stevenson (1978) found that visual attention was more strongly related to recognition of information that had been presented on the visual track than of information presented on the auditory track.

Also using viewers of *Sesame Street*, Lorch, Anderson, and Levin (1979) found no differences in segment comprehension across experimental conditions that manipulated attention. Possibly this result was due to large within-segment variations on one or both measures. Their subsequent within-group analyses used much smaller time frames as the unit of analysis and did indicate a significant relationship between the two variables. The authors believe that this outcome is an argument for comprehension producing visual attention (i.e., the children watched the episodes that they found comprehensible). This argument has been tested experimentally by Anderson, Lorch, Field, and Sanders (1981) who found that auditorally incomprehensible programs (foreign language or backward speech) received less visual attention than normal programs. They also obtained mixed support for a partially comprehensible program (intact scenes edited together randomly) obtaining somewhat lower visual attention than a normal program. It should be noted that comprehensibility as measured by Anderson *et al.* (1981) is essentially a program attribute, whereas comprehension is an attribute of the individual viewer. It is possible, for example, that program comprehensibility contributes to visual attention which in turn may help to produce some level of comprehension in the viewer.

Welch and Watt (1982) examined the impact of viewer visual attention on both verbal recall and nonverbal recognition. Visual attention proved to be modestly related to recall and more strongly related to recognition. These differential results were interpreted in terms of the predominant channel used to carry the messages tapped by the questions. Recognition questions almost always reflected material presented on the visual track whereas recall questions predominantly reflected material presented on the audio track.

Evidence for the visual attention–comprehension link is by no means overwhelming, but this brief review indicates that it is at least consistently found, if modest and arguable in terms of causal direction. The next question, is then: If one could control the modest effects due to visual attention, what kind of impact would program complexity have on learning?

Visual Complexity and Learning

Based on the limited research on this topic, there is reason to suppose that static visual complexity and dynamic visual complexity may affect learning differently. The early work by Friedlander, Wetstone and Scott (1974) suggests that irrelevant visual background material impedes recall. Among other variables studied, Flagg, Allen, Geer, and Scinto (1976) examined one that is akin to static visual complexity. Their discussion of its impact on eye gaze patterns suggests that it might hinder learning. Welch and Watt (1982) found static visual complexity to be fairly strongly negatively related to both verbal and nonverbal learning.

Little is known at this point about the impact of dynamic visual complexity on learning. Watt and Krull (1977) obtained a slight negative relationship between form complexity and recall. Welch and Watt (1982) found that dynamic visual complexity was positively related to recognition and not significantly related to recall. They speculated that the cognitive processing of information required in providing a verbal response (recall) might be qualitatively different from the processing of information requiring visual recognition, and that form complexity occurring over time would affect this processing differently than form complexity occurring statically.

A number of researchers have studied the learning impact of various camera techniques (e.g., Acker & Tiemens, 1981; Salomon & Cohen, 1977), with conflicting results. However, Acker and Tiemens (1981) pro-

vide evidence that young children perceive changes in the size of televised images that are due to camera changes as being actual changes in
the images themselves. In other words, they do not conserve the images. Furthermore, they apparently learn the conservation of televised
images at a later age than that of physically tangible objects. This finding may have negative implications for the use of visually complex
programming for young children, since televised information may be
generally more difficult for young children to learn than information
for which the referents are physically present in the child's environment.

There are several mechanisms by which visual complexity may affect learning, independent of visual attention. One is the simple idea of
information overload. Berlyne (1971, p. 149) suggested that the larger
the number of elements contained in a pattern, the more complex that
pattern would be. A visual field with more elements will be harder to
process and make sense of. Important elements may be missed in the
act of decoding the picture. This is especially true of young children
whose cognitive developmental abilities may not yet include efficient
information selection strategies (cf. Collins, 1970; Wackman & Wartella, 1977). Another process at the other extreme of information overload is boredom. Overly simple visual fields may lead to what Berlyne
terms "negative hedonic value," or the uncomfortable feeling of
boredom [p. 80]. One response to boredom with the external environment is to switch to internal information processing, that is, to
daydream. This has obvious implications for learning. It is likely that
presentations whose form neither bores nor overloads the viewer will
lead to higher levels of learning.

Auditory Complexity and Learning

This area brings us into the realm of the unknown. Watt and Krull
(1977) found that one complexity variable associated with the audio
track, verbal time entropy, was significantly negatively related to recall.
Furthermore, research in the area of language learning indicates that
the presence of acoustic information (via an audio channel or subject
vocalization) enhances short-term memory (cf. Crowder, 1970). These
results are merely suggestive, however, in the absence of more extensive evidence, although we may speculate that the audio track may be
highly influential in the learning process. The same processes previously discussed for the visual channel may be at work in the auditory
channel. Auditory overload and boredom are likely outcomes when
dealing with extremes of auditory complexity. Silence may produce

boredom on the part of the viewer, with resultant reduced learning. A full orchestra and chorus may produce overload, also with resultant reduced learning. Ordinary dialogue, however, may represent an effective, moderate level of auditory complexity for learning purposes.

Definitions of Complexity

A difficulty with much of the literature on the form aspects of television is in the definition of variables—variables that are labeled differently but have some conceptual overlap often appear. This confusion makes detection and description of general effects of television form difficult, as the results of different studies are not easily comparable. Form variables also often suffer from being either too abstract or too specific. Abstract variables, while being generally applicable to most programming, are often difficult to define operationally. Highly abstract form variables are also generally useful only in the prediction of similarly abstract viewer behavior variables, limiting their usefulness. "Pace" is a good example of this kind of variable. Variables that are very specific do not suffer from these drawbacks, but their lack of generality limits their usefulness both pragmatically and theoretically. "Presence of puppets" is a very specific nominal variable, but it is applicable only to certain programs. It is also difficult to specify the theoretical process by which this variable might affect viewers.

What is needed is a set of mutually exclusive concepts that are sufficiently general to approach being an exhaustive set, while not being restricted to particular programming types. One very useful technique is to extract modal primitive terms that can be used to build up a set of derived concepts (Hage, 1974). For example, a television stimulus can be split into an audio and a visual mode. It can also be characterized in terms of form and content. Combining these two modes gives us four classifications of television variables: audio form, audio content, visual form, and visual content. This process can be continued until very specific variables are defined. The virtue of the process is that it produces concepts that are mutually exclusive and exhaustive. In the preceding example, there is no overlap among the classes of variables, and, if one could measure all variables in all classes, the original concept (television stimuli) could be completely characterized.

Clearly one modal distinction being made is that between television form and television content. Form is restricted to the medium itself. Any concept which is defined as formal must be applicable to all television programming, from *Captain Kangaroo* to *NFL Football* to *Master-*

piece Theater. Any concept that is defined as purely content must be completely independent of the production techniques used to convey the meaning.

Both modes can be used to define some concepts, but some degree of confusion is bound to result. In fact, most of the measured concepts (or variables) used in the studies cited previously are somewhat mixed, for example the Lichty *et al.* "variety" variable. Variety could be introduced by television production techniques such as editing or camera movement (form variety), or it could be introduced by plot intricacies (content variety).

A mode that is so self-evident that it is often overlooked is "channel". Television is both an auditory and a visual medium, but the two sensory channels are very different in their operation, and concepts that are defined for the auditory channel may behave quite differently than similar variables defined for the visual channel.

The stimulus provided to the receiver is different in each television channel: auditory signals are unidimensional (sound pressure as a function of time), whereas visual signals are bidimensional (being changes in luminance which have both height and width characteristics as a function of time). There are also many perceptual processing differences within the receiver. Auditory processing is more general. It is difficult (although not completely impossible) to concentrate on a stimulus in the presence of other competing stimuli. In the visual field, where the eye can select and sample from the visual stimuli available, one can focus on one stimulus and ignore competing stimuli more easily.

Another modal distinction is that between simplicity and complexity. Moles (1968) provides a useful set of synonyms for the simplicity–complexity distinction. These may be particularly useful in considering television form: simple–complex; order–disorder; predictable–unpredictable; banal–original; redundant–informative; intelligible–novel; structured–random. If one considers complexity as a continuum, the definitional term becomes *degree of complexity*. The degree of complexity of a concept (such as a television visual) could range from simple (ordered, predictable, structured) to complex (disordered, unpredictable, random). The idea of complexity as disorder and unpredictability underlies the whole of mathematical information theory.

The usefulness of information theory in Moles's (1968) definition of complexity cannot be overstated. "In every message, 'information' is nothing other than a *measure of the complexity* of the temporal *Gestalten* presented: [entropy] measures complexity, which is very important in all theories of form, that until now have lacked an instrument with which to compare forms [p. 33]."

The basic formula for entropy is

$$H = -\sum_{i=1}^{k} p_i \log_2(p_i),$$

where H is entropy, a measure of information or complexity; p_i is the probability of appearance of symbol i; and k is the total number of symbols in the system. This formula shows the information theory measure to be sensitive to the total number of symbols being used, as well as their probability of appearance. If all are equally probable, entropy, and thus complexity, is maximized and predictability of the appearance of a particular symbol is minimized. A full discussion of information theory is not called for here, but those unfamiliar with its basic concepts are referred to Shannon and Weaver (1949) and Pierce (1961) for the basic papers and a readable interpretation of the formulas.

A final mode that is less evident is that of static–dynamic. Static concepts are time invariant; dynamic concepts are functions of time. There has been serious lack of attention to the differences between the two in much of the literature. For example, the Watt and Krull (1974) measures of program form do not make this distinction for either visual or verbal variables. Yet there is clearly a distinction to be made between stimuli that differ only in speed of presentation (i.e., over time) and those that differ only in complexity of pattern (i.e., over space). The Watt and Krull variables, since they are concerned primarily with the randomness of presentation of visuals and character verbalizations over an entire program, are primarily dynamic complexity measures. It is not at all clear, however, that dynamic and static processing of stimuli lead to the same outcomes. The Welch and Watt (1982) results for static and dynamic visual complexity suggest that cognitive processing mechanisms involved with visual memory operate differently for the two types of complexity. The concepts should be separated so that static effects are not confused with dynamic effects.

From this analysis, we obtain the following modal terms with which to define some concepts: form–content; simplicity–complexity; audio–visual; and static-dynamic. As we are interested here in the form of programming, we will eliminate the content term and discuss combinations of the other terms. From these combinations will come definitions of television form variables, which are mutually exclusive and which can be applied to all television programming, as they are based on these very general modal concepts. The combination of terms gives some very specific variables to be defined: degree of audio static complexity; degree of audio dynamic complexity; degree of visual static complexity; and degree of visual dynamic complexity.

Audio Static Complexity

The first task in defining audio static complexity is the choice of the symbol set for audio. We are constrained in this choice by the fact that we are operating within the form, rather than content, mode. The digit chosen must be applicable across all types of television content, that is, it must be content independent.

An audio signal is a composite of sound waves of different frequencies, with each frequency having an associated intensity. If we break up the audio signal into frequency bands, or ranges of frequencies, and measure the loudness, or intensity, of the frequencies in each band, we have defined a symbol set which can be used in an information theory definition.

Imagine 10 boxes laid in a row on a table top. Each of the boxes represents a band of audio frequencies. In each box is a slip of paper with a number on it; this is the intensity of the frequencies within the band at a single point in time. The representation is thus static. If we add another row of 10 boxes behind the first, with another set of intensities, we can represent the audio signal at another point in time. By adding rows of boxes, we can completely describe the whole audio stimulus sequence.

Let us first consider only the set of boxes at one point in time. How might we characterize a simple (i.e., low complexity) audio stimulus? In information theory terms, the signal would be simple if the intensity in one box could predict those in the other 9 boxes. For example, if all intensities were identical, one could predict all the rest by knowing the value of one band intensity. Silence, an obviously simple stimulus, would be an example of this. As the intensities in each box become increasingly different (i.e., unordered), the complexity of the sound increases.

Suppose we have an automatic machine that will create the frequency band boxes once each second, measure the intensity of frequencies in each, and put a slip in each box corresponding to the intensity, ranging from 0 (silence in this frequency band) to 9 (very loud intensity). At three time points the machine measures (a) silence; (b) a solo flute playing a note; and (c) a crescendo of a full orchestra. The pattern of measurements might look like this:

$$
\begin{array}{cccccccccc}
0 & 0 & 0 & 0 & 0 & 0 & 0 & 0 & 0 & 0 \\
0 & 8 & 0 & 0 & 0 & 0 & 0 & 0 & 0 & 0 \\
2 & 2 & 6 & 3 & 3 & 5 & 5 & 8 & 6 & 4
\end{array}
$$

The first measurement is utter simplicity. The second is slightly more complex. The last is a truly complex sound, with little apparent order or predictablity.

This intuitive approach leads us to a formal theoretical and operation definition. Static audio complexity is defined as the degree of randomness (or unpredictability) of the pattern of sound intensities measured in a finite number of frequency bands at a single point in time.

Operationally, we can use a modified information theoretical formula:

$$
H_{\substack{\text{audio} \\ \text{static}}} = \sum_{i=1}^{k} H_i ;
$$

$H_i = -(p_i \log_2 p_i) - (q_i \log_2 q_i);$

k = number of audio bands

$q_i = 1 - p_i;$ and

p_i = percentage of frequency bands adjacent to band$_i$ with differing sound intensity.

The symbol set in this formula has actually been reduced from a set of band intensities to two symbols: SAME and DIFFERENT. The probabilities for each frequency band are computed by determining the percentage of intensities of each neighboring band which are the same and which are different. This distinction is important. If all the frequency bands are present at the same intensity (all 9s, for example), the operational formula will give 0 complexity. One might intuitively think that the presence of many frequencies is a more complex situation than the presence of only one; but the presence of all frequencies at the identical intensity is a very ordered situation and hence is of low complexity. In fact, it describes "white noise," which sounds like the interstation noise from an FM radio receiver. White noise is not perceived as complex, and in fact it is used by enterprising insomniacs to mask more random and distracting sounds.

Audio Dynamic Complexity

In considering audio static complexity, all frequencies at a single point in time were considered as a kind of snapshot of the audio. In audio dynamic complexity we examine *change* in a single frequency band over time. Thus the time dimension is substituted for the frequency dimension. Results for all frequency bands can be aggregated, but the basic definition concerns change within a single frequency band across all time points. Audio static complexity, by contrast, was concerned with differences within a single time point, across all frequency bands.

Using the analogy from the previous section, we can examine the box on the left side of each row, over several rows (which correspond to different time points). If the intensities in each box remain constant over time, the situation is very ordered, and we can predict the intensity at a later time point by knowing the current intensity. This is a low complexity situation. If the intensity changes, we lose this predictability and say that the audio signal within the particular frequency band (box) being investigated is more complex. The longer the intensity stays at its new value, however, the less random and therefore the less complex the audio signal becomes.

From this verbal statement, we can formally define *audio dynamic complexity* as the randomness over time of the intensity of an audio frequency band. The following operational formula corresponds to this definition, with the addition of summing the audio dynamic complexity over all frequency bands to produce a summary value for the variable at each time point.

$$H_{\substack{\text{audio} \\ \text{dynamic}}} = \sum_{m=1}^{k} H_m;$$

$$H_m = -(r_m \log_2 r_m) - (s_m \log_2 s_m);$$

k = number of audio bands;

$s_m = 1 - r_m;$

$r_m = \dfrac{1}{2^D}$; and

D = total time points for which frequency band $_m$ has had an identical sound intensity.

This formula is again based on information theory but has been modified to respond to a symbol set of SAME and DIFFERENT over time. The probabilities are computed by a bit of mathematical trickery as a geometrically decreasing series that operates in the following way: At the time point immediately after a change in intensity of the audio signal in a band, the D value will be 1, and thus the probability of SAME and DIFFERENT will be set to 1/2, giving the maximum value for audio dynamic complexity in this band at this time point. If the intensity then remains unchanged at the next time point, D will be 2, and probability of DIFFERENT will be 1/4 and SAME will be 3/4. At the next time point, assuming no change in intensity, the probabilities will be 1/8 and 7/8, 1/16 and 15/16, and so on. When substituted in the information theory formula, these values will cause the audio dynamic complexity to rapidly drop toward 0, as the situation is becoming increasingly predictable (the next time point will be the same as the current time point). When the intensity in the frequency band changes, however, the probabilities jump back to 1/2 and 1/2 once again, as D is reset to 1, and the geometric series begins again. The result is a sharp rise in audio dynamic complexity at the point of change, followed by a smooth but rapid drop unless there is further change in the intensity.

Visual Static Complexity

We must first define the basic visual symbol set in content independent terms. A visual signal is a set of luminances or light levels which occur on a two-dimensional spatial surface and which vary over time. If we break up the spatial surface into small areas and measure the light intensity in each area, we can describe the visual field completely. If a number representing luminance is assigned to each area, we have a set of symbols that can be used in information theory measurements of complexity. Note that we are talking about measuring the light levels at a single instant in time and across both spatial dimensions. This makes the summary results static in nature, as they do not depend upon measurement across time.

If all luminances are the same (a gray screen, for example), the static complexity should be 0, as the luminance of every cell could be predicted from knowledge of a single cell. If one cell has a different luminance (a single white dot, for example), the visual field becomes somewhat more complex. As other cells take on different luminance values, the complexity increases again. Here we note a difference from the audio static complexity. Because the visual field is two-dimensional, the *spatial location* of luminances is important. If the left half of the screen is black and the right half white, the complexity is not greatly different from that of a single white dot on a black field, even though there is a great difference in the numbers of black and white areas involved. A checkerboard pattern, however, which is also made up of half white and half black cells, is much more complex.

One method of incorporating spatial patterns in the measurement of static visual complexity was originally suggested by Shea (1974). It involves consideration of the neighbors of each individual visual cell. If the neighbors of a cell are identical in luminance to the cell itself, that is, if their luminance values are predictable from the luminance value of the cell being examined, the cell contributes nothing to the total visual complexity of the picture. As the surrounding cells become different in luminance, the complexity contributed by the cell increases until the number of luminances that are the same is equal to those that are different. At this point, knowledge of the luminance of the cell being examined will not allow one to predict the luminance of a particular neighboring cell at better than chance levels. Maximum disorder has thus been reached, and complexity for this cell is at its highest. If most neighboring cells are different in luminance from the cell being examined, complexity is reduced, as once again one can predict the luminance levels in the surrounding cells with a better than 50% accuracy from knowledge of the target cell's luminance. If all surrounding cells differ in luminance from the examined cell, complexity is again 0. By examining all cells in a display and summing the complexity about each, an estimate of the static visual complexity for the entire picture can be constructed.

If we examine the operation of this procedure in the three simple visual fields described earlier (a white dot on a gray background; a half white, half black screen; and a checkerboard), we see that complexity is found only at the boundaries of different luminance levels. The procedure thus implicitly equates static visual complexity to visual contours. This is very desirable, as it parallels an intuitive definition of static visual complexity, namely, complexity as the number of different objects depicted, which is exactly the definition of visual complexity given by Moles (1968). Objects are represented on the television screen as luminance contours (e.g., a white box on a gray table), so this measurement procedure will be sensitive to the number of objects on the screen.

Visual static complexity can be formally defined as 'the degree of unpredictability of the luminance contours of the entire visual field'. The operational definition, based on information theory, that assesses visual static complexity is

$$H_{\substack{\text{visual} \\ \text{static}}} = \sum_{i=1}^{r} \sum_{j=1}^{c} H_{ij};$$

$H_{ij} = -(p_{ij} \log_2 p_{ij}) - (q_{ij} \log_2 q_{ij});$
r = number of rows in grid;
c = number of columns in grid;
$q_{ij} = 1 - p_{ij};$ and
p_{ij} = percentage of cells adjacent to cell$_{ij}$ with differing light intensity.

Visual Dynamic Complexity

In defining and measuring visual dynamic complexity, we ignore changes across the spatial dimensions (visual contours) and measure changes in luminance across the time dimension within each area on the screen. If a picture remains motionless on the screen, the luminance levels in every cell will remain constant over time. This will happen regardless of the visual static complexity of the picture. Since there is no change over time, there is complete predictability of luminance levels in each cell at future time points, and thus the visual dynamic complexity is 0.

Let us take the example of a white ball on a black background. The visual static complexity of this picture will be fairly low, as the number of contours is small. If the ball remains motionless, there will be no changes in the luminance levels in individual cells and thus no visual dynamic complexity. If the ball rolls across the screen, however, some cells will change in value. Suppose the ball rolls from the left side to the right side of the screen. Cells on the left which had previously been white (high luminance) because they were part of the ball will become black background when the ball vacates their part of the picture, and cells on the right which were black background will become white ball cells. This change in luminance over time is dynamic complexity. Note that the visual static complexity has not changed. A snapshot of the screen at two time points will show identical visual contours, although they will be located at two different places on the screen. By examining single cells over time for the SAME or DIFFERENT levels of luminance, we can use the same strategy in defining and measuring visual dynamic complexity as was used in the definition of audio dynamic complexity, by simply substituting the luminance level in a cell for the sound intensity in a frequency band.

Visual dynamic complexity is formally defined as the degree of unpredictability of the luminance levels over time in a set of spatial cells which make up the visual display. Operationally, the formula for this definition is:

$$H_{\substack{visual \\ dynamic}} = \sum_{m=1}^{r} \sum_{n=1}^{c} H_{mn}$$

$H_{mn} = -(r_{mn} \log_2 r_{mn}) - (s_{mn} \log_2 s_{mn});$

r = number of rows in grid;

c = number of columns in grid;

$s_{mn} = 1 - r_{mn};$

$r_{mn} = \dfrac{1}{2^D};$ and

$D =$ total time points for which cell$_{ij}$ has had an identical luminance level.

An Example of Research Using Static and Dynamic Complexity

The definitions derived earlier were used in a study that illustrates their utility. The research consisted of a detailed analysis of two children's programs: *Sesame Street* and *Mister Rogers' Neighborhood*. This research was undertaken for two purposes.

The first was descriptive. *Sesame Street* has been accused by some researchers and critics of overstimulating young audiences by its use of fast-paced production techniques (e.g., Halpern, 1975; Singer & Singer, 1979). By contrasting episodes of each of these programs on the complexity measures we may either confirm or contradict some of these assertions concerning the form complexity of each program. The second purpose was to test the adequacy of the flow of effects model outlined earlier. By examining the strength of the hypothesized relationships in two very different programs, we may draw conclusions about the accuracy and adequacy of the hypothesized model.

Experimental Procedures

Stimulus materials were two black-and-white videotapes. One consisted of a 30-minute edited version of 12 *Sesame Street* segments. The other was an off-the-air tape of *Mister Rogers' Neighborhood*. In addition, another tape was prepared that reversed the order of the *Sesame Street* segments to control for possible effects due to the order of segment presentation. The ongoing narrative of the *Mister Rogers' Neighborhood* program precluded making a reversed order version, insofar as events occurring later in the program often referred to or depended on information presented in earlier scenes.

Of the 12 *Sesame Street* segments, 7 were analyzed for present purposes. These 7 were chosen because they were judged to reflect sufficient variability on the independent measures and would not overtax the attention spans of the subjects. The *Mister Rogers' Neighborhood* tape was broken down into 8 separate segments, of which data on 6 were analyzed. The 2 omitted segments involved the singing of familiar songs and were judged unsuitable for present purposes.

Synchronizing pulses at 1-second intervals were placed on the second audio track of each videotape. These pulses were used to insure that all audio and video measurements were made at identical points in the tapes. Luminance readings for visual complexity were taken each second on a 4-row, 5-column grid placed over the screen of a monitor. A photocell at the center of each grid provided a luminance reading that was recorded by a lab computer. Calibration error was less than 1% between the photocells, and mean test–retest error in the readings was .5%.

Audio intensities for the audio complexity measure were taken at the same 1-second intervals. An analog filter was used to separate the audio track into the following frequency bands:

$$
\begin{array}{rl}
20- & 100 \quad \text{Hz} \\
100- & 200 \\
200- & 300 \\
300- & 400 \\
400- & 500 \\
500- & 750 \\
750- & 1000 \\
1000- & 1500 \\
1500- & 2000 \\
2000- & 3000 \\
3000- & 5000 \\
5000- & 7500 \\
\end{array}
$$

These frequency bands were chosen to correspond roughly to those found to be of value in distinguishing between human speakers. This should make the measurements more sensitive to the use of different speakers on the audio track. Also, as most power in the audio spectrum is concentrated in the lower frequencies, the specification of increasingly larger bandwidths as frequency increases should equalize the intensities found in each band and eliminate the need for rescaling at higher frequencies.

The intensities of the frequencies within each band were averaged by a hardware device which computed a moving average of the peak intensities. A moving average is computed at a time point by weighting data according to its recency and averaging the weighted data over time. This gives more weight to recent data and eventually discards data further back in time. The hardware averager had a .5-second time constant, meaning that frequency intensity data decreased in importance exponentially until it disappeared from the average after about 1.5 seconds.

The luminance and sound intensity data were used in the operational definitions given earlier to produce estimates of visual static dynamic complexity, and audio static and dynamic complexity on a 1-

second basis for each entire program. Descriptive statistics for the complexity variables were computed on this second-by-second basis. In addition, each of the complexity variables was averaged over each segment of each program, providing a single value per variable for that segment. These values were used in tests of the models, and descriptive statistics based on these segmental values were also computed.

There were 48 subjects (25 males and 23 females) viewing *Sesame Street*, with half viewing each order, and 50 subjects (19 males and 31 females) viewing the single version of *Mister Rogers' Neighborhood*. The subjects were obtained from three preschools; all subjects except one ranged in age from 4 years 0 months to 6 years 0 months (the single exception was a subject aged 3 years 7 months). All but four of the subjects were white.

Experimental procedures were identical for both programs. Subjects viewed the tape alone in a room with a variety of toys and other activities alternative to viewing, while an experimenter observed and recorded the subject's attention through a one-way window. The experimenter administered a learning posttest immediately after the program ended. This test included both a recall measure requiring verbal responses from the subject and a recognition test requiring only that the subject select from a set of objects one correct object, which had appeared in the segment under test (cf. Welch & Watt, 1982, for a full description of the procedure and its scoring). The entire procedure took approximately 1 hour.

Since this was a repeated measures design in which subjects served as their own control group, all statistics were corrected for between-subjects variance (Cohen & Cohen, 1975). Thus the relationships reported here are based on the within-subject variance and should be interpreted as the relationship obtained when individual differences between subjects are held constant.

Linear causal analysis was used to estimate the strength of relationships (Heise, 1975; Kenney, 1979). In causal diagrams, such as Figure 3.2, an arrow represents a causal relationship, pointing from cause to effect, and a curved, double-headed arrow represents a noncausal covariance between variables. These covariances were computed as partial correlations, and the causal coefficients were beta weights from linear regression (see Heise, 1975, for a full discussion of the procedure). The resulting path model was tested for plausibility by testing its ability to reproduce the observed zero-order correlations among all variables (cf. Watt, 1980, or Duffy, Watt, & Duffy, 1982, for a detailed description of this procedure). All models were found to be plausible, indicating that no serious structural or coefficient estimation errors were made in the modeling process.

Sesame Street *and*
Mister Rogers' Neighborhood *Contrasted*

Table 3.1 summarizes the differences between the two programs' complexities and the differences in viewer responses. All second-by-second measurements produced significant differences between shows. However, with the large number of observations, this is not surprising. Since even trivial differences will be statistically significant, it is the size of the differences that is important. The situation with the segment comparisons is reversed. As there are only 13 segments (7 for *Sesame Street* and 6 for *Mister Rogers' Neighborhood*), only very large differences will be statistically significant.

The audio static complexity was somewhat higher for *Sesame Street* then for *Mister Rogers' Neighborhood*. The probable reason is the use of more music in *Sesame Street*, which will result in a wider range of frequencies being present at any static time point, thus increasing the static audio complexity. The audio dynamic complexity was much higher for *Sesame Street* than for *Mister Rogers' Neighborhood*. The higher audio dynamic complexity for *Sesame Street* indicates a greater change in sound frequencies and amplitudes over time. This is proba-

Table 3.1

Descriptive Statistics Contrasting Sesame Street (SS) *and* Mister Rogers' Neighborhood (MN)

Variable	Segment		Second-by-second[a]	
	MN	SS	MN	SS
Audio static	9.49	10.26	9.35	10.70
(SD)	(.835)	(.715)	(3.39)	(2.34)
Audio dynamic	7.187	9.63[b]	7.66	9.64
(SD)	(.863)	(1.40)	(1.71)	(1.80)
Visual static	31.6	26.62[b]	31.73	27.99
(SD)	(2.17)	(3.01)	(5.51)	(5.98)
Visual dynamic	12.06	11.85	11.99	12.36
(SD)	(2.06)	(1.79)	(3.89)	(4.33)
Visual attention	63.0	68.9	58.3	68.1
(SD)	(27.8)	(28.8)	(19.6)	(16.5)
Recall	4.49	3.44		
(SD)	(1.81)	(1.88)		
Recognition	5.36	4.01		
(SD)	(1.50)	(1.76)		

[a]All differences between shows significant at $p < .01$; $N = 1722$ for MN; $N = 1629$ for SS.
[b]$p < .02$; $N = 6$ for MN; $N = 7$ for SS. All other differences n.s.

bly a result of *Sesame Street's* use of sound effects and many different characters whose voices change from segment to segment.

Visual static complexity for *Mister Rogers' Neighborhood* is much higher that that for *Sesame Street*. The *Mister Rogers' Neighborhood* sets are visually quite "busy." *Mister Rogers' Neighborhood* also tends to use a number of medium and long shots that include several persons. This places much detail on the screen at any one time and thus increases the visual static complexity. *Sesame Street*, by contrast, often uses simple sets, especially for Muppets segments. *Sesame Street* also makes extensive use of cartoons, which are low in detail. The two programs differed quite substantially in this complexity measurement. (The segments chosen from *Sesame Street* accentuated the difference somewhat, as the mean for the segments is somewhat lower than the whole program mean based on the second-by-second analysis. The *Mister Rogers' Neighborhood* segment mean is very close to the second-by-second mean, however.)

The visual dynamic complexity results are surprising. On the segments chosen, *Mister Rogers' Neighborhood* was actually slightly higher in visual dynamic complexity that *Sesame Street*. (Over the whole program, *Sesame Street* was slightly higher, but the difference is quite small.) The result conflicts with the general belief that *Sesame Street* is visually faster paced than *Mister Rogers' Neighborhood*. Through camera switching and editing techniques and by moving the characters about on the sets, *Mister Rogers' Neighborhood* produces visual dynamic change about equal to *Sesame Street*. It should be noted that the definition of visual dynamic change used here is not identical to less formally defined concepts like "pace," which are usually operationally defined in terms of camera and editing techniques. We would argue that the effects attributed to pacing are usually described in terms of sensory stimulation (cf. Halpern, 1975; Singer & Singer, 1979), which is precisely what visual dynamic complexity measures.

Over the whole program, *Sesame Street* produced much higher levels of visual attention that did *Mister Rogers' Neighborhood*, but, on the segments chosen to test the models, this difference is reduced. The *Mister Rogers' Neighborhood* segments selected were somewhat higher in visual attention than the average for the whole *Mister Rogers' Neighborhood* program.

Because the recall and recognition questions had different operational definitions, they cannot be directly compared. There is no assurance that the questions for one program were not harder to answer than the questions for the other. Viewers consistently scored higher on the *Mister Rogers' Neighborhood* questions than on the *Sesame Street* questions, however.

In summary, *Mister Rogers' Neighborhood* differed from *Sesame Street* in having a less complex audio track, both statically and dynamically, and in having a more complex static visual track. The two programs were very close in visual dynamic complexity. *Sesame Street* provided an audio track that might result in more viewer stimulation; *Mister Rogers' Neighborhood* provided a visual track that might produce the same result. There appears to be only a modest difference in total sensory stimulation provided by the programs. The general belief that *Sesame Street* provides many more flashing lights, bells, and whistles than does *Mister Rogers' Neighborhood* does not appear to be well founded in the segments tested. If this result was found to be consistent across a larger sample of show segments, it would imply that any statements about differential viewer arousal produced by the two programs would have to be based on some cognitive or emotional mechanism beyond that of simple perceptual stimulation.

Table 3.1 also points out a problem in the analyses described in the next section. Because viewer recall and recognition scores could only be obtained for entire segments, the complexity scores and visual attention score had to be averaged over entire segments. This change of measurement unit resulted in mean complexity scores for the selected segments that did not equal the means of the second-by-second measurements for the entire program. The *Sesame Street* segments chosen were a little lower in visual complexity, and the *Mister Rogers' Neighborhood* segments were higher in visual attention. The aggregation also reduced the variation in complexity scores but increased it for visual attention. The result in the following analyses is to decrease the variation of causal variables while increasing that of the effect variable, which will reduce the size of the estimated relationships. This introduction of error is unavoidable, as there is no satisfactory way to measure recall and recognition on a second-by-second basis, forcing the aggregation of the complexity and attention values. It should be realized, however, that the values for relationships reported later are probably lower in magnitude than the actual values.

Tests of Flow of Effects Model

Because of the low number of segments in each program, there were some very large correlations between complexity variables. Although this is a normal situation when using a sample with a very small number of observations, it made inclusion of all complexity variables in tests of the flow of effects model for the individual programs impossible. Technically, the problem is one of high multicollinearity, which makes the regression results unstable and sometimes overestimates the independent effects of collinear variables. It is intuitively easy to see what is wrong: If two variables always appear together (high correlation, or multicollinearity), how are we to estimate the effect of either independently of the other?

To reduce this problem, visual only and audio only models were initially developed for each of the programs. This is somewhat of an ostrich approach. We know from the simple correlations that the audio and visual complexity variables are related; to ignore one while examining the other is bound to be incorrect to some degree, but we also wanted to contrast the two shows in order to see if the production styles of each lead to different effects on viewers. Although the overall model may produce somewhat different results when the deleted mode is introduced and thus controlled for, the errors made for one program should be similar to the errors made for the other, and thus contrasting the two results on the same sensory mode should be legitimate. Any sweeping interpretation of the individual coefficients is probably not warranted due to the exclusion of some of the complexity variables. We will not discuss the individual models, except in conjunction with the model described in Figure 3.2. This model, which is structurally the same as the one presented in Figure 3.1, is based on the combined data for *Sesame Street* and *Mister Rogers' Neighborhood*. The combination removes enough of the collinearity between complexity variables to permit better (although still not perfect) estimation of independent relationships between variables, which are given by the path coefficients in Figure 3.2.

To aid the interpretation of five path models (audio only and video only for both *Mister Rogers' Neighborhood* and *Sesame Street*, plus the combined model), Table 3.2 was constructed. It summarizes the relationships of the complexity variables to the recall and recognition variables in two ways: first, directly; and, second, indirectly via a visual attention process. Path analysis permits this comparison to be made simply (cf. Heise, 1975). To estimate the indirect effect, one merely multiplies the the first path coefficient (such as from audio dynamic complexity to visual attention) by the next path coefficient in the causal chain (such as visual attention to recall). The result is the indirect effect of the first variable on the third via the second (audio dynamic complexity on recall via visual attention). These indirect effects are of interest, because they may modify the direct effects. If they subtract, one might observe no overall simple correlation between the initial cause and final effect, but find significant direct effects coupled with independent significant, but canceling, indirect effects. An elaboration of the microprocesses relating television complexity variables to the

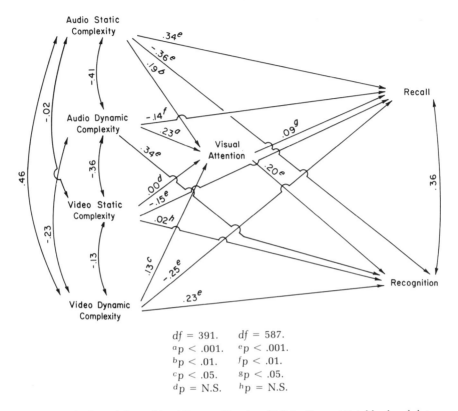

df = 391.   df = 587.
[a]p < .001.   [e]p < .001.
[b]p < .01.   [f]p < .01.
[c]p < .05.   [g]p < .05.
[d]p = N.S.   [h]p = N.S.

Figure 3.2 *Path model, combined Sesame Street and Mister Rogers' Neighborhood data.*

ultimate learning variables is thus possible, with the result being better explanation of the whole process.

Attention Processes

Audio static complexity was strongly associated with visual attention in *Mister Rogers' Neighborhood* but showed no relationship to visual attention in *Sesame Street*. When the data for the two shows were combined, the relationship remained positive, but at a moderated level. The difference between shows may have occurred as a result of differences in audio static complexity. *Sesame Street,* which averaged higher on this variable, may have been nearer the optimum level for eliciting or maintaining visual attention, so that increases in audio static complexity were not associated with any increases in visual attention. *Mister Rogers' Neighborhood,* which scored lower on this vari-

Table 3.2

Summary of Results of Test of Models

Attention processes	MN		SS		Combined	
Audio static—visual attention	.47	(+)	.00	(null)	.19	(+)
Audio dynamic—visual attention	.17	(null)	.14	(null)	.23	(+)
Visual static—visual attention	.49	(+)	−.32	(−)	.00	(null)
Visual dynamic—visual attention	.58	(+)	.30	(+)	.13	(+)
Learning processes						
Audio static—recall	.33	(+)	.09	(null)	.34	(+)
Indirect via attention	.09	(+)	.00	(null)	.02	(+)
Audio dynamic—recall	−.03	(null)	.12	(null)	−.14	(−)
Indirect via attention	.03	(null)	.01	(null)	.02	(null)
Visual static—recall	−.57	(−)	−.14	(null)	−.15	(−)
Indirect via attention	.20	(+)	.01	(null)	.00	(null)
Visual dynamic—recall	−.25	(−)	−.16	(null)	−.25	(−)
Indirect via attention	.23	(+)	.01	(null)	.01	(null)
Audio static—recognition	−.57	(−)	.03	(null)	−.36	(−)
Indirect via attention	.16	(+)	.00	(null)	.04	(+)
Audio dynamic—recognition	.01	(null)	.27	(+)	.34	(+)
Indirect via attention	.06	(null)	.04	(null)	.05	(+)
Visual static—recognition	.21	(+)	−.52	(−)	.02	(null)
Indirect via attention	.10	(+)	−.07	(−)	.00	(null)
Visual dynamic—recognition	.28	(+)	.59	(+)	.23	(+)
Indirect via attention	.12	(+)	.06	(+)	.03	(+)

Note: MN refers to *Mister Rogers' Neighborhood*; SS refers to *Sesame Street*. (+) indicates significantly positive value. (−) indicates significantly negative value. (null) indicates no significant relationship.

able, would thus experience increases in visual attention in the segments that approached the optimum audio static complexity level, that is, had higher audio static complexity.

Audio dynamic complexity shows a positive path coefficient in both *Mister Rogers' Neighborhood* and *Sesame Street*, but in neither is the coeffieient statistically significant. With the greater numbers of observations in the combined data, the result is significantly positive. It is also larger than either individual show coefficient. This indicates the effect of controlling for the visual complexity variables while estimating the audio coefficients. We can conclude that changes in the audio track over time produce higher levels of visual attention, possibly by an "orienting response" that directs attention to novel or strange stimuli in the viewer's environment.

The relationship of visual static complexity to visual attention was inconsistent in the two programs. In *Mister Rogers' Neighborhood*, an increase in the visual field complexity was associated with a large increase in visual attention. In *Sesame Street*, a similar increase was associated with a large decrease in visual attention. When the data were combined, there was no relationship between visual static complexity and visual attention. The lack of consistency in the individual program results probably means that the null relationship for the combined data is the best estimate of the general relationship. In contrast, the results for visual dynamic complexity were consistent across both programs and the combined data. The greater the visual change on the screen, the higher the visual attention level.

Learning Processes

AUDIO STATIC COMPLEXITY

Audio static complexity is related to learning in an interesting way. In *Mister Rogers' Neighborhood*, increases in audio static complexity produced modest increases in recall due to increased visual attention and also produced a fairly large increase in recognition due to increased visual attention. When visual attention was controlled, however, audio static complexity still produced increases in recall (which required some verbal processing on the part of the child) but produced larger decreases in recognition (which did not require verbal processing). In *Sesame Street*, there was no relationship between audio static complexity and either learning measure, either directly or indirectly via visual attention. The combined model, which included all complexity variables, gave results that are a moderated version of the *Mister Rogers' Neighborhood* results: (a) increases in audio static complexity produced small increases in both recall and recognition by increasing visual attention; and (b) when visual attention was controlled, increases in audio static complexity produced increases in recall while simultaneously producing decreases in recognition.

Interestingly, the indirect effect of audio static complexity via visual attention on both learning measures was significantly positive, but quite small. In the case of recall, it added to the positive effect, and, in the case of recognition, it countered some of the negative effect. The net effect on recognition, however, which is just the sum of the direct and indirect paths, was still highly negative.

The audio track appears to have facilitated the process of verbal learning (or at least learning that involves later verbal processing), while inhibiting visual learning. The effect is most apparent at lower values of audio static complexity, seeming to indicate that there is a ceiling effect beyond which changes in audio static complexity no longer significantly affect recall or recognition. *Mister Rogers' Neighborhood*, with lower audio static complexity, shows strong effects, whereas *Sesame Street*, which is higher in audio static complexity, shows no effects at all.

At this point, we can only speculate about what causes one type of learning to be enhanced by audio static complexity whereas another is retarded by it. Segments higher in audio static complexity are more likely to have used extensive verbalization and music. The verbal model provided by these segments may have facilitated the verbal response later required of subjects in the recall measure or the use of music may have cued some memory process. Likewise, we may speculate that visual memory may be impeded somewhat by the transfer of cognitive processing effort from the visual to the verbal (or at least auditory) mode. Kahneman (1973) has proposed that individuals possess a finite information processing capacity that is allocated among attentional tasks. The level of general capacity is proportional to the drive or arousal level of the individual at any point in time and is variable. However, if the combined processing task exceeds the capacity at some time point, one would expect reallocation of processing resources, which would result in the kind of impedance of one processing mode combined with the enhancement of another observed here.

AUDIO DYNAMIC COMPLEXITY

Only one of the paths from audio dynamic complexity to learning was significant in the individual program models—the direct path between audio dynamic complexity and recognition in *Sesame Street*. With the increase in observations in the combined data, we found a small negative direct relationship between audio dynamic complexity and recall and a large positive effect of audio dynamic complexity on recognition. This positive effect was further enhanced by a small indirect visual attention effect.

The interesting finding here is that audio dynamic complexity produced a pattern of direct effects on the two learning measures that was opposite to that of audio static complexity. Apparently across time complexity is not handled within the perceptual and cognitive processing apparatuses of the individual in the same way as within time complexity. Why this should be so is not clear. In any event, the depression of recall by increases in audio dynamic complexity was much smaller than the corresponding increase in recognition.

The visual static complexity results were as contradictory in their impact on the learning processes as they were on the attention processes. Visual static complexity produced large decreases in recall for *Mister Rogers' Neighborhood*, but they produced no significant change in recall for *Sesame Street*. The combined data showed a small but significant decrease in recall with increases in visual static complexity. The recognition results were directly contradictory, with visual static complexity increasing recognition in *Mister Rogers' Neighborhood* and decreasing it dramatically in *Sesame Street*. Combining the data, not surprisingly, results in a null relationship. Indirect results via visual attention for the combined data are 0 for both learning measures, even though visual static complexity is positively related to both measures in *Mister Rogers' Neighborhood*.

The visual static complexity–recall direct effect appears to be another example of possible "modal blocking," whereby more complex visuals interfere with memory processes involving verbal retrieval. Overall, visual static complexity impinges on the learning process in a moderately negative way. This finding somewhat contradicts earlier conclusions about the role of visual static complexity in learning (Welch & Watt, 1982). The earlier results were based solely on the visual complexity variables of *Sesame Street*. As Table 3.2 shows, visual static complexity had a strong negative effect on recognition in *Sesame Street*. With the addition of controls for audio complexity and the increase in the number of segments observed, however, this conclusion must be modified to weaken the apparent role of visual static complexity in depressing learning scores. Visual static complexity still leads to either null or negative results, depending on the learning measure applied, so the recommendation that producers avoid complex visuals and sets still holds, but to a lesser degree. This finding underscores the importance of accounting for the impact of audio stimuli when assessing the impact of visual stimuli in televised materials.

The visual dynamic complexity results are consistent across both programs and the combined data. Visual dynamic complexity depressed recall scores when visual attention was controlled, but it increased recognition scores at the same time. Again we find results that point to a visual complexity variable interfering with a memory process involving verbal processing.

An interesting finding here is that indirect effects of visual dynamic complexity via visual attention are very small in the combined data. For the *Mister Rogers' Neighborhood* data, increases in recall due to this indirect effect almost offset decreases due to the direct effect on recall. No such canceling effect appears in *Sesame Street*. Since both shows scored similarly in visual dynamic complexity, individual differences in variables not included in the models must account for this difference, and thus the combined data result of a null indirect effect is probably the most plausible.

Implications

To the degree one is willing to assume that a combination of *Sesame Street* and *Mister Rogers' Neighborhood* segments runs the gamut of children's programming in general, we can conclude the following:

1. Complexity variables have only a modest relationship to visual attention, which in turn has only a fairly small relationship to either of the learning measures. Combined, this seems to indicate that the emphasis on the importance of increasing visual attention by program production techniques is misplaced. The largest impact on a learning measure which a complexity measure produced via visual attention was only 5% (in standard score units). By contrast, differences in complexity produced by differences in production techniques had a 36% maximum direct effect on learning when visual attention levels were controlled. If one desires to maximize the learning by manipulating production techniques, it appears that one should worry less about modifying visual attention levels and more about the direct effects of program form complexity on the memory processes of young viewers.[1] It must be stressed that this statement applies only to visual attention,

[1]It might be argued that the low values for the indirect effects of complexity via visual attention are statistically induced. The path coefficients reported are not corrected for unreliability of the measurements. Thus the two-stage indirect effects are subject to cumulative unreliability, whereas the direct effects have only one stage of unreliability to contend with. But the complexity variables are highly reliable (better than 99% reproducible), however, as is the visual attention measure (different tests of the procedure with redundant coders have averaged about 95% reproducible). Thus only the recall and recognition measurements are likely to have significant unreliability, but these variables are present in both the direct and indirect analyses, so the actual degree of unreliability is the same for both, and we can conclude that comparisons between the size of coefficients for direct and indirect effects are legitimate. We will underestimate both direct and indirect path coefficients in this case, and the figures reported are conservative.

not to auditory attention. Some production techniques may produce auditory attention without affecting visual attention. The reported research does not assess auditory attention.

2. There seems to be a difference between the effects of program complexity on memory tasks requiring verbal responses (recall) and those requiring only nonverbal responses (recognition). Complexity that enhances one kind of response appears to retard the other in some instances.

Increasing audio static complexity by introducing music, sound effect, strange voices, etc., increases recall but decreases recognition by an almost identical amount in the combined data. Increasing audio dynamic complexity by adding speaking characters, staccato sound effects, switching from one "auditory setting" to another (such as by *Sesame Street's* short segment juxtaposition) decreases recall but increases recognition to a somewhat greater degree.

The verdict on static visual complexity is less ambiguous. Increasing detail on the screen by use of complex sets, elaborate graphics, and long shots that include many objects of reduced size decreases recall while leaving recognition unaffected. Static visual simplicity thus seems called for in all instances. Dynamic visual complexity gives completely different results according to the type of learning. Increases in visual dynamic complexity produce decreases in recall coupled with increases in recognition.

It appears that both the visual and audio form components can be manipulated to enhance learning but that the type of learning involved (primarily visual recognition versus verbal recall) will determine the appropriate levels of complexity on the audio and visual tracks. For example, suppose a producer is attempting to communicate curriculum material that is primarily visual and desires to produce recognition of this material by children (for example, recognition of simple geometric shapes or letters of the alphabet). The producer would be more successful with a highly active visual track consisting of only a few elements (an animation of a simple object, for example). The accompanying audio track should consist of simple sounds that change rapidly over time (narration interspersed with periods of silence, for example). If the producer is attempting to communicate material that is more verbal in nature, a different approach is called for. The visual track should be kept simple and calm (a close-up without much camera switching, for example). The audio track should not show much change over time but should consist of a number of frequencies (narration with background music, for example).

3. A number of the speculations about relationships in this chapter

have implied that some nonlinearities must be present, but all modeling was based on linear relationships. Nonlinear tests of the flow of effects model are quite difficult but are clearly called for, as it appears that some of the inconsistencies found between programs could be resolved by relaxing the linearity restriction.

Summary

We have presented definitions of television audio and visual complexities which formalize the idea of form complexity. The definitions encompass the essential ideas found in other researchers' definitions of television form which are derived from television production techniques. Because the present definitions are based on the very general concepts of difference within and across time in both the audio and visual tracks, and because they use information theory for basic operational definitions, they can be more easily linked by human information processing theory to viewer responses such as visual attention and learning.

An in-depth analysis of two popular children's educational programs was provided as an example of the utility of the definitions. One notable result was the counter intuitive finding of equal visual complexity for *Mister Rogers' Neighborhood* and *Sesame Street*. The value of the definitions is illustrated by the fact that children's television analysts and critics have assumed that *Sesame Street* was providing much more visual stimulation. When analyzed in the completely content-independent fashion provided by the definitions, this assumption is found to be questionable.

In analyzing the entire viewing process, it was found that visual attention was of small importance in the learning process but that static and dynamic complexities were quite important. Complexities were found to have different effects on learning that involved a verbal recall process than on learning that required only visual recognition. Producers of televised instructional material would thus be advised to tailor production techniques to enhance the particular mode of learning desired rather than to enhance visual attention.

References

Acker, S. R., & Tiemens, R. K. Children's perceptions of change in size of televised images. *Human Communication Research*. 1981, 7, 340–346.

Alwitt, L. F., Anderson, D. R., Lorch, E. P., & Levin, S. R. Preschool children's visual attention to attributes of television. *Human Communication Research*, 1980, 7, 52–67.

Anderson, D. R., & Levin, S. R. Young children's attention to *Sesame Street*. *Child Development*, 1976, 47, 806–811.

Anderson, D. R., Lorch, E. P., Field, D. E., & Sanders, J. The effects of TV program comprehensibility on preschool children's visual attention to television. *Child Development*, 1981, 52, 151–157.

Arnheim, R. *Entropy and art*. Berkeley: University of California Press, 1971.

Berlyne, D. E. Uncertainty and conflicts: A point of contact between information theory and behavior theory concepts. *Psychological Review*, 1957, 64, 329–339.

Berlyne, D. E. *Aesthetics and psychobiology*. New York: Appleton-Century-Crofts, 1971.

Berlyne, D. E., Craw, M. A., Salapatek, P. H., & Lewis, J. L. Novelty, complexity, incongruity, extrinsic motivation, and the GSR. *Journal of Experimental Psychology*, 1963, 66, 476–483.

Cohen, J., & Cohen, P. *Applied multiple regression/correlation analysis for the behavioral sciences*. Hillsdale, N.J.: Erlbaum, 1975.

Collins, W. A. Learning of media content: A developmental study. *Child Development*, 1970, 41, 1133–1142.

Crane, E., & MacLean, M. S. Live dimensions of style in educational TV programs. *Audio Visual Communication Review*, 1962, 10, 158–168.

Crowder, R. G. The role of one's own voice in immediate memory. *Cognitive Psychology*, 1970, 1, 157–178.

Duffy, J. R., Watt, J. H., & Duffy, R. J. Path analysis: A strategy for investigating multivariate causal relationships in communication disorders. *Journal of Speech and Hearing Research*, 1982, 24, 64–80.

Flagg, B. N., Allen, B. D., Geer, A. H., & Scinto, L. F. *Children's visual responses to Sesame Street: A formative research report*. Unpublished research report. New York: Children's Television Workshop, 1976.

Friedlander, B., Wetstone, H., & Scott, C. Suburban preschool children's comprehension of an age-appropriate information television program. *Child Development*, 1974, 45, 561–565.

Hage, J. *Techniques and problems of theory construction in sociology*. New York: Wiley, 1974.

Halpern, W. I. Turned-on toddlers. *Journal of Communication*, 1975, 25, 66–70.

Hazard, W. R., Moriarty, J. D., & Timmons, V. C. A nontopical system of program categories. *Audio Visual Communication Review*, 1964, 12, 146–163.

Heise, D. R. *Causal analysis*. New York: Wiley, 1975.

Hofman, R. J., & Flook, M. A. An experimental investigation of the role of television in facilitating shape recognition. *Journal of Genetic Psychology*, 1980, 136, 305–306.

Huston, A. C., Wright, J. C., Wartella, E., Rice, M. L., Watkins, B. A., Campbell, T., & Potts, R. Communicating more than content: Formal features of children's television programs. *Journal of Communication*, 1981, 31(3), 32–48.

Kahneman, D. *Attention and effort*. Englewood Cliffs, N.J.: Prentice-Hall, 1973.

Kenny, D. A. *Correlation and causality*. New York: Wiley, 1979.

Krull, R., & Husson, W. Children's attention: The case of TV viewing. In E. Wartella (Ed.), *Children communicating: Media and development of thought, speech, understanding*. Beverly Hills, Calif.: Sage, 1979.

Krull, R., & Husson, W. Children's anticipatory attention to the TV screen. *Journal of Broadcasting*, 1980, 24, 35–47.

Krull, R., Watt, J. H., & Lichty, L. W. Entropy and structure: Two measures of complexity in television programs. *Communication Research*, 1977, *4*, 61–86.

Lesser, G. S. *Children and Television*. New York: Vintage Books, 1974.

Lichty, L. W., & Ripley, J. M. *American broadcasting*. Madison, Wisc.: College Printing and Typing Co., 1970.

Lorch, E. P., Anderson, D. R., & Levin, S. R. The relationship of visual attention to children's comprehension of television. *Child Development*, 1979, *50*(3), 722–727.

Minton, J. H. The impact of *Sesame Street* on readiness. *Sociology of Education*, 1975, *48*, 141–151.

Moles, A. *Information theory and esthetic perception*. Urbana: University of Illinois Press, 1968.

Pierce, J. R. *Symbols, signals and noise*. New York: Harper & Row, 1961.

Salomon, G., & Cohen, A. Television formats, mastery of mental skills and the acquisition of knowledge. *Journal of Educational Psychology*, 1977, *69*, 612–619.

Shannon, C. E., & Weaver, W. *The mathematical theory of communication*. Urbana: University of Illinois Press, 1949.

Shea, C. *Measuring the information content of a video signal*. Unpublished manuscript, University of Connecticut, 1974.

Singer, J. L. & Singer, D. G. Come back, Mister Rogers, come back. *Psychology Today*, March 1979, 56–57, 59–60.

Sprigle, H. Who wants to live on *Sesame Street*? *Young Children*, 1972, *27*, 91–108.

Wackman, D. B., & Wartella, E. A review of cognitive development theory and research and the implication for research on children's responses to television. *Communication Research*, 1977, *4*, 203–224.

Wartella, E., & Ettema, J. S. A cognitive developmental study of children's attention to television commercials. *Communication Research*, 1974, *1*, 69–88.

Watt, J. H. Television form, content attributes, and viewer behavior. In M. J. Voigt, & G. J. Hanneman (Ed.), *Progress in Communication Sciences* (Vol. 1). Norwood, N.J.: Ablex, 1979.

Watt, J. H. *Evaluating causal models*. Paper presented to the Communication Theory and Methodology Division, the Association for Education in Journalism, Boston, 1980.

Watt, J. H., & Krull, R. An information theory measure for television programming. *Communication Research*, 1974, *1*, 44–68.

Watt, J. H., & Krull, R. *Form complexity and children's physiological responses, attention and recall*. Unpublished research report. New York: Children's Television Workshop, 1977.

Welch, A., & Watt, J. H. Visual complexity and young children's learning from television. *Human Communication Research*, 1982, *8*, 133–145.

Zuckerman, P., Ziegler, M., & Stevenson, H. W. Children's viewing of television and recognition memory of commercials. *Child Development*, 1978, *49*, 96–104.

chapter **4**

Children Learning
to Watch Television[1]

ROBERT KRULL

Introduction

The purpose of our research is to explain in detail how children watch television. Our efforts have been applied mainly to children's visual attention to program form. The purposes of this chapter are to describe our theoretical framework, the relationship of the framework to methodology, and to provide illustrations of our findings. The chapter is organized into the following sections: common assumptions about television viewing and the different assumptions of our framework; measures for television programs and children's viewing; research findings about relationships of program attributes to viewing behavior; and implications of our findings for producers and researchers.

Variables for Analyzing Children's Television

Framework

Our approach is similar in intent to that of other researchers who are trying to explain how children relate to television. However, with the

[1]This project was supported by National Institute of Mental Health grant No. MH 34836-2.

103

exception of Watt and Welch's work (described in Chapter 3, this volume), our theoretical framework is different. The particular area we have examined is children's visual attention to program form. Our study of attention is not unusual. We have concentrated on attention because it should indicate preference for program materials and reflect cognitive development, and it is a prerequisite for the success of educational television series. Our concentration on program form and our assumptions about children's attending to form are unusual. We have concentrated on program form because television seems more unique in its form than its content (Huston, Wright, Wartella, Rice, Watkins, Campbell, & Potts, 1981; Salomon, 1979; Watt & Krull, 1974). Our assumptions about viewing are different from the common, often implicit, assumptions about television viewing one sees in the research literature. The latter seem to include the following:

1. The content of programs is more important to viewers than the form. This assumption seems implicit in the heavy concentration in television research on program content attributes. For example, studies of programs have often been concerned with program types (e.g., Lyle & Hoffman, 1972; Steiner, 1963) or with the social roles of program characters (Gerbner, 1972).

2. Logical reasoning about the meaning of program sequences is the dominant mode of active processing by viewers. This assumption underlies some of the explanations of program effects. For example, some studies of television violence have argued that viewers' assessments of the effectiveness of violence in a film will affect their use of violence as a problem-solving technique in their own lives (e.g., Bandura, Ross, & Ross, 1963). The key here is that viewers are expected to see the logical implications of what they see on television.

3. Children, as well as viewers of other ages, can verbalize accurately about what they do while viewing. This assumption is implicit in research relying on viewers' verbal responses and particularly in research using open-ended questions that require viewers to construct an answer (cf. Greenberg, 1974). Some kinds of information can only be obtained with such techniques, but the resulting data may be affected strongly by viewers' verbal abilities. For example, viewers could use the label "entertainment" to refer to television programs as different as drama, nightclub performances, and college ski-racing meets. What they mean by entertainment is unlikely to be the same for each program because they may have difficulties specifically describing what they find entertaining. This would be particularly true for children.

4. When viewers are not doing something that is easily described

verbally, they are doing little perceptual or cognitive processing. This assumption underlies some of the popular criticism that television makes viewers lethargic due to passive viewing (Winn, 1977).

The research based on these assumptions has provided us with a considerable understanding of television and its viewers. However, research limited to analysis of program content and viewer verbalization may not have taken into account all of the ways viewers may process television materials.

Our research program is based on a related but different set of assumptions:

1. The form and content of programs are both important to viewers. If television's form of presenting information did not have some appeal, viewers might look for the same material in another medium. For example, television viewing seems to substitute for the functions of several other media- and nonmedia-related activities (Brown, Cramond, & Wilde, 1974; Robinson, 1969). Since the content of these activities (e.g., sleeping, interacting with friends, traveling, reading comic books) is different, it may be that television can substitute for their form characteristics.
2. Thinking about programs can be spatial, time-dependent, and concrete as well as verbal and abstract (Salomon, 1979). This assumption points to an additional way in which viewers could process visual and auditory displays such as those provided by television.
3. Viewers may be quite active mentally when in engaged in spatiotemporal information processing. This assumption is a corollary of the preceding one and is the converse of content-oriented assumption Number 4. For example, Radlick (1980) found that viewers' electroencephalograph patterns showed indications of comparatively greater amounts of processing for some instructional televised materials than for reading.
4. Viewers may not be able to verbalize well about their processing of form even though they can do the processing. For example, children emphasize more action and emotion in their nonverbal depictions of programs than when they are asked to verbally describe what they have seen (cf. Meringoff, 1980; Smith, 1981).

Together these assumptions direct research into avenues different from those explored ordinarily. To carry out such research one needs measures of program form, measures of viewer behavior that require little verbal skill, and a system of causal analysis that taps the temporal flow of program form rather than the logical flow of program content. The next three sections describe each of these items in turn.

Program Form Variables

We have concentrated on form variables that are concrete and production-oriented. Terms commonly used in this area are *camera cut* and *zoom*. Our terminology is somewhat different because our conceptualization of variables emphasizes the processing load that television viewing provides. Materials supporting our framework have come from information processing work in engineering and from perception and cognition research. Information processing variables are discussed first; variables based on theories of cognition are discussed in the next section, "Program Content Variables."

The work of engineers on Information Theory (Shannon & Weaver, 1949) led to a large number of perception studies in the social sciences (Garner, 1962, 1974). A nonmathematical overview of theoretical ideas in this area has been provided by Berlyne (1971). The information theory approach emphasizes one aspect of messages in particular—the variety that is possible in them. In the perception literature, the variety of messages (or stimuli) has been linked to their surprise value, the uncertainty of their occurrence, and their complexity (Garner, 1962). In applying information theory to television we have looked at the complexity in programs. Since information processing load increases as the variety of complexity in messages increases, one would expect that television viewers' processing load would increase as the complexity of programs increases. For example, if a television program contained only one kind of program format, the processing load would probably be lower than if the program contained a variety of formats.

The information theory way of assessing complexity is closely related to the concept of statistical variance. Variance is calculated by assuming a set of items has a middle value that occurs very frequently, the mean, and the deviations occur with a frequency specified by a particular distribution, the normal curve. Information theory does not assume there is a frequently occurring "middle" value and does not assume there is a particular distribution of values. The information theory concept of complexity is called entropy and can be seen as a measure of variance for nonnormal distributions. One computational formula for entropy is as follows:

$$H = -\sum_{i=1}^{n} p_i \log_2 p_i$$

where p_i is the probability of a given event's occurring. Entropy scores, based on this formula, are low when only a few kinds of things appear in a program or when one kind of thing dominates a program. Entropy scores are high when many kinds of things appear in a program and they occur with equal likelihood. Although we use entropy computations to generate scores, we refer to "complexity" scores to avoid the somewhat mystical connotations of the word *entropy*.

We have used a large number of variables in our studies. Several variables have been eliminated because of redundancy or lack of conceptual clarity; others have been used in only a few studies and are being refined. Watt and Krull developed some of these variables for studies of adolescent and mature viewers (Krull & Watt, 1975; Krull, Watt, & Lichty, 1977; Watt & Krull, 1974, 1975, 1976). This chapter describes only those variables for which we have a considerable data base.

Shot complexity is the randomness of the apparent distance between the camera and the objects in view. Coders are required to assess if the camera is showing a close-up, medium, or long shot and to depress a push button as long as each kind of shot lasts. A minicomputer is used to keep track of the number of coders' responses and to perform complexity calculations after coding is completed. The range of values for shot complexity is continuous from 0, indicating that the camera showed only one kind of shot, to 1.5, indicating that the camera showed an even balance of long, medium, and close-up shots. The purpose of this variable is to determine the effect of changing the camera's view of a scene. One would expect that as the shot changes increase, viewer processing load would increase. Shot complexity probably correlates with visual variables that are operationalized quite differently, such as Huston's *et al.* (1981) visual change variable, and with indicators of the source of visual change, such as camera cut. For example, high shot complexity may also be accompanied by a large number of camera cuts.

Set complexity is the randomness of visual duration of physical locations in a program. Coders are required to determine which of the shooting locations (or sets) that appear in a program is in view and to depress a push button assigned to the location. The procedure of computing complexity scores from the raw data is analogous to that for shot complexity. If a program contains only a few sets, set complexity scores are low; if a program contains many sets, each appearing for about the same amount of time, set complexity is high. The purpose of this variable is to see the effect of adding locations for action. One could expect that, as the number of settings increases, the effort required of viewers to understand how each setting relates to others would increase and that processing load would increase as a result. Set complexity can correlate with several other television program measures. For set complexity to increase there must be transitions from one set to another. Therefore, set complexity may correlate with measures of the number of transitions such as variability and tempo (Huston et al., 1981), and with bit changes (Alwitt, Anderson, Lorch, & Levin, 1980).

Verbal interaction complexity is the randomness of characters' making audible sounds. Coders are required to press a push button when a particular character makes an audible sound (not just speech). The complexity of the interaction (its randomness) is determined by means of the entropy calculations. The objective of this variable is to see the effect of spreading dialogue (and other audible behavior) among a number of characters. As the number of characters with dialogue increases, one would expect the effort required of viewers to keep the characters distinct would increase. This variable is conceptually unrelated to other auditory television measures but is likely to correlate empirically with several of them. For example, verbal complexity is likely to correlate with the amount of adult and child dialogue and with the number of characters visible on the screen (Anderson & Levin, 1976; Huston et al., 1981).

Modal complexity is the randomness of the program's message being carried by the visual or verbal track. Coders already are required to press push buttons to assess the amount of verbalization to score verbal interaction complexity. Modal complexity is determined by indexing coders' responses in a different way. Rather than keeping the amount of verbalization of different characters separated, modal complexity is computed by aggregating the total amount of audible behavior produced by all characters and comparing that to the total amount of time during which there is no verbalization. The purpose of this variable is to see the effect of presenting information both visually and verbally. If a program's action is presented visually only, viewers can understand the action just by paying visual attention. If the action is presented aurally only, viewers can understand just by listening. If the program alternates between the two modes, viewers should be required to both watch and listen, and their processing load should increase as a result. This variable is conceptually distinct from other television measures but is likely to correlate to a small extent with other measures of character verbalization.

Each of the preceding measures of program form is based on information theory. We do not maintain that they exhaust all dimensions of program structure or even of complexity measures of structure. We have developed additional electronically coded measures that tap the complexity of individual visual images and of the variability in the auditory volume of soundtracks. Watt and Welch (see Chapter 3, this volume) have developed similar measures of visual complexity, which they call static and dynamic complexity. Our auditory complexity measure is similar in purpose to variables such as liveliness or brightness of the soundtrack (Anderson & Levin, 1976; Huston et al., 1981).

In a few studies these measures have correlated with children's attention and with television viewers' physiological responses (Radlick, 1980). However, we have also found their covariance with the other complexity measures to be quite high. We are continuing to refine these variables. An analysis of programs based only on form would be incomplete, so we have turned our attention to program content. As our starting point, we have developed several measures of the relationship between the verbal content and visual images of programs.

Program Content Variables

We have tried to consider viewers' information processing foremost in developing our content variables, but our basis here has been Piaget's theory of intellectual development (Ginsburg & Opper, 1969; Piaget, 1969). According to Piaget, young children may be able to perceive logical relationships among objects that are physically present but may not be able to perceive the same relationships when the objects are absent. One might say that children find it more difficult to think abstractly than concretely. Since television programs can vary in abstractness, this aspect of programs may affect children's viewing behavior. We have developed several measures of language concreteness in programs, two of which are described here.

Visual presence of speakers is the extent to which characters speaking are shown on the screen. Coders score programs by pressing one of four push buttons—many speaking characters on screen, one character on screen, one character offscreen, and many characters offscreen (see Husson & Hughes, 1981, for a full description of the coding procedure). An index, formed from the raw scores, has high values if there are many characters speaking and visible. The index has very low scores if many characters are speaking offscreen.

The objective of this variable is to assess the effect of tying verbalization to its source. One would expect that, as the source of verbalization becomes more remote, viewers would have greater difficulty relating what is said to who says it. For example, a large number of disembodied voices might not be integrated with a program's visual material by the children watching. However, one would also expect a limit to the number of characters who can be shown on camera simultaneously, let alone verbalizing at the same time. The relationship of this variable to children's preference should be curvilinear, although the general effect is likely to be positive. This variable is not related to many other program attributes conceptually, but it is likely to correlate with attributes assessing the kinds of characters (such as adult males) who are present in a program (Anderson & Levin, 1976).

Visual–verbal congruence is the number of instances per unit time that the object referred to by verbalization is present on the screen. Coders assess whether segments of verbalization have a visible, concrete referent and press a push button to record each occurrence of such verbalization. In early studies we measured this variable by coding written transcripts of programs (Husson & Hughes, 1981).

The objective of this variable, like that of visual presence of speaker, is to see the effect of visual support for verbalization. However, this variable assesses the relationship between the object spoken about and visual support, rather than that between the subject speaking and visual support. Congruence is most likely to increase when characters speak about physical objects; congruence is most likely to decrease when characters speak about abstractions such as the justness of social relationships. One would expect that, particularly for children, congruence (concreteness) requires less complex cognitive processing than abstraction. Visual–verbal congruence is similar in some respects to a measure of verbal "immediacy" developed by Anderson, Lorch, Field, and Sanders (1981).

In addition to these measures of the relationship between verbal content and visual images, we are developing new measures of the more abstract aspects of program content. The variables we have used for a few test programs include the extent to which characters have human form, the intensity of emotion displayed by characters, and the explicitness of program segments' goals. Preliminary results indicate that these variables affect children's attention, but data analyses are not yet complete.

Viewing Variables

Program complexity has been correlated with several measures of viewer appeal and effects. Our work with children has focused on their visual attention to the television screen. Studies of other viewer variables will be discussed briefly in the next section. In exploring children's television viewing, we sought reliable variables that required little verbal skill on the part of children and little interpretation on the part of coders. In addition, we needed viewer measures that were able to fluctuate in response to changes in form complexity occurring within programs. Children's visual attention to the screen seemed to be a variable that met these requirements (visual attention also has limitations, which will be discussed). We were fortunate that several researchers had done studies of visual attention to television. The Children's Television Workshop (CTW) has collected test data on visual attention for many programs. By analyzing the same programs, it was possible for us to obtain a direct comparison with the findings of other researchers. Several authors of other chapters in this volume have used these data.

Children are tested in a room that allows them to pay attention either to the television set or some alternate stimulation. The alternatives, or "distractions," can be a slide projector, toys, other children, or some combination of these. Coders rate the amount of visual attention children pay to the screen. They can tell with high reliability if the children are looking at the screen; however, they cannot tell at which part of the screen children are looking. Eye-movement studies provide the latter information but require more physical restraint on the part of children (Flagg, 1978; also see discussion of this issue by Anderson & Lorch, Chapter 1, this volume).

Rating of attention is done on a continuous basis using push buttons connected to mechanical recording devices. Either the onset and offset of attention or the average attention during an interval are noted (Krull & Husson, 1979). Often these data are aggregated over some time interval, such as a program segment, and over a number of children (Anderson & Levin, 1976). The resulting data represent an average response to programs rather than point estimates for individuals. One must be careful in extrapolating from these data to the responses of individual children.

Although the coders' estimates of attention are quite reliable, the data have peculiarities that must be taken into account during analysis. First, the intergroup stability of the data is not very high. For example, two groups of equivalent children watching the same program do not show precisely the same levels of attention during the viewing period. One group of children can be somewhat quicker than another in reacting to the program as a consequence of viewing experience (Krull & Husson, n.d.). Second, there can be a strong trend in attention during an hour's viewing that seems independent of program attributes and may be related to the test setting (Epstein, 1977; Husson & Hughes, 1981). Third, children may show attention spillover, or inertia, from one point during a viewing period to the next. As a result of these three factors, children's reactions to programs attributes are not clear cut, and accurate causal assessments may be difficult to obtain. Techniques for handling these data are described next.

Causal Relationships in Television Viewing

Framework

Many television analyses require simplifying assumptions about causality. If a study includes many variables, one assumption may be that all causes take the same time to affect the dependent variable. If such a study is a survey, an additional assumption is that effects do not decay rapidly. If the study is an experiment, as assumption is that effects occur sufficiently quickly to be observed during an experimental session. When these assumptions are applied to children watching television, one is limited to a rather rigid formulation of how children behave. In reality, children viewing television in natural settings might show considerable flexibility in behavior.

Viewers are likely, for example, to develop an efficient style of paying attention to the television screen. One kind of efficiency would be the flexibility to react to different aspects of programs with different degrees of swiftness; viewers might rapidly turn toward the television set when an unusual and sharp sound occurs. On the other hand, viewers might turn away from the set for long periods when the program material is a conversation. Viewers could expect little change in visual material while a conversation continues and could monitor the program material just by listening. By running simple correlations between the occurrence of sharp sounds, conversations, and visual attention, a researcher is likely to conclude that viewers pay attention to sharp sounds and not to conversation. The effect seen may actually be an artifact of the timing of viewers' reactions.

An additional feature of viewers' flexible reactions to programs could be their anticipation of program occurrences. Neisser (1976) argues that perception in general is made more efficient through anticipation. It seems reasonable to expect some anticipation by television viewers as well. However, the pattern of anticipation and the effects of age and viewing experience on anticipation are not known.

Since the speed of viewers' reactions is not known, in our work we have used a quasi-experimental design that allows us to examine a range of causal delays. We use data on programs and children's attention gathered on a continuous basis and then analyze relationships using a technique called Time Series Analysis (TSA). TSA is used commonly in engineering as a companion to the information theory measures we have described. In the social sciences, TSA techniques are used in economics and to some extent in EEG (electroencephalogram) work (Box & Jenkins, 1970; Chatfield, 1975; Krull & Paulson, 1977). Their application to children's viewing has been quite effective.

To summarize our assumptions about causal relationships in children's television, we expect that children may react to a wide variety of program attributes, that the reactions may not be linear, and that the causal delay in reactions to program attributes may vary with the attribute under consideration. Our assumptions derive in part from studies conducted by Watt and Krull regarding the appeal and effects of program form complexity for adolescent and adult viewers. Krull and Watt tested several measures of viewer appeal for relationships with program complexity. They found that young adults liked and viewed the highest levels of program form complexity (Krull, Watt, & Lichty, 1977). They also found that program complexity correlated strongly with the ratings of public television programs and to small extent with the ratings of commercial television programs (Krull & Watt, 1975). These findings suggest that program complexity is associated with the appeal of programs to viewers.

Watt and Krull examined several viewer effects variables, including viewer aggression and physiological response. They found that aggression of adolescents correlated moderately with program form complexity (Watt & Krull, 1976) and that the physiological arousal (GSR) of college students varied as a curvilinear function of program form complexity, with moderate levels of complexity producing the highest arousal (Watt & Krull, 1975). In a related study, Radlick (1980) found that EEG patterns of young adults varied as a function of program form complexity.

These studies support the expected relationship between program form complexity and some aspects of television viewing. The following sections summarize findings and provide concrete examples from a series of studies of children's attention. We have studied 3–5-year-old Sesame Street viewers and 7–8-year-old Electric Company viewers. It is not feasible to describe analyses in detail. More complete descriptions of our findings are available elsewhere (Husson & Hughes, 1981; Krull & Husson, 1979, 1980; Krull, Husson, & Paulson, 1978).

Findings on 3–5-Year-Olds

THE VIEWING SITUATION

Young children seem to react quite strongly to the viewing situation itself. If they are tested in a slide-distractor condition, their attention often shows a consistent rise during an hour's viewing period (they appear to get bored with the slides). If they are tested in small groups in a toy distraction condition, children pay progressively less attention during an hour's viewing period.

Another situational effect is a change in children's reaction to program attributes during an hour's viewing. Although we have not yet done a comprehensive analysis of this effect, so far it seems children react differently to program attributes during the first half of a viewing period than they do during the second half. In some cases, program attributes at first eliciting greater attention depress attention later (Husson & Hughes, 1981).

ATTENTION INERTIA

Stronger even than the situation effect is the spillover in attention from one point in the program to the next. Young children tend to change in attention rather slowly compared to older children. It appears young children are not able to discriminate rapidly whether or not they are going to like a particular program segment. They tend to watch slightly longer before turning away if they do not like what they see. Conversely, if young children are not watching, it takes them a comparatively longer time to return to viewing than it does older children. (The same pattern has been observed by Ward, Levinson, & Wackman, 1972, in children watching television commercials.)

We call this effect attention inertia (Krull & Husson, 1980). Anderson independently developed a related concept which he also calls attention inertia (Anderson & Lorch, 1979). Anderson's concept of attention inertia involves a trend in the duration of children's segments of attention and inattention to the television screen. Our conceptualization involves short-term interdependencies in attention and is based on a TSA statistic called the autocorrelation (Box & Jenkins, 1970; Krull & Paulson, 1977).

The autocorrelation indicates the strength of the interdependence among adjacent points in a sequence of events. In this case, the autocorrelation indicates that about half of the attention paid by young children to the television screen is based on their level of attention 30 seconds earlier in the viewing period. In general we have found that for young children the combined effects of the viewing situation and attention inertia to be stronger than those of any program attribute. Whether children react differently in natural viewing situations may be determined by Anderson's videotaping of viewers (see Anderson & Lorch, Chapter 1, this volume).

REACTIONS TO PROGRAM ATTRIBUTES

Young children react to a fairly restricted number of program attributes. One could interpret this as meaning that young children do not have wide viewing tastes. They also react to program attributes in a fairly simple way.

One of the program attributes to which young viewers react fairly consistently is the length of the content segment or "bit." Generally, as bits increase in length, children's attention falls. *Sesame Street* is a magazine format show with distinct divisions, so children could be expected to react to these divisions. A dramatic program is divided into scenes and some reaction by children to scene length should be expected as well.

Among the program complexity attributes, young children seem to prefer the verbal ones. This is surprising since one would expect that if young children do not understand what is said, they might still pay attention to the visuals. However, there may be two reasons why children seem to be more affected by audio than video attributes. One is that young children may be more likely than older viewers to pay attention to the audio for its interesting surface qualities without dealing with its meaning. Bright sounding audio materials might therefore draw attention even though the content is not particularly interesting. Anderson, Lorch, Field, and Sanders (1981) found that distorted sound tracks affected younger children's attention less than older children's attention (cf. Friedlander, Wetstone, & Scott, 1974). The other reason is that audio materials may be easier to monitor at a superficial processing level. For example, children may be able to ignore the television set and only turn towards it if they hear an unusual sound effect. Monitoring visual effects would be much more difficult. Since visual attributes do not announce themselves to inattentive viewers, with the exception of gross brightness changes that affect general illumination of a viewing room, viewers cannot expect to pay low levels of attention and still see the interesting parts of programs. Young children might, therefore, pay consistently high attention to be sure not to miss anything.

One way to monitor visuals is to sample the television screen regularly, looking at it occasionally to see if anything of interest is transpiring. We have proposed a viewing style like this for 7–8-year-olds and have observed it in some 6-year-olds (Krull & Husson, 1979). If this viewing strategy is beyond younger children's abilities, visual attributes may appear to have little correlation with attention even though the general level of visual attention is quite high.

Another feature of younger children's attention is that it shows little evidence of anticipation of program occurrences. This may be because younger children are acquainted with a small number of production techniques and therefore have limited basis for anticipation. One might expect that younger children would eventually develop more elaborate viewing styles through viewing experience. We have tested quite recent versions of *Sesame Street*. The children watching these programs presumably would have had a great deal of opportunity to watch the series in their homes. We found the attention patterns for these programs to be quite similar to patterns of attention for much earlier series. The sophistication of children this age may have reached a ceiling, at least for this particular television series.

Table 4.1 illustrates the preceding points by showing the regression results for a sample *Sesame Street* program. Although there is variability in the results for different sample programs, the patterns are comparable to the one shown in this table.

The table shows the relationship over time among several program attributes and attention. The time lag (negative subscripts) or lead (positive subscripts) of the predictor terms is taken into account in the model. One can see that the largest effect is that of attention at one point in the program on attention 30 seconds later. Additional predictors are visual presence of speakers and time in show (the trend effect) and a pair of complexity variables accounting for a small amount of variance. Although the complexity terms are statistically significant for this model, there is relatively little consistency in the complexity coefficients among programs. The overall predictive power of the regres-

Table 4.1

Regression for Program Attributes and Attention for Sesame Street

Predictor variable	Beta	Multiple R	F value	df	p <
Attention$_{t-30}$	.45				
Set complexity$_{t-120}$	−.15				
Shot complexity$_{t-60}$	.17				
Time in show$_t$	.18				
Visual presence of speakers$_{t-30}$	.25				
		.74	26.66	5/110	.001

Note: Subscripts for predictors indicate by how many seconds the predictor term precedes (−) or follows (+) children's attention.

sion model is considerable $(R = .74)$, but most of this is the attention inertia effect.

We are continuing to examine the attention patterns of 3–5-year-olds. We are trying to determine if the apparent lack of correlation for visual program attributes is a function of the difficulty of monitoring visuals. We are trying to find the effects of program content attributes on attention; and finally, we are looking at children's comprehension of what they see.

Findings on 7–8-Year-Olds

VIEWING SITUATION

By comparison to younger children, 7–8-year-olds are more sophisticated viewers. This can be seen in their reaction to the viewing situation. Younger children regularly show a continuous trend in attention during a viewing period. Older children generally show a smaller reaction to the situation and instead react more to specific attributes of the program they are watching. There are special circumstances in which older children react like younger ones, however. We have found that 7–8-year-olds who have little experience with a particular program are likely to react more to the situation and less to program attributes. Apparently, the more elaborate viewing style of 7–8-year-olds develops through viewing experience (Krull & Husson, n.d.).

ATTENTION INERTIA

Older children show less attention inertia. They seem able to respond quickly to programs, particularly after they have had some experience with a television series. Where one-half the variance in young children's attention at any point is due to attention inertia, only about 10% of the variance in older children's attention is inertial.

REACTIONS TO PROGRAM ATTRIBUTES

Older children react to a comparatively wide range of program attributes. They react positively to both visual and auditory complexity and seem able to follow the rhythm in some production attributes. They also appear to anticipate changes in some program attributes. Older children watching a new series react like younger children in showing both higher attention inertia and a more restricted taste for program attributes. Younger children appear not to gain to the same extent from their experience. The difference probably is due to differences in cognitive development.

Table 4.2 shows a typical regression model for children's attention to *The Electric Company*. One can see the large number of terms in the model, indicative of a wide range of viewing interests and the long span of time over which the terms act. The model suggests that 7–8-year-olds react based on what they have seen, what they are seeing, and what they expect to see. Children's reaction to rhythms in production is not clearly illustrated in this type of regression model. The only indication of cycling is several set complexity terms. The children's reacting to the rhythm in set complexity is the reason the betas oscillate from positive to negative (Krull & Husson, 1979).

To summarize our results, we have found that young children show a fairly restricted viewing style indicating they have only begun to develop a vocabulary of viewing techniques. Older children have a more elaborate viewing style that allows them considerable flexibility in viewing. They are probably able to obtain much of what they want from programs without paying attention the entire time they are in front of the set. At least as far as reacting to program form is concerned, they seem to show a fairly mature viewing style. What they understand about program content is a matter for future studies.

Implications for Producers and Researchers

Implications for Producers

A few implications of these findings for the production of educational television series are summarized in this section. Application of findings to the development of a specific series would require considerable interaction between researchers and producers.

1. Children learn from viewing a television series over time. Their initial reactions to programs may not be the same as their later reactions, particularly if the children are 7 years of age or older. Producers might consider planning for a learning period during which children could become acclimatized to program formats, characters, and stock plot devices.
2. Children's ability to handle program material changes with age. As they mature, they are progressively more likely to pay attention only during segments which they find appealing. Producers could take advantage of this trend by allowing time for young

Table 4.2

Regression for Program Attributes and Attention for The Electric Company

Predictor variable	Beta	Multiple R	F Value	df	p <
Attention$_{t-30}$	−.23				
Set complexity$_{t-90}$	−.65				
Set complexity$_t$	.22				
Set complexity$_{t+120}$	−.41				
Set complexity$_{t+150}$	−.63				
Shot complexity$_{t-60}$	−.51				
Modal complexity$_{t+90}$	−.35				
Visual–verbal congruence$_t$	.48				
Time in show$_t$	.48				
Visual presence of speakers$_{t-90}$	.62				
		.93	29.33	10/45	.001

Note: Subscripts for predictors indicate by how many seconds the predictor term precedes (−) or follows (+) children's attention.

children's attention to build, overcoming attention inertia, before covering the most important aspects of program segments. For older children producers might make it clear on the audio track that something visually interesting and important is about to occur. Children who otherwise might miss such material due to inattention then might not do so.

3. Younger children are less sensitive to rhythms in production and seem less able to anticipate program occurrences than older children. Producers might provide several cues to young children that interesting material is coming up in a program. Young children's limited understanding of program formats might preclude their coming to the same conclusion on their own.

4. Young children prefer concrete verbalization. Producers could provide concrete visual representations for many verbal referents and could illustrate complex ideas with examples. An abstract term like *physical forces*, for example, is unlikely to mean anything to a 5-year-old. An example like dropping a ball or a person's falling off a chair would probably be much clearer. Although older children are likely to understand more abstract terminology, they may be monitoring the audio track purely for superficial features such as the "brightness" of the sound. Concrete illustrations may lead them to pay more than superficial attention and may aid in their recalling the material.

Implications for Researchers

Implications of our findings for researchers included the following:

1. Since there are strong attention trends during viewing periods, researchers ought to be cautious about how they interpret results of analyses based on comparing segments from the front to those from the back of programs. For example, if attention rises steadily during a viewing period, program segments occurring at the end of programs would receive higher attention as a function of their position rather than as a result of their intrinsic interest for children.
2. Since young children show high attention inertia, researchers should be careful about comparing program segments to one another without taking their length into account. A program segment shorter than 60 seconds might show an attention score that is largely the result of attention to the segment preceding it in the program. A very long program segment may have several attention peaks and valleys, and an average level of attention for the segment may not be a meaningful assessment of children's reaction to the attributes of the segment.
3. Older children show cyclical reactions to program attributes. As a result, their attention level at any point in the program could be affected by program material at surrounding points. A simple bivariate correlation between a program attribute and attention may not accurately reflect a child's reaction to the attribute.
4. The delay in children's reacting to program attributes varies with the attribute in question. Researchers ought to allow for some time variability in children's reacting to programs when making causal assessments.
5. Since children learn about programs as they view, their initial reactions may not represent their experienced reactions. Negative initial reactions could later change to positive reactions if the new material is complex. Positive initial reactions could change to negative reactions if the new material is simple. This instability may jeopardize causal inferences made on children's viewing of test programs.

Limitations

The work done at Rensselaer Polytechnic Institute is limited. We have examined the effects of a small number of program complexity and visual–verbal interaction attributes on children's attention. We have barely looked at either program content or viewer comprehension. Our research designs have not answered all of the questions to which they have been applied. We have found variability among different children's reactions to the same programs. Until we can specify with a high degree of certainty how children will react to specific programs, our findings will have limited value in the production of new educational series. Additional predictive power may come from broadening our studies. We have not yet explained why visual program attributes explain little variance in young children's attention even though their visual attention is high. We have proposed some reasons for this seeming contradiction, but validation of that reasoning is required.

To summarize, we have looked in detail at a small area and have been able to explain it moderately well. It remains for us to explore further implications of this area and to expand our efforts into new areas. Expansions already underway include measures of program content, refined measures of structure, and measures of children's comprehension.

Acknowledgments

Several Rensselaer Polytechnic Institute students aided in collection and analysis of data discussed in this chapter: William Husson, Carol Hughes, Elaine Lewis, Mehmet Kuccukurt, Susan McDermott, and Juanita Ciraulo.

References

Alwitt, L. F., Anderson, D. R., Lorch, E. P., & Levin, S. R., Preschool children's visual attention to attributes of television. *Human Communication Research*, 1980, *7*, 52–67.

Anderson, D. R., & Levin, S. R. Young children's attention to *Sesame Street*. *Child Development*, 1976, *47*, 806–811.

Anderson, D. R., & Lorch, E. P. *A theory of the active nature of young children's television viewing*. Paper presented at the Society of Research in Child Development Biennial Meeting, San Francisco, 1979.

Anderson, D. R., Lorch, E. P., Field, D. E., & Sanders, J. The effects of TV program comprehensibility on preschool children's visual attention to television. *Child Development*, 1981, *52*, 151–157.

Bandura, A., Ross, D., & Ross, S. Imitation of film-mediated aggressive models. *Journal of Abnormal and Social Psychology*, 1963, *66*, 3–11.

Berlyne, D. E. *Aesthetics and psychobiology*. New York: Appleton-Century-Crofts, 1971.

Box, G. E. P., & Jenkins, G. M. *Time series analysis: Forecasting and control*. San Francisco: Holden-Day, 1970.

Brown, J. R., Cramond, J. K., & Wilde, R. J. Displacement effects of television and the child's functional orientation to media. In J. G. Blumler & E. Katz (Eds.), *The uses of mass communications*. Beverly Hills, Calif.; Sage, 1974.

Chatfield, C. *The analysis of time series: theory and practice*. London: Chapman and Hall, 1975.

Epstein, S. L. A comparison of two methods for measuring children's attention to television program material. *Report to the Children's Television Workshop*, New York, 1977.

Flagg, B. N. Children and television: Effects of stimulus repetition on eye activity. In J. W. Senders, D. F. Fisher, & R. A. Monty (Eds.), *Eye movements and higher psychological functions*. Hillsdale, N.J.: Erlbaum, 1978.

Friedlander, B., Wetstone, H., & Scott, C. Suburban preschool children's comprehension of an age-appropriate informational television program. *Child Development*, 1974, 45, 561–565.

Garner, W. R. *Uncertainty and structure as psychological concepts*. New York: Wiley, 1962.

Garner, W. R. *The processing of information and structure*. New York: Wiley, 1974.

Gerbner, G. Violence in television drama: Trends and symbolic functions. In G. A. Comstock, E. A. Rubinstein (Eds.), *Television and social behavior* (Vol. I), *Media content and control*. Washington, D.C.: U.S. Government Printing Office, 1972.

Ginsburg, H., & Opper, S. *Piaget's theory of intellectual development: An introduction*. Englewood Cliffs, N.J.: Prentice–Hall, 1969.

Greenberg, B. S. Gratifications of television viewing and their correlates for British children. In J. G. Blumler & E. Katz (Eds.), *The uses of mass communication: Current perspectives on gratifications research*. Beverly Hills, Calif.: Sage, 1974.

Husson, W. G., & Hughes, C. *A time series analysis of children's attention to television in a naturalistic environment*. Paper presented to the Association for Education in Journalism, East Lansing, Mich., 1981.

Huston, A. C., Wright, J. C., Wartella, E., Rice, M. L., Watkins, B. A., Campbell, T., & Potts, R. Communicating more than content: Formal features of children's television programs. *Journal of Communication*, 1981, 31, 32–48.

Krull, R., & Husson, W. G. Children's attention: The case of TV viewing. In E. Wartella (Ed.), *Children communicating: Media and development of thought, speech, understanding*. Beverly Hills, Calif.: Sage, 1979.

Krull, R., & Husson, W. G. Children's anticipatory attention to the TV screen. *Journal of Broadcasting*, 1980, 24, 36–47.

Krull, R., & Husson, W. G. Children learning to watch *The Electric Company*, Submitted for review to *Journal of Broadcasting*, 1982.

Krull, R., Husson, W. G., & Paulson, A. S. Cycles in children's attention to the television screen: A time series analysis. In B. D. Ruben (Ed.), *Communication yearbook* (Vol. 2). New Brunswick, N. J.: Transaction, 1978.

Krull, R., & Paulson, A. S. Time series analysis in communication research. In P. M. Hirsch, P. V. Miller, & F. G. Kline (Eds.), *Strategies for communication research*. Beverly Hills, Calif.: Sage, 1977.

Krull, R., & Watt, J. H. *Television program complexity and ratings*. Paper presented to the American Association for Public Opinion Research, Itasca, Ill., 1975.

Krull, R., Watt, J. H., & Lichty, L. W. Entropy and structure: Two measures of complexity in television programs. *Communication Research*, 1977, 4, 61–86.

Lyle, J., & Hoffman, H. R. Explorations of patterns of television viewing by preschool-age children. In E. A. Rubinstein, G. A. Comstock, & J. P. Murray (Eds.), *Television and social behavior* (Vol. 4), *Television in day-to-day life: Patterns of use*. Washington, D.C.: U.S. Government Printing Office, 1972.

Meringoff, L. K. Influence of the medium on children's story apprehension. *Journal of Educational Psychology*, 1980, *72*(2), 240–249.

Neisser, U. *Cognition and reality: Principles and implications of cognitive psychology*. San Francisco: Freeman, 1976.

Piaget, J. *The mechanisms of perception*. New York: Basic Books, 1969.

Radlick, M. S. *The processing demands of television: Neurophysiological correlates of television viewing*. Unpublished doctoral dissertation, Rensselaer Polytechnic Institute, 1980.

Robinson, J. Television and leisure time: Yesterday, today and (maybe) tomorrow. *Public Opinion Quarterly*, 1969, *33*, 310–222.

Salomon, G. *Interaction of media, cognition, and learning*. San Francisco: Jossey-Bass, 1979.

Shannon, C. E., & Weaver, W. *The mathematical theory of communication*. Urbana: University of Illinois Press, 1949.

Smith, R. *Preschool children's comprehension of television*. Paper presented to the Society for Research in Child Development, Boston, 1981.

Steiner, G. A. *The people look at television*. New York: Knopf, 1963.

Ward, S., Levinson, D., & Wackman, D. Children's attention to television advertising. In E. A. Rubinstein, G. A. Comstock, & J. P. Murray (Eds.), *Television and social behavior*. (Vol. 4), *Television in day-to-day life: Patterns of use*. Washington, D.C.: U.S. Government Printing Office, 1972.

Watt, J. H., & Krull, R. An information theory measure for television programming. *Communication Research*, 1974, *1*, 44–68.

Watt, J. H., & Krull, R. *Arousal model components in television programming: Form activity and violent content*. Paper presented to the International Communication Association, Chicago, 1975.

Watt, J. H., & Krull, R. An examination of three models of television viewing and aggression. *Human Communication Research*, 1976, *3*, 991–112.

Winn, M. *The plug-in drug*. New York: Viking, 1977.

chapter **5**

Interpretation and Inference in Children's Television Viewing[1]

W. ANDREW COLLINS

The study of television influences includes two irreducible elements: the content of the medium and the viewer who perceives and interprets the images and messages. Throughout most of its history, mass media research has focused primarily on the former (e.g., Gerbner, 1972; Liebert, Neale, & Davidson, 1973). The frequency of occurrence of a behavior or event on the screen—not viewers' perception of its function or significance within a narrative—has been considered the major determinant of media effects. In this "dominant-image" model (Collins, in press-a), viewers are implicitly pictured as passive recipients of a series of salient images from which they make no attempt to extract unique social meanings. To be sure, television effects have also been seen partly as a function of age and social group correlates of the expected outcomes of viewing (e.g., Comstock, Chaffee, Katzman, McCombs, & Roberts, 1978; Feshbach & Singer, 1971; Leifer, Gordon, & Graves, 1974; Liebert et al., 1973; Maccoby, 1964; Siegel, 1975; Stein & Friedrich, 1975). For example, aggressive behavior following a violent program may be influenced not only by program content, but also by

[1]Preparation of this chapter was facilitated by a grant to the author from the National Institute of Mental Health.

antecedent social learning, and states and circumstances subsequent to viewing. Neither this view nor the dominant-image view gives the viewer an active role, however; in both, media effects are assumed only to reflect complex mixtures of external forces. Questions of how viewers perceive salient images and how their cognitive and motivational characteristics might contribute to the influence of particular content upon subsequent behavior have rarely been addressed.

The focus of this chapter is a program of research undertaken to assess how viewers of different ages encode, interpret, and make inferences about the contents of typical programs. A major premise of the research is that viewers' interpretations and inferences contribute to a variety of possible effects of television dramatic fare. In the following sections, I will discuss two related aspects of television content and young viewers' cognitive and emotional responses to them. The first aspect is children's comprehension of plots from commercial television dramatic programs. The second is the nature of inferences and evaluative responses to television characters, their actions, and significant social events by viewers of different ages and capabilities and with different social and personal histories.

Comprehension of Dramatic Plots

In order to understand television's effects, we must first consider some characteristics of television as a medium for potentially influential social content. Dramatic television programs offer a panoply of social actions, events, and situations. In this respect, they are much like the real world in which children and adults live and also like the contents of other mass media. Nevertheless, a written version or radio play presenting the same contents shown on television probably does not have the same behavioral or psychological effects. In this section, I discuss some characteristics of the television stimulus and describe some recent findings about children's comprehension of social information conveyed in typical programs.

The Television Stimulus

Television programs consist of sequences of visual and auditory stimuli that are organized in particular ways. In children's programs like *Sesame Street*, the organization consists of a series of disconnected brief episodes consisting of one or a few scenes; in dramatic programs, the sequence of scenes is subordinated to a plot or narrative. In both cases, programs share two general characteristics: (a) irrelevant information, as well as information that is relevant, to the theme of the program; and in most cases, (b) relevant information that is in some instances explicitly presented and in others implied by events shown on the screen. In typical dramatic programs, the series of discrete scenes implies interrelationships from which coherence must be inferred. For example, there may be an early scene in the plot involving two characters (e.g., a verbal disagreement) and a later scene in which the same two characters are portrayed in somewhat altered circumstances (e.g., one character physically attacks the other). The information that something has occurred to cause a change from the first to the second is only implicit, however; viewers must infer it. Often these linkages are important for understanding plots—as in the case of the inference that an early program event *caused* a later event. Thus, program comprehension involves both attention to and retention of explicitly portrayed relevant events and inferences in which viewers go beyond on-screen events to grasp the relations among them. Simon (1976) has recently characterized cognitive tasks such as those presented by television as "ill-structured problems" that require considerable attentional , organizational, and inferential activity by the viewer. In this respect, television programs are quite different from the simple laboratory analogs used in most studies of basic modeling and social-inference processes (Collins, 1975, 1979). Consequently, the results of those studies may often be poor indicators of children's responses to television.

Specifying and Assessing Program Content

The foregoing analysis implies that the first step in understanding young viewers' comprehension must be careful specification of the content of programs. In our research, we have "parsed" programs using the following procedure. First, *event analyses* of program plots (Omanson, in press; Warren, Nicholas, & Trabasso, 1979) are used to identify plot-essential content items and relations between them. In contrast to analyses developed in the study of prose narratives (e.g., Stein & Glenn, 1979), these event analyses are designed for deriving the structure of narratives, rather than fitting narrative content to predetermined, idealized story structures. Next, using the event analyses, we prepare lists of events to give to groups of adults, usually volunteers from community groups or undergraduate classes. We then ask these adults to select those events without which the plot "could not be understandably retold." Interrater agreement on the central on-screen events in studies of television comprehension has ranged from .76 to .94 (Collins, in press-a).

The event analyses and adult ratings then serve as a basis for measuring understanding of the explicit and implicit information contained in programs. The primary measure in most studies consists of recognition items about the essential elements of plots. The first step in constructing these items involves detailed interviews with children and adults during pretesting. Children's answers are used to devise wording for correct and incorrect alternatives for the recognition items. An example from a recent study may clarify the nature of the recognition measure. One explicit content item concerned a salient program event ("When Luke was walking in the alley, he . . . saw a man steal some money"). Another concerned a later act of violence ("When Luke walked into the office, another man . . . jumped on him from behind"). A subsequent question then addressed the cause of the act ("The man jumped on Luke . . . because Luke knew he had stolen money"). The first two questions assess retention of explicit content. The third concerns an inference about the implicit cause–effect relation between them. Children's responses to these recognition items taps their abilities to verify the occurrence of onscreen events and the implicit relations among them.

We also use this recognition-item format to examine certain errors of comprehension and inference. Incorrect alternatives for the recognition items are constructed to represent specific misperceptions of the plot. Patterns of errors enable us to analyze particular types of difficulties in understanding programs and also to assess effects of guessing and response bias. Other nonrecognition procedures, selected according to the purposes of individual studies, are used to supplement the recognition measure.

Developmental Patterns of Retention and Inference

This approach to specifying program content and constructing measures of children's comprehension has now been used in a number of studies. I will review one of them (Collins, Wellman, Keniston, & Westby, 1978) briefly to illustrate the research strategy and findings. The study was designed to examine effects of plot organization and complexity on processing by children of different ages. The stimulus was an hour-long action–adventure show composed of two parallel subplots edited into four different versions. The *simple* version consisted of one of the plots. The *complex* version contained the same plot, intermingled with the other subplot, which was not necessary for comprehension of the basic story line. We also prepared jumbled versions of both the simple and complex plots in which the scenes were randomly, rather than chronologically, ordered. These four versions were shown to groups of second-, fifth-, and eighth-grade children (N = 292).

Viewers of different ages showed quite different levels of comprehension of the edited programs. Second graders correctly recognized significantly less of the explicit central information than did older children, adolescents, and adults. The average proportion for second graders was only 66% of the content that adults had judged as central to the plot. Corresponding proportions of comprehension for fifth and eighth graders were 84% and 92%. Similar age differences occurred across all four versions of the program, despite the different organizations and different numbers of scenes they contained. The age differences have been replicated in other studies in which the stimuli were situation comedies (Collins, 1970; Newcomb & Collins, 1979) or other types of action–adventure programs, including a period western (Collins, 1981). In short, children as old as 8 years retain a relatively small proportion of central actions, events, and settings of typical programs. Substantial improvement occurs from the ages 8 to 14, however (Collins, in press-a).

Even when they retained explicit content, younger children often failed to infer the interscene relations in programs. On the recognition measure of implicit information, second graders had an overall mean score of fewer than half (47%) of the items that adults had agreed upon as important; and fifth and eighth graders scored 67% and 77%, respectively. This poor performance on inference items is not an artifact of second graders' poor knowledge of individual scenes. To rule out this possibility, we calculated conditional probabilities for correct inferences, given that both of the relevant premise scenes, or only one of them, or neither one, were known at the time the children were tested. The white bars in Figure 5.1 represent the conditional probability for inferences when children knew both requisite pieces of explicit information. For second graders, the probability is less than 50%. The probabilities for fifth and eighth graders are significantly higher (68% and 75%, respectively). By contrast, the likelihood of correct inferences when children knew only one or neither of the premise scenes (shown in Figure 5.1 by the shaded bars) is marginally greater than the chance at all three grade levels. Thus, when the explicit scenes are known, older children are more likely than second-grade children to infer the implied relationships among on-screen events. Like our findings of age differences in retention, this developmental pattern has been replicated in studies of a number of different types of television shows (e.g., Col-

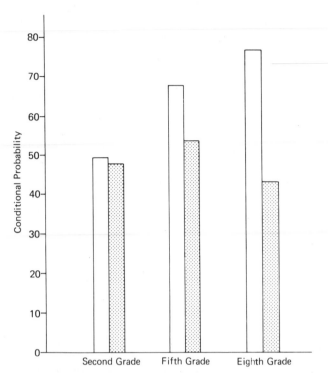

Figure 5.1. *Conditional probabilities for correct inferences about relations between program events, given that both premises of the inference are known or that only one or neither of the premises is known. (White bars refer to participants who know two premises; shaded bars refer to participants who know 0–1 premise.) (Adapted from Collins, Wellman, Keniston, & Westby, 1978.)*

lins, 1981; Collins & Westby, 1981; Newcomb & Collins, 1979; Purdie, Collins, & Westby, 1979).

Children's Representations of Television Programs

Since younger viewers apparently have both a less complete and less accurate representation of plots than more mature viewers, they may perceive and evaluate the content of many typical programs quite differently than older children and adults. Their representations partly reflect age-related differences in cognitive abilities, including capabilities for selective attention, information processing, and inferential reasoning. In addition, two other factors affect understanding: (a) the degree of difficulty of the "ill-structured task" presented by a program; and (b) the extent of viewers' own prior knowledge and expectations pertinent to the content of programs. In the following sections, I discuss these two determinants of children's interpretation and inferences about program content.

Effects of Program Characteristics

Program difficulty, complexity, and abstractness account for many of the difficulties young viewers experience. Most programs are not produced for an audience of children, but for a general audience including adults. Consequently, stories must be somewhat complex and subtle in order to hold adult attention. In the case of dramatic presentations, at least three cognitive tasks are involved in comprehension: (a) selective attention to central program events; (b) orderly organization of the program events; and (c) *temporal integration* (Collins, 1979), involving inferences about implicit relations among explicit scenes (Collins, Wellman, Keniston, & Westby, 1978). In our research, we have emphasized the third task.

Children's difficulties with tasks are apparent from additional analyses of data from the study described earlier (Collins et al., 1978). in these post hoc analyses, we assessed the nature of the inferences required by each item in the recognition test of implicit information. All of these implicit content items were rated independently within three different taxonomic frameworks: (a) types of content involved (i.e., inferences involving cues about motives, action, goals, or consequences); (b) relations among the separate events relevant to the inferences (e.g., physical or psychological causes, enablement); and (c) number and abstractness of inferential steps required to answer each item. Interrater reliabilities for the three sets of ratings were .92, .96, and .88, respectively. Next, we independently and arbitrarily identified as difficult items those that fewer than 45% of the second-grade children in the study had answered correctly. The item categories were then compared to the difficulty ratings. Neither content category nor nature of the relations among events were related to item difficulty. However, items rated as notably complex, in terms of number and abstractness of intermediate inferential steps, overlap significantly (80%) with the set of items that were difficult for second graders. Thus, one factor in younger children's generally poorer comprehension may be the difficulty of the processing task in many typical programs.

One factor in program complexity undoubtedly is the number and kind of formal features, such as camera angles, background music, and visual techniques for compressing time and signaling breaks in action. These noncontent features nevertheless carry considerable information for those viewers whose experience permits their meaning to be recognized (e.g., Rice, Huston, & Wright, in press). In studies of prose narratives, the explicitness with which story elements are stated and their grammatical forms can be relatively easily controlled. Control is less feasible in audiovisual narratives because of the dramatic and cinematic techniques that sometimes result in inexplicit or complex portrayals of important information. As a result, formal features often confound attempts to assess comprehension. To date, no systematic means of characterizing both content and presentation features has been developed. However, the role of presentation features in comprehension has been documented, most extensively by Huston-Stein and Wright and their colleagues, whose research is described in Chapter 2 of this volume.

Surprisingly, however, young children's processing difficulties do not appear to be due simply to the length of programs nor to the presence of extraneous intervening information in plots. We have recently investigated forgetting and interference effects, using a procedure of interrupting viewing at different points for different subgroups of children. When interrupted, the children were tested on their knowledge of explicit content and inferences in the program thus far. The procedure calls for one group of children to see the entire program without interruption to provide a check on possible contamination of post interruption answers in the other three interruption groups. The procedure is diagrammed in Table 5.1. In several studies with this procedure (Collins & Westby, 1981; Purdie, Collins, & Westby, 1979), children who were tested on content they had seen only minutes before performed no better than children who were asked the same question at a much later time. Throughout the program, second graders' performance was poorer than fifth and eighth graders'. Similar findings were reported in a study of retention of *Sesame Street* content (Friedlander, Wetstone, & Scott, 1974). Thus, despite the difficulty of programs, young viewers'

Table 5.1

The Interruption Design: Points at which Initial Comprehension and Evaluation Measures Are Taken

Condition	Time line of the plot		
Before-motive group	↓ Motive portrayal[a]	Aggressive action	Consequences
Before-action group	Motive portrayal	↓ Aggressive action	Consequences
After-action group	Motive portrayal	Aggressive action	↓ Consequences
No interruption group	Motive portrayal	Aggressive action	Consequences ↓

[a] ↓ denotes point of interruption.

comprehension problems cannot reasonably be attributed to simple forgetting of information. Rather, as indicated earlier, young viewers appeared to select and encode program content inadequately during viewing, and this is probably the primary reason they retain essential content so poorly.

Nevertheless, the nature and structure of typical television programs present a number of unique perceptual and cognitive tasks to viewers, whose knowledge and general cognitive skills may be inadequate to the task demands. Although we have tentatively ruled out some program factors as sources of comprehension difficulties in the shows used in our studies, much additional information is needed about the interaction of task characteristics and viewer skills involved in interpretations and inferences from television.

The Role of "World Knowledge"
and Social Expectations

Children's representations of programs are also affected by the general background of knowledge and experience they bring to viewing. Since television programs include a wide range of common and uncommon portrayals, including much implicit information, comprehension necessarily draws upon knowledge derived from general experience of perceptual, cognitive, linguistic, and social phenomena.

The contribution of differences in general knowledge to age differences in comprehension is apparent from further analyses of the data gathered by Collins, Wellman, Keniston, and Westby (1978). In these analyses (Collins & Wellman, in press), we examined two categories of program content. *Common knowledge* refers to generally familiar information in programs that is likely to be understood by viewers of all ages. *Program-specific knowledge* refers to information that is idiosyncratic or peculiar to the particular plot being viewed. To apply these distinctions to the program studied by Collins *et al.*, the show probably evoked *common knowledge* about (a) policemen; (b) acts of murder; (c) a murderer's being shot or apprehended by the police; and (d) buying groceries—which the protagonist did repeatedly in order to cash his forged checks; buying groceries is likely to be understood by even young children (Nelson, 1978). *Program-specific knowledge* included information that (a) some nonuniformed characters were policemen; (b) the murder at the beginning occurred because the victim surprised the villain during a theft (a motive inference); and (c) the purpose behind buying groceries was cashing "fake" checks to get money.

Collins and Wellman examined these categories of content in inter-

view protocols from the children in the Collins et al. (1978) study. The
children had been asked to retell the narratives "so that someone who
hasn't seen the show would understand what happened." We first had
two adults code content propositions into either the program-elicited
common knowledge or the program-specific knowledge category. Proportion of agreements was .98. We then noted the frequency with
which children mentioned one or the other category of content in their
narrative. Among second graders, 81% of children mentioned the content commonly known by all age groups, but only 16% of these younger
children mentioned the more specialized knowledge. Fifth and eighth
graders were just as likely as the younger children to mention the
common-knowledge content, but many more fifth graders than second
graders mentioned the program-specific knowledge—55% and 98%
were the mean proportions in fifth and eighth grades, respectively,
compared to 16% for second graders. Both younger and older viewers
probably recognize common-knowledge sequences. Older viewers may
also recognize—and perhaps also note the potential importance of—
events that deviate from common expectations, whereas younger viewers appear less likely to notice such deviations or to appreciate their
significance within the plot.

Two additional analyses further substantiated the role of age differences in knowledge. First, we examined children's errors on the
recognition items. The items had been constructed so that alternatives
reflected two different types of incorrect inferences: (a) common or
stereotypical events; or (b) confusions about the relationships among
events that were actually portrayed in the program. For example, in the
program viewed by the children in this study, the protagonist was
asked by an old panhandler for a quarter. The protagonist, guilt-ridden
over his murder of a similar elderly derelict earlier in the show, im-
pulsively gives the panhandler $40. In the recognition-item measure,
children were told the following item: "The man is just walking along
when an old man asks him for a quarter. When this happens, he . . . (a)
gives the old man $40; (b) tells him he doesn't have a quarter; (c) hits
the old man on the head." Answer (a) is correct. When second-grade
viewers answered incorrectly, however, they strongly preferred answer
(b), the stereotyped response. Older viewers were equally likely to
choose the confusion response (c). In short, younger viewers not only
more often made errors in comprehending the program, but also, in a
higher proportion of instances, they filled in gaps in their knowledge
with stereotypes of common action sequences.

Second, the intrusion of event stereotypes was also seen in younger
children's predictions about plot sequences. The interruption pro-

cedure (cf. Figure 5.2) was used to interview children at one of two points during viewing. These were points that adult judges had identified as plot junctures after which something important seems likely to happen. Children were asked to predict "what will happen next" in the show and to give reasons for their predictions. Their verbatim answers were coded into two categories according to whether a sequence of events from the plot, rather than just the immediately preceding event, was mentioned as a basis for their predictions. Predictions based on frequently occurring events instantiated by some aspect of the scene immediately prior to interruption were coded as *stereotypes*. Answers that were based on details from the sequence of prior scenes in the program were coded as *program-specific* predictions. Three independent coders achieved intercoder reliabilities ranging from .85 to .91.

The majority of fifth and eighth graders (78% and 68%, respectively) made predictions that invoked the sequence of plot occurrences prior to interruption (program-specific predictions). Second graders rarely (28% of the cases) predicted events that followed from the preinterruption scenes but instead made stereotyped predictions. A typical stereotyped prediction followed the scene in which an elderly panhandler approached the protagonist. One young viewer guessed that the protagonist would "tell the old man to go away." By contrast, older youngsters usually recognized the similarity of the panhandler to the derelict murdered earlier in the show and drew implications accordingly, "He'll think it's the old man he killed, and he'll hit him again."

Prior social knowledge also accounts for individual, as well as developmental, differences in children's comprehension. In a recent study (Newcomb & Collins, 1979), differences among second graders in understanding of typical programs apparently reflected different social experiences of the individual children. The experiment involved equal numbers of children from both lower- and middle-socioeconomic samples at grades 2, 5, and 8. One representative group of children viewed an edited version of a commercial network show featuring middle-class characters. A second group saw a similar plot featuring lower-class characters. Comprehension of explicitly portrayed and implicit events differed for second-grade youngsters as a function of the match between their own previous experience and the characters and settings portrayed in the program. Both white and black lower-class children understood the lower-class family plot better than the middle-class second graders, whereas middle-class children of both races understood the middle-class family plot better than their lower-class counterparts did. Apparently, for second-grade viewers the general knowledge available to the different social-class groups resulted in differential understanding of the programs. At the two older ages, however, viewers from all groups understood both programs equally well, perhaps because more extensive and varied social knowledge made it possible to understand aspects of portrayals that were unlike their own common experiences. Thus, within the younger age group, in which understanding is generally unreliable, individual differences in children's understanding may often reflect differences in the knowledge gained in social learning.

The effect of individual differences in social expectations was directly assessed in a recent study by List, Collins, and Westby (1981). Third graders who either held conventional sex-role expectations or less stereotyped expectations viewed both a program featuring a traditional female character and a second show featuring a nontraditional female. Representations of the two plots, as tested by a recognition measure, were clearly affected by the children's different sex-role expectations. When high-stereotype children made recognition errors, the errors significantly reflected traditional sex-role expectations, whereas low-stereotype viewers more often made errors that were consistent with less traditional expectations. A separate group of high- and low-stereotype third graders who answered the recognition items without having seen the program chose between the incorrect alternatives at chance level. Apparently, viewers' sex-role expectations were activated by the content of the program and, in turn, influenced children's perceptions of the show's content. Individual differences in other areas of knowledge and expectations may similarly bias children's processing of social roles, attitudes, and behaviors in television programs.

In summary, children's representations of the content of typical programs reflect not only their age-related cognitive abilities, but also the difficulty of the program material to be comprehended and the store of general knowledge and social expectations built up through experiences prior to viewing. In the remaining sections of the chapter, I consider some implications of varying representations for cognitive and emotional responses to persons, behaviors, and events portrayed in typical television dramatic programs.

Inferences about Characters, Their Actions, and Events

Television programs portray varied persons, behaviors, roles, attitudes, situations, and events that are drawn from a range of social strata and circumstances (e.g., Leifer et al., 1974). Effects of viewing these social exemplars probably include not only overt behavior patterns, but also social knowledge and expectations that are only indirectly, rarely, or subtly apparent in overt action—for example, children's expectations about adults' behavior, including the normativeness of crime, family conflict or its absence, appropriateness of various roles and behaviors, and so forth (Gerbner, 1972; Leifer et al., 1974). Furthermore, this social content is embedded in sometimes complex plots. Difficulties in understanding plots undoubtedly affect perceptions of social information and its influence upon viewers.

Two common instances of television content illustrate this point. First, consider an often portrayed character in dramatic programs: the "double dealer," who appears benevolent but is subtly and gradually revealed to be malevolent instead. Preschool and young grade-school children may well fail to comprehend the duplicity in such a portrayal (Collins & Zimmermann, 1975) and, in many instances, may evaluate the character's behavior more positively than the details of the plot warrant. Prevailing theories of behavioral effects (e.g., Bandura, 1965) imply that a duplicitous character would probably be more readily emulated than one about whom consistently negative cues were shown. Young viewers in particular might be affected by such a model, since older, more experienced viewers would be apt to recognize the pertinent negative cues, discount the apparently positive ones, and evaluate the character negatively. On the other hand, even young children who are especially familiar with an ambiguous character's social role and the circumstances in which he appears may more readily recognize and weigh conflicting cues. Such evaluative effects are often attributed to perceived similarity between viewers and television characters, but the effects of the similarities between model and viewer often may also include such cognitive factors such as the attention-directing function of similarity and preference (cf. Bartlett, 1932; Krebs, 1970) and the facilitative effects of prior knowledge in processing character and plot information.

A second example—perhaps a more common one in typical programming—involves the social context for judging social information in plots. Television dramas often involve one or more distinctive, salient acts (e.g., aggression), along with information relevant to evaluations of the acts and the characters who perform them. If violent fighting or shooting is perpetrated by a character who clearly wishes to harm his victim and who is obviously punished for what he does, the character and his behavior are likely to be evaluated negatively. On the other hand, aggression for the purpose of freeing a hostage which earns the perpetrator a medal of bravery would be viewed much more positively. This contrast is familiar from laboratory studies (e.g., Berndt & Berndt, 1975; Costanzo, Coie, Grumet, & Farnill, 1973; King, 1971; Piaget, 1965), in which characters are judged to be naughty, nice, good, or bad because of the motive or consequences that are described along with their actions. The same factors have been shown to affect observers' imitative behavior after watching aggressive models in observational learning experiments (e.g., Bandura, 1965; Berkowitz & Geen, 1967; Berkowitz & Rawlings, 1963). Motives or reasons for social acts and their consequences are potentially important modifiers of children's evaluative responses and of their postviewing behaviors.

In several early studies in our research program (e.g., Collins, 1973; Collins, Berndt, & Hess, 1974), however, we found that kindergarten and second-grade children had difficulty remembering the relations of the motive and consequences cues in connection with the aggressive actions in an action–adventure program. Collins (1973) further reported behavioral differences that ostensibly reflect cognitive-processing differences like those described earlier. When commercials were inserted between the aggressive action and scenes of negative motives and negative consequences, third graders' tendencies to choose aggressive responses increased, in comparison to children of the same age who saw the three scenes close together in time. Although comprehension was not adequately assessed in this study, the task of inferring relations between aggression and pertinent motive and consequences cues was probably more difficult for the first group than the second because of the temporal separations imposed by the commercials. There was no evidence of behavioral differences among the sixth and tenth graders who saw these two versions of the program. Thus, comprehension of plots potentially affects understanding of influential social cues that form the context of modeled action.

Age-related Patterns of Comprehension and Evaluation

The implications of comprehension difficulties for children's evaluation of social models were tested in a study recently completed by Purdie, Collins, and Westby (1979). In this study, the stimulus was an edited version of a commercial network action–adventure drama. The plot involved a man searching for his former wife to prevent her from testifying against him in a kidnapping case. He finds the house where she is hiding and shoots at her, but his goal is thwarted by the arrival of officers, and he is taken away in handcuffs. The program was edited into two versions, retaining the main events of the plot, but deleting some extraneous materials and all commercials. In the *distal-motive version*, the protagonist's motives and aggression appeared in scenes that were approximately 4 minutes apart. In the *proximal-motive version*, the motive and aggression information were presented adjacent to each other. One or the other of the two versions was shown to 200 randomly selected second- and fifth-grade girls and boys.

As in our other research, there were pronounced grade differences on the recognition measure of comprehension. At both grade levels, however, children who saw the motive and aggression cues in immediate sequence understood the implicit motive–aggression relationship better than children who saw the cues separated from each other by extraneous material. Apparently, reducing the distance between relevant cues facilitated incorporation of information about the protagonist's motive and aggression, with special benefit to the second graders. The conditional probability for correct inference items, given that children answered both discrete premise items correctly, was .52 for proximal-motive viewers in the second grade; distal-motive viewers in the second grade made correct inferences at chance level (.29). Fifth-graders' probabilities were higher and essentially equal in both viewing conditions. Both age groups performed at chance level when only one or neither explicit premise was known. The data are shown in Figure 5.2.

Recognition of explicit and implicit information about motives and action influenced the children's impressions about the goodness or badness of the aggressor. Evaluations were assessed using the graduated squares procedure developed by Costanzo *et al.* (1973), in which six size-graduated squares are labeled from "very bad" to "very good." Participants point to the square that shows how good or bad a character is. Children who answered all three motive–aggression inference questions correctly were significantly more negative in their evaluation of the aggressor than were children who understood two or fewer inferences. Whether motives and aggression were proximally or distally portrayed also affected evaluations. At both grades, distal-motive viewers evaluated the character less negatively than proximal-motive viewers, particularly following portrayal of the aggressive action. Thus, children's inferences about critical links were correlated with their evaluative responses.

Moral Judgments of Characters

Why do children as old as 7 or 8 years fail to perceive important linkages among scenes? Several possibilities can be suggested: Perhaps

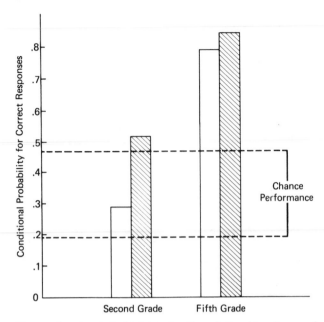

Figure 5.2. *The results of a study to determine the relationship of age and comprehension of a specially edited version of a commercial network action–adventure drama. (White bars refer to distal motive; shaded bars refer to proximal motive.) (Adapted from Collins & Westby, 1981.)*

young viewers' lower level of knowledge simply impairs all aspects of processing new instances for which the knowledge is relevant. Or, as suggested by Collins and Wellman (in press), perhaps young viewers, even when they have the relevant information that should facilitate comprehension, apply it less flexibly than older children. Once information has been instantiated by salient cues (for example, the label "police" for seeing uniformed characters), younger children may perceive the program in terms of a standard, preset sequence of events that is already familiar to them. As a result, they may fail to notice or may ignore ways in which the program varies from familiar sequences. Consequently, explicit and implicit details of particular events may be short-circuited by rigid expectations of actors and actions (Schank & Abelson, 1977). More mature or more knowledgeable viewers may be likely to recognize the significance of departures from expected sequences and to process them as significant aspects of stories that override usual occurrences.

This hypothesis has recently received suggestive support in a study of children's moral judgments of television characters (Collins & Westby, 1981). Most studies of moral judgment involve laboratory studies of reactions to brief stories. The basic assumption behind this work is that moral judgments of characters depend on comprehension and weighting of information about motives and consequences of their action. Television dramas, however, involve numerous evaluation-relevant cues presented explicitly and over a longer period of time than the simple stories used in most moral judgment research. Thus, in the study described later, we used the interruption procedure (see previous section, Effects of Program Characteristics) to trace the formation of and change in evaluations over the course of viewing a program. We also examined emerging evaluations in relation to comprehension of evaluation-relevant cues. The stimulus was the program about the kidnapping suspect searching for his wife to prevent her testifying against him. We interrupted 88 second- and fifth-grade children at one of the four interruption points and asked them to evaluate the "goodness" or "badness" of the character. We also tested their comprehension of the program up to the point of interruption.

The usual grade-level differences in comprehension between second and fifth grade were found, as well as parallel differences between the two grades in the degree to which children evaluated the antisocial character as "bad." The most pertinent findings, however, concern the patterns of evaluation that emerged from the beginning to the end of the show (see Figure 5.3). Second graders who evaluated the character negatively did so only after seeing the consequences, whereas fifth graders were generally negative at earlier points in the program. At the first two interruption points, second and fifth graders' evaluations were

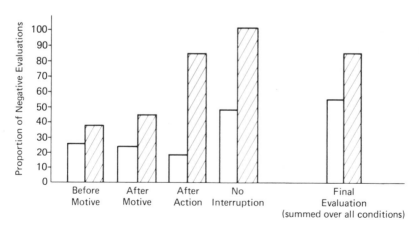

Figure 5.3. *Proportion of second- and fifth-graders who evaluated antisocial character as negative at different points in viewing of an action–adventure program. (White bars refer to second grade; shaded bars refer to fifth grade.) (Adapted from Collins & Westby, 1981.)*

not significantly different from each other and were generally positive. Only about 25% of the second graders and 40% of the fifth graders gave negative evaluations after these scenes. However, by the third interruption—after the aggressive action—fifth grader's evaluations were overwhelmingly negative (83%), whereas the proportion of second graders giving negative evaluations did not change. Only at the end of the program—after the protagonist had been arrested by the police—did the proportion of second-graders evaluating him negatively increase significantly, and then only to 46%. Whether their first evaluation of the protagonist was positive or negative, by the end of the program nearly all fifth-graders evaluated the characters negatively, as compared to only 56% of the second-graders.

Why did some second graders eventually change from positive to negative evaluations of the protagonist, although others did not? Two pieces of evidence are pertinent. First, second graders whose evaluations were positive both during and after the program (nonchangers) were compared to those whose evaluations were initially positive but ultimately negative (changers). However, changers understood the implicit causal links among motives, actions, and consequences scenes better than nonchangers, although changers and nonchangers were not different in their knowledge either of the motive scene or aggressive action alone. Thus, evaluation differences among second graders apparently reflected differences not in comprehension of necessary explicit cues, but in understanding the aggressive action in relation to the motive scenes. Differences among second graders in the comprehension of the important later scenes in the show are not attributable to differences in verbal ability, which we had controlled in covariance analyses. Nor did they reflect some limitation in acquiring information from the program generally. Nonchangers actually performed better than changers on tests of content that had been presented early in the program but was unrelated to the character's motives.

Second, post hoc analyses showed that children who were initially positive appear to have formed and applied hypotheses about the character's behavior differently. For example, changers and nonchangers gave markedly different reasons for their initial evaluation (coded as either positive or negative; interrater agreement = .94). Although participants interrupted during the motive scene gave uniformly positive evaluations, 75% of those who remained positive explicitly justified their initial judgments with incorrect, but positive, interpretations of ambiguous events occurring early in the program (i.e., "he is trying to help the girl," or "he is trying to find her so she won't be scared.") By contrast, children who eventually changed their evaluations often gave initially noncommittal answers (80%), indicating that they did not have a reason for their evaluation. After the program, nonchangers continued to explain evaluations in terms of the positive interpretation of early cues (83%), whereas changers focused on the negative motives or action (73%).

Thus, both changers and nonchangers gave initially positive evaluations, but they apparently selected and retained plot information differently as a function of the explicitness of their early instantiated expectations about the actor. Nonchangers' initial positive perceptions may have affected retention of some plot events, much as social prototypes or schemata have been found to create conformity biases in memory for social information (e.g., Hastie, 1981; Nisbett & Ross, 1980; Schneider, Hastorf, & Ellsworth, 1980). Furthermore, their expectations may well have interfered with recognition of negative consequences to the protagonist. By contrast, changers' less explicit initial assumptions, although not facilitating overall comprehension, may have permitted assimilation of later-occurring negative cues.

Different inferences by children who change evaluations in response to a sequence of cues about an actor's behavior and those who do not change emphasize the need for closer analyses of what viewers do when they encounter new instances of others' behavior. This need can partly be met by studies of comprehension in which viewers' knowledge or expectations about on-screen actions and events are carefully controlled and manipulated. However, we also must understand better the motivations and knowledge that are likely to be elicited in television viewing outside the laboratory and how such elicited motivations and knowledge guide responses in typical viewing. For example, the moral judgment findings described earlier would be illuminated by independent assessments of young children's usual expectations about "good guys" in shows, and their specific predictions about event sequences in which the setting and actor cues are like those presented in the program they saw in the study. It is possible that the differences between changers and nonchangers depend on the extent to which such expectations are initially well formed or the extent to which only one (as compared to several) alternative event sequences seem plausible to them.

Comprehension and Social Effects

These findings imply that the social influences of television cannot be considered a simple function of on-screen content, since they may also involve the perception of actors and events by viewers of different ages with different experiences. After watching typical dramatic pro-

grams, grade-school and preadolescent children construct interpretations that vary considerably in how accurately and completely they
reflect the content of the programs. Evaluations of the portrayed characters and actions appear to vary concomitantly with comprehension.
The implications of these comprehension variations for behavioral effects have so far been addressed in relatively few studies, and those in
which direct measures of comprehension and behavior have been taken
(e.g., Leifer & Roberts, 1972) have yielded null findings. In this regard,
the literature parallels discouraging attempts to demonstrate attitude–behavior relationships (e.g., Ajzen & Fishbein, 1977) and social
cognition–behavior correspondences (e.g., Shantz, 1975). Nevertheless, in several studies behavioral differences have been found that are
suggestive of links between children's representations of programs and
subsequent behavior that warrant further examination. Although it is
impossible to estimate what proportion of the variance in the social
impact of television is due to incomplete inferences or distorted interpretations, age-related and individual differences in cognitive processing of typical programs underscore a need to consider these processes in future research on television's social influence.

Discussion and Implications

Up to now, the working premise of the present research program has
been derived from general social learning models of television effects.
We have attempted to document the role of viewers' subjective interpretation of television content as a mediating factor in postviewing
responses. Rather than focusing on the content of the model's behavior
per se, we have emphasized the perception of that behavior by the
viewer. Taken together, the studies undertaken in our program of research indicate that children's understanding and evaluations of television content are embedded in cognitive development and in the social
experiences from which knowledge and expectations about persons
and events are built.

In the future an even broader view of possible effects is needed. Not
only behavioral patterns, but also social expectations, knowledge, and
evaluative responses should be considered possible outcomes of television viewing that may be important in their own right and that may also
mediate a range of possible behaviors. Television should be viewed as a
source of general social information, rather than as a mere purveyor of
certain highly salient images, such as violence (cf. Collins, in press-a).
Several implications for the study of television effects follow from this

suggestion. For example, Gerbner and Gross (1976) have suggested that television "cultivates" social reality. Viewers' subjective transformation of television portrayals may be an important mediating factor in the cultivation process (Hawkins & Pingree, 1980); but, to date, the viewer's role has neither been tested nor conceptualized by researchers interested in cultivation effects. A broader view of television effects and the processes by which they occur opens the possibility of contrasting the interpretations and inferences of viewers whose views of reality have been heavily influenced by television with those whose views of reality correspond less closely to the television world. In addition, recognizing individual differences in social knowledge and expectations may provide an approach to the study of individual differences in responses to television. Previous research has primarily emphasized group differences, despite evidence of considerable variation within groups (cf. Collins, in press-a; Comstock *et al.*, 1978). Several questions should be addressed: How do children represent social information from typical shows? What inferences, evaluations, attributions, and expectations about persons and behavior are formed during viewing? Under what conditions are portrayals perceived as relevant to self and/or others? How do patterns of social inferences and evaluations vary across age periods?

This broader approach requires a framework for studying social inferences from television in which responses to characters, actions, and events are examined as a function of viewers' knowledge and expectations, within the general constraints imposed by developmental and individual capabilities for acquiring, retaining, and retrieving social information. The role of knowledge and expectations in understanding new instances of stimuli has received surprisingly limited attention in psychology (cf. Simon, 1976), however. In most developmental and cognitive studies, knowledge has been treated either as error variance (e.g., Trabasso, 1975) or as an independent variable to be manipulated by the researcher (e.g., Bransford & Nitsch, 1978; Brown, 1977). Relatively rarely has the nature of knowledge been assessed in connection with an analysis of the pertinent cognitive task (exceptions include Newell & Simon, 1973, and Chi, 1978). In particular, little precedent exists for assessing knowledge and its use in "ill-structured" cognitive tasks. By examining social-cognitive processes in the complex task of television viewing, it should be possible to extend and elaborate laboratory-based findings and to understand their application in more complex tasks.

Recent work in social psychology (reviewed in Nisbett & Ross, 1980; Schneider, Hastorf, & Ellsworth, 1980) provides some beginning points for assessing knowledge and its uses in social inference and evaluation tasks. In general, these studies support the view that preexisting knowledge and expectations affect perception of and memory for persons and events. Constructs like *schemata*, which refer to structures of knowledge, preference, or attitudes in terms of which incoming information is processed, help to account for the apparently systematic ways in which individuals process and respond to new social stimuli (Hastie, 1981). At least three categories of general knowledge structures have emerged from experimental analyses that are pertinent to the complex stimuli exemplified by dramatic television plots: (a) knowledge about sequences of events or actions (e.g., scripts; common goals or purposes of others); (b) knowledge about attributes of persons and their relationships (e.g., interpersonal relation schemes; intrapersonal correlations of traits; person prototypes); and (c) knowledge of causal or other relational rules for inferring connections among actors and settings [e.g., Kelley's (1967) causal schemata; Jones & Davis's (1965) principles of correspondence]. When applied to complex actions and situations, these categories may often be overlapping and interrelated, rather than distinct as they are in experimental analyses. With respect to television viewing, such categories are spontaneously elicited and used by viewers in the attempt to understand quasi-natural depictions of persons, situations, and events (Collins, in press-b).

It is still too early to propose a formal model of the nature and use of social knowledge and expectations in viewing. However, Hastie and Carlston (1981) and Wyer and Srull (1981) have recently drawn on the experimental literature to propose information-processing formulations that acknowledge the role of perceiver knowledge. These formulations include two general categories of knowledge: (a) conceptual social memory, generally corresponding to the abstract categories of knowledge listed previously; and (b) social event memory, or relatively specific memories about social events, in particular, temporal and spatial locations. The two are highly interdependent. For example, after viewing typical programs, attributions of causality and predictions about future behavior reflect not only the content of the stimulus, but also what viewers know about the types of characters and incidents portrayed, the conditions under which causality is appropriately imputed, and expectations about the temporal stability of behaviors or traits, as well as skills for processing the implicit and explicit contents, per se. The categories of conceptual social memory and social event memory provide an analytic framework for specifying and assessing relevant knowledge in such cases. Although somewhat noncommittal theoretically, this formulation offers an approach that is both useful and appropriate for initial attempts at examining social knowledge and its use in television viewing.

A relatively idiographic research strategy is appropriate within this framework. Selection and careful analysis of individual stimulus programs and postviewing measures should be the basis for determining what viewer knowledge is relevant and how it should be assessed. In the research program described in this chapter, this general approach is being used to examine children's abilities to comprehend and make inferences about the plots of typical programs. Thus far, the strategy has led us to conclude that the nature and operation of cognitive and affective factors and their influence on children's representations of typical programs may be an important key to understanding the social influences of television. Processes of interpretation and inference have begun to emerge not simply as an alternative consideration in the study of television effects, but as a significant vantage point on the meaning and significance of television content itself.

Acknowledgments

The helpful editorial suggestions of Jennings Bryant and Daniel Anderson are gratefully acknowledged, as are the pervasive contributions of Sally Westby and Andrea Easter to the work reported herein.

References

Ajzen, I., & Fishbein, M. Attitude–behavior relations: A theoretical analysis and review of empirical research. *Psychological Bulletin*, 1977, 84, 888–918.

Bandura, A. Influence of models' reinforcement contingencies on the acquisition of imitative responses. *Journal of Personality and Social Psychology*, 1965, 1, 589–595.

Bartlett, F. C. *Remembering*. Cambridge, England: Cambridge University Press, 1932.

Berkowitz, L., & Geen, R. The stimulus qualities of the target of aggression: A further study. *Journal of Personality and Social Psychology*, 1967, 5, 364–368.

Berkowitz, L., & Rawlings, E. Effects of film violence on inhibitions against subsequent aggression. *Journal of Abnormal and Social Psychology*, 1963, 66, 405–412.

Berndt, T., & Berndt, E. Children's use of motives and intentionality in person perception and moral judgment. *Child Development*, 1975, 46, 904–912.

Bransford, J., & Nitsch, K. Coming to understand things we could not previously understand. In J. Kavanaugh & W. Strange (Eds.), *Speech and language in the laboratory, school, and clinic*. Cambridge, Mass.: MIT Press, 1978.

Brown, A. The development of memory: Knowing, knowing about knowing, and knowing how to know. In H. W. Reese (Ed.), *Advances in child development and behavior* (Vol. 10). New York: Academic Press, 1977.

Chi, M. Knowledge structures and memory development. In R. Siegler (Ed.), *Children's thinking: What develops?* Hillsdale, N.J.: Erlbaum, 1978.

Collins, W. A. Learning of media content: A developmental study. *Child Development,* 1970, *41*(4), 1133–1142.

Collins, W. A. The effect of temporal separation between motivation, aggression and consequences: A developmental study. *Developmental Psychology,* 1973, *8*(2), 215–221.

Collins, W. A. The developing child as viewer. *Journal of Communication,* 1975, *25*(4), 35–44.

Collins, W. A. Children's comprehension of television content. In E. Wartella (Ed.), *Children communicating: Media and development of thought, speech, understanding.* Beverly Hills, Calif.: Sage, 1979.

Collins, W. A. *Developmental and individual differences in children's responses to television.* Manuscript in preparation, University of Minnesota, 1981.

Collins, W. A. Social antecedents, cognitive processing, and comprehension of social portrayals on television. In E. T. Higgins, D. Ruble, & W. Hartup (Eds.), *Social cognition and social behavior: Developmental perspectives.* New York: Cambridge University Press, in press. (a)

Collins, W. A. Inferences about the actions of others: Developmental and individual differences in using social knowledge. In J. Masters & J. Harvey (Eds.), *Boundary areas in psychology: Developmental and social.* Hillsdale, N.J.: Erlbaum, in press. (b)

Collins, W. A., Berndt, T. J., & Hess, V. L. Observational learning of motives and consequences for television aggression: A developmental study. *Child Development,* 1974, *45,* 799–802.

Collins, W. A., & Wellman, H. Social scripts and developmental changes in representations of televised narratives. *Communication Research,* in press.

Collins, W. A., Wellman, H., Keniston, A., & Westby, S. Age-related aspects of comprehension and inference from a televised dramatic narrative. *Child Development,* 1978, *49,* 389–399.

Collins, W. A., & Westby, S. *Moral judgments of TV characters as a function of program comprehension.* Paper presented at the Society for Research in Child Development Biennial Meeting, Boston, April 1981.

Collins, W. A., & Zimmermann, S. A. Convergent and divergent social cues: Effects of televised aggression on children. *Communication Research,* 1975, *2,* 331–347.

Comstock, G., Chaffee, S., Katzman, N., McCombs, M., & Roberts, D. *Television and human behavior.* New York: Columbia University Press, 1978.

Costanzo, P. R., Coie, J. D., Grumet, J. F., & Farnill, D. A reexamination of the effects of intent and consequence on children's moral judgments. *Child Development,* 1973, *44,* 154–161.

Feshbach, S., & Singer, R. *Television and aggression: An experimental field study.* San Francisco: Jossey-Bass, 1971.

Friedlander, B., Wetstone, H., & Scott, C. Suburban pre-school children's comprehension of an age-appropriate informational television program. *Child Development,* 1974, *45,* 561–565.

Gerbner, G. Violence in television drama: A study of trends and symbolic functions. In G. Comstock & E. Rubinstein (Eds.), *Television and social behavior* (Vol. 1). Washington, D.C.: U.S. Government Printing Office, 1972.

Gerbner, G., & Gross, L. Living with television: The violence profile. *Journal of Communication,* 1976, *26*(2), 173–199.

Hastie, R. Schematic principles in human memory. In E. T. Higgins, C. Sherman, & M.

Zanna (Eds.), *The Ontario Symposium on Personality and Social Psychology: Social Cognition*. Hillsdale, N.J.: Erlbaum, 1981.

Hastie, R., & Carlston, D. Theoretical issue in person memory. In R. Hastie, T. Ostrom, E. Ebbesen, R. Wyer, D. Hamilton, & D. Carlston (Eds.), *Person memory: The cognitive basis of social perception*. Hillsdale, N.J.: Erlbaum, 1981.

Hawkins, R. P., & Pingree, S. Some processes in the cultivation effect. *Communication Research*, 1980, 7(2), 193–226.

Jones, E. E., & Davis, K. From acts to dispositions: The attribution process in person perception. In L. Berkowitz (Ed.), *Advances in experimental social psychology* (Vol. 2). New York: Academic Press, 1965.

Kelley, H. H. Attribution theory in social psychology. In D. Levine (Ed.), *Nebraska Symposium on Motivation*. Lincoln: University of Nebraska Press, 1967.

King, M. The development of some intention concepts in young children. *Child Development*, 1971, 42, 1145–1152.

Krebs, D. L. Altruism: An examination of the concept and a review of the literature. *Psychological Bulletin*, 1970, 73, 258–302.

Leifer, A. D., Gordon, N. J., & Graves, S. B. Children's television: More than mere entertainment. *Harvard Educational Review*, 1974, 44, 213–245.

Leifer, A., & Roberts, D. Children's responses to television violence. In J. Murray, C. Rubinstein, & G. Comstock (Eds.), *Television and social behavior* (Vol. 2), *Television and social learning*. Washington, D.C.: U.S. Government Printing Office, 1972.

Liebert, R., Neale, J., & Davidson, E. *The early window: Effects of television on children and youth*. New York: Pergamon Press, 1973.

List, J., Collins, W. A., & Westby, S. *Comprehension and inferences from traditional and nontraditional sex-role portrayals*. Unpublished manuscript, University of Minnesota, 1981.

Maccoby, E. Effects of the mass media. In M. Hoffman & L. Hoffman (Eds.), *Review of child development research* (Vol. 1). Chicago: University of Chicago Press, 1964.

Nelson, K. How children represent knowledge of their world in and out of language: A preliminary report. In R. Siegler (Ed.), *Children's thinking: What develops?* Hillsdale, N.J.: Erlbaum, 1978.

Newcomb, A. F., & Collins, W. A. Children's comprehension of family role portrayals in televised dramas: Effects of socioeconomic status, ethnicity, and age. *Developmental Psychology*, 1979, 15(4), 417–423.

Newell, A., & Simon, H. *Human problem solving*. Englewood Cliffs, N.J.: Prentice-Hall, 1973.

Nisbett, R., & Ross, L. *Human inference: Strategies and shortcomings of social judgment*. Englewood Cliffs, N.J.: Prentice-Hall, 1980.

Omanson, R. C. An analysis of narratives: Identifying central, supportive and distracting content. *Discourse Processes*, in press.

Piaget, J. *The moral judgment of the child*. New York: Free Press, 1965.

Purdie, S., Collins, W. A., & Westby, S. *Children's processing of motive information in a televised portrayal*. Unpublished manuscript, Institute of Child Development, University of Minnesota, 1979.

Rice, M. L., Huston, A. C., & Wright, J. C. The forms and codes of television: Effects on children's attention, comprehension, and social behavior. In D. Pearl, L. Bouthilet, & J. Lazar (Eds.), *Television and behavior: Ten years of scientific progress and implications for the eighties*. Vol. 2. Washington, D.C.: U.S. Government Printing Office, in press.

Schank, R., & Abelson, R. *Scripts, plans, goals, and understanding.* Hillsdale, N.J.: Erlbaum, 1977.

Schneider, D., Hastorf, A., & Ellsworth, P. *Person perception* (2nd ed.). Reading, Mass.: Addison–Wesley, 1980.

Shantz, C. U. The development of social cognition. In E. M. Hetherington (Ed.), *Review of Child Development Research* (Vol. 5). Chicago: University of Chicago Press, 1975.

Siegel, A. Communicating with the next generation. *Journal of Communication,* 1975, *25,* 14–24.

Simon, H. Cognition and social behavior. In J. Carroll & J. Payne (Eds.), *Cognition and social behavior.* Hillsdale, N.J.: Erlbaum, 1976.

Stein, A., & Friedrich, L. Impact of television on children and youth. In E. M. Hetherington (Ed.), *Review of child development research* (Vol. 5). Chicago: University of Chicago Press, 1975.

Stein, N. L., & Glenn, C. G. An analysis of story comprehension in elementary school children. In R. Freedle (Ed.), *New directions in discourse processing* (Vol. 2). Hillsdale, N.J.: Erlbaum, 1979.

Trabasso, T. Representation, memory and reasoning: How do we make transitive inferences? In A. Pick (Ed.), *Minnesota Symposia on Child Psychology* (Vol. 9). Minneapolis: University of Minnesota Press, 1975.

Warren, W., Nicholas, D., & Trabasso, T. Event chains and inferences in understanding narratives. In R. Freedle (Ed.), *New directions in discourse processing* (Vol. 2). Hillsdale, N.J.: Erlbaum, 1979.

Wyer, R., & Srull, T. The processing of social stimulus information: A conceptual integration. In R. Hastie, T. Ostrom, E. Ebbesen, R. Wyer, D. Hamilton, & D. Carlston (Eds.), *Person memory: The cognitive basis of social perception.* Hillsdale, N.J.: Erlbaum, 1981.

chapter **6**

How Is Children's Learning from Television Distinctive? Exploiting the Medium Methodologically[1]

LAURENE K. MERINGOFF
MARTHA M. VIBBERT
CYNTHIA A. CHAR
DAVID E. FERNIE
GAIL S. BANKER
HOWARD GARDNER

Introduction

How did *Star Wars*'s audiovisual delivery contribute to its success? What is gained or lost by seeing what characters like r2d2 actually look like? What would an illustrator and an author select from this story to highlight in a picture book? What would children who only heard this saga on public radio draw upon in imagining what these unfamiliar characters and settings looked like? Would the sound effects and music accompanying the verbal radio content enhance children's story understanding? How did inclusion of both more and less realistic characters affect children's engagement with them? The overall objective of the research we present in this chapter was to investigate the distinctive cognitive consequences for children of their experience with television and other story-bearing media.

In this chapter, we begin by making explicit the assumptions that underlie our research hypotheses and methods. We then identify the diverse literature in psychology, the arts, and the humanities that have

[1]The conduct of this research was supported by a grant from the John and Mary R. Markle Foundation.

151

informed and provided support for these assumptions. A series of studies are described, and examples are given of methods we have used to reveal learning outcomes which may be specific to television and to other media. Stimulus materials and response measures are discussed in terms of the specific problems and opportunities they present for answering the research questions being raised. Select findings are reported from each study. We conclude the chapter by reviewing our initial assumptions in light of these research findings.

Assumptions Guiding Research

Certain premises have shaped and been tested by our research. They pertain to the distinctiveness of each medium's messages, the use of stories as content, the ability to measure medium differences in children's story learning, and the usefulness of such research.

DISTINCTIVE MEDIUM MESSAGES

Television delivers to child audiences messages that are qualitatively different from those of other media. This distinctiveness derives from:

1. The medium's particular physical inheritance, that is, its combination of pictures, print, and sound (speech), sound effects, and music
2. The symbol systems or languages that pictures and sounds make use of to represent content, such as verbal language
3. The particular rules and conventions in use regarding the treatment of material, such as jump cuts used to indicate changes in time and place
4. The kinds of programming it makes available

Other reasons of more sociological, economic, and political nature are not addressed here.

Learning from television comes to be distinctive in two ways. The first pertains to the cognitive processes that are (or are not) called into play in the act of watching and listening. The repeated utilization of certain mental activities allows children opportunities to practice and cultivate them as skills; as such, they are an end in themselves, as Salomon (1979) has documented. Activation of these processes or skills also is a means to other ends such as remembering and using aspects of television content in reasoning. For example, bringing to mind images of previously viewed behavior may help children to interpret the motives, temperament, and emotional states of the characters who were seen performing. Our research has focused on these latter kinds of learning outcomes.

Stories are ideal stimuli to use for studying medium effects on children's learning. The prevalence of the narrative marks it as an important source of information and entertainment for children. Television now constitutes one of the dominant media in which stories are presented to children. However, given the recent proliferation in media, the same story line also routinely crosses medium boundaries. Exposure to a story in more than one form already may be the more common experience for children. Furthermore, the substantive richness and wide range of content presented in stories permits examination of diverse learning outcomes.

It is possible to study the differential cognitive effects on children of television and of other media. Procedures for measuring such differences are discussed here.

Analysis of Materials. The distinguishing physical features and production techniques attributable to a given medium like television are identified; then the content offered via these features needs to be analyzed. Certain kinds of information are more likely to be better conveyed by some means (e.g., visual or aural) than by others. For example, no matter in what minute detail an author describes the protagonist's facial features, costume, and posture, the text will not provide as comprehensive a description as will television's moving visual display of the character. In doing such an analysis, one constructs an operational definition of a given television presentation as an independent variable or set of variables whose effects on learning potentially can be measured.

Research Design: Across-Medium Comparisons. How will one determine whether what children learn from televised material is distinctive for having been conveyed in this particular format? One way to find out is to contrast the presentation of this television material with comparable material delivered via another medium whose treatment of content has been similarly assessed. Each time a new medium is held up against television for comparison, a different set of television's attributes and potential effects is highlighted. For example, one might assume that features common to two media, such as verbal language which is common to radio and television, are learned equally well from both. In this case, however, one needs to take into consideration the fact that television offers visual as well as verbal information, and these dual sources may reinforce each other or compete for children's attention.

Obviously, the greater the overlap in physical makeup between television and another medium, film for instance, the less potential there is for learning differences to result that are attributable to the medium. Still, questions of medium effects can be addressed to finer distinguishing attributes; for example, comparing television with film raises questions about the impact of image size and scale in relation to the viewer.

The nature and treatment of the story play a critical role in determining the extent of potential medium effects. In the first place, selection of stories to produce has a built-in bias toward material that lends itself to optimal treatment, given the physical resources available to the medium. For example, producers of stories whose major content can be conveyed via actions can take advantage of many camera and editing techniques to portray characters' movements through space. Even then, each story brings with it a particular balance between elements that can or cannot readily be expressed. In addition, the extent to which medium-specific techniques are used varies from production to production.

For the purposes of cross-medium research, there is a dilemma between the necessity of attaining a level of comparability across medium presentations sufficient to permit their comparison experimentally and that of having each medium take advantage of the means of production at its disposal. Early research on the relative effectiveness of instructional television in comparison to live classroom teaching is a classic example of too little use being made of television as an instructional medium on its own terms. It is not surprising that little evidence of medium effects was found (Schramm, 1977). How a balance is struck in research between these two demands and the implications this has for the validity and generalization of the findings is a recurring theme in this chapter.

Response Measures. It is important to take into consideration at least three sources of variation in the response measures used to tap learning from television and other media. One source of variation is on a continuum from more open-ended and spontaneous to more structured tasks. Providing children with more freedom to respond necessarily limits one's control over the responses offered and permits children to reveal more of what is salient to them. Obviously, the converse is true for measures where more structure is imposed. Relatedly, the extent to which the task is structured influences the performance demands made upon children. For example, even when children understand something they have heard on a sound track, they may not be able to explain it to someone else.

The second source of variation is the modality in which tasks are couched. One needs to be sensitive to the relationships that exist between the modalities in which a story is related and the form in which children are asked to respond (Meringoff, 1981). For example, because much of what children remember and understand from a televised story has been conveyed pictorially, this knowledge may be tapped readily with methods that include a nonverbal dimension. At least it should be recognized that having children rely solely on verbal or written language to report their learning from a highly visual story entails translation from one symbol system to another. Matches in modality between story presentation and response measure tap one kind of learning; differences between modality, another.

A third variable pertains to the kind of learning that one solicits about a story, that is, the content of the task, whether a detailed description of the story line, a summary, or inferences beyond the given content. For example, medium differences found in the endings that children provided to either television or radio stories (Greenfield, Geber, Beagles-Roos, Farrar, & Gat, 1981) may have been facilitated by the creative nature of the task. As another example, summarizing a story delivered either in a film or in written prose has been found less likely to produce medium differences (among adults) than the task of retelling the story in full detail (Baggett, 1979). Such similarities in the responses across medium may be a function of the more general nature of the learning being tapped, such as summarizing a story or assessing its main point.

Child Audiences. The extent to which medium differences appear in story learning also may be predicted on the basis of the developmental level of the audience. For instance, preschool children may not be as good candidates for obtaining common knowledge from different media as older school-age children. Their less well-developed ability to override the superficial appearance of visual displays (Piaget, 1973) may make them more vulnerable to the perceptually salient features of different media.

Research Design: Within-Medium Comparisons. An alternative way to examine learning from television is to compare two or more presentations in which some specific feature has been manipulated within the medium. Elements to be manipulated can include the balance of modalities in which content is conveyed—visually, auditorily, or both (e.g., Wartella & Ettema, 1974); how a given modality is used—whether zooms or cuts from long shots are used to arrive at close-ups (Salomon, 1979); and how information is organized over time—how shots (Frith, 1975) and episodes (Collins, 1979) are ordered. Such comparisons facilitate well-controlled studies of the influence on learning of very specific features, which is especially useful in formative research. However, it is difficult to identify effects which are distinctive to television when the control as well as the experimental material are televised.

The research we report in this chapter has studied the influence of television and other media by comparing children's learning across medium and by varying features within the same medium (including radio and television).

IMPLICATIONS AND UTILIZATION OF THE RESEARCH

Findings from such research investigations of children's learning from television can have important implications for academic and applied audiences. To theorize accurately about cognitive development, it is necessary to know how different medium presentations influence children's learning. To the extent that children repeatedly exposed to given media use different cognitive skills to extract information from the forms in which it is represented and acquire different kinds of information, then, as Olson and Bruner (1974) have suggested, knowledge about children's media usage implies knowledge about the development of intelligence.

In assessing learning effects among a target audience, television producers can take good advantage of research that adequately accounts for both the form and content of given material. In light of the increasing adaptation of children's books for the screen and the adaptation of television stories into print (Duke, 1979), across-medium comparisons between printed and televised stories are especially germane.

Such research also has great potential value to parents and professionals who work with children on a daily basis. More useful than a set of absolute givens about likely medium effects (which may be unrealistic anyway), researchers can identify important questions to consider when offering story materials to children. The choice of prior and follow-up activities with children also is informed by knowing as much as possible about the teaching "biases" of television and other media. Research methods can be thought of as extremely self-conscious and systematically applied curricula. In short, knowledge about the unique strengths and limitations of every story-bearing medium seems essential, in order to know how each medium can best be used and how learning from it can be maximized.

Drawing upon the Literature

Our research has been informed by psychology, the arts, and the humanities. This is in part a necessity, given the interdisciplinary nature of the work. Each discipline brings to bear a conceptual framework and/or empirical research relevant to certain of the questions under investigation.

Drawing upon disparate literatures has the advantage of offering varied kinds of information. points of view, and values. This diversity can help prevent research from becoming too narrow-minded and limited in its generalization. On the other hand, the amount and breadth of potentially applicable material demands that one exercise selectivity in utilizing information from these sources. When very different sources are consulted, more conflicting ideas also may have to be reconciled, such as about how to parse story content or analyze its audiovisual presentation on television.

THE MEDIUM

To know what reliable differences to expect in the learning outcomes of different medium presentations, or even to know what questions to raise about presentation of one medium as opposed to another, requires taking into account a medium's physical makeup, its symbol systems, and the specific tools of production used.

Theorists and practitioners whose focus is a single medium have much to offer media researchers. For example, semiotic analyses of film (and television) have helped us to define the combination of symbolic codes that distinguish these media from others (e.g., Kjørup, 1977; Metz, 1974). Descriptions of the specific ways that editing techniques are used to suggest associations between shots (e.g., Eisenstein, 1949) and to imply transitions in time and place (e.g., Burch, 1973; Reisz & Millar, 1968) have aroused our curiosity about children's ability to "read" across film and television story lines. For instance, dissolves and jump cuts imply the passage of time only to those audience members who understand the meaning of these conventions. However, the power of such analyses to predict what are meaningful units of film ultimately needs to be tested against the perceptions of child audiences.

Therefore, the research literature on television and children clearly pertains. Studies identifying formal features that recur on television programs that children watch (e.g., Huston, Wright, Wartella, Rice, Watkins, Campbell, & Potts, 1981) and studies relating the presence of specific features and techniques to children's responses (e.g., Levin & Anderson, 1976; Salomon, 1979) have given us clues about attributes to look for when selecting materials.

Also invaluable to us are studies that examine learning from narrative content presented on television or film. For example, given our use of inference-making as a response measure, it is important to take into account developmental studies indicating that younger school-age viewers exhibit less ability than older ones to draw inferences about the meaningful relationships between discrete televised events (e.g., Collins, 1979) and that they base inferences about film story content more on behavior viewed than on inferred psychological states (e.g., Flapan, 1968). Such findings alerted us to developmental differences in children's inferential reasoning about stories that might interact with potential medium effects.

Previous television research with children also has influenced our choice of response measures, as much by what has not been done as by what has. In particular, the bias toward verbal measures has directed us to adopt nonverbal methods for assessing visually based learning from film and television.

STORY CONTENT

In this research one needs to be aware both of options for analyzing story content, and of the kinds of story-related learning to anticipate in children. In terms of analysis, theoretical and critical writing on the narrative can contribute important insights, by advancing a specific approach to analysis (e.g., Propp, 1968), as well as by offering comparative observations about the handling of narrative by print and by film (e.g., Bluestone, 1973; Chatman, 1980). Critical works focused specifically on literature to which children are exposed have influenced our selection of story materials, for example, by discussing differences in book illustration styles (e.g., Lanes, 1972) and by discussing why certain genres of children's literature have such lasting value (e.g., Bettelheim, 1977).

The research literature on children's learning from oral or written stories has increased our awareness of what responses to expect from the children to whom we present stories in aural forms. For instance, studies that have imposed grammars on the analysis of story content and on children's retellings of these told stories have suggested what aspects of simple stories children remember at different ages (e.g., McConaughy, 1980; Mandler & Johnson, 1977; Stein & Glenn, 1977). Specifically, actions and outcomes have been shown to be better recalled (and recalled at an earlier age) than internal reactions like the emotions characters express. Given a similar bias among younger film viewers toward using overt behavior as bases for story inferences (Flapan, 1968), one wonders whether any medium differences should be expected in recall of story actions among young audiences.

Also of interest have been studies concerned with children's inference-making in response to textual story content [e.g., Bartlett, 1932 (adults); Fitzhenry-Coor, 1977; Paris & Mahoney, 1974; and Trabasso, Nicholas, Omanson, & Johnson, 1977]. For example, explanations for how children make inferences range from application of simple logical reasoning (e.g., Paris & Mahoney, 1974) to developmental differences in story comprehension (e.g., Fitzhenry-Coor, 1977). As previously mentioned, developmentally based explanations for how children infer about narratives also have been applied to film and television presentations. However, without comparison to other media presentations of like content, it remains uncertain to what extent age differences are attributable to limited cognitive skills and to what extent they are due to particular demands imposed by the medium.

THE AUDIENCE

For information about child audiences, we have consulted cognitive developmental theory and research (e.g., Bruner, 1973; Piaget, 1973). At different times we also have paid especial attention to more specific information, for example, about visual perception (e.g., Arnheim, 1971) and about children's artistic development (e.g., Gardner, 1980; Golomb, 1974; Goodnow, 1977; Wilson & Wilson, 1977). Concepts from other psychological theories occasionally have been applied, the conditions under which observed behavior is modeled, for example, as discussed in social learning theory (e.g., Bandura & Walters, 1965).

Empirical Work

Many of the studies we have conducted will be briefly described. Our discussion of measures and findings is intended to highlight methodological issues. Unless otherwise indicated, the reported differences are statistically significant at $p \leq .05$.

Initial Across-Medium Comparisons:
Measuring Story Apprehension at Different Ages

An initial study investigated medium differences by comparing children's apprehension of an African folktake presented either as an animated televised film or read aloud from a picture book (Meringoff, 1980).

In pitting picture book and television against one another, it became evident that both use verbal language and visual imagery ordered over time to deliver narrative content. However, they differ in the extent and nature of their visualization. Although book illustrations can suggest or imply movement (Friedman & Stevenson, 1975), each image remains discrete and static. In contrast, the illusion of movement is inherent in television's and film's continuous display of images. Moreover, some narrative elements lend themselves more readily than others to both visualization and movement. For example, characters' actions (e.g., the nuances of their gestures and facial expressions, as well as what they actually do) are particularly accessible to visual representation, whereas an author's use of figurative language (e.g., phonetic refrains) usually eludes illustration.

These differences in story materials suggested possible differences in learning. It was hypothesized that television's dynamic depiction of story actions and the potential visual reinforcement of the corresponding text would make more salient the visible and behavioral features of story characters. On the other hand, the book's provision of more limited and static pictorial information might allow for greater auditory attention to the text and to figurative language in particular.

In order to study the impact of this variation in the illustrations, the two story versions needed to be highly comparable, both in the text and in the graphic style used for the illustrations. Fortunately, existing story materials required only minor changes to achieve this level of parity. Some film and television production companies, Weston Woods notable among them, go to great lengths to preserve maximum consistency with the literature they adapt (see Deitch, 1978).

There were 48 children participating in the study—24 6–7year-olds and 24 9–10-year-olds. They were randomly assigned to one of the two medium conditions and individually presented one version of the story. To determine what children remembered of the story, their verbal recall of the story was examined on both a spontaneous and an aided basis. To tap learning beyond the explicit story content, children were asked to draw diverse story-relevant inferences (e.g., about physical features of a character, such as strength; about a character's feelings;

and about dimensions of events, such as the difficulty of performing them.

The inference questions posed to children pertained to aspects of story content hypothesized to vary in the relative impact of their delivery across these two media. Two types of information were solicited about each question: the specific inference drawn ("Was it a hard job or an easy job to tie the leopard up in the tree?") and the evidence used to substantiate each inference ("How do you know?"). In addition to such experimenter-imposed tasks, certain behaviors that children generated spontaneously during the interview were monitored; these included any clearly visible physical gestures used to illustrate their verbal recounting of the story.

The findings of this study revealed a distinctive learning profile for each medium. For example, children exposed to the televised story included more of characters' actions in their verbal retellings and did more physical gesturing to elaborate their recounting, usually by demonstrating depicted actions. In addition, the television viewers relied more on visual content (e.g., "It was a hard job to tie up the leopard because he looked like he was struggling") as the basis for inferences. In comparison, children who were read the story in picture-book form recalled more figurative language and based their inferences more on textual content and outside-story information (e.g., prior knowledge like "It was a hard job because leopards are heavy").

These and other observed medium differences provided support for the hypothesis that material differences in these media—such as differences in their relative visualization of a story—influence what content is conveyed more effectively to children. The consistency of findings noted across different responses measures added to their validity; for example, evidence of the greater salience of depicted behavior for the television audience was found in their free verbal recall, in their further reasoning about the story, and their unsolicited behavior. Being able to look for such "layered" evidence of specific kinds of learning is one major advantage of using multiple response measures within the same study.

To replicate this research, a second study was conducted using a different set of story materials with preschool and school-age children (Kelly & Meringoff, 1979). A total of 88 children participated in this study—60 preschoolers and 28 9–10-year-olds. Again, all children were randomly assigned to either a television or picture-book presentation of the story, a simple adventure about three robbers. The two versions delivered the same narration, and all of the book's illustrated content appeared in the film.

A similar array of response measures was used as in the earlier study, with some additions respectful of developmental differences between the two age groups. For example, preschoolers' free recall of the story, often very spare, was followed up with an aided form of story recall and with language recognition items.

The findings from this study replicated the pattern of medium differences reported earlier. Particularly striking was the significantly better performance on measures of language recall by preschoolers who were read the story than by those who watched the story on television, even though children heard the same language in both formats. Perhaps there is more competition among modalities for younger children, with a concomitant loss of information from the underloaded auditory modality. Alternatively, the younger children may be even more susceptible than older ones to the power of live narration.

There is some evidence of greater story comprehension (i.e., more complete verbal retellings) among children following a live rather than a recorded version (Campbell & Campbell, 1976). In a subsequent study of story recall across three medium presentations (recorded narration, recorded narration plus book illustrations, and televised film), there was only a slight trend toward greater recall of figurative language among the listeners (Char & Meringoff, 1981). Taken together, these two studies' findings suggest that live presentation of the picture book was an important, initially overlooked factor in generating better language recall among children than the recorded television text.

If it is the case that children who watch stories on television and film remember the visual and behavioral content especially well, and also use this pictured content to help them interpret stories, then we reasoned that one of the functions story illustrations serve is to provide children with a repertoire of mental visual imagery.

Subsequent Across-Medium Comparison:
Measuring Visualization of Story Content

A study was conducted to compare children's picturing and related inference-making for a Grimm's fairy tale, presented either as an animated film or as an audio recording (Vibbert & Meringoff, 1981). Audio versions of stories can describe the way characters and settings look in literal or nonliteral language and can suggest appearances indirectly by such auditory means as tone of voice, music, and sound effects. Moreover, authors can choose the extent and placement of such descriptive information. In contrast, the depiction of characters and settings is necessary and more continuous in film and television stories. Such visible story content includes details of character figure and costume; qualities of character movement; displays of emotion in facial expression; and location of characters in space. For example, a character's physical orientation within a setting and in relation to the viewer is evident whenever he appears on the screen.

How will the extent and nature of children's visual images for a story be influenced by the provision of such information in dynamic illustration and how by its provision in either literal or nonliteral verbal form? How will related inferences children make about characters (e.g., age and affect) and settings (e.g., time and place of story) be affected by this difference between visual depiction and verbal description? As an example, it was hypothesized that children exposed to vivid close-up shots of a character's face at an emotionally charged moment in this story would be more likely to include observed facial features in their own drawings of this character. We also predicted that film viewers would make more appropriate inferences about the character's feelings at that moment than children who had her facial expression described to them in words.

To test for such medium-based differences, we selected a sound film version of the tale "The Fisherman and his Wife" that made good use of pictorial and cinematic techniques, specifically in the depiction of distinctive costumes, repeated movements, close-ups of facial expression, and unusual orientations. Then we recorded two versions of the film soundtrack in which verbal descriptions of this visualized content (the protagonist's appearance, his carrying out of a repeated action, his wife's facial expression, and the magic fish's orientation) were inserted in either literal language or nonliteral similes. For instance, the selected close-up of the wife's face in the film was described either in literal terms ("She turned to him and opened her mouth wide, showing her big white teeth. Her eyebrows turned down . . .") or in nonliteral form ("She turned to him. Her face looked like a hungry wolf . . ."). Note that neither verbal description makes explicit reference to the character's affective state; this is because it is assumed that viewing children need to infer a feeling state from depicted gestures and facial expression.

There were 45 9–10-year-old children participating in the study. They were randomly assigned to one of three story conditions (sound film, literal audio, or nonliteral audio) and individually presented the story. Although it is difficult to define precisely the relationship between graphic and mental imagery (e.g., Kosslyn, Heldmeyer, & Locklear, 1977), it still seems essential to provide children with optimal opportunities to report learning of story content in modalities that share important features with those of the stimulus. Therefore, nonverbal as well as verbal response measures were developed to tap children's visual imagery for this story. For example, once cued verbally to specific points in the story (e.g., "Think about what the wife looked like when she made that last wish, when she wanted to be ruler of the universe"), children were instructed to " . . . draw, as best you can, how the wife looks to you then in your mind." Following each drawing exercise children could verbally describe any discrepancy between their drawing and the way they imagined things would look. To test whether access to visual depiction or comparable verbal description of select content affected their interpretation of the story, children were asked to make and substantiate varied story-related inferences during the interview. After they completed their drawing (and discrepancy comment) about the wife, for instance, they were asked to evaluate how she felt at the same moment as their drawing of her depicted. To establish a standard of reference against which to compare the experimental data, baseline drawings of analogous content were obtained from children who were not presented the story. In the case of the wife, the instructions were: "Draw a woman who has everything she wants in the world and is demanding she be given one more thing. Draw what she would look like when she asked for that last thing."

When children's drawings were compared across groups, some significant differences were observed. For example, children who viewed the film were more likely to just draw the wife's face (as if in close-up), as opposed to the more conventional full figure favored by both listening and baseline groups. When filling in facial features, those who saw the film were more likely to open the wife's mouth and expose bared teeth than those in either the listening or baseline groups.

Independent ratings of the emotional expression conveyed in the drawing revealed that a small percentage of children in all groups rendered an angry face (e.g., teeth gritted, turned down eyebrows). However, the remainder of drawings done by film viewers were more likely to be judged as indistinguishable (e.g., display of affect confused or ambiguous) than as happy (e.g., smiling mouth), whereas the opposite was true for children in baseline and nonliteral audio groups. Children in the literal group were just as likely to draw the more prototypical happy figure as one judged to be indistinguishable.

Children's verbal inferences about her feelings were more clearly differentiated than their graphic responses. Most film-viewing children perceived the wife as being angry, whereas the majority of listening children labeled her feelings as happy. Furthermore, in substantiating their assessments, children who saw the film relied almost exclusively on visual content specific to the moment in the story when she made the last wish (e.g., "angry, by the mean way she looked at him"), whereas audio children tended to base their inferences on textual content drawn from across the story line (e.g., "happy, because she had everything, a castle, a husband, she could rule the weather, a black dress, hall painted . . ."). These children rarely referred to the language offered to describe the wife's facial expression at that moment, although most of them recognized having heard it.

Such observed medium differences suggest two of the ways that access to film (and television) imagery informs children. The first relates to their understanding of a story. As observed in the previous studies, children who saw the animated story used the visual content to make appropriate inferences about characters' internal states. Even a single remembered film image may provide children with adequate and compelling evidence about characters' feelings. By way of comparison, children who heard this story roamed the story line for legitimate textual (and auditory) bases for their inferences. Their seeming disregard of the specifically applicable text information raises the issue of what makes verbal description dramatic and salient enough for children to incorporate it into their schema for story characters.

The second function of film imagery relates more to children's artistic and aesthetic development. In all the drawing tasks, pictures made by film viewers tended to differ the most from those produced in the baseline condition. The differences observed usually could be interpreted by comparing the film viewers' drawings with the animation. In the case of the wife's face, for example, the film audience succeeded in reproducing film information about scale and specific facial features. Perhaps conveying the angry emotion children said she felt was a more difficult effect for them to achieve graphically, given that the emotions exhibited in their drawings were the least distinguishable to adult judges.

Children's attempts to draw what they have seen in film may be construed simply as imitative and even inhibiting—"Well, of course, they saw the face one way, and that's why they drew it that way. So what?" However, that albeit logical interpretation does not take into account another piece of evidence. Children of school age exhibit canonical ways of dressing people, situating them in space, making them happy, etc., as observed in their baseline drawings. Access to a single film screening mitigated this being done by children. Thus, when compared to prototypical drawings of like content, such divergent efforts also may indicate that memorable film imagery inspired in children the practicing of new graphic means, and even new perceptions of familiar things.

Subsequent Across-Medium Comparison:
Measuring the Meaningfulness of Stories
Conveyed by Visual Means

If the visual content offered by film and television supplies children with a comprehensible body of information, then even a strictly visual execution of a story should be meaningful. A study was conducted to compare children's physical enactment of story content, their verbal telling, and related inference-making for an Eskimo legend presented either as a nonverbal animated film or as an audio recording (Banker & Meringoff, 1982). This research was designed to address two general questions: Do children read visual story images meaningfully? and How is the meaning they may derive from story images distinctive for having been visualized? Although there is evidence that even young children are inclined to construct a sensible story line from picture narratives (e.g., Messaris & Gross, 1977; Poulsen, Kintsch, Kintsch, & Premack, 1979), we wondered whether children's understanding would go beyond grasp of the sequence of central events and include such aspects of meaning as inferred motives, feelings, and thoughts for the characters. In order to document the extent and nature of children's understanding of a story conveyed visually, we chose an animated story film that could be screened either silent or "intact," (i.e., with occasional Eskimo dialogue and sound effects). The sophistication and subtlety of the story derived both from the story line, a deceptively simple legend about an owl who marries a goose and tries to follow her ways, and from the minimally detailed style used to represent the animal characters (animated in sand and filmed in black and white).

To establish a textual standard against which to evaluate the adequacy and distinctiveness of children's learning from this pictorial format, two worded versions of the story were prepared. One was constructed (using adult consensus) to serve as a verbal description of the behavior depicted in the film. The other was written by a storyteller and asserted many things agreed to be implied in the film. For example, at the point where the owl stumbles into the pond, the version describing his response states: "He looked up, rolled his eyes, and, cringing, took a small step away from the water, blinking, shrugging his shoulders and talking to himself." The storyteller version indicates his reactions to the water, e.g., "it was cold . . . it was wet . . . owl thought, it's too deep." The descriptive aural version was intended to provide a more experimentally valid control for the film, and the storyteller version a more real-world source of literary comparison.

In order to use nonverbal means in eliciting learning from nonverbal story materials, we included a task where children acted out selected story events in which characters' affective response could be inferred either from the animated images or from the text. For instance, when the owl accidentally got his foot wet, children might reasonably infer a reaction of aversion or surprise. Children were asked to use physical gestures alone to show how the character looked or reacted in each situation. This behavior was videotaped and later scored for the specific means used (e.g., parts of the body, changes of pace, defining of physical context) and for communication of recognizable emotions. Given the inherently greater degree and vividness of the information provided visually as compared with prose (e.g., Perkins, in press) and evidence of more spontaneous gesturing following televised stories than readings from picture books (Kelly & Meringoff, 1979; Meringoff, 1980), we expected to find medium differences in children's gestural responses to this story. For example, it was hypothesized that exposure to the film would enhance the affective expressiveness of children's miming of character behavior.

The sample was composed of 60 10–11-year-olds randomly assigned to one of the four story versions: silent film, nonverbal film, descriptive aural, or storyteller aural. All children were individually presented the story and administered all tasks. Two groups' interviews (intact film and descriptive aural) were videotaped for later scoring of children's gesturing. Contrary to our expectations, however, there was little indication of medium effects in children's miming, although the means used necessarily varied somewhat depending upon the behavior content of the question. In general, children were just as likely to use as many means and to use them as effectively to convey recognizable emotions following the prose description as they were following the animation. For example, children's typical reactions for the owl at the pond included remaining seated and hugging their arms together in a shiver or opening their eyes wide and backing away.

Several factors may help to explain the apparent similarity in the children's nonverbal performance. The first pertains to the story materials. The film imagery was pictorial (not photographic) and relatively abstract. Furthermore, the behavior modeled in the film was both subtle and familiar (e.g., a slight shrug of the shoulders, eyes widening). The second pertains to the audience. By this age, children could make logical and appropriate inferences about the characters' reactions in these situations. Given their grasp of the story line and their prior experience, it apparently was not difficult for them to figure out how a character was likely to feel; as a consequence, they could generate as adequate a performance without ever seeing the characters. A third factor relates to the response measure. While confining the task to specific events made children's behavior comparable and amenable to analysis across groups, it also seriously limited the range of behavior the children showed us.

The likelihood of documenting the distinctive impact that film displays may have on children's behavior (e.g., on such qualitative features of body movement as pace, intensity, and affect) probably would be increased by presenting more novel and conspicuous behaviors. Much of the early television violence research with children attests to the presence of the modeling phenomenon in terms of content but without giving much consideration to these more expressive features of behavior or to the meaningfulness to children of the behavior they perform (e.g., Bandura, Ross, & Ross, 1963). We still believe that children exposed to visually conveyed stories are potentially equipped to display more expressive, more detailed information nonverbally than children presented prose. Conversely, the performance of story-related behavior may contribute importantly to children's understanding and appreciation of a story's events and characters.

Thus far we have discussed studies which have contrasted one medium's presentation of a story against another medium's delivery of like content. Such investigations facilitate examination of what features are distinct to each format and whether such differences affect children's story understanding. In comparison, research that manipulates format or content variables within a single medium permits a closer and more self-contained study of how individual features or productions techniques function for child audiences. To conclude the reporting the research, two such within-medium studies—one focused on radio stories and one on television characters—will be briefly discussed.

Manipulating Variables within Radio:
Measuring Story Comprehension at Different Ages

A study was carried out to examine children's understanding of radio stories and to study the extent to which this understanding may be enhanced when a story text is accompanied by sound effects and music (Char, 1982). Given the purely aural nature of radio stories and the frequent use of sound effects and music in aural media (Arnheim,

1972), it is important to know more about how these two auditory and nonlinguistic features function for children who hear stories. Specifically, although there is evidence that the presence of such auditory features in television sound tracks influences children's visual attention (e.g., Levin & Anderson, 1976; Wartella & Ettema, 1974), there has been little investigation of whether these features also provide children with meaningful clues about story settings, actions, and overall mood.

To measure the effects of sound effects and music on story comprehension, two test stimuli were prepared. In one, the first episodes of a classic adventure, *Treasure Island*, were presented intact, with verbal text, sound effects, and music; the second, a control version, presented the verbal text alone. These episodes were taken from a radio series of stories produced for children.

Greater comprehension of story material among children exposed to text with sound effects can be explained either by sound effects' provision of meaningful information or their heightening effect on audio attention to the text. Thus, an audiotape of sound effects was prepared to test how well children derive meaning from sounds alone and how well they recognize sounds as being previously presented in, or appropriate to, a particular story. All the children and an additional group of "story-naive" subjects listened and responded to this tape. Questions also were posed to pinpoint whether these strictly auditory cues served as bases for knowledge or inferences reported about story actions or settings.

There were 30 third and fourth graders and 30 sixth graders recruited for the study. Children were randomly assigned to hear one of the two story versions and then were individually interviewed. The response measures used varied in the degree to which they attempted to focus children's attention on the story's sound effects. For example, in the most unstructured task, children were asked for their spontaneous verbal recall of the story. This task assessed whether the story content accompanied by sound effects was more salient and frequent in the recall of children exposed to the sound-effects version. Next, open-ended and multiple-choice questions were asked concerning content that had been accompanied by sound effects. These questions examined more directly the role that sound effects play in children's story comprehension, inferences, or rationale for story knowledge or inferences. For example, the last episode is described as occurring during the winter, either through only textual references (e.g., "It was a bitter cold winter, with long hard frosts and heavy gales..."), or with an additional extended sound of wind blowing in the sound-effects version. The influence of such a sound on children's story understanding was tapped by seeing whether such information appeared spontaneously in a child's retelling (e.g., "Then it was winter and this guy came . . .") and was evidenced by a correct response to the multiple choice question concerning in what season the scene took place and in the rationale for such an answer (e.g., "winter, because I heard the wind blowing real hard").

Note that when multiple response measures like this are used, the order in which tasks are administered needs to be organized carefully, so as to minimize the influence of the questions themselves on children's subsequent responses. One solution is to always lead with the less structured items. In addition, proceeding through the story in chronological order helps to preserve the logical continuity of the story and of the children's recall.

The most compelling argument for the influence of sound-effect information on story comprehension would be an effect in the most spontaneous and least sound-effect-focused tasks. Such evidence would indicate that sound effects were salient enough for children to volunteer or draw upon their content without directly being asked to do so. At the same time, inclusion of more structured tasks enables the researcher to minimize underestimations of children's meaningful grasp of sound effects; for example, perhaps the lack of attention sound-effect information is given in standard classroom listening comprehension exercises discourages children from reporting it.

Preliminary results indicate the influence of sound effects on story understanding tapped by a number of different measures. Using the wind sound example, analysis of children's free story recall revealed a slightly greater tendency for children who heard the elaborated version to mention either the season or weather in their description of this scene. In response to the multiple choice question, "In what season did the scene take place?", the older children presented the sound-effect version were more likely to correctly identify the season than those who listened to the text alone. Of the children who correctly identified winter as the season, all those exposed to the sound-effect version based their answers on what they heard at that point in the story. In contrast, rationales offered following the text alone were evenly divided between referring to story content and simply guessing. Later, when directly questioned, a number of children who heard the intact version also were able to name wind as one of the sounds they heard in the story. Finally, baseline data indicated that almost all children could identify wind when they heard it.

Thus in the case of the wind sound, the evidence for children's use of this auditory content in understanding the story was more prominent in the more focused measures. Given findings such as these, it becomes clear that multiple measures not only allow the researcher to test the robustness of a phenomenon by seeing if consistent evidence can be obtained across different tasks, but their use also enables one to become aware that the degree of focus required to elicit this learning may be another independent variable and lead to the presence or absence of an observed outcome.

Manipulating Variables within Television:
Measuring Children's Assessment
of Familiar Characters at Different Ages

A study was conducted to examine children's understanding of television characters of varied reality status and "real" people (Fernie, 1981). Fictional characters vary widely in their realism. In the course of their television viewing, for example, children are likely to encounter characters who range in reality status from fantastic superheroes (like the building-leaping Superman) to implausible characters (like the ultracool Fonz) to more realistic characters (like the "fatherly" Tom Bradford). Given young children's difficulty in distinguishing between the real and the fantastic (e.g., Klapper, 1979; Winner & Gardner, 1979) and television's tendency to present all these characters with equivalent visual realism, we wondered how well young viewers could assess the realism and other personality attributes of fictional television characters. Here, then, is a case where the consistency and potency of a medium's feature—that is, photographic imagery—may mask important differences in the veracity of narrative content.

As in the previous studies reported, all the television people selected for use were fictional characters from narrative programming. However, instead of representing a single story, these characters appeared in series (e.g., superhero adventures, situation comedies). We reasoned that such characters are prevalent as well as popular on television and therefore can provide continuing and important sources of social knowledge and psychological identification among regular viewers. To tap children's cumulative memory and understanding of these familiar characters, photographs of the characters were used as visual cues for tasks and questions. In comparison, we assumed that viewing of specific episodes (as in our other studies) would more likely elicit responses drawn from this more limited data base. To better gauge the meaningfulness and potential influence of these television personna on children, photographs of familiar real people (e.g., their teachers) were added to the sample of more and less realistic characters. This addition both extended the parameters of the reality–fantasy continuum with which the children dealt and served as a real-world standard of reference against which to evaluate children's response to televised fiction.

The interview addressed several aspects of children's understanding of characters and real people. Included among these were questions in which children assessed these models in terms of various physical and psychological abilities and vulnerabilities. The responses were analyzed so as to describe both particular attributes and the overall degree of realism associated with each character. For example, it could be determined whether a positive and extreme assessment of Superman's strength (e.g., "strong enough to lift a truck with his bare hands") was related to a similarly positive but unrealistic evaluation of his feelings (e.g., "always feels happy"). The children's more affective involvement with these people also was explored by asking them to select the persons they wished they were (fantasy identification) and the persons who were similar to them (realistic identification).

Participating in the study were 70 boys: a younger group (5–6-year-olds), a middle group (8-year-olds), and an older group (11–12-year-olds). The findings revealed many noteworthy differences in the assessments that children of different ages made of these select television characters and real people. For example, although boys at all three ages attributed unique physical abilities to unrealistic characters, it was the younger children who were apt to generalize this uniqueness to other attributes, stating for example that a superhero could live forever ("because he's so strong") or is always happy ("because he can fly"). For some children, then, what is salient and unusual in these fantastic portrayals (e.g., super-strength or flying) may become the index for judging other attributes. The younger boys also selected these bigger-than-life characters as both the people they wished to be and, surprisingly, as the people most similar to themselves. At this age, real people seem to serve a less visible role against which to evaluate the appeal of fictional characters than they do at an older age.

In comparison, the older children described even unrealistic characters more realistically and separated their physical ability from their psychological vulnerability; they now seemed fully cognizant that even flying does not insure a person's continued happiness. Perhaps relatedly, although the older boys joined the younger ones in ranking the most unrealistic and implausible characters highest as people they wished to be, with age they increasingly selected realistic characters and real people as the models most similar to themselves. Thus, older children were more discriminating, both in assigning individual attributes to characters and in assessing their own relationships to these models. With age and viewing experience, fantastic television characters fade somewhat in importance as children become more grounded in real-world knowledge and concerns.

By systematically varying select character dimensions (e.g., reality status) within-medium, it was possible to monitor ways in which this feature is interpreted by children and how it relates to their comprehension of the narratives to which these characters are central. Although keeping the medium constant facilitated in-depth study of content, it also required that one be sensitive to the relationship between form and content. Here, television's veridical treatment of superhuman feats of strength and magic accentuated the illusion that these performances actually take place. As one consequence, the combined means of filmed movement, special visual effects, skillful editing, sound effects, and music may heighten young children's appreciation for the physical omnipotence of these characters at the cost of other more subtle and less visible traits.

Conclusion

Assumptions Reconsidered

Now let us return to the assumptions stated at the beginning of the chapter and reconsider them in light of the research methods and findings which have been reported. This procedure should help us both to evaluate the validity and usefulness of the premises that have shaped these investigations and to summarize key points.

The first assumption asserts that *television delivers to child audiences messages that are qualitatively different from those of other media*. In fact, we have found considerable evidence for medium effects on what children learn. For example, televised stories have elicited greater use of character actions than picture book stories, both in children's verbal recounting of story material and in their own spontaneous gesturing. In addition, television and film viewers alike made frequent use of visual content, such as qualities of character movements and facial expressions, in making story-related inferences, whereas children presented less highly illustrated (or nonillustrated) materials necessarily based their inferences either upon the aural text or upon information not given in the story at all. Such differences suggest not only which kinds of story content children may remember better following exposure to alternative media, but also how children apply this learned information in their further reasoning about the material presented.

However, the extent and nature of such medium effects also depends upon other factors, most importantly how the content is produced, how learning outcomes are evaluated, and which cognitive skills are available to the child audience. For example, no medium differences were found in children's miming of character behavior when the pictorial treatment of these actions was subtle and minimally representational, the task circumscribed, and the audience highly competent at interpreting the story.

The second premise states that *stories are ideal stimuli to use for studying medium effects on children's learning.* Since we relied exclusively on stories in our research, it is difficult to make any relative judgments about their value as stimulus materials. However, working with stories did make it possible to examine many important cognitive outcomes, including children's ability to retell stories, their visualizations of story content, their reasoning about characters' internal states and reality status, and their identification with various fictional figures. Furthermore, sampling existing stories from a wide range of narrative genres increased the validity and generalization of the research. Not, however, as will be indicated later, that working with stories entails taking into account the various content elements that narratives use to organize and impart information, such as presenting content by means of dialogue between characters or via a narrator or assigning characters either dialogue or nonverbal behavior at different times.

The next assumption claims that *it is possible to study the differential cognitive effects of television and other media on children.* Procedures are also recommended for analyzing story materials and for selecting research methods, response measures, and child audiences.

With regard to the analysis of story materials, categorizing stories on the basis of their actions, dialogue, and figurative language content yielded significantly different learning profiles when television and picture-book presentations were compared. For example, children who were read picture books included more figurative language in their accounts of the stories, whereas television viewers favored actions in their retellings of the same story line. In the study of children's visualization of story content, a priori selection of specific content elements (e.g., character appearance or facial expression) enabled us to conduct a more focused comparison between the memorability of analogous content delivered by verbal description or filmic depiction.

Early identification of content and format variables worthy of analysis and manipulation is essential both to tapping medium differences and to interpreting them appropriately. For example, the live (versus recorded) presentation of the picture-book story was an important, initially overlooked factor in generating better language recall among children than was found in response to the television version.

In considering alternative methods for conducting media research, we have distinguished between making comparisons across different media presentations of like content and focusing on a single medium. As suggested, both approaches have specific uses and limitations. In the case of across-medium studies, comparisons made between television (or film) and both picture books and aural stories permitted investigation of the functions that still and moving images serve in children's story apprehension. In this way, comparative media studies do facilitate examination of which features comprise each format and whether its specific composition affects children's learning. However, this approach also is constrained by having to achieve adequate comparability of content across media to permit their experimental comparison. This requirement has limited our choice of story materials to those products which make more conservative use of the production means available. In our more recent studies, we dealt with this dilemma by producing our own alternative story versions. Still, although use of one's own stimulus materials helps satisfy demands of the research design and allows for more flexibility in the selection of stories, it also compromises the real-world validity of the study findings.

By way of comparison, manipulation of these same format variables within the television medium, such as the presence of either still or moving images, would be a less informative test of television's potential (or even typical) performance. Instead, such within-medium studies have permitted close examination of how individual format or content features function. For example, varying the presence (or absence) of sound effects and music in a radio story enabled us to assess the memorability and meaningfulness to children of these nonlinguistic auditory features. In this case, we learned that children did use sound effects to help them interpret the story, although obtaining this outcome depended upon using more structured probes.

In working to develop effective response measures to use in media research with children, we have emphasized the need to take several factors into consideration. For example, the extent to which tasks are structured by the investigator has acted as an independent variable in tapping medium effects. When the information being tapped was not called forth spontaneously, use of more closed-ended items has helped to elicit evidence for children's use of format or content features (e.g., sound effects, characters' reality status) in interpreting narratives.

However, under different circumstances the use of a highly focused task also may have inhibited children's miming of character behavior and undermined demonstration of potential medium effects.

The modality in which tasks are presented also has proven to be an important factor in our research. For instance, many of the medium differences we observed in children's graphic depictions of story content would be unlikely to emerge using a less visual response mode. For example, film viewers' use of a close-up shot to represent a character, as opposed to the more conventional full figure favored by listening (and baseline) children, is the kind of information not readily obtained in a verbal interview.

As a final example, the incorporation of multiple response measures in these studies has proven to be well worth the effort. Evidence from more than one kind of measure allowed us to test the robustness of a phenomenon, as well as to monitor the degree of focus, the modality, and the task content necessary to elicit given learning.

With regard to the predictive value of developmental level on the presence of medium effects, we have some evidence that format variables have greater impact on younger children than on older children. For example, when television and picture-book presentations were compared, preschoolers' memory for figurative language was increased dramatically by having a picture book read to them, as opposed to their language recall after watching the televised story. However, our evidence is limited. Rather than suggesting that medium differences decline with age, it seems more likely that the form that medium effects assume simply changes depending upon the age of the audience. In the case of language acquisition, although older audiences may be equally as adept at remembering language from television stories as they are from stories read aloud, they instead may be sensitive to a narrator's skill in delivering that language in each of these media.

The final assumption pertains to the usefulness of this research: *Findings from such research investigations of children's learning from television can have important implications for academic and applied audiences.* This premise may impose the greatest responsibility on the investigator. We have made efforts to interpret and share the results of our research with as wide an audience as possible. This has entailed addressing very different kinds of information needs, including directors' interest in the appeal of specific production techniques, researchers' interest in methodological issues, and parents' concern about medium effects on their children's behavior. For example, researchers are clearly in a position to give parents good ideas about how to use television more effectively with their children. Moreover, we should not expect the public's concerns and beliefs about media effects on children to be fully informed unless relevant research is made available to them. Therefore, in order to affirm this assumption it is incumbent upon researchers to make the product of their work accessible to all those who can most benefit from it.

Acknowledgments

The authors also wish to thank Gerald Lesser and Courtney Cazden for their support and encouragement at the outset of this research. The assistance of Mary Caulfield, Barbara Flagg, Patrick McGee, Erin Phelps, Carole Smith, and Joseph Walters in data collection and analysis is gratefully acknowledged. Sincere thanks are also expressed to Frank Peros and to participating principals, teachers, and children at the Watertown, Massachusetts, public schools.

References

Arnheim, R. Art and visual perception: A psychology of the creative eye. Berkeley: University of California Press, 1971.

Arnheim, R. Radio: An art of sound (2nd ed.). New York: DeCapo, 1972.

Baggett, P. Structurally equivalent stories in movies and text and the effect of the medium on recall. Journal of Verbal Learning and Verbal Behavior, 1979, 18, 333–356.

Bandura, A., & Walters, R. H. Social learning and personality development. New York: Holt, Rinehart & Winston, 1965.

Bandura, A., Ross, D., & Ross, S. Imitation of film-mediated aggressive models. Journal of Abnormal and Social Psychology, 1963, 66, 3–11.

Banker, G. S., & Meringoff, L. K. Without words: The meaning children derive from a non-verbal film story. Technical Report, Harvard Project Zero, Harvard University, 1982.

Bartlett, F. C. Remembering: A study in experimental and social psychology. Cambridge, England: Cambridge University Press, 1932.

Bettelheim, B. The uses of enchantment: The meaning and importance of fairy tales. New York: Vintage, 1977.

Bluestone, G. Novels into film: The metamorphosis of fiction into cinema. Berkeley: University of California Press, 1973.

Bruner, J. Beyond the information given: Studies in the psychology of knowing. New York: W. W. Norton, 1973.

Burch, N. The theory of film practice. New York: Praeger, 1973.

Campbell, D. E., & Campbell, T. A. Effects of live and recorded story telling on retelling performance of preschool children from low socioeconomic backgrounds. Psychology in the Schools, 1976, 13(2) 201–204.

Char, C., & Meringoff, L. K. Stories through sound: Children's comprehension of radio stories, and the role of sound effects and music in story comprehension. Technical Report, Harvard Project Zero, Harvard University, 1982.

Char, C., & Meringoff, L. K. The role of story illustrations: Children's story comprehension in three different media. Technical Report, Harvard Project Zero, Harvard University, 1981.

Chatman, S. What novels can do that films can't (and vice versa). *Critical Inquiry*, 1980, 7(1), 121–140.

Collins, W. A. Children's comprehension of television content. In E. Wartella (Ed.), *Children communicating: Media and development of thought, speech, understanding*. Beverly Hills, Calif.: Sage, 1979.

Deitch, G. The picture book animated. *The Horn Book Magazine*, April 1978, pp. 144–149.

Duke, J. S. *Children's books and magazines: A market study*. White Plains, N.Y.: Knowledge Industry Publications, 1979.

Eisenstein, S. *Film form*. New York: Harcourt Brace, 1949.

Fernie, D. E. Ordinary and extraordinary people: Children's understanding of television and real-life models. In H. Kelly & H. Gardner (Eds.), *New directions for child development*. San Francisco: Jossey-Bass, 1981.

Fitzhenry-Coor, I. *Children's comprehension and inference in stories of the intentionality*. Paper presented at the Society for Research in Child Development Biennial Meeting, New Orleans, March 1977.

Flapan, D. *Children's understanding of social interaction*. New York: Teachers College Press, 1968.

Friedman, S., & Stevenson, M. Developmental changes in the understanding of implied motion in two-dimensional pictures. *Child Development*, 1975, 46, 773–778.

Frith, U. Perceiving the language of films. *Perception*, 1975, 4, 97–103.

Gardner, H. *Artful scribbles: The significance of children's drawings*. New York: Basic Books, 1980.

Golomb, C. *Young children's sculpture and drawing: A study in representational development*. Cambridge, Mass.: Harvard University Press, 1974.

Goodnow, J. *Children drawing*. Cambridge, Mass.: Harvard University Press, 1977.

Greenfield, P., Geber, B., Beagles-Roos, J., Farrar, D., & Gat, I. *Television and radio experimentally compared: Effects of the medium on imagination and transmission of content*. Paper presented at the Society for Research in Child Development Biennial Meeting, Boston, April 1981.

Huston, A. C., Wright, J. C., Wartella, E., Rice, M. L., Watkins, B. A., Campbell, T., & Potts, R. Communicating more than content: Formal features of children's television programs. *Journal of Communication*, 1981, 31(3), 32–48.

Kelly, H., & Meringoff, L. K. *A comparison of story comprehension in two media: Books and television*. Paper presented at the Convention of the American Psychological Association, New York, September 1979.

Kjørup, S. Film as a meeting place of multiple codes. In D. Perkins & B. Leondar (Eds.), *The arts and cognition*. Baltimore: Johns Hopkins University Press, 1977.

Klapper, H. L. Children's perceptions of televised fiction. *California Management Review*, 1979, 22(2), 36–49.

Kosslyn, S. M., Heldmeyer, K. H., & Locklear, E. P. Children's drawings as data about internal representations. *Journal of Experimental Child Psychology*, 1977, 23, 191–211.

Lanes, S. G. *Down the rabbit hole: Adventures and misadventures in the realm of children's literature*. New York: Atheneum, 1972.

Levin, S., & Anderson, D. The development of attention. *Journal of Communication*, 1976, 26(2), 126–135.

McConaughy, S. H. Using story structure in the classroom. *Language Arts*, February 1980, pp. 157–165.

Mandler, J. M. & Johnson, N. S. Remembrance of things parsed: Story structure and recall. *Cognitive Psychology*, 1977, 9, 111–151.

Meringoff, L. K. Influence of the medium on children's story apprehension. *Journal of Educational Psychology*, 1980, 72(2), 240–249.

Meringoff, L. K. Viewpoints. *Language Arts*, March 1981, pp. 281–282.

Messaris, P., & Gross, L. Interpretations of a photographic narrative by viewers in four age groups. *Studies in the Anthropology of Visual Communication*, 1977, 4(2), 99–111.

Metz, C. *Language and cinema*. The Hague: Mouton, 1974.

Olson, D., & Bruner, J. Learning through experience and learning through media. In D. Olson (Ed.), *Media and symbols: The forms of expression, communication and education*. Chicago: National Society for the Study of Education, 1974.

Paris, S. G., & Mahoney, G. T. Cognitive integration in children's memory for sentences and pictures. *Child Development*, 1974, 45, 633–642.

Perkins, D. Imagery in minds and poems. *Poetics Today*, in press.

Piaget, J. *The psychology of intelligence*. Totowa, N.J.: Littlefield & Adams, 1973.

Poulsen, D., Kintsch, E., Kintsch, W., & Premack, D. Children's comprehension and memory for stories. *Journal of Experimental Child Psychology*, 1979, 28, 379–403.

Propp, V. *Morphology of the folktale* (2nd ed.). Austin: University of Texas Press, 1968.

Reisz, K., & Millar, G. *The technique of film editing* (2nd ed.). New York: Hastings House, 1968.

Salomon, G. *Interaction of media, cognition, and learning*. San Francisco: Jossey-Bass, 1979.

Schramm, W. *Big media, little media: Tools and technologies for instruction*. Beverly Hills, Calif.: Sage, 1977.

Stein, N. L., & Glenn, C. G. An analysis of story comprehension in elementary school children. In R. Freedle (Ed.), *Multi-disciplinary approaches to discourse comprehension*. Hillsdale, N.J.: Erlbaum, 1977.

Trabasso, T., Nicholas, D., Omanson, R., & Johnson, L. *Inferences and story comprehension*. Paper presented at the Society for Research in Child Development Biennial Meeting, New Orleans, March 1977.

Vibbert, M. M., & Meringoff, L. K. *Children's production and application of story imagery: A cross-medium investigation*. Harvard Project Zero, Harvard University, 1981. (ERIC Document Reproduction Service No. ED 210682)

Wartella, E., & Ettema, J. S. A cognitive developmental study of children's attention to television commercials. *Communication Research*, 1974, 1(1), 69–88.

Wilson, B., & Wilson, M. An iconoclastic view of the imagery sources in the drawings of young people. *Art Education*, January 1977, pp. 5–12.

Winner, E., & Gardner, H. (Eds.). Fact, fiction, and fantasy. *New Directions for Child Development*. San Francisco: Jossey-Bass, 1979.

chapter **7**

Television Watching and Mental Effort: A Social Psychological View[1]

GAVRIEL SALOMON

Resnick (1981) shows how the parent disciplines of educational psychology—child development and differential psychology—have affected the assumptions made by and questions asked and ignored by researchers in that field. The same seems to be true for research on children and television. Its major roots are the two scholarly traditions of child development and the study of mass media effects. The reliance on child development has introduced into the field such assumptions as the biological basis of growth, hence the strong influence of Piaget's work on the field (cf. Wartella, 1980), and the widespread attempts to plot the ways in which children develop into mature television users. The child development tradition has also brought with it a strong emphasis on individual growth and a great respect for it, to the relative deemphasis of social and cultural influences on developments that are not necessarily universal (for more detailed discussions see Feldman, 1980; Resnick, 1981).

The tradition of research on mass media's effects has introduced into the field somewhat different assumptions. One such assumption con-

[1]The research reported here was supported by a grant from the John and Mary R. Markle Foundation, given jointly to Don Roberts of Stanford University and the author of this chapter.

181

cerns the influence of external forces—particularly television—on knowledge acquisition, attitudes, behaviors, and even on cognitive skill mastery. Another assumption is that these external forces exert their influences through the mediation of already existing cognitive structures, which set the limits on the magnitude and qualitative nature of the external effects. Thus, these two traditions, or parent disciplines, are fairly compatible. They suggest a clear path for research on children and television: One looks for the critical or, at least, typical elements of the medium (commercials, aggressive contents, formal features, realism, and the like) and then explores how children of varying ages and ability levels come to handle them.

While this kind of research continues to provide an increasing number of intriguing findings, research in other relevant fields, such as cognitive sociology, interpersonal communication, and particularly cognitive social psychology, offers ideas which, if adhered to, could be of great interest to researchers in the field of children and television. The work done in these fields is relevant for it deals with the commerce between people and social environments, much like the field of children and television. However, unlike the latter field, cognitive social psychology is based, in part at least, on a different set of assumptions. Most important and relevant among them is the assumption that people actively affect their environment (of which television is certainly an important part) through their personal and socially shared perceptions, and they experience the consequences of their activity in a reciprocal, rather than linear fashion (e.g., Bandura, 1978; Wieck, 1979). In what follows I wish to discuss the relevance of this aspect of social psychology and related disciplines to the field of children and television, offer a few concepts that link the fields, and provide a number of illustrative research findings from our lab.

The Child's Active Role

People, as we well know, are not only affected by their environments, but they influence their environments as well in a number of ways: They choose situations, stimuli, places, and roles; they act on their environment; they influence the behaviors and self-concepts of their peers; and they interpret and reinterpret events, and the like. Often, the various ways in which people affect their environment are based on their a priori expectations, perceptions, attributions, and interpretations. For example, people often interpret the behavior of others as caused by dispositions, despite available veridical evidence suggesting that situational forces are at work, thus committing the "basic attribution error" (Ross, 1977). Similarly, as Wilhoit and de Bock (1976) show in their research on *All in the Family*, authoritarian Dutch viewers interpret Archie Bunker's behavior differently from nonauthoritarian ones. Clearly, preexisting beliefs, perceptual sets (including those about one's self), consensually held notions, and personality dispositions strongly influence one's perceptions. These in turn affect selections and actual behaviors.

Research on children and television has not ignored such conceptions. Indeed one can witness in recent years an impressive increase in the number of studies that examine not only how television affects children, but also what effects children's abilities, knowledge, sex, or socioeconomic status (SES) have on the way it affects them. Increasingly more researchers follow the suggestion by Schramm, Lyle, and Parker (1961) to attend to what the child brings to the medium (e.g., Collins, 1979).

The incorporation of the child's active part is however a tricky issue, for there are a number of ways in which "active" can be conceptualized. One can assume that active part of the child to serve as a mediator, moderating the effects of the medium's attributes, as an a priori determiner of the medium's effects (as in disposition-determined selective attention), as an addition to the medium's part, or in other ways. Thus although most people would tend to agree with the initial generalization, its translation to specific instances in the field of children and television becomes somewhat problematic. We are quite accustomed to studying how children with certain levels of ability or specific dispositions respond to external stimuli and how television's attributes differentially affect them. We are less accustomed to studying how children's beliefs, world views, or a priori perceptions shape the way they experience the medium.

The question of what it is that a child brings to television has at least two aspects. One aspect, which follows appropriately from the root assumptions of the field, perceives the child as an active responder to the medium's demands. The medium can be said to differentially activate or trigger cognitive or emotional responses from children with particular cognitive abilities and tendencies. The exact nature of these responses depends jointly on the attributes of the medium and on those of the child. The other aspect is more phenomenological in nature and follows more directly from a social psychological perspective. The child is perceived not only as a responder, but also as a potential determiner of the TV experience. The child does not always or necessarily respond to the "real" attributes of the medium but applies to it

his or her often culturally shared perceptions and attributions (themselves the partial results of prior exposure to the media), which in turn
affect the kind of experiences he or she encounters. Thus, seen from
one point of view, what the child brings to the screen is taken to set the
limits to what and to how television elicits from him or her; seen from
the other point of view, what the child brings to the screen—in terms of
perceptions and expectations—is taken to influence what the medium
is experienced to be. In the latter case the medium, as perceived, can be
said to be the party that "responds" to the child.

Obviously, the two perspectives are complementary. From one perspective we learn what children of different ages can learn from the
screen and to which of its elements they respond in what fashion. For
example, we learn that younger children attend to salient but not particularly informative features and that older ones come to attend to less
salient and more informative features [Calvert, Huston, Watkins, &
Wright, 1981 (but see Huston & Wright, Chapter 2—editors' note)].
From the other perspective, we learn what perceptions and expectations children acquire from the medium and from their social milieu
and how they apply them to the screen. For example, Greenberg (1972)
found that black people seen on television were rated as "real to life"
by white children who had had previous contact with black children
more often than by those who lacked such contact.

One may, however, question the importance of adding a cognitive
social psychological perspective to the already well-established tradition of research on children and television. Are children's perceptions,
expectations, and attributions that forceful in affecting their encounters
with the medium? There is little research in the field to warrant either a
positive or negative answer, but research in social psychology, while
rarely concerned with television or children, does show how important
people's beliefs, perceptions, and socially shared outlooks are in their
daily encounters with their environment (e.g., Nisbett & Ross, 1980). It
would be unreasonable to assume that children's encounters with television are exempt from such biases and other expectation-determined
behaviors.

It is often implicitly assumed by researchers and lay people alike
that children's behaviors on a given task reflect their mastery of relevant skills and knowledge. When children fail at a task, their failure is
taken to indicate a lack of such mastery. Although nobody would question this assumption on general grounds, it can nevertheless be argued
that it lacks an important component—namely, the choice that is often
involved in the application of particular skills or knowledge structures
to a particular instance or class of instances. Taylor and Fiske (1978)

criticized the implicit assumption in many attribution theories that, because information is presented to subjects, it is necessarily utilized by them. Langer (1978) similarly argues that, while it is taken as a given that people move through their environment thoughtful of other people, events, objects, and relationships, there is a growing body of evidence to suggest that they often behave "mindlessly." It is not unreasonable to expect children to exercise at least a modicum of choice whether or not to behave more "mindlessly" when encountering television and, by so doing, to determine the nature of their experience.

Meringoff (1980) found that children were likely to base their inferences on their own personal experiences when a story was read to them. They relied more heavily on the visually presented material when observing the animated story on television. It could be argued that such differences are due to the differential nature of the two media, but in light of the previous information and in light of findings to be reported later, it can be hypothesized that children, while capable of basing their inferences on personal experiences, choose (not necessarily consciously) to rely more heavily on the available, vivid stimulus. They could have, if so instructed, behaved differently.

Perceptions and Some of Their Consequences:
The Investment of Mental Effort

Assume that a priori perceptions, preconceptions, anticipatory schemata, or scripts affect the way children treat the medium. What are these perceptions? Where do they come from? How sensitive are they to the medium's inputs? How do they change with age? And what do they actually affect? The list of questions that comes to mind is very long, and, as research along these lines is still in its infancy, one can only generate hypotheses and speculations, illustrating them with a few initial findings. I will limit myself in this chapter to the identification of a possible factor that seems to be affected by a priori perceptions. For if nothing of importance is so affected, then there would be no compelling reason to add a social psychological viewpoint to the already utilized ones.

To be affected by any material one needs to process it. Processing can proceed in two directions which usually act in concert. It proceeds in a top-down fashion, guided by anticipatory schemata typical of search behavior (e.g., Wright & Huston, 1981), and in a bottom-up fashion, guided mainly by the saliency of stimulus properties, (e.g., Langer, 1978; Neisser, 1976; Rumelhart, 1975) typical of exploratory behavior. Apparently, the more one knows about a topic, and the better a new unit of material fits into a preexisting frame, conception, or schema, the more top-down processes dominate (assimilation); when the material is relatively novel (but not too novel) and being handled by impoverished schemata, bottom-up processes dominate (accomodation).

Prior knowledge affects the way the material is processed in a number of already known ways such as offering meaning, suggesting how to bridge gaps, how to organize and structure the material, what to emphasize and deemphasize in it, and the like. Prior knowledge, however, can also tell the individual how novel the material is and how much or how deeply it needs to be processed. Langer and her associates show in a series of studies (cf. Langer, 1982) how often adults engage in mindless behavior when they encounter events that appear to them as highly familiar, overlearned, and repetitious. For example, in one study (Langer & Abelson, 1974) therapists were shown a tape of either a "job applicant" or a "patient." Therapists who more routinely used labeling of patients, described the "patients" in quite mindless ways independently of the actual person they viewed on tape. In another study (Langer & Benevento, 1978), subjects were found to comply with unjustified, even ridiculous requests, which had the appearance in structure of familiar or "typical" requests.

Mindlessnes takes place even in the absence of well-mastered tasks or in the absence of prior knowledge; providing an individual with a conceptual category that appears credible and sensible is enough to make him or her forgo mindful processing upon encountering an instance of that category. Mindlessness is defined by Langer as the absence of active conscious processing, as when the individual relies on a structure of the situation which represents its underlying meaning (Langer, 1982). More specifically: "Attention is not paid precisely to those substantive elements that are relevant for the successful resolution of the situation. It has all the external earmarks of mindful action, but new information actually is not being processed. Instead, prior scripts, written when similar information was once new, are stereotypically reenacted [Langer, Blank, & Chanowitz, 1978, p. 636]."

There is a great similarity between the construct of mindlessness (versus mindfulness) and the more veteran concept of shallow (versus deep) processing. Elsewhere, and for reasons unrelated to the present argument, I have introduced the concept of AIME—the amount of invested mental effort in nonautomatic elaboration of material (Salomon, 1981a, 1981b). The concept of AIME encompasses the essential idea of mindfulness or depth and its opposites but is less judgmental than mindlessness; it also avoids some of the conceptual pitfalls of the concept of depth (Baddley, 1978). AIME can be expected to increase when a unit of material cannot be easily fitted into existing schemata. When it can, one would expect AIME to decrease, as the individual feels, rightly or wrongly, that there is little in the encountered material that warrants the investment of his or her mental efforts. If the material is perceived to fit into existing schemata well (Does the reader feel that these arguments are already well-known to him or her?), then one can use easily available automatic processing. This, as Abelson (1981) points out, is the great advantage and limitation of scripts for under- standing or action. Although there is now evidence to show that greater AIME expension leads to more learning (e.g., Kane & Anderson, 1978), particularly where nonautomatic elaborations are involved (Salomon, 1981c), one may wonder how a priori perceptions of a class of material or of a medium influence the process. For after all, more difficult or novel material may indeed demand more effort, and to the extent that relevant skills are available, it should lead to better learning, regardless of perceptions.

Attributes of material, difficulty included, are not just inherent qualities exerting their autonomous influence on processing. What a unit of material is greatly depends on the kinds of schemata one brings to bear on it, and this need not reflect only the "true" nature of the material as determined by outside judges. This may apply in particular when ambiguous attributes such as "difficulty," "novelty," and "depth" are concerned. Is All in the Family a "deep" program? And what about Maude?

Generally speaking, the better one feels acquainted with a class of materials, a source, or a medium, the stronger one's preconceptions of it and its demands are. (We know that a Bergman film entails great symbolic depth and expend AIME accordingly.) The stronger these preconceptions, or more easily available to processing, the greater the chance that these will preempt the unbiased examination of the pre- sented material (Nisbett & Ross, 1980). In such cases, it can be argued, top-down processing dominates. The extent to which strong precon- ceptions include beliefs or expectations about the AIME required, may affect the amount and nature of nonautomatic elaboration of the mate- rial by such a priori perceptions. The film Being There nicely and humorously illustrates this point.

Here, however, the present conceptual outline faces a difficulty. Pri- or knowledge per se need not lead to decreased AIME. There is some evidence to show that prior knowledge even increases AIME. For exam- ple, experienced uncertainty leading to information search cannot real- ly take place in the presence of ignorance (Berlyne, 1971). Similarly, it has been shown that older children, who are certainly more knowledgeable about television and its typical portrayals than younger ones, can handle it more elaborately (e.g., Rice, Huston, & Wright, 1982). A contradiction? First, what children can do is not necessarily what they actually do (an issue already raised by Collins, 1979). This, indeed, is the whole idea of mindlessness or AIME. A source of information we perceive to be well-known to us, easily handled, and routine, allows us, so to speak, to treat it with the minimum AIME we can expend to get our pleasures. Second, we need to distinguish between prior knowledge and skills, which are stored in our schemata and available for processing, and metarules or metacognitions, which tell us when, under what conditions, and for what purposes we are to apply them. The preconceptions about a source of information that affects AIME are of the latter type, and their development with age causes the shift from exploration to search behavior and from attention to salient television features to more focused and selective attention. Thus, mindless behavior, or processing with little AIME, is not a simple function of knowledge but of those metacognitions.

Flavell (1979) suggested in this respect that children's metacognitions should be trained to improve their "critical appraisal of message source, quality of appeal, and . . . consequences needed to cope with these inputs . . . [p. 910]." Abelson (1981) argues that scripts, or schemata, do not always lead to totally automated responses, for they often include such heuristics as "now think." In addition there are also "metascripts" which are of a higher order of abstraction than the scripts themselves. (There may be a script for *Sesame Street* and a metascript for television; the latter may entail higher order heuristics of the "now think" type.) A metascript pertaining to television can suggest whether the events to which it pertains should be handled with more or with less AIME, leaving the fine tuning to the more specific scripts. In sum, it is not knowledge per se that affects AIME but the metarules, metacognitions, or metascripts that govern and supervise the application of the available knowledge to particular instances.

The Perception of Television, AIME, and Learning: Initial Findings

Children, it appears, develop skills necessary for elementary comprehension of television fairly early and without tutelage (Gardner & Meringoff, 1981). It is reasonable to assume that they also develop a general conception of the medium and thus learn to differentiate between it and other media. The nature of their developing conceptions reflect in part their parents' conceptions and ways of handling the medium (Cojuc, Watkins, & Tan, 1981). As television is dominated by pictorials and as even the verbal discourses it presents are "real" in appearance, one would expect children (and even adults) to perceive the medium as lifelike in its representational modes and thus as relatively uncontrived.

Morison, Hope, and Gardner (1981) studied children's attributions of reality to television and their reasoning about it. They found that, although there were age-related changes in children's modes of reasoning about the medium's reality, many criteria were applied by only a few children even at sixth-grade level. Thus, for example, only 10% of the sixth graders (versus 5% of the younger ones) invoked in their responses the purpose or intention of programs. Thus "contrary to expectation, critical consideration of the quality, authenticity, and veracity of television representations was rarely expressed, even among the oldest subject. Apparently, mastery of these 'meta-medium' concerns has not been accomplished by the majority of sixth graders [Morison et al., 1981, p. 16]."

Instead, it seems, there are other meta medium concerns, or preconceptions, that guide the child to treat the medium as "real." Given such perceptions of the medium (unlike those of books; Landry & Gardner, 1981), one can expect children to approach it as relatively undemanding and easy and to perceive themselves as highly efficacious in handling it with little effort. It follows that such perceptions could guide them to actually invest little effort in also processing material that demands greater AIME, resulting in relatively poor performance on postviewing tasks that require nonautomatic elaborations.

We have thus far carried out four studies designed to test these and related hypotheses. In one study (Salomon, 1981b, 1981c) we first tried to measure the perceptions that 124 sixth graders have of television and of print, as well as their causal attributions of success and failure with each. Second, we examined the extent to which their learning from either source depends on their self-reported AIME and whether AIME depends on their preconceptions.

As expected, we found that television is perceived to be a much "easier" and a more lifelike medium, demanding far less effort for comprehension than printed material of the same content. Children also expressed more self-efficacy with television than with print. Although failure to comprehend print was attributed by most children to its difficulty, failure with television was attributed to "dumbness." On the other hand, success with print was attributed to "smartness" and with television to its ease. All of this could be explained as no more than children's accurate perception of the real differential nature of the two media. However, the results of the exposure manipulation suggest otherwise. Contrary to common sense, those children to whom we showed the film *A Day of a Painter* manifested poorer comprehension than those who read the equivalent version in print; yet the former reported expending less AIME than the latter. Indeed, the correlation between self-reported AIME and elaboration-achievement was .67 for the television group and .64 for the print group, suggesting that AIME was an important correlate, if not determiner, of learning. Most importantly, AIME in the print group correlated .37 with initial self-efficacy but $-.49$ in the television group. (The latter correlation suggests that too high self-efficacy is related to the relinquishment of AIME.) In other words, the way children perceive a medium (and their own efficacy in handling it) is quite strongly related to their investment of mental effort in processing its material, which in turn is related to how much they actually learn from it. If indeed the children's perceptions would have reflected only the real demands of each medium, the television group, rather than the print group, should have demonstrated better learning.

A second study was carried out with 49 sixth graders in Israel. The study replicated the first study in general outline, using educational instead of entertainment material, and included a pretest measure of reading ability. As in the first study, children reported expending less AIME in television than in printed material of the same nature and perceived television to be more "realistic" than print.

Unlike the first study in which a negative correlation of about $-.30$ was found between lifelikeness attributed to television and AIME in it, none was found in the second study. We also found only a slight difference in achievement scores between the television and reading groups (no inferential questions were asked, and most children reached ceiling in the memory posttest). Two important phenomena emerged, however. First, we found that the poorer readers expressed a relatively high level of self-efficacy in learning from both television and print, reported the expension of the smallest AIME in both, and got the poorest achievement scores. It appeared that these children, perhaps for defensive reasons, played down the perceived demand characteristics of televiewing and reading by inflating their perceived self-efficacy. In so doing they could avoid the investment of effort in processing, and yet they failed to learn much from either source. When given feedback concerning their achievement scores, these children adjusted their perceived self-efficacy and reported AIME the least. (The others changed their perceptions to accommodate the feedback information.)

Second, and most importantly, we failed to replicate the pattern of intercorrelations obtained in our American study. Although general AIME pertaining to either print or television correlated in this study with specific AIME pertaining to the material seen or read, the latter variable did not correlate with achievement. Rather, achievement correlated with initial perceived self-efficacy, which itself was related to ability. Controlling for ability, the correlation dropped to .10 in the print group but to only .30 ($p < .05$) in the television group. It became evident that, while preconceptions play an important role in determining AIME, particularly when applied to television, the measure of self-reported AIME, when used with Israeli children, is flawed. It also became apparent that effort investment can exert its influence on learning only where nonautomatic processes become involved; a simple recognition test hardly taps such processes.

The two studies, viewed together, lend some support to the general theses—namely, preconceptions of the medium and of one's efficacy in handling it satisfactorily are related to effort invested in processing its material and to inferential learning. The findings leave other questions wide open, however. One such question pertains to the perception of television as a medium. Could it be that an individual has no global perception of television but makes one up as a response to global questions? A second question relates to the measure of AIME. How valid a measure is it? Another question pertains to the role played by what we have globally called "perceived demand characteristics" (PDC) of a medium, task, or context. For example, does television's perceived "depth" of typical materials relate to reported AIME?

In the next study we tested 96 freshmen in the school of education at the Hebrew University. Using a counterbalanced design, we questioned them about the AIME they generally expend in print, in television, and in each of a number of content areas (e.g., adventure, sports, news, science, and crime stories). We also asked them, in a similar fashion, about their perceived self-efficacy with each medium and content area within it, as well as about the "depth" they attributed to each (the latter was seen as a reasonable measure of PDC). We reasoned that if we failed to find overall perceptions of television, or failed to substantiate the measure of AIME with university students, then we would have good reason to question the whole idea when applied to children.

The results were quite clear and supported our expectations. First, as with the children in the previous studies, efficacy with television was higher and AIME was lower than with print, when both overall measured and category-specific ones were compared. The only exception was the news: Television news was seen as "deeper" than news in print, thus demanding more AIME. The students also felt less efficacious about it. Second, reports of content-specific AIME and general AIME in television correlated .49, and with respect to print, .55. Thus, it appears that our general measure of AIME reflects the average perception of different content areas. Similar results were obtained with respect to the measures of efficacy and attributed "depth."

Last, we developed a measure of relative homogeneity of responses, that is, "stereotyping" in the way a medium is perceived. Since students responded to various content areas within each medium, we could compute for each student his or her standard deviation (one for AIME, one for efficacy, and one for PDC) and then compute a group average for each variable. What we found was not surprising at all. There was far less variance in the responses to television than to printed material of the same kind. Thus, one may say that television is more homogeneously or stereotypically perceived than print (holding content areas constant), in terms of students' perceptions of the AIME they typically expend, the "depth" they attribute, and the efficacy they feel. Moreover, the stereotypical scores of AIME in television (how well or poorly students differentiated between the AIME expended in different kinds of television content) correlated .35 with the average AIME they reported expending in television. No such correlation was found with respect to print, suggesting that AIME in television is related to how well its repertoire is differentially perceived. The more stereotyped the perception of the medium, the less effort is invested in it.

With these findings in mind we turned to address other questions. While preconceptions of television may influence how much effort is invested in processing, this kind of influence could be marginal if the effort one invests is highly responsive to the specific nature or demands of the material presented. Obviously one does accomodate the amount and qualitative nature of mental effort to the material observed. One would not be expected to totally ignore the specific demands of a program unless one's anticipatory schemata are highly loaded emotionally or very central in one's overall cognitive apparatus. Thus, despite the existence of preconceptions, children would not be expected to be totally insensitive to material variations. But, given the existence of preconceptions and metarules concerning the AIME typically needed to process television, how much influence do input-variations have on the AIME actually expended?

Another issue involved here pertains to PDC. If effort investment depends to a significant extent on the perceived demands of the medium, the task to be performed, or the context (Salomon, 1981a), then a change of one of its components, experimentally induced, should be reflected in AIME and in learning. If such changes can be introduced, then we would have better grounds to claim that preconceptions of, say, task, and not just the specific nature of the medium, affect the commerce between child and television.

Our fourth study was designed to examine these issues. A group of 120 sixth graders took part in the study. One major variable was PDC, defined in terms of the instructions given to the subjects. Half of them were told to attend to the material (a televised film or an equivalent text) "just for fun" (PDC-1), a situation that we assumed is typical of home viewing. The other half were told "to watch (or read) carefully as we want to see how much you can learn from it." The latter condition (PDC-2) was assumed to induce greater AIME and lead to better inference-making.

The second variable was the structure of the material. One-third of the subjects viewed a well-structured story on television, while another third watched the same film, spliced and reedited at random. We wanted to see how sensitive AIME and postviewing performance are to such unusual changes in the stimulus, relative to the effects of preconceptions and PDC. The last group read in print the equivalent of the well-structured film. We expected AIME in print to exceed that in television and to be less responsive to the manipulation of PDC. Again we found overall reports of AIME to correlate with the average AIME concerning specific content areas—AIME in print to exceed that in TV and efficacy with TV to exceed that with print.

Reported AIME pertaining to the story was higher in the print groups than in the regular television groups, and this difference was accompanied by better and richer inferences made by the print group. This finding replicates the finding of our first study, as well as that of Meringoff (1980). The manipulation of PDC had the expected effect: PDC-2 groups, television and print alike, reported investing more effort and showed better performance than PDC-1 groups, but the effect was more pronounced in the television group. The print group achieved relatively high achievement scores even without being told to learn the material. Thus, a change in PDC had a positive effect on the televiewers, suggesting that their typical way of viewing does not reflect what they can do with such a program.

Comparing the regular- with the scrambled-television groups, we found, as one would expect, the scrambled-television groups to report more AIME but to perform less well than the regular television groups. The manipulation of PDC had no noticeable effect on the scrambled-television groups, the AIME of which was high anyway due apparently to the unusualness of the presentation.

Children, then, tend to show sensitivity to stimulus variations and to abandon their preconceptions, provided the material deviates sufficiently from their expectations. When they encounter a typical show of the familiar, even overlearned kind, and, in the absence of instructions that change their usual perception of the material, they tend to invest little effort in processing it in accordance with their preconceptions. Indeed, in the latter case they do not invest much of their ability and rely more heavily on their preconceptions, or mental scripts, that were written earlier: Ability correlated more highly with achievement in the PDC-2 than in the PDC-1 groups (.43 versus .16 in the television groups and .65 versus .53 in the print groups). Similarly, a priori perceived self-efficacy with print (but not with television) correlated .65 with achievement in the television PDC-1 group but only .17 in the television PDC-2 group (controlling for initial AIME reduced the correlations to .57 and .08, respectively).

Additional evidence to corroborate our findings is provided in a recent study by Kwaitek and Watkins (1981). As in our study they manipulated children's task perceptions and obtained essentially the same results. Subjects instructed to learn the televised material reported more story elements in their reconstructions and displayed higher levels of abstraction and a more detailed understanding of the story than subjects instructed to view the program as entertainment. The former also took more time to complete the task.

Tentative Conclusions and Open Questions

The findings of the studies reported tend to support the general theses that children approach television equipped with specific preconceptions about the medium and about their ability to handle it. They treat television as an easy source of information and perceive themselves to be highly efficacious in processing its messages. The findings of the last two studies lend evidence to the contention that the perceptions of the medium's demands affect effort investment, and, that unless children are specifically instructed to treat the stimulus differently than usual, they invest little effort in it and extract little inferential knowledge from it. In other words, they appear to be relatively effortless televiewers, performing below their real levels of ability.

Elsewhere (Salomon, 1981d) I have argued that televiewing, like the processing of other kinds of material, entails roughly three phases: recoding, chunking, and elaborating. The skills needed range from the more symbol-specific ones, required by the first phase, to the more general, required by the third phase. Although the skills needed for the first phase are easily acquired and reach automatic mastery early on, those needed for elaboration are effort-demanding. As our fourth study and the one by Kwaitek and Watkins (1981) show, the application of such skills is not automatic.

If children tend to process typical television shows with little AIME and are relying more heavily on the already well-mastered skills of the earlier phases of processing, they may be missing the opportunity to further the development of higher order skills while televiewing, but these skills, being of the more general type (e.g., inference-making), are likely to be the ones most appropriate for transfer to other sources of information. Acquiring the matarule that information can be satisfactorily processed at only the lower levels, children—when acting voluntarily—may then turn to other sources expecting them to allow the same. Morgan (1980) noticed that heavy televiewers, while reading more, seek out reading material that reflects the common television fare, and Watkins, Cojuc, Mills, Kwaitek, and Tan (1981) found that heavy television consumers produce narratives that are choppier, entail fewer words per sentence, and are more descriptive of external, surface elements than those produced by light television users. The former seem to describe events like remote observers, leaving out elements that require inferential processing, and they do this not only when producing television narratives, but also when they produce "real-life" narratives. In other words, the preconceptions that are successfully applied to television may be transferred to other kinds of information.

The data presented thus far are not conclusive and could be interpreted in other ways. I described the findings mainly to illustrate my point: Children actively influence the way they experience the medium, not just through the skills and knowledge the medium evokes in them, but also through their a priori metacognitions, metascripts, or metarules that they apply to it. To an extent it is the child who determines how "deeply" or "shallowly" televised material is to be processed. This of course does not rule out the question of how the medium, through its symbols and forms and through its typical contents, affects these conceptions. Quite likely, what parents teach a child about television, what it actually offers, and what preconceptions a child learns to apply to it, may all turn out to be reciprocally interrelated.

Once we are willing to entertain the possible active roles that children play with respect to television, we have to consider the social and cultural settings (rather than only the universal cognitive developments) in which children grow up and which may have strong influences on their television-related metacognitions. In other words, we might shift from a view of the individual child who responds to television to a view of the child in a social context who also makes the medium respond to him or her.

This raises the question of development in interaction with culture. Langer (1982) argues that the younger child, still lacking well-established mental categories and metacognitions, may be more mindful in processing familiar classes of information than at an older age. It can be argued, however, that, as children mature, increasingly more categories become available to them, allowing them not only more top-down processing, but also more alternative ways to choose in mindful, nonpredetermined ways. This, though, may be quite culture specific. While in one culture there may be strong prevailing views of television imposing early closure, in another culture television may be seen as a medium the details of which one should pay close attention to. The study by Cohen and Salomon (1979) suggests that the former is more typical of the United States and the latter of Israel. Far more research is needed, however, before firm cross-cultural conclusions can be reached.

One implication is that, rather than change the medium of television, one should change through educational means children's typical way of processing televised material. Indeed, a number of such attempts have been published (e.g., Dorr, Graves, & Phelps, 1980; Prasad, Rao, & Sheikh, 1978) which suggest that children can be taught to invest more mental effort in televiewing. None of the studies so far has shown any lasting effects manifested when the children voluntarily watch television at home on their own. Children may not need to learn all the skills of elaboration anew, as they have mastery of many of them; rather, they would need to learn how to apply them to television. It may also be important for them to acquire new metacognitions, or metarules, of the kind suggested by Flavell (1979), which tell them when to invest more processing effort ("now think") and when to process the material more automatically.

Acknowledgments

The studies described here were carried out with the help of Mati Weissberg, Tami Leigh, Mike Halpern, Miri Ben-Moshe, and Giorah Tzeder.

References

Abelson, R. P. Psychological status of the script concept. *American Psychologist*, 1981, *36*, 715–726.

Baddley, A. D. The trouble with levels: A reexamination of Craik and Lockhart's framework for memory research. *Psychological Review*, 1978, *85*, 139–152.

Bandura, A. The self system in reciprocal determinism. *American Psychologist*, 1978, *33*, 344–358.

Berlyne, D. E. *Aesthetics and psychobiology*. New York: Appleton-Century-Crofts, 1971.

Calvert, S. L., Huston, A. C., Watkins, B., & Wright, J. C. *The effects of selective attention to television forms on children's comprehension of content*. Paper presented at the Society for Research in Child Development Biennial Meeting, Boston, 1981.

Cohen, A., & Salomon, G. Children's literate television viewing: Surprises and possible explanations. *Journal of Communication*, 1979, *29*(3), 156–163.

Cojuc, J. R., Watkins, B., & Tan, Z. *Children's perceptions about television: Its evaluation, its effects*. First annual report to the Spencer Foundation. Children's Media Project, The University of Michigan, 1981.

Collins, W. A. Children's comprehension of television content. In E. Wartella (Ed.), *Children communicating: Media and development of thought, speech, understanding*. Beverly Hills, Calif.: Sage, 1979.

Dorr, A., Graves, S. B., & Phelps, E. Television literacy for young children. *Journal of Communication*, 1980, *30*(3), 71–83.

Feldman, D. H. *Beyond universals in cognitive development*. Norwood, N.J.: Ablex, 1980.

Flavell, J. H. Metacognition and cognitive monitoring: A new area of cognitive-developmental inquiry. *American Psychologist*, 1979, *34*, 906–911.

Gardner, H., & Meringoff, L. K. *Children stories media*. Fourth annual review to the Markle Foundation. Harvard Project Zero, December 1981.

Greenberg, B. S. Children's reactions to TV blacks. *Journalism Quarterly*, 1972, *49*, 5–14.

Kane, J. M., & Anderson, R. C. Depth of processing and interference effects in the learning and remembering of sentences. *Journal of Educational Psychology*, 1978, *70*, 626–635.

Kwaitek, K., & Watkins, B. *The systematic viewer: An inquiry into the grammer of television*. First annual report to the Spencer Foundation. Children Media project, The University of Michigan, July 1981.

Landry, M. O., & Gardner, H. *Reality–fantasy discriminations in literature: A developmental study*. Harvard Project Zero, Technical Report # 21, 1981.

Langer, E. J. Rethinking the role of thought in social interaction. In J. Harvey, W. Ickes, & R. Kidd (Eds.), *New directions in attribution research* (Vol. 2). Hillsdale, N.J.: Erlbaum, 1978.

Langer, E. J. Playing the middle against both ends: The usefulness of adult cognitive activity as a model for cognitive activity in childhood and old age. In S. R. Yussen (Ed.), *The development of reflection*. New York: Academic Press, 1982.

Langer, E. J., & Abelson, R. A patient by any other name . . . : Clinician group differences in labelling bias. *Journal of Consulting and Clinical Psychology*, 1974, *42*, 4–9.

Langer, E., & Benevento, A. Self-induced dependence. *Journal of Personality and Social Psychology*, 1978, *36*, 886–893.

Langer, E. J., Blank, A., & Chanowitz, B. The mindlessness of ostensibly thoughtful action: The role of "placebic" information in interpersonal interaction. *Journal of Personality and Social Psychology*, 1978, *36*, 635–642.

Meringoff, L. K. Influence of the medium on children's story apprehension. *Journal of Educational Psychology*, 1980, *72*(2), 240–249.

Morgan, M. Television viewing and reading: Does more equal better? *Journal of Communication*, 1980, *30*, 159–165.

Morison, P., Hope, K., & Gardner, H. Reasoning about television: A developmental study. Harvard Project Zero, 1981.

Neisser, U. Cognition and reality: Principles and implications of cognitive psychology. San Francisco, Calif.: Freeman, 1976.

Nisbett, R., & Ross, L. Human inference: Strategies and shortcomings of social judgment. Englewood Cliffs, N.J.: Prentice-Hall, 1980.

Prasad, V. K., Rao, T. R., & Sheikh, A. A. Mothers vs. commercials. Journal of Communication, 1978, 28, 91–96.

Resnick, L. B. Social assumptions as a context for science: Some reflections on psychology and education. Educational Psychologist, 1981, 16, 1–10.

Rice, M. L., Huston, A. C., & Wright, J. C. The forms and codes of television: Effects on children's attention, comprehension, and social behavior. In D. Pearl, L. Bouthilet, & J. Lazar (Eds.), Television and behavior: Ten years of scientific progress and implications for the eighties. Washington, D.C.: U.S. Government Printing Office, 1982.

Ross, L. The intuitive psychologist and shortcomings: Distortions in the attribution process. In L. Berkowitz (Ed.), Advances in experimental social psychology (Vol. 10). New York: Academic Press, 1977.

Rumelhart, D. E. Notes on a schema for stories. In D. G. Bobrow & A. Collins (Eds.), Representation and understanding: Studies in cognitive science. New York: Academic Press, 1975.

Salomon, G. Communication and education: Social and psychological interactions. Beverly Hills, Calif.: Sage, 1981. (a)

Salomon, G. Introducing AIME: The assessment of children's mental involvement with television. In H. Gardner & H. Kelly (Eds.), Children and the worlds of television. San Francisco, Calif.: Jossey-Bass, 1981. (b)

Salomon, G. TV is "easy" and print is "tough": The role of perceptions and attributions in the processing of material. Manuscript submitted for publication, 1981. (c)

Salomon, G. Television literacy and television vs. literacy. Paper presented at the conference on Literacy in the 80's, University of Michigan, June, 1981. (d)

Schramm, W., Lyle, J., & Parker, E. B. Television in the lives of our children. Stanford, Calif.: Stanford University Press, 1961.

Taylor, S. E., & Fiske, S. T. Salience, attention and attribution: Top of the head phenomena. In L. Berkowitz (Ed.), Advances in experimental social psychology (Vol. 11). New York: Academic Press, 1978.

Wartella, E. Children and television: The development of the child's understanding of the medium. In G. C. Wilhoit (Ed.), Mass communication review yearbook. Beverly Hills, Calif.: Sage, 1980.

Watkins, B., Cojuc, J. R., Mills, S., Kwaitek, K., & Tan, Z. Children's use of TV and real-life story structure and content as a function of age and prime-time television viewing. First annual report to the Spencer Foundation. Children's Media Project, The University of Michigan, July 1981.

Weick, K. E. The social psychology of organizing. Reading, Mass.: Addison-Welsley, 1979.

Wilhoit, D. C., & de Bock, H. "All in the Family" in Holland. Journal of Communication, 1976, 26, 75–84.

Wright, J., & Huston, A. The forms of television: Nature and development of television literacy in children. In H. Gardner & H. Kelly (eds.), Children and the worlds of television. San Francisco, Calif.: Jossey-Bass, 1981.

chapter **8**

No Shortcuts to Judging Reality[1]

AIMÉE DORR

Introduction

Among the many developmental tasks facing children is that of learning how to recognize which ideas, beliefs, attitudes, and behaviors to take seriously and which to regard lightly. In face-to-face situations, children need to learn to recognize such contexts as joking, lying, teaching, and fantasizing and to discriminate in *each* context the content to take seriously. Similarly, in mediated situations children need to learn to recognize content that should be taken as informative, persuasive, or simply entertaining, whether it is presented in the context of instruction, news, public affairs, advertising, entertainment, or social influence. Although they oversimplify and to some extent obscure the distinctions, the terms *real, realistic,* and *reality* can be made to stand for that content and those ideas and behaviors that one ought to take seriously.

Of all the mediated experiences children have, television is probably the most similar to "real" life. This should lead children to take its

[1]The research upon which this chapter is based was supported by grant No. 90-C-247 from the Office of Child Development to Aimée Dorr Leifer, Sherryl Browne Graves, and Neal J. Gordon. Subsequent coding and analyses were supported by the Annenberg School of Communications at the University of Southern California.

CHILDREN'S UNDERSTANDING
OF TELEVISION

content more seriously than they otherwise might. In live action programming things look and sound normal. People and animals usually behave as they ordinarily do in real life. When they do not, their behavior is still convincingly realistic in appearance. Settings seem natural. People, places, and events are usually seen repeatedly and formulaic plots are commonplace, giving one a comfortable feeling of intimacy and predictability. The problems facing characters are often those of everyday life—or at least the more interesting and dramatic parts of everyday life. Clearly, the forms of nonanimated programming lend an aura of reality to all its content.

Animated programming, in contrast, does not look real and often does not sound real; yet it too may seem quite realistic. Sesame Street, The Electric Company, and short segments presented Saturday morning by the networks all use animation to teach counting, letter recognition, reading skills, arithmetic facts, grammar, history, and the like. Young children know this is content that we adults consider real, even if its form (or context) is clearly fantastic. There are also animated series that focus on the quite real social concerns of children. Fat Albert and the Cosby Kids examines sibling rivalry, stereotyping, and sex roles. Davey and Goliath examines loneliness, fear, and religiosity. Children recognize the ideas as being wholly appropriate to the human condition. Thus, even the unrealistic images and sounds of animation may convey content that children would judge to be accurate or realistic or worth taking seriously.

These characteristics of television content and context point to complexities inherent in studying viewers' judgments of television reality, of what to take seriously. Simple distinctions such as information–entertainment (Schramm, Lyle, & Parker, 1961) and fantasy–reality (Berkowitz & Alioto, 1973; Feshbach, 1972; Lyle & Hoffman, 1972a, 1972b) can certainly be made. Respondents can usually categorize programming accordingly. Yet such distinctions may considerably simplify what viewers actually experience. After all, Sesame Street is filled with fantastic Muppets and unrealistic animation; yet some children understand that much of its content is facts, skills, social attitudes, and social behaviors which they should take seriously. Good Times is clearly a scripted, acted, entertainment series; yet thousands of black men took an episode about heart disease seriously enough to see a doctor soon after it was broadcast. The CBS Evening News clearly purports to convey facts; yet many refuse to accept them all as believable.

A variety of factors is likely to influence children's perceptions of television's reality. Children who understand something of the economic structure of the television industry or of the mechanics of television production may be more likely to discount the reality of what they see. They will understand that most of the programming they watch is not designed to inform and that the technology of television permits the production and broadcasting of apparently realistic content. If such knowledge is used as the basis for judging television's reality, then the judgment process becomes a simple one. It could also be simplified by relying on gross characteristics of context such as genre, specific production technique, setting in time, or specific statements about reality status that precede or succeed programming. If such broad criteria are not employed, then children must decide about the reality of individual programs, characters, events, objects, and settings. To do so they must use their existing knowledge of physical and social reality, new knowledge they are motivated to obtain from nonprogram sources (e.g., parents, books, other programs), and their ability to integrate and relate program and nonprogram elements properly, as well as some information from programming itself. This is clearly a much more complex process than any of the simpler judgment methods just described. It should lead to more situation- and viewer-specific judgments.

For several years colleagues, students, and I have been studying children's understanding of television content. We have been interested in what they think is fantasy and reality, what they find believable or worth learning or remembering, and what guided their judgments. We have confined ourselves to judgments made upon reflection, recognizing that viewing enjoyment often comes from the *willing—but temporary—suspension of disbelief*. With a few minor sidetrips we have focused on entertainment programming broadcast on commercial stations. Most of the illustrations and data in this chapter are derived from interviews conducted in the Boston area in the late 1970s (Dorr, 1980; Dorr, Graves, & Phelps, 1980; Forté, 1976; Graves, 1976a, 1976b; Leifer, 1976; Leifer, Graves, & Gordon, 1975; Lemon, 1976; Phelps, 1976). Some results come from analyses carried out soon after the data were gathered; others are derived from more recent coding and analyses. Together they provide interesting insights into viewers' understandings of television's reality.

The Meaning of Reality

Any collective effort to study reality—or fantasy—makes it painfully evident how complex and elusive the concept is. A research staff can debate endlessly how to define and operationalize the concept. The approach we took, once failure to achieve unanimity and simplicity of definition was accepted, was to consider three possible meanings of the judgment that something on television was real. Data were then examined to determine which meanings were likely to be used by viewers of different ages.

At the most concrete definitional level, one may say that something on television is real and mean that it is exactly as it is without television. The chair in which a character sits is a real chair. The drawings which make up an animated program are real drawings. The people who are acting out a drama are real people. The events of what we adults would call a drama are really happening just as one sees them on the television screen. This is the definition one would use if one saw television as "Magic Window Reality," to use Hawkins' (1977, p. 309) term. Adopting such a definition, however, does not necessarily mean one believes television is a magic window. One may restrict those things judged as real on television to those that are truly exactly as they are in unmediated circumstances—some props, the drawings in animation, the live actors. Here little of television content, and certainly little of that which social scientists study and critics critique, would be judged to be real.

The other two definitions of *real* accept that programming is fabricated but do not use that as the basis for judging reality. Instead, reality means a fabricated experience in which characters, actions, messages, or themes somehow conform to real life. Such definitions were common among people we interviewed. Edith Bunker of *All in the Family* and Mary Richards of *The Mary Tyler Moore Show* were both known to be portrayed by actresses, but Edith was judged more realistic than Mary. Portrayals of white women as flighty were judged real, because that was the perceived character of most white women. Pebbles Flintstone was clearly an animated girl unrealistically living in prehistoric times, but she still demonstrated something believable about cooking for one's father.

Two somewhat different meanings can be found within this second general definitional approach. In one, something is judged real if it is deemed possible. In the other, it is only judged real if it is deemed probable or representative. The former is likely to extend considerably the range of characters, events, messages, and themes that could be judged real. The bionic man could be real, because it is possible, though uncommon, for modern medicine to provide excellent prosthetic devices. Charlie Chaplin's boiling and eating a shoe could be real, because it is possible to soften leather by boiling and to be hungry enough to eat strange things. Tarzan's talking to the apes is real, because it is possible for human beings to teach apes to talk. None of these would be judged real, however, if one restricted one's definition to probable rather than possible.

Use of possibility or probability as the criterion for reality requires extensive reference to one's general knowledge of physical and social reality. If one is familiar only with household pets and animals at the zoo, it probably does not seem possible for Tarzan and the apes to converse. If one is familiar with the work of those who have trained apes to talk with them, it may seem possible. Under either definition, possible or probable, the judgments one makes ot the reality of television content ought to reflect such general knowledge. They ought also to be tempered by the realism of the portrayal. A live-action bionic man who looks and acts in lifelike ways should seem more possible than an animated collection of microcomputers, wires, and flashing lights.

Having developed these three meanings for *real*, we examined interview responses to learn what children, adolescents, and adults mean when they say something on television is real. Three sets of responses were used. One was responses to an explicit question about what they meant. The second was suggested explanations to a younger child puzzled about how to decide what was real on television. The third was explanations given for each of a series of judgments interviewees made about the reality of television content. All three measures were obtained from coding of lengthy semistructured individual interviews about television (see Dorr, Graves, & Phelps, 1980; Graves, 1976b; and Leifer, Graves, & Gordon, 1975, for descriptions of the coding; manuals are available on request).

When asked what they meant when they said something on television was real, children gave many different answers—as well as some puzzled looks. It was not until sixth grade that they were generally able to explain what they meant. The majority of kindergartners said they did not know what they meant, and the rest gave a synonym for *real* or an idiosyncratic response. The great majority of the second–third graders either said they did not know or gave an idiosyncratic response. In contrast, none of the sixth graders said they did not know what their definition was, and only some gave a synonymous or idiosyncratic definition. About half said that *real* meant something that could possibly happen, and only a very few said it was something that had happened to them or an acquaintance.

There are two age trends in the explanations children gave for what they mean when they say something on television is real. There is a reduction in children not being able to explain what they mean by *real*, and there is an increase in children meaning "possible" when they say *real*. These two trends are also apparent in children's responses to a question about what they would tell a younger child who was puzzled about how to decide what to believe on television. The percentage of children not knowing what to say decreased markedly over the three grade levels (59%, 20%, and 18%, respectively); those giving idiosyncratic responses decreased (24%, 5%, and 0%); and those referring to a decision based on possibility increased (0%, 15%, and 18%). Most of the change clearly occurred between kindergarten and second–third grade.

The increasing importance of possibility in evaluating television reality is further illustrated in the reasons children gave for the reality judgments they made throughout the interview. When reasons based on the possibility (or impossibility) of a character, action, setting, prop, or plot were expressed for each child as a percentage of all reasons given, the mean percentages increased significantly from kindergarten to sixth grade (17%, 28%, and 47%, respectively). Possibility or plausibility was the most frequent reason among second–third and sixth graders and the third most frequent among kindergarteners (after "don't know" and "television is made up").

Although the interviews with adolescents (13- and 16-year-olds) and adults were somewhat different from those with the children, some interesting comparisons are suggested. One is that almost half the 16-year-olds and adults defined *real* as something that was probable, something that had happened to them or to acquaintances. Another is that only about a quarter of the adults defined *real* as something that could possibly happen. This suggests they define *real* as probable rather than possible. The reasons that adolescents and adults gave for their reality judgments throughout the interview did not, however, show the same strong reliance on personal experience as did their definitions. Reasons based on possibility—not probability—were the most frequent for the adolescent and adult sample just as they had been for children. However, reasons based on personal experience, or probability, were second most frequent for all three ages in the adolescent and adult sample, whereas they were fourth most frequent for the children. Thus probability is a more important basis for judging television's reality for adolescents and adults than for children, although it is not quite as important for adolescents and adults as their definitions of *real* would suggest. Over the entire age range, there is a general increase in the use of probability in defining *real* and an increase and then a decrease in the use of possibility.

Thus, the meaning of the statement "X on television is real" changes considerably from kindergarten to adulthood. The youngest children cannot really explain what they mean. Others must ferret meaning out of their judgments and reasoning. Our own work and that of others (Fernie, 1981; Hawkins, 1977; Lyle & Hoffman, 1972b) suggest that at this age *real* is most likely to mean as it is in unmediated circumstances. When it does not mean this, it is likely to mean fabricated, but depicting something possible. However, many young children do not completely understand that most of what they watch is fabricated (see the section under "Knowledge of Production or Economics"). Consequently they are not as likely to operate with the second meaning of *real* as with the first. By the latter half of elementary school, children realize that at least some of what they watch is fabricated, but this does not become the primary basis for judging reality of the content. Rather the possibility that what has been fabricated for television *could* happen in real life is the criterion for judging reality. *Real* means made up, but possible in real life. This meaning of *real* remains important for adolescents and adults. However, with increasing maturity comes increasing stringency in the requirements for content judged real. More and more, *real* means made up, but probable in real life, representative of real life, like something personal acquaintances or I have experienced.

Simple Approaches to Judging Reality

Much thinking and research has assumed that viewers use simple criteria to decide about television content reality. Entertainment programming is considered fantasy not reality; informational programming is considered reality not fantasy; programming based on actual events is real; programming based on a writer's imagination is pretend. Criteria such as these require simple dichotomous judgment: discriminate entertainment from informational programming or "only the names have been changed" from "written and produced by" programming. Much of my early thinking about television reality judgments and some of our curriculum development effort (Dorr, Graves, & Phelps, 1980) reflected this perspective.

Let us explore the evidence we have since garnered for the use of simple criteria in judging what is real or realistic in television program content. As suggested in the introduction to this chapter, there are several methods that could be used to simplify the judgment process. One would utilize knowledge of television production techniques or the economics of the television industry to produce a summary judgment that entertainment programming was not real because it was made up or because it was produced and broadcast primarily to make a profit (rather than to inform or educate). Another set of methods would utilize contextual or formal features as cues to the reality of the content associated with them. Judgments could be made solely on the basis of genre, production style (animation versus live action), setting time, and so on.

Knowledge of Production or Economics

Several lines of evidence suggest slow development throughout childhood and adolescence in the knowledge that most television programming is fabricated drama whose essential purpose is to turn a profit. Adolescents and adults understand that entertainment programming is fabricated, although they may lack sophisticated knowledge of specific production techniques. However, they are generally underinformed about the primary pecuniary motivations for most programming they watch. Where knowledge about production or economics does not exist, it obviously cannot be used as a guide to judging television's reality. On the other hand, knowing about television production or industry economics does not necessitate using that knowledge to judge television reality. To have a simple judgment method based on knowledge of television production or economics, one must both have such information and also use it as the basis for one's judgments.

Work by Fernie (1981), Hawkins (1977), and others (Dorr, Graves, & Phelps, 1980; Greenberg & Reeves, 1976; Lyle & Hoffman, 1972a, 1972b) suggests that the knowledge that most television programs are made up develops during the elementary school years, although it is certainly not part of the curriculum of the school. Among working-class boys, Fernie (1981) found age-related changes throughout the elementary school years in their knowledge that television characters were portrayed by actors. Among 5- and 6-year-olds, 58% did not understand this at all. Among 8-year-olds, 45% completely understood that characters were actors; another 26% partially understood it, and only 29% did not understand it. Among 11- and 12-year-olds, 65% had complete understanding. Thus, in Fernie's data a major jump in knowledge occurred between the beginning and middle of elementary school, but, by the end of elementary school, about one-third of the boys still did not completely understand about actors. Hawkins' (1977) data also show a major jump in knowledge around the age of 8. Children older than 8 infrequently thought of television as a magic window on the world. They understood something about the fabricated nature of programming. Given the nature of Hawkins' data, however, one cannot assess how well they understood. Other studies of perceived television reality also indicate that by the time children are about 8 years old they are generally aware that television programming is made up. How completely they understand this varies, depending on the children studied and on what criteria are established for awareness.

Understanding of television as an economic system develops more slowly and less completely throughout childhood and adolescence. As reported by Phelps (1976), among those we interviewed, only adults were more likely than not to evidence complete understanding of the interrelationships among the three crucial television industry elements of ratings, advertising, and income. Only slightly more than one-half of them ever showed such complete understanding in their responses to several questions about how the industry worked. Moreover, one-half made one or more assertions that were coded as actual misconceptions.

Naturally, adults were more knowledgeable about the television industry than were children and adolescents. When each interviewee's utterances were categorized as to the degree of understanding each reflected (three levels of relevant knowledge, one of irrelevant knowledge, one of misconceptions, and one of no ideas proferred), it was possible to identify the most and least sophisticated levels of understanding ever displayed and the most frequently displayed level. All these changed significantly with age. The most sophisticated understanding ever displayed by the largest percentage of interviewees was understanding the relationship of two elements for adolescents and sixth graders, understanding one element for second–third graders, and understanding correct but irrelevant facts for kindergartners. The most frequently expressed levels of understanding were lower than the most sophisticated level ever displayed: isolated facts or misconceptions for the adolescents and sixth graders, misconceptions for the second–third graders, and no proferred ideas for kindergartners. Subsequent work with another sample of kindergartners and second–third graders found significant increases with age in knowledge about the television industry as expressed in response to closed-ended and open-ended questions. The absolute level of understanding was still low; incorrect ideas were expounded more than correct ones in the free-response situation, and there was no significant decrease with age in the number of incorrect ideas expressed (Dorr, Graves, & Phelps, 1980).

These findings suggest several things about viewers' opportunities to use knowledge of television production or economics as a guide to judging the reality of television content. First, younger children have little such knowledge to guide their judgments. Second, sometime around the age of 8, a majority of children have some understanding that entertainment programming is fabricated, an understanding that could be used to guide reality judgments. Third, by the beginning of adolescence virtually all viewers understand the fabricated nature of entertainment programming and have understood it for some time. Fourth, not until somewhere in adolescence is there any understanding of the economic motivations guiding production and broadcasting. Fifth, even in adulthood understanding of the economics of the television industry is often incomplete. Thus, reality judgments based solely on the knowledge that television is a fabricated experience could be present in kindergartners and could increase in frequency from then until adolescence; judgments based solely on the motivations for producing and broadcasting programming could only first occur in adolescence and would be unlikely to occur often at any age. To say, however, that knowledge is *available* to use as a guide to reality judgments is not to say that it *is* used. That depends on viewers' decisions about what knowledge is best used as a guide to judging the reality of television content.

Several findings from interviews with children, adolescents, and adults (Graves, 1976b; Leifer, Graves, & Gordon, 1975) and from an evaluation of two television literacy curricula for children (Dorr, Graves, & Phelps, 1980) pertain to this issue of how much production and industry knowledge are used. Those relating to use of knowledge of the television industry conform most closely to the assessments of amount of knowledge. In the interview study no children (of 54) ever referred to industry economics in explaining why they believed any television content was real or pretend. In the curriculum evaluation, 7 kindergartners and second–third graders (of 88) referred to industry economics as a reason for a fantasy–reality judgment. Of the 7, 4 had participated in a curriculum designed to teach industry economics and its import for reality judgments. The remaining 3 children were part of the 58 who had participated in a different curriculum or a control condition. Overall, the data support the idea that children very infrequently use industry economics as a basis for deciding about television content reality.

Adolescents and adults sometimes did use knowledge of industry economics to guide their reality judgments. With increasing age, such reasoning constituted an increasing percentage of all reasons given for fantasy–reality judgments, being about 10% of all reasons given by 13-year-olds and about 25% of all reasons given by adults. It should be noted, however, that these ideas were never as important a basis for judging reality as were the more complex comparisons of television content with physical and social reality (possibility and probability reasons). For 13- and 16-year-olds, references to industry economics were much less frequent than references to possibility or probability (roughly 10% for industry economics, 22% for probability, and 43% for possibility). Among adults these three bases for judgment were used more nearly equally, although industry knowledge was still the least frequently used (roughly 25% for industry economics, 30% for probability, and 35% for possibility as reasons for fantasy/reality judgments). Thus, although not the main weapon in the judgment arsenal, knowledge of the motivations for producing and broadcasting programming serves as a criterion for reality judgments beginning in early adolescence (in untutored samples) and becomes a more important criterion as viewers mature.

Knowledge of television production, in contrast, was practically never used as a basis for reality judgments by adolescents and adults. Given that every adolescent and adult interviewee probably knew that entertainment programming was fabricated, one concludes that by adolescence this fact is so accepted that it is not even commented upon. Rather, what is evaluated is the extent to which the fabrication is related to real life. The same cannot be said for elementary school-age children. They sometimes referred to the fact that television programming was made up—usually commenting at that level of generality—as a basis for the reality judgments they had just made. Such knowledge constituted 15% of the reasons kindergartners gave for their reality judgments, 23% of second–third-graders' reasons, and 19% of sixth-graders' reasons. The only more frequently given reason for a reality judgment was "don't know" which constituted 40% of kindergartners' responses and 22% of second–third-graders' responses. These figures suggest that understanding that television is a fabricated experience is a relatively important judgment criterion for young television viewers, but its importance should not be overestimated. If this knowledge were a prepotent criterion for younger children's assessments of television reality, then one would expect them to find more television content to be pretend than would older children. Such is not the case. There were no significant changes over the three ages in the percentage of children's judgments that were pretend.

Television Form or Context

Like knowledge of television production or economics, context or formal features of television programming may be used as a guide to the reality of the content embedded in them. Our data have suggested some interesting possibilities about children's use of such features to simplify the process of deciding what television content is real. In all cases we have been interested in the consistent use of a form cue to decide that specific content is real or pretend, but not both. What the cue signified (real or pretend) was determined by how children chose to use it. As shown in Table 8.1 the percentage of children ever using any form cue increases dramatically between kindergarten and second–third grade. The number of different forms that children report utilizing also increases with age. All kindergartners find cartoons to be fantasy, and a few find witches and genies to be pretend and news and crime-drama programs to be real. Second–third and sixth graders utilize all four of these form cues and six others as well. Television genre clearly serves as a useful cue to reality for the older children. Interestingly, many sixth graders feel a simple statement that a program is based on facts is a reliable indicator that it is real. Fully 50% of those who mentioned any form cue at all spontaneously mentioned this one. This is almost as many as spontaneously stated that a news format was a cue that content was real.

Other analyses of our data provided additional support for the ideas that children use form as a guide to reality and that there are age

Table 8.1

Percentage of Children by Age Using Television Forms as Cues to Reality

	Kindergarten (N = 11)[a]	Second–Third (N = 38)	Sixth (N = 28)
Children ever using any form cue	55	84	88
Genre			
Cartoons (pretend)[b]	100[c]	82	61
Comedy (pretend)	0	13	21
Crime drama (pretend)	0	19	10
Crime drama (real)	18	21	7
News (real)	10	37	57
Sports (real)	0	5	43
Characters			
Ghosts, monsters, vampires (pretend)	0	26	18
Witches, genies (pretend)	10	24	11
Time			
Past or future (pretend)	0	11	11
Disclaimer			
This story true (real)	0	21	50

[a]Number of children who spontaneously gave at least one response in which television form was the reason for a reality judgment.

[b]Read as "Cartoons as a cue that content is pretend."

[c]Percentage of children giving any form cue who gave this one.

changes in its use. For instance, there are clear age changes in children's understanding that reality may vary according to program type. Nearly all sixth graders (94%) report that there are some kinds of programs they can believe more than others, whereas 44% of the kindergartners and 75% of the second–third graders so report. Also, there is a slight increase with age in children's suggestions that program type would be a good guide to television reality for a younger child (0%, 10%, and 18%, respectively), and some use of other form cues as well. Finally, over age, program type constituted an increasingly larger percentage of the content whose reality was judged. For children the percentages were 6%, 9%, and 12%, respectively. Comparable percentages for adolescents and adults were roughly 15%, 18%, and 25%.

Our data suggest that children sometimes use form cues to judge television reality. Kindergartners made infrequent explicit reference to doing so in the interview. Only about one-half could be scored as ever using a form cue, and they only mentioned four such cues. By second–third grade most children made some reference to using form cues, and a wide variety of such cues were mentioned. Kindergartners seemed to think content was pretend when it looked fantastic—cartoons, witches, and genies—and real when it looked realistic and was not humorous—news and crime dramas. Second–third graders relied on similar types of cues with witches, genies, ghosts, monsters, and vampires often being singled out. They more often used genres as a cue to reality and appreciated the information contained in program disclaimers. By sixth grade the most visually unrealistic elements—cartoons and fantasy characters—were not mentioned so often as form cues. It is unlikely that sixth graders do not recognize these cues, rather they are probably so well accepted that they are not even mentioned.

The full extent of children's use of any form cues, such as the use of animation as a cue by sixth graders, cannot be determined because of certain characteristics of our data:

1. Only those children who clearly indicated that their reality judgments were based on television form were included in the analyses.
2. Only those aspects of form that were brought up spontaneously by a child were coded.
3. Only those television forms with which children were familiar were discussed.

These choices made in gathering and coding data mean that the number of kindergartners included in analyses is smaller than desirable. They also mean we cannot conclude that children never use or cannot use a particular form as a basis for judgment. Had we chosen to ask them about various forms, rather than rely on what they spontaneously brought up, we would be better able to decide if they could or did use a form as a cue to reality. As it is we can identify some form cues children use, but we cannot be sure we have identified them all. Undoubtedly, more structured testing would show the older children, adolescents, and adults recognized and used cues such as cartoons and witches, but it would be unlikely to show that younger children recognized and used the cues older children spontaneously mentioned.

Thus with age there is increasing ability to use, and actual use of, form cues as a simple heuristic for judging the reality of television content. However, our data also show that form cues never serve as the predominant criterion for assessing reality. This again suggests that more complex judgment techniques may frequently be used by viewers. The next section presents more direct evidence that this is indeed the case.

Complex Approaches to Judging Reality

I have now suggested that simple approaches to judging the reality of television content are used by viewers, that their availability for use increases with age, and that there is some increase with age in their use. It is possible for viewers to summarily dismiss cartoons as fantasy, dramas set in the future as made up, monsters and genies as unreal, and even all entertainment programming as fabricated. The characters, actions, settings, objects, and messages in each of these contexts can therefore be dismissed as things not to be taken seriously. It is equally possible for viewers to take characters, actions, settings, objects, and messages seriously because they are in a live-action format (which is deemed real), because entertainment programming is designed to teach and inform (which many youngsters believe), or because noncomedic approaches mean people are serious about the content (which several children told us). In both cases the methods for deciding about the reality of television content are relatively simple, whether or not they lead to accurate decisions. The criteria are few and rather easy to apply; once made, each judgment applies to much content. A viewer need make relatively few independent judgments.

Our data suggest, however, that viewers are not so economy-minded. Television is not a near monolith. Its content is not usually evaluated at the level of production technique or purpose or formal feature. Rather it is evaluated at the level of characters, what they do, what happens to them, what their surroundings are, and so on. In our interviews, respondents were mostly free to select the aspects of television content they judged. No interviewee selected only one or two and confined his or her discussion to them. No one simply stuck to the fact that entertainment programming was made up, although at the time the interviews were done we were looking for such simple approaches. Overall children did not focus on broad criteria and summary judgments.

In the interviews everyone was asked to make one judgment about the reality of entertainment programming, one about all programming, one about an entertainment program we had shown them, and one about an entertainment program they said they especially liked to watch. Other than that, nearly all the content to be judged was chosen by the interviewee during the course of the interview. On the average, an interviewee made about 40 separate judgments of content during the interview. The content categories listed in Table 8.2 are all those judged at least once by at least one-half the children in at least one of three age groups (kindergarten, second–third grade, sixth grade). There are 11 such content categories, exactly one-half the total number for which we originally coded. (The other 11 content categories were monsters, objects, sets–costumes–props, plot, human characters and nonhuman acts, nonhuman characters and human acts, production techniques, specific science fiction programs by name, specific news–sports–documentary programs by name, situation comedy as a genre, and science fiction as a genre.) At least 75% of the children at each age talked about television in general, entertainment programming, characters, specific incidents, and particular situation comedies. The remaining 6 categories of content listed in the table were mentioned at least once by between one-third and two-thirds of the children at any age. There is a small but significant age-related increase in the number of different content categories mentioned by each child (9.2, 11.3, and 12.6, respectively).

One noteworthy aspect of the data presented in Table 8.2 is how few decisions children made about most content categories, despite the fact that the average total number of judgments was about 40. For 7 of the 11 categories in Table 8.2 (remember, these were the most commonly mentioned of 22 coded categories), the average number of comments per child, given that the category is mentioned at all, is just slightly more or less than two. The remaining 4 content categories are mentioned more often. Characters, specific situation comedies, and specific crime dramas are all likely to be brought up 3 or 4 times by any child who mentions them at least once. Incidents are brought up 7.3, 9.6, and 14.5 times, respectively per kindergarten, second–third-grade, and sixth-grade child who mentions incidents at all. Children's changing viewing

Table 8.2

Percentage of Children by Age Mentioning a Content Category and Average Number of Mentions by Them

	Kindergarten (N = 17)	Second–Third (N = 20)	Sixth (N = 17)	All (N = 54)
People real, acting pretend	41[a]	70	53	56
	(2.4)[b]	(2.0)	(1.8)	(2.0)
Characters	88	85	76	83
	(3.3)	(3.6)	(3.8)	(3.6)
Incidents	94	100	100	98
	(7.3)	(9.6)	(14.5)	(10.5)
Programs by name				
Cartoons	65	40	18	41
	(1.9)	(1.8)	(1.3)	(1.8)
Situation comedies	82	90	100	91
	(2.9)	(4.0)	(4.2)	(3.7)
Crime dramas	18	35	65	39
	(1.7)	(3.3)	(3.2)	(3.0)
Program genres				
Cartoons	47	65	65	61
	(1.4)	(1.5)	(1.3)	(1.4)
Crime dramas	41	55	35	44
	(1.3)	(1.5)	(2.0)	(1.5)
News–sports–documentary	18	25	53	31
	(1.3)	(1.4)	(2.0)	(1.7)
Entertainment programs	94	75	82	83
	(1.6)	(1.3)	(1.3)	(1.4)
All television	88	100	82	91
	(2.3)	(2.4)	(1.9)	(2.2)

[a]Percentage of children in the age group who ever mentioned this content category.

[b]Numbers in parentheses indicate average number of mentions of this content category by those children who ever mentioned it.

patterns are reflected by a significant increase with age in mentions of specific crime dramas and a significant decrease in mentions of specific cartoons. Taking into consideration the kinds of content the interviewer asked about (all television programming and entertainment programming), the proportion of children bringing up a category of content, and the average number of judgments about it, one concludes that television content and its reality are thought about primarily in terms of incidents, events, or actions carried out by characters. Most of these are in specific situation comedies, whose reality may itself be judged.

In examining the fantasy–reality decisions children made about the content categories presented in Table 8.2, one finds that much content is simultaneously judged real, pretend, and both real and pretend by the three age groups combined (see Table 8.3). The notable exceptions to this are that cartoons as a genre and as specific programs are generally considered to be pretend, news–sports–documentary as genres are real, crime dramas as a genre and as specific programs are real, and entertainment programming in general is pretend. Judgments about the reality of characters, incidents, specific situation comedies, and television in general are more mixed. Judgments about actors and acting (people are real; acting, pretend) are also mixed, but this is an artifact of coding a judgment "real" if a child seemed to be focusing on the actor and "pretend" if focusing on the acting.

Table 8.3

Average Number of Decisions Made for Each Reality Judgment and Content Category and Number of Children on Whom Average Is Based

	Real	Mostly real	Real and pretend	Mostly pretend	Pretend	Don't know
People real, acting pretend	2.0[a]	—	1.0	—	1.2	—
	(20)[b]	(0)	(1)	(0)	(21)	(0)
Characters	1.9	1.0	1.0	1.7	2.4	1.8
	(29)	(8)	(5)	(6)	(37)	(4)
Incidents	3.1	2.9	2.0	2.3	4.2	1.5
	(45)	(41)	(21)	(15)	(46)	(18)
Programs by name						
Cartoons	1.1	1.0	—	—	1.5	1.7
	(8)	(1)	(0)	(0)	(16)	(3)
Situation comedies	2.2	1.0	1.2	1.0	2.0	1.4
	(23)	(14)	(11)	(4)	(33)	(28)
Crime dramas	1.6	1.8	1.0	1.0	2.8	1.2
	(13)	(4)	(4)	(1)	(9)	(8)
Program genres						
Cartoons	1.0	—	1.0	1.3	1.3	1.5
	(1)	(0)	(2)	(3)	(29)	(2)
Crime dramas	1.3	1.0	1.1	1.3	1.2	—
	(11)	(3)	(10)	(3)	(8)	(0)
News–sports–documentary	1.6	—	1.0	1.0	1.0	1.5
	(17)	(0)	(2)	(1)	(1)	(2)
Entertainment programs	1.0	0.7	1.0	1.0	1.0	1.2
	(6)	(3)	(9)	(4)	(27)	(13)
All television	1.1	1.0	1.2	1.1	1.4	1.3
	(7)	(3)	(21)	(9)	(25)	(25)

[a]Average number of decisions made for the indicated reality judgment and content category by children who ever made such a decision.

[b]Number of children who ever made the indicated reality judgment about the indicated content category.

On inspecting these data for the three ages separately, only one age difference was apparent. Older children were more likely to perceive specific crime dramas to be realistic. Although in this one instance children's judgments that content is real increase with age, this is not true over all the judgments children made. As shown in Table 8.3, reality judgments were categorized into five decisions (real, mostly real, real and pretend, mostly pretend, and pretend), don't know, and no answer. There was a significant increase with age in the number of different types of decisions made (4.6, 5.5, and 6.1, respectively), a significant increase in the percentage of all decisions which were mostly real, real and pretend, and mostly pretend (12.5, 18.7, and 28.8, respectively), rather than entirely real or entirely pretend, and no significant changes by age in the percentages of real, pretend, or don't know decisions. Very similar findings about age changes in fantasy–reality decisions were obtained in subsequent work with kindergartners and second–third graders (Dorr, Graves, & Phelps, 1980).

Our data on the television content children choose to judge and on the reality decisions they make show no monolithic view of television reality. Children between the ages of 5 and 12 talk about many different types of content and make both real and pretend judgments about nearly every type. Characters, actions and events, and particular situation comedies are the most frequent types of content judged by children. Each seems to invite particularistic reality judgments, and the data show this. Some exemplars of each of these types of content are realistic; some are not, and some are both real and pretend. Television as a whole and all entertainment programs are also frequently judged by the children, but mainly because we asked them to do so. They invite broader reality judgments, which are shown in the data. When asked to judge at this level, children find entertainment programs to be mostly pretend and television in general to be either pretend or both real and pretend.

There are few age differences in these findings. Older children are likely to talk about more different types of content, to use more mixed reality judgments, to use genre more often as a guide to television reality, and to talk about more crime drama, news, and sports programming and about fewer cartoons. Their changing viewing preferences, from children's programming to prime-time, are reflected in the programs and genres they choose to talk about. They become more diverse, moderate, and sophisticated in their views, but they still talk most about actors and actions. The picture that emerges is one of all children focusing on the heart of storytelling—characters and what happens to them—and judging reality in a rather particularistic fashion. This approach to judgment and the variety of reality judgments made indicate that more often than not children adopt complex strategies for judging the reality of television programming.

Reality Is Always There to Judge

Evaluating the reality of entertainment programming is apparently accomplished through the use of complex judgments. Most programming is realistic in format, with real people engaged in realistic behaviors and events. Children consume such programming as stories about what protagonists do and what happens to them. The reality of characters and incidents is largely judged within the context of the program and the child's knowledge of the world. Reality is that which is plausible or that which has actually been experienced by the child or an acquaintance. This is so even when the child recognizes that entertainment programming is the product of other people's imaginations.

Recent work has suggested that all the children we interviewed would be aware of the process and products of imagination (Silberstein, Winner, Cadogan, & Gardner, 1980). They could have accurately discussed what they imagine, why they imagine, and whether other people imagine. Yet there would be marked age differences in their ability to apply this knowledge to such products of imagination as entertainment programs. In particular, our kindergartners and second–third graders would be less likely to recognize a program as a fantasy, because it does not explicitly show that it is someone's imaginings. Children of this age have difficulty supplying such information themselves. As Hawkins (1977) suggests, the youngest children in our studies might even still consider entertainment programming to be a "magic window" on reality. Moreover, for all the children, fantasy versus reality is apparently not a prepotent criterion for classifying things (Morison & Gardner, 1978). These factors, however, will not fully explain our findings.

The magic window conception of programming would be unlikely among the second–third and sixth graders we interviewed. It probably did not even occur among the majority of the kindergartners. If it had, we should have obtained age differences in children's judgments that television content was real and in their overall evaluation of the reality of entertainment programming. We did not. At the same time we do not find the majority of children's judgments about television content to be that it is fantasy. They may all know that imagination creates stories and that television is not a magic window, but these are not their bases for judging the reality of television content.

Television's reality is mostly judged through content-specific evaluations of its social reality, a factor that Hawkins (1977) also did not find changing during childhood. For the younger children in our sample, willingness to judge some entertainment content as real is probably heightened by the fact that much of it looks real. They are not repeatedly remained by animation, voiceover, or some other technique that it is the product of someone's imagination. Under such circumstances, as Silberstein et al. (1980) have noted, the younger children might know the content was fantasy yet have difficulty recognizing that all characters' attributes, actions, and cognitions were the product of others' imaginations. Imaginings once brought to life tend to have lives of their own. Second–third graders in our studies best illustrated this. They asserted such things as that actors and actresses who play married couples must certainly be very close friends and that those engaged in violence wear bulletproof vests just in case the bullets are not fake. Even adults fall prey to the realism of the portrayals. As related earlier in this chapter, one asserted that Edith Bunker was more realistic than Mary Richards. This was so because we saw Edith in her own home where one is more revealing of self but saw Mary at work where one is more reserved. What ever happened to scripts and sets?

Most of children's thinking about television does not seem to relate context writ large to content writ small. Entertainment programming is not interpreted all of a piece, even if nearly all children recognize it to be a created product. Even specific genres are not interpreted all of a piece much of the time. Characters and incidents within genres are evaluated. Genre may influence the final reality decision, but it is not often its major determinant. Animation, at least as it is represented in current children's programming, is one exception to this generalization. Children often, but not always, use the presence of animation as a cue that program content is fantasy. News and sports are genres that are recognized as presenting reality, but because they have not been explored in any depth in our work we cannot say much about the extent to which content in those genres is consistently viewed as realistic.

The realistic aspects of television form and/or content present challenges to children, who need to decide what content to accept, and to adults, who need to help children learn how to do this well. These challenges would be less if our television system had become the educational one once envisioned or if our culture were a much more homogeneous one. In these circumstances all content would be more useful for children and/or more compatible with adult values. Things have not turned out that way, however. The programs children watch are usually not designed as responsible instruction, and the social values in our culture are quite heterogeneous. In such an environment it becomes important to understand children's judgments about the realism, believability, or utility of television content.

Our work shows that, when judging television's reality, children use contextual cues some of the time and that the number of children using such cues and the number of different cues utilized increase with age. Clearly those who produce television and those who guide children's use of it should provide more contextual cues and increase children's use of them. They should also teach children about television production and industry economics. Increasing such knowledge and providing more contextual cues would surely help children better decide what television content to take seriously. It is unlikely, however, that context or television knowledge would be the basis for the majority of children's decisions. Instead children will look at characters and incidents in each program and evaluate them based somewhat on program characteristics and more on what they know or guess to be possible or probable in the real world. The belief that entertainment programming represents social reality does not seem to change much with greater life experience or exposure to television (Hawkins, 1977). Such programming may be recognized as fantasy, but it is fantasy grounded in or applicable to social reality. As such, children's views of television reality largely reflect their viewing patterns (for what is judged) and their world knowledge (for how realistic it is judged to be). Identifying which program content to take seriously more often than not requires a complex judgment process. It is only somewhat simplified by understanding the contexts of genres, production processes, and industry economics within which the content occurs. Children simply take few shortcuts in deciding which televised ideas, beliefs, attitudes, and actions to take seriously.

Acknowledgments

I am particularly grateful to Cynthia Char, Catherine Doubleday, Peter Kovaric, and Erin Phelps for their assistance with various portions of the work reported here.

References

Berkowitz, L., & Alioto, J. T. The meaning of an observed event as a determinant of its aggressive consequences. *Journal of Personality and Social Psychology*, 1973, *28*, 206–217.

Dorr, A. When I was a child, I thought as a child. In S. B. Withey & R. P. Abeles (Eds.), *Television and social behavior: Beyond violence and children*. Hillsdale, N.J.: Erlbaum, 1980.

Dorr, A., Graves, S. B., & Phelps, E. Television literacy for young children. *Journal of Communication*, 1980, *30*(3), 71–83.

Fernie, D. E. *Ordinary and extraordinary people: Children's understanding of television and real-life models*. Paper presented at the Society for Research in Child Development Biennial Meeting, Boston, April 1981.

Feshbach, S. Reality and fantasy in filmed violence. In J. P. Murray, E. A. Rubinstein, & G. A. Comstock (Eds.), *Television and social behavior* (Vol. 2), *Television and social learning*. Washington, D.C.: U.S. Government Printing Office, 1972.

Forté, M. *Cognitive processes for evaluating the credibility of television content*. Paper presented at the American Psychological Association Meeting, Washington, D.C., September 1976.

Graves, S. B. *Content attended to in evaluating television's credibility*. Paper presented at the American Psychological Association Meeting, Washington, D.C., September 1976. (a)

Graves, S. B. *Overview of the project*. Paper presented at the American Psychological Association Meeting, Washington, D.C., September 1976. (b)

Greenberg, B. S., & Reeves, B. Children and the perceived reality of television. *Journal of Social Issues*, 1976, *32*, 86–97.

Hawkins, R. P. The dimensional structure of children's perceptions of television reality. *Communication Research*, 1977, 4(3), 299–320.

Leifer, A. D. *Factors which predict the credibility ascribed to television*. Paper presented at the American Psychological Association Meeting, Washington, D.C., September 1976.

Leifer, A. D., Graves, S. B., & Gordon, N. J. *When people think television is a window on their world*. Paper presented at the American Educational Research Association Meeting, Washington, D.C., April 1975.

Lemon, J. *Teaching children to become more critical consumers of television*. Paper presented at the American Psychological Association Meeting, Washington, D.C., September 1976.

Lyle, J., & Hoffman, H. R. Children's use of television and other media. In E. A. Rubinstein, G. A. Comstock, & J. P. Murray (Eds.), *Television and social behavior* (Vol. 4), *Television in day-to-day life: Patterns of use*. Washington, D.C.: U.S. Government Printing Office, 1972. (a)

Lyle, J., & Hoffman, H. R. Explorations in patterns of television viewing by preschool-age children. In E. A. Rubinstein, G. A. Comstock, & J. P. Murray (Eds.), *Television and social behavior* (Vol. 4), *Television in day-to-day life: Patterns of use*. Washington, D.C.: U.S. Government Printing Office, 1972. (b)

Morison, P., & Gardner, H. Dragons and dinosaurs: The child's capacity to differentiate fantasy from reality. *Child Development*, 1978, *49*, 642–648.

Phelps, E. M. *Knowledge of the television industry and relevant first-hand experience*. Paper presented at the American Psychological Association Meeting, Washington, D.C., September 1976.

Schramm, W., Lyle, J., & Parker, E. B. *Television in the lives of our children*. Stanford, Calif.: Stanford University Press, 1961.

Silberstein, L., Winner, E., Cadogan, P., & Gardner, H. *Fantasy's source: Children's awareness of imagination*. Paper presented at the American Psychological Association Meeting, Montreal, September 1980.

chapter **9**

Entertainment Features in Children's Educational Television: Effects on Attention and Information Acquisition[1]

JENNINGS BRYANT
DOLF ZILLMANN
DAN BROWN

Introduction

During the early years of research on *Sesame Street*, the Children's Television Workshop (CTW) staff identified three viewing styles among 3–5-year-old consumers of their program (cf. Lesser, 1972): (*a*) children who "view television for hours with their eyes rarely leaving the set," the so-called "zombie viewer" (Reeves, 1970, p. 11); (*b*) "those who constantly keep a check on all outside activities in the room while they view" (Reeves, 1970, p. 11), the "dual attention viewer" (Maccoby, 1967); and (*c*) children who display "overt, active physical, and verbal participation in the televised action" (Lesser, 1972, p. 114), perhaps best identified as the "modeling viewer." When presenting these descriptions, the CTW staff frequently issued a caveat: There appears to be little systematic relationship between viewing style and learning (e.g., Reeves, 1970, p. 11).

Numerous scholars, most notably several of the contributors to this volume, have apparently accepted this CTW caveat as a challenge, as

[1]The authors' research discussed in this chapter is part of a program of research into the uses and effects of elements of entertainment in educational television that was supported by grant APR77-13902 from the National Science Foundation.

221

they have paid considerable attention to specifics in the relationship between watching television and learning from its educational messages. In fact, the research reported in this chapter specifically examines the effects on attention and learning of a phenomenon popularized by *Sesame Street*, the use of entertainment in educational material. This marriage of education with entertainment is one of the recent revolutions in teaching, a union which has yielded progeny that might be called "learning can be fun," "learning while they laugh," and "education by entertainment." Why was this marriage arranged? Largely because of necessity.

Capturing and holding an audience in the face of competition from commercial entertainment programming has been and is a major concern of educational television. Viewers have the option of switching at any time from educational content to comedy, drama, games, or sports. Audiences for television, unlike textbook readers, tend to be relatively unmotivated by interest or obligation and tend to seek content that is immediately gratifying and of little practical utility. Viewers, especially children, who do not find immediate gratification for educational programs should be expected to watch alternative programs which provide such fare. Therefore, educational programmers have incorporated humor, special effects, background music, and other entertaining features to attract viewers to their television teaching.

In 1977, the National Science Foundation funded a project to assess the uses and effects of entertainment features in educational television. Nearly 30 studies were conducted during the course of this investigation. Many of these studies assessed, among other things, the effects of the use of humor and other entertainment devices on selective exposure to the educational message, on attention to particular portions of the message, and on information acquisition. These findings will be reported in this chapter.

Levels of Attention

Watching television involves different levels of attention. For example, *selective exposure* pertains to attention to one particular televised message rather than another (i.e., channel selection) or choosing to view a particular television program versus engaging in other activities. This type of attention typically involves gross motor activity (e.g., changing channels, body locomotion). Factors involved in selective exposure to television programs have only recently been investigated.

On the other hand, attention to educational programs has frequently been assessed at a more refined (i.e., fine motor) level. Investigators have examined "eyes to the screen" or to a specific portion of the screen or object on the screen as indices of *visual attention*. The relationship between visual attention and selective exposure is largely unknown, and the more frequently examined relationship between visual attention and information acquisition is a topic of considerable debate. The notion that viewers who pay more attention to a television program will learn more from it may appear intuitively attractive, but the CTW finding that viewing style is apparently unrelated to learning serves as a warning against premature conclusions in this regard. Furthermore, some investigators have argued forcefully that message comprehensibility more likely facilitates attention than visual attention improves message comprehension (see Chapter 1 by Anderson & Lorch). It should be noted that the bulk of the research to be presently reviewed deals with information acquisition, rather than comprehension, as an index of learning, and so is of limited utility in clarifying the causal direction between visual attention and comprehension. Whenever possible, however, the strength of the association between these variables will be noted.

Entertainment Features and Selective Exposure

The producers of educational television programs for children frequently employ entertainment features (Bryant, Hezel, & Zillmann, 1979) as a facilitator of initial attention; many believe a program's success in attracting an audience depends on it (Lesser, 1974). However, until very recently, no evidence existed to support or refute the presumed beneficial effects of entertainment on selective exposure to educational fare. The first investigation to address this issue was conducted by Wakshlag, Day, and Zillmann (1981).

Humor as a Facilitator of Selective Exposure

In the investigation by Wakshlag, Day, and Zillmann, educational programs were manipulated to create versions without humor and versions with humor in a slow, intermediate, and fast pace. The amount of humor was kept constant in all humor versions by combining episodes into blocks (12 individual episodes in the fast-pace versions; six blocks of 2 episodes in the intermediate-pace versions; three blocks of 4 episodes in the slow-pace versions). The variation could thus be described as "cluttering" versus "clustering" of humor in an educational message. These manipulated messages competed against two others that were simultaneously available for display on the television monitor. Ostensibly in a waiting period, first- and second-grade schoolchildren could watch any of these programs for as long as they pleased; or they could, just like at home, turn off the set. Unknown to the children, their program selections were automatically recorded. This experimental procedure had proved useful as a simulation of noncaptive audience conditions in the study of preferences for different types of entertainment programs (cf. Zillmann, Hezel, & Medoff, 1980).

It was found, first of all, that the presence of humor in educational programs greatly facilitated selective exposure. Both boys and girls spent much more time watching the programs when they were embellished with humorous tidbits than when they were presented in unadorned form. The study, then, leaves no doubt that children who are not coerced into watching certain programs and who are free to watch as they please will favor humorous over nonhumorous educational television. Or put another way: The findings show that nonentertaining educational television is likely to compete very poorly with other programs, especially with entertaining ones, whenever the respondent is free to choose from several available offerings.

Second, and more important to the message designer, the study revealed significant differences in selective exposure as the result of the particular distribution of humorous episodes in an educational message. As can be seen from Figure 9.1, the fast pacing of humorous stimuli—presumably because in the initial sampling of available programs such stimuli were more frequently encountered and because the more frequent encounter prevented further sampling of competing programs—attracted the viewers more rapidly and held them more effectively to the program. Successively slower pacing of humorous stimuli proved successively less effective in both regards. Clearly, if attracting an audience were the sole objective of educational television, humorous stimuli should be frequently interspersed in educational messages, ideally without disrupting the flow of the message. The continuity of the educational message is, of course, imperative; and, to assure this continuity, the limits to placing humorous stimuli need to be recognized. However, for preschoolers, demands on attention span have to be kept to a minimum anyway, and the frequent employment of humorous stimuli is unlikely to be disruptive. Similarly, many educational messages to children in the lower grades (e.g., messages designed to teach spelling) are composed of short, self-contained units and can readily tolerate the frequent insertion of humorous stimuli. Generally

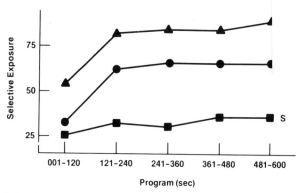

Figure 9.1. *Selective exposure to educational programs as a function of differently paced humorous inserts. The programs, one at a time, competed with two others that were simultaneously available for display on a television monitor. The fast-paced interspersion of humor (F, triangles) proved more effective in attracting and sustaining an audience than the interspersion of the same humorous materials at an intermediate pace (I, circles); the latter, in turn, proved more effective than the interspersion of humor at a slow pace (S, squares). (Adapted from Wakshlag, Day, & Zillmann, 1981.)*

speaking then, it appears that, as long as essential message continuities are not disrupted, the employment of humorous tidbits in a rapid pace—the so-called cluttering—is superior to any slower-pace "time-outs for humor"—the so-called clustering—in attracting and sustaining a broadcast audience.

The audience-drawing capacity of rapidly paced humor has also been demonstrated for adolescents. In an investigation that used high school seniors as subjects (Schleicher, Bryant, & Zillmann, 1980), it was found that the fast pacing of humorous stimuli in educational programs attracted more students for longer periods of time to the screen than did the interspersion of the same stimuli at a slower pace.

Background Music as a Facilitator
of Selective Exposure

Not only does humor facilitate selective exposure to educational television programs, background music also has that effect. Wakshlag, Reitz, and Zillmann (1981) reasoned that appealing music should attract viewers to television and hold them once they have been attracted. Since fast music seems to elicit more active and positive moods, and, since programs with fast, appealing music should be more immediately gratifying than the same programs without such music, viewers tuning in programs with more gratifying music constantly in the background should be less likely to sample other programs containing less gratifying music or no music.

To test the effect of background music on selective exposure, pretested music was dubbed into the background of nonhumorous educational films, which were systematically rotated. The experiment involved (a) one program with fast, appealing background music; (b) a second with slow, unappealing music; and (c) a control with no background music. In a procedure that was virtually identical to that employed by Wakshlag, Day, and Zillmann (1981), first- and second-grade children were given an opportunity to choose from the simultaneously available programs. The findings indicated that after a short scanning of all available programs, boys and girls settled on one program and typically remained with it for some time. Similar to the attentional inertia described by Anderson, Alwitt, Lorch, and Levin (1979), the findings indicate that there appears to be an exposure inertia such that the longer a child views the program, the less likely he or she is to search for another. Appealing music of fast tempo produced exposure time significantly above the levels associated with the no-music control and the program with unappealing background music of slow tempo. Exposure times of the latter two programs did not differ significantly.

Entertainment Features and Visual Attention

The Wakshlag, Reitz, and Zillmann (1981) study provided for the first time in a single study a useful operational distinction between selective exposure and visual attention. Selective exposure was assessed by the length of time a subject chose to tune in and remain tuned to a particular television message; visual attention was assessed in the inverse of the traditional manner—length of time of eyes on screen—by measuring the time subjects had their eyes off of the television screen. As this measurement differentiation suggests, exposure does not dictate visual attention—the subject could tune to a particular channel without ever looking at the picture. Nor does visual attention necessarily influence selective exposure, at least not in many of the protocols employed to assess visual attention. Viewers in many studies have been placed in a stimulus-sparse environment with little potential for actual exposure selection (e.g., Zillmann, Williams, Bryant, Boynton, & Wolf, 1980). What has been assessed under such conditions is whether or not viewers watched the material presented by the experimenter. The possibility exists that entertainment features may facilitate selective exposure to educational messages, yet impair and have little impact on visual attention. Recent evidence indicates, however, that entertainment features are excellent attractors of attention and typically facilitate attention to educational messages as well as to entertaining inserts.

Humor as a Facilitator of Visual Attention

In an experiment by Zillmann, Williams, Bryant, Boynton, and Wolf (1980), conducted with 5- and 6-year-old boys and girls, which examined both visual attention and information acquisition as a function of differently paced humorous inserts, various experimental programs were created by inserting humorous stimuli that are characteristic of children's fare. Similar to the investigation by Wakshlag, Day, and Zillmann (1981) reported earlier, humorous episodes were edited into the educational message proper, and these episodes were distributed differently to create a condition of fast pace (individual episodes) and a condition of slow pace (two episodes blocked together, without changing either the sequence of presentation or the amount of material). Since the humorous materials were added to the message proper, the humorous versions of the program were necessarily longer. Also, since the two distributions of humorous stimuli can be construed as different sets of message disruptions that may uniquely affect information acquisition, controls for both time and particular distribution of humorous inserts were necessary. However, these additional controls produced effects that did not appreciably differ from the effect produced by the message proper, and it consequently suffices here to compare the humor versions against the message proper alone.

The study, then, explored not only the effect of the involvement of humor, but the effects of the pacing of humorous episodes throughout an educational television program as well. The variation in pace should be of particular interest to the message designer, because it is a variable that lends itself to arbitrary manipulation. In this connection, it should be pointed out that in the discussed investigation the humorous episodes employed bore no particular semantic relationship with the educational message. Pace manipulations using such "unrelated" humor are obviously virtually unlimited.

The children paid close attention to the educational segments, regardless of the involvement of humorous episodes. They kept their eyes on the screen for 95% of the exposure time, perhaps because of the experimental procedure that limited distraction through the presence of supervisors, materials that were especially designed for child au-

le anticipation of questions about the segments. In spite
high level of attention, differently paced humerous epi-
in differential effects on attention to the screen during
on of the identical educational segments. Fast pacing of
episodes enhanced attention sooner than did slow pac-
ing. According to the duration data, both humor conditions produced a
greater degree of visual attention to the semantically unrelated educational message than did the controls. The findings, which are summarized in Figure 9.2, strongly support the notion that interspersed humor
in educational television programs for children increases visual atten-
tiveness to the educational materials in which it is presented.

Background Music as a Mediator of Visual Attention

Attention to the screen was also examined in a second experiment
included in the report by Wakshlag, Reitz, and Zillmann (1981). First-
and second-grade children were shown segments containing background music dubbed into an educational television program segment,
with music tempo and appeal manipulated in a factorial design. The
experimental segments were especially written and produced for the

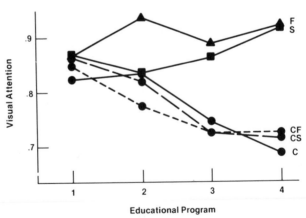

Figure 9.2. Visual attention to educational programs as a function of the involvement of
differently paced humorous inserts. The fast-paced interspersion of humor (F, triangles)
proved most effective. The effect of interspersing humor at a slow pace (S, squares)
developed more slowly. However, both versions containing humor proved to be more
effective than any of the three nonhumorous control versions (circles). Of the controls,
the solid line identifies the educational message proper (C), the short-segment broken
line identifies the version that controls for the fast-paced insertion pattern (CF), and the
long-segment broken line identifies the version that controls for the slow-paced insertion
pattern (CS). (Adapted from Zillmann, Williams, Bryant, Boynton, & Wolf, 1980.)

children's age group, and the educational materials covered were novel to the subjects. The experimental conditions were composed with music that was either fast and appealing, fast and unappealing, slow and appealing, or slow and unappealing. A control group saw segments without background music. The children viewed an educational segment prior to being exposed to the experimental presentation, and measures of attention, information acquisition, and appeal and interest for the segment were obtained for use as covariates.

The investigators found that the tempo of background music markedly affected visual attention to educational television programs. The declining attention noted for all groups near the end of the presentations was stronger for the fast music conditions and strongest with fast and appealing music. One possible explanation is that the children grew tired of either the background music or of the entire program. Alternatively, however, the children may have been attracted by the background music sufficiently to try to "act it out" and to learn it, to the detriment of attention to the screen. The slow music did not produce the diminution in attention observed in the fast music condition.

Entertainment Features and Information Acquisition

Attracting and sustaining an audience, although critically important, are of course only first steps in the process of educating by means of television. The necessary next step is to get the educational message across—that is, to make sure that the information to be acquired is indeed being acquired by the viewers. And it is this issue that has produced most of the controversy over the use of entertainment features in contemporary educational television. In particular, the Singers (Singer, 1980; Singer & Singer, 1979) have taken issue with the fast pace of most educational television programs for children, arguing that such rapid-fire expositions prevent vital rehearsal processes and ultimately stunt the development of cognitive skills that are essential to learning. Notwithstanding such projections of long-term consequences that are most difficult to ascertain (cf. Zillmann, 1980), concerns that elements of entertainment in education can only distract from the educational message and thus impair the acquisition of information have been voiced for some time.

Humor as a Facilitator of Information Acquisition

Examining the effects of humor as a mediator of information acquisition more specifically, Schramm (1973) speculated that the respondents' enjoyment of humor might extend into subsequently presented educational segments. The assumed cognitive preoccupation with humor would then interfere with the reception of educational information; or, should the information be received, it would hamper the rehearsal and storage of this information. Early research on the effects of humor in instructional films, mainly conducted with captive and presumably very attentive military audiences (e.g., Lumsdaine & Gladstone, 1958; McIntyre, 1954), indeed tended to support the conclusion that the involvement of humor is more a hindrance than a help in accomplishing educational objectives (cf. Schramm, 1972). Schramm (1973) further speculated that viewers might perceive educational segments in sharp contrast to any enjoyable humorous stimuli associated with them and thus be more dissatisfied with the educational segments and possibly pay less attention to these segments than to the same educational segments without humor. Recently, McGhee (1980) added the suggestion that humor in educational television might create a playful frame of mind that could interfere with the acquisition of novel information mainly because it would make any rehearsing, which could be construed as effort and labor, seem undesirable or unnecessary.

McGhee's speculations are in line with Bateson's (1972) theory of play and fantasy which holds that humor identifies signs that material to come is play and should not be taken seriously. Material associated with play may, therefore, not be valued by the receiver. Educational material should be processed in the "serious mode" and receive more careful attention than material containing humor.

Theoretical considerations, then, led mainly to the projection of negative effects of the involvement of humor on information acquisition from educational messages (cf. McGhee, 1980). Even writers who promoted fast-paced, entertaining educational programs for children seemed to concede that, on the whole, humor might be distracting. However, they tended to insist that humor that is well integrated in the educational message (i.e., that directly relates to it semantically) might have beneficial effects (e.g., Lesser, 1972, 1974). The only aspect of humor use associated with unqualified positive projections concerned quizzes and exams and apprehensions connected with them. Based on Freudian reasoning (1905/1958), humor has been expected to alleviate tensions and anxieties. Consequently, it should relax students who are nervous about exams and improve their performance. The evidence on this point (e.g., Horn, 1972; Mechanic, 1962; Smith, Ascough, Ettinger, & Nelson, 1971; Terry & Woods, 1975; Weinberg, 1973) is quite inconsistent, however (cf. Chapman & Crompton, 1978; McGhee, 1980).

Evidence suggesting that, counter to the distraction concerns, the involvement of humor in educational television might actually facilitate information acquisition comes from investigations by Hauck and Thomas (1972), Kaplan and Pascoe (1977), Davies and Apter (1980), and Chapman and Crompton (1978). The latter two of these investigations, in particular, pertain to educational television. In both these studies slide presentations were used that can be regarded as acceptable simulations of standard educational television fare, and in both studies it was found that information acquisition from the humorous version of a program was superior to that from its nonhumorous counterpart. In the investigation conducted by Chapman and Crompton, there was a very close correspondence between humor and the information to be acquired. Children (5- and 6-year-olds) who had been exposed to zoo animals that were drawn either in a "funny" or "serious" fashion had to retrieve as many species as possible upon a letter cue. For example, the initial presentation of a camel was connected with the statement, "c is for camel"; and in the test for retention, "c" was the cue for retrieval. Because of this linkage between humor and the item of recall, is can be argued that in this investigation it was the humorous item itself (not a potentially nonhumorous, educational item) that was better recalled. However, in the investigation by Davies and Apter in which somewhat older children (8- to 11-year-olds) served as subjects, the humorous stimuli were only minimally relevant to the topics being taught, and it appears that the humorous format alone effected superior retention of the educational items presented.

Zillmann, Williams, Bryant, Boynton, and Wolf (1980), in a study previously discussed, explored the effects of humor on information acquisition from educational television more directly than other investigations. In order to test for information acquisition, tests were constructed to determine the extent to which subjects recall items and comprehend significant relationships.

As will be recalled, the investigation employed humor that was semantically unrelated to the educational message, whereas only the involvement of humor that relates directly to the educational message has been viewed as having a chance to facilitate the learning of educational materials. But is any beneficial effect of humor on the acquisition of information from educational television really limited to "related" humor? Does "unrelated" humor necessarily function as a distractor? It seems that in the past much of the reasoning on humor in educational television was based on the premise that audiences are highly attentive to educational programs. Indeed, if this premise is adopted, it is difficult to see how humor can enhance information acquisition because, regardless of particular message characteristics, information acquisition should always be at a high level. This premise can readily be challenged. In general, television audiences are all but fully attentive; and children, in particular, may watch a cut-and-dried educational program with little interest and be semiattentive at best. Just as the most motivated college student may find it difficult to be fully alert through a lengthy lecture, so may the child watching educational television, even if essentially interested in the contents, become nonalert, if not drowsy at times, and as the experienced lecturer might be able to break the monotony and regain the attention of the audience by saying something funny or doing something amusing, so might children's attention to the screen be revived by an occasional humorous episode.

If, then, one accepts the premise that attention cannot be at maximum levels for long periods of time and that educational messages are often met with less than maximum interest—a condition conducive to the rapid fading of alertness—it becomes possible to project positive effects on information acquisition as the result of the involvement of humor, especially of humor that is rapidly paced. In line with this reasoning, Zillmann, Williams, Bryant, Boynton, and Wolf (1980) proposed that the interspersion of humorous stimuli in an educational program, whether or not the humor is semantically related to the educational materials covered, is likely to serve an alerting function. The respondent who vigilantly reacts to a humorous episode will remain vigilant and alert for some time thereafter (cf. Berlyne, 1960, 1970; Tannenbaum & Zillmann, 1975; Zillmann, 1980); during this period, he or she may more closely attend to the educational portions of a program and process incoming information more actively. As a result, the presence of humor should facilitate learning, especially when vigilance is revived often through the fast-paced placement of humorous stimuli.

The findings of the investigation by Zillmann, Williams, Bryant, Boynton, and Wolf (1980) are entirely consistent with such a projection. As can be seen from Figure 9.3, the interspersion of "unrelated" humorous stimuli in an educational program resulted in information acquisition that was superior to that from the educational message proper. The fast pacing of humorous episodes proved to be particularly effective: It produced the facilitating effect on learning more rapidly and, mostly because of this early effect, tended to produce a stronger overall facilitation. The vigilance interpretation is further supported by the findings on visual attention that were presented earlier and summarized in Figure 9.2. Humor-induced vigilance apparently carried over into the subsequently presented portions of the educational message. There can be no question, then, that "unrelated" humor, especially

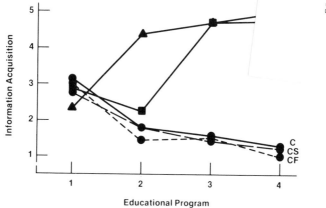

Figure 9.3. *Acquisition of information from educational programs as a function of the involvement of differently paced humorous inserts. All effects paralleled those on visual attention (see Figure 9.2). The nomenclature of Figure 9.2 applies. (Adapted from Zillmann, Williams, Bryant, Boynton, & Wolf, 1980.)*

when paced rapidly, can enhance children's acquisition of information from educational television programs.

Bryant, Zillmann, Wolf, and Reardon (1981) carried out essentially the same investigation with somewhat older children (7- and 8-year-olds). The findings were consistent with those of the earlier study, but there was some indication that the learning-facilitating effect of humor becomes weaker as the child's age increases.

Although research on the effects of the distribution of humorous stimuli in educational television programs for children has produced clear-cut results, many aspects of the use and the effects of humor in such programs have remained obscure. Variations in the funniness of humor, for example, failed to produce strong effects (Sapolsky, 1981). There are indications, however, that only mildly funny humor has a facilitory effect on information acquisition, whereas the involvement of highly enjoyable humor had no appreciable effect on learning. It is thus conceivable that humor that triggers intense mirth reactions—because, as Schramm (1972, 1973) had suggested it preoccupies the re-spondent—might interfere with information acquisition to the point where it is inferior to that from the educational message without humor.

Research on the funniness of the source of educational information (i.e., the speaker or presenter) also failed to exhibit strong effects on learning (Sapolsky & Walker, 1980; Wakshlag, 1981). All a funny source seems to accomplish is to make the experience of watching

.ducational materials somewhat more enjoyable. On the other hand, a study conducted by Cantor and Reilly (1980) showed that a teacher's use of a jocular language style enhanced information acquisition. At the same time, however, the joking teacher was less favorably evaluated by the children (sixth-, seventh-, and eighth-grade students).

Cantor and Reilly's investigation also included a variation in the use of "related" humor. Compared to a no-humor control, the use of such humor (i.e., humor that is relevant to the concepts taught by the educational message) had no appreciable effect overall. Tracing the effect of the various humorous stimuli that were employed suggested that the use of irony, in particular, may have been confusing and may have caused misinterpretations that impaired information acquisition. Since irony and similar message-distorting techniques are heavily used in children's educational television, this observation may prove highly significant. One immediate consequence is that it now appears that the classification of humor as "related" is a confusing oversimplification. Finer distinctions within this class are necessary. In fact, making these finer distinctions holds promise of clarifying and reconciling findings on the effects of "related" humor in children's educational television.

The issue of humor that is related versus humor that is unrelated to educational messages is significant in yet another way: It seems to define a turning point in the effects of the involvement of humor in educational television programs for children versus for adult audiences. For one thing, humor is usually not well-integrated, semantically, with educational materials in programs for children. Visual and auditory humorous cues are, by and large, as often lacking correspondence with topics taught as they are directly related (Bryant, Hezel, & Zillmann, 1979). In lectures delivered by college professors, in contrast, the use of humor that helps to make educational points dominates other uses, the involvement of "unrelated" humor being comparatively rare (Bryant, Comisky, & Zillmann, 1979). These uses seem to reflect a good intuitive grasp of the effects of humor in educational endeavors— that, at least, is what recent research suggests. Totally "unrelated" humor in educational programs, on the other hand, can greatly facilitate information acquisition in children. With age, this beneficial effect seems to weaken. The involvement of "related" humor, on the other hand, poses a risk for children in that, while some forms of relatedness may achieve highly beneficial effects, many other forms such as irony, cyncism, and sarcasm—because they distort the related educational point—may foster misconceptions and thus impair information acquisition. It can be assumed that adult audiences, because of superior information-processing skills, are far less likely to misinterpret reality-distorting forms of humor, and "related" humor can thus be expected to be devoid of the discussed ill effects. Additionally, one might expect that adult audiences respond unfavorably to the involvement of obviously forced-in "unrelated" humor. Humor that is well-integrated and used to make points of interest can readily be accepted, but humor that has no apparent connection to the educational message, obviously interspersed to liven things up, may be met with impatience, if not with annoyance. Be this as it may, recent research on adult audiences (college students) shows that in televised lectures the use of "unrelated" and "somewhat related" humor has detrimental effects on information acquisition (Hezel, Bryant, Harris, & Zillmann, 1981). According to this research, only humor that is well-integrated with critical educational statements—that virtually helps to make important points—does not produce such negative effects and seems to hold promise of enhancing the learning process.

Special Effects as a Facilitator of Information Acquisition

An experiment designed to test the vigilance explanation of the observed facilitory effect of humor on learning more directly has been conducted by Bryant and Zillmann (1981) with children (5- and 6-year-olds) as subjects. These investigators argued that, if humor has its effect through the stimulation of vigilance, nonhumorous stimuli, as long as they have a similar effect on vigilance, should similarly facilitate learning. Consequently, nonhumorous stimuli that are commonly used as attention-getters (the audiovisual "fireworks" of children's television—i.e., fast-moving colorful objects accompanied by unusual noises, exploding stars, and the like) were sampled, and their attention-getting potential and hedonic value (neutral versus pleasant) were determined in a pretest. Humorous stimuli were similarly pretested. Nonhumorous and humorous stimuli were then matched on these criteria. In the main experiment, it was found that the interspersion of stimuli with a high potential to attract attention, whether humorous or not and whether pleasant or not, facilitated the acquisition of information from an educational program. No appreciable differences were found in the effect of humorous and nonhumorous stimuli. There was a tendency, however, for pleasant stimuli to be more effective than hedonically neutral ones of a similar attention-getting capacity.

The same investigation was carried out with 7- and 8-year-olds. Once again, the effects of humorous and nonhumorous stimuli were comparable. However, in this investigation, the effect of hedonic valence was stronger than that observed for the younger children. The more pleasant stimuli yielded substantially greater information acquisition than the less pleasant ones. Additionally, the effect of the variation in attention-getting potential was somewhat weaker than in the prior investigation.

Surely, these two investigations lend strong support to the vigilance explanation. Their practical implications are less clear, however. The studies show that audiovisual fireworks may do as good a job as humorous stimuli in recapturing the attention of an audience whose alertness is fading. This should not be taken to mean that both types of stimuli function equally well in the facilitation of learning from educational television. It should be remembered that in the investigations by Bryant and Zillmann the children could not turn to another program. Had they not been a captive audience, they may well have turned away from the fireworks presentations. Content-free audiovisual displays or displays with little meaning are unlikely to attract and sustain selective exposure as effectively as humorous materials, and their beneficial effects on learning may well be limited to captive audiences or to messages that feature these displays infrequently enough to be tolerated by a noncaptive audience.

Effects of Background Music
on Information Acquisition

The faciltiative effects on information acquisition produced by humor were not observed for background music in children's educational television programs (Wakshlag, Reitz, & Zillmann, 1981). In fact, rhythmic background music, especially when appealing, significantly impaired information acquisition. A crucial difference in the stimulus presence of humor and music should be recognized, however. Although the humorous stimuli were placed intermittantly, the background music was present continuously. The music, but not the humorous stimuli, thus competed for attention with the educational messages. The intermittant use of music might produce entirely different effects. In fact, under the assumption that rhythmic, lively music produces marked vigilance reactions, there is every reason to expect that the intermittant use of such music functions analogously to the intermittant use of humor. Definitive statements about these likely effects must await further research, however.

Summary

The use of entertainment features in educational television programs clearly facilitates children's *selective exposure* to the programs. Humor and background music consistently attract children's attention to the educational material, with "fast pace" and "appealing" being the most desirable attributes for the entertaining stimuli. Practically speaking, since most program selecting occurs early in the program, it appears critically important for exposure to load the educational message with such entertainment devices during the opening sequences.

Visual attention is greatly facilitated by humor and special effects, with fast pace (humor and special effects) and high appeal (special effects) providing the winning combination. In marked contrast, visual attention is impaired, over time, by the inclusion of continuously presented fast and appealing background music, whereas slow tempo music has negligible effects on attention. Although a number of explanations can be offered to explain the discrepancy in these findings (cf. Wakshlag, Reitz, & Zillmann, 1981), it seems most likely that the children got caught up in the rehearsal and performance of the frequently presented appealing tune at the expense of attention to the screen. That is, the distraction potential of the memorable music overpowered its vigilance-producing qualities. If these assumptions are correct, then it seems likely that the format that proved successful with other entertaining features—short inserts rapidly paced—would be amenable to the presentation of music as well.

The findings for *acquisition of information* from educational programs parallel those of visual attention. The facilitative effects produced by intermittently placed stimuli such as humor (Bryant, Zillmann, Wolf, & Reardon, 1981; Zillmann, Williams, Bryant, Boynton, & Wolf, 1980) and special effects (Bryant & Zillmann, 1981) seem not to extend to continuously presented stimuli such as background music (Wakshlag, Reitz, & Zillmann, 1981). The latter findings are in line with the notion that fast, appealing background music interferes with the educational message. It should be anticipated, however, that the *intermittent* use of music would function analogously to other intermittently employed entertaining stimuli. If that be the case, then the appropriate generalization is that the intermittent use of attention-getting and appealing educational materials provides an effective facilitation of learning from educational programs for children.

Acknowledgments

Joanne R. Cantor, University of Wisconsin–Madison; Kenneth D. Day, State University of New York–Buffalo; Richard T. Hezel, University of Huston; Barry S. Sapolsky, Florida State University; and Jacob J. Wakshlag, Indiana University, all of whose research is cited, collaborated with the authors.

References

Anderson, D. R., Alwitt, L. F., Lorch, E. P., & Levin, S. R. Watching children watch television. In G. Hale & M. Lewis (Eds.), *Attention and cognitive development.* New York: Plenum, 1979.

Bateson, G. *Steps to an ecology of the mind.* New York: Ballantine, 1972.

Berlyne, D. E. *Conflict, arousal and curiosity.* New York: McGraw-Hill, 1960.

Berlyne, D. E. Attention as a problem in behavior theory. In D. I. Mostofsky (Ed.), *Attention: Contemporary theory and analysis.* New York: Appleton-Century-Crofts, 1970.

Bryant, J., Comisky, P., & Zillmann, D. Teacher's humor in the college classroom. *Communication Education,* 1979, *28*(2), 110–118.

Bryant, J., Hezel, R., & Zillmann, D. Humor in children's educational television. *Communication Education.* 1979, *28,* 49–59.

Bryant, J., & Zillmann, D. *Humor and audiovisual fireworks in educational television: Effects on learning.* Unpublished manuscript, 1981. (Available from Jennings Bryant, Department of Communications, University of Evansville, Evansville, IN 47702.)

Bryant, J., Zillmann, D., Wolf, M. A., & Reardon, K. K. *Learning from educational television as a function of differently paced humor: Further evidence.* Manuscript in preparation, 1981.

Cantor, J., & Reilly, S. *Jocular language style and relevant humor in educational messages.* Paper presented at the Second International Conference on Humor, Los Angeles, 1980.

Chapman, A. J., & Crompton, P. Humorous presentations of material and presentations of humorous material: A review of the humor literature and two experimental studies. In M. M. Gruneberg, P. E. Morris, & R. N. Sykes (Eds.), *Practical aspects of memory.* London: Academic Press, 1978.

Davies, A. P., & Apter, M. J. Humor and its effect on learning in children. In P. E. McGhee & A. J. Chapman (Eds.), *Children's humor.* New York: Wiley, 1980.

Freud, S. *Der Witz und seine Beziehungzum Unbewussten.* Frankfurt: Fischer Bucherei, 1958. (Originally published, 1905.)

Hauck, W. E., & Thomas, J. W. The relationship of humor to intelligence, creativity, and intentional and incidental learning. *Journal of Experimental Education,* 1972, *40,* 52–55.

Hezel, R. T., Bryant, J., Harris, L., & Zillmann, D. *The relationship between humor and educational information: Lectures and learning.* Manuscript in preparation, 1981.

Horn, G. Laughter . . . a saving grace. *Today's Education,* December 1972, pp. 37–38.

Kaplan, R. M., & Pascoe, G. C. Humorous lectures and humorous examples: Some effects upon comprehension and retention. *Journal of Educational Psychology,* 1977, *69,* 61–65.

Lesser, G. S. Assumptions behind the production and writing methods in "Seasame Street." In W. Schramm (Ed.), *Quality in instructional television.* Honolulu: University Press of Hawaii, 1972.

Lesser, G. S. *Children and television: Lessons from Sesame Street.* New York: Random House, 1974.

Lumsdaine, A. A., & Gladstone, A. I. Overt practice and audio-visual embellishments. In M. A. May & A. A. Lumsdaine (Eds.), *Learning from films.* New Haven, Conn.: Yale University Press, 1958.

Maccoby, E. E. Selective audiotry attention in children. In L. P. Lipsett & C. C. Spiker (Eds.), *Advances in child development and behavior* (Vol. 3). New York: Academic Press, 1967.

McGhee, P. E. Toward the integration of entertainment and educational functions of television: The role of humor. In P. H. Tannenbaum (Ed.), *The entertainment functions of television*. Hillsdale, N.J.: Erlbaum, 1980.

McIntyre, C. J. *Training film evaluation: FB 254-Cold weather uniforms* (Technical Report SDC 269-7-51). Port Washington, N.Y.: U.S. Naval Special Devices Center, 1954.

Mechanic, D. *Students under stress: A study of the social psychology of adaption*. New York: Free Press of Glencoe, 1962.

Reeves, B. R. *The first year of Sesame Street: The formative research*. New York: Children's Television Workshop, 1970.

Sapolsky, B. S. *The degree of funniness of humor accompanying informative messages and its effect upon children's rote learning*. Manuscript in preparation, 1981.

Sapolsky, B. S., & Walker, B. A. *The effect of mood and source on children's attention, enjoyment, and learning from educational television*. Paper presented at the Second International Conference on Humor, Los Angeles, August 1980.

Schleicher, M. P., Bryant, J., & Zillmann, D. *Voluntary selective exposure to educational television programs as a function of differently paced humorous inserts*. Manuscript in preparation, 1980.

Schramm, W. What the research says. In W. Schramm (Ed.), *Quality in instructional television*. Honolulu: University Press of Hawaii, 1972.

Schramm, W. *Men, messages, and media: A look at human communication*. New York: Harper & Row, 1973.

Singer, J. L. The power and limitations of television: A cognitive–affective analysis. In P. H. Tannenbaum (Ed.), *The entertainment functions of television*. Hillsdale, N.J.: Erlbaum, 1980.

Singer, J. L., & Singer, D. G. Come back, Mister Rogers, come back. *Psychology Today*, March 1979, 56, pp. 59–60.

Smith, R. E., Ascough, J. C., Ettinger, R. F., & Nelson, D. A. Humor, anxiety, and task performance. *Journal of Personality and Social Psychology*, 1971, 19, 243–246.

Tannenbaum, P. H., & Zillmann, D. Emotional arousal in the facilitation of aggression through communication. In L. Berkowitz (Ed.), *Advances in experimental social psychology* (Vol. 8). New York: Academic Press, 1975.

Terry, R. L., & Woods, M. E. Effects of humor on the test performance of elementary school children. *Psychology in the Schools*, 1975, 12, 182–185.

Wakshlag, J. J. *Effect of humorous appearance of teacher on effectiveness of televised educational programs*. Manuscript in preparation, 1981.

Wakshlag, J. J., Day, K. D., & Zillmann, D. Selective exposure to educational television programs as a function of differently paced humorous inserts. *Journal of Educational Psychology*, 1981, 73(1), 27–32.

Wakshlag, J. J., Reitz, R., & Zillmann, D. *Selective exposure of and acquisition of information for educational television programs as a function of appeal and tempo of background music*. Unpublished manuscript, 1981. (Available from Dolf Zillmann, Institute for Communications Research, Indiana University, Bloomington, IN 47405.)

Weinberg, M. D. *The interactional effect of humor and anxiety on academic performance*. Unpublished doctoral dissertation, Yeshiva University, 1973.

Zillmann, D. Television viewing and arousal. In D. Pearl, L. Bouthilet, & J. Lazar (Eds.), *Television and behavior: Ten years of scientific progress and implications for the eighties*. (Vol. 2). Rockville, MD: NIMH, 1982.

Zillmann, D., Hezel, R. T., & Medoff, N. J. The effect of affective states on selective exposure to televised entertainment fare. *Journal of Applied Social Psychology*, 1980, 10(4), 323–339.

Zillmann, D., Williams, B. R., Bryant, J., Boynton, K. R., & Wolf, M. A. Acquisition of information from educational television programs as a function of differently paced humorous inserts. *Journal of Educational Psychology*, 1980, *72*(2), 170–180.

chapter 10

Formative Research on Appeal and Comprehension in 3–2–1 CONTACT[1]

KEITH W. MIELKE

Introduction

This chapter deals with appeal and comprehension of television programming from the viewpoint of formative research applied to the design and production of *3–2–1 CONTACT*.

The Children's Television Workshop (CTW) premiered this series of 65 half-hour programs in January 1980, with the aim of motivating interest in science and technology among its target audience of 8–12-year-olds. More specifically its aim was to communicate the joy of science and some beginning familiarity with scientific modes of thought, and, with special appeal to girls and minorities, to show that science and technology are open to a wide range of participation.

The management model for *3–2–1 CONTACT* placed major responsibility for series design and production in three staff units: Scientific Content, Formative Research, and Production. Basically, the content

[1]This chapter is based in part on an extensive overview of formative research on *3–2–1 CONTACT*, supported by National Science Foundation award No. 8020774 (Mielke & Chen, 1981). Any opinions, findings, conclusions, or recommendations expressed herein are those of the author and do not necessarily reflect the views of the National Science Foundation.

241

staff was responsible for the accuracy, relevance, and organization of the scientific content of the series. The Formative Research staff represented the target audience as an in-house advocate and as a provider of research feedback while the series was in its formative stages. The production staff had responsibility for coordinating inputs from content and research and putting it all together on the screen.

Formative research, therefore, functioned as a member of a team that had a project orientation and production goals. Compared with typical settings for theoretical research on appeal and comprehension, this environment is sufficiently different to call for more elaboration later. Understanding the distinctive context and mission of formative research will be helpful in understanding its insights into appeal and comprehension issues.

Formative and theoretical research do share similar problems in drawing generalizable connections between (a) principles of message design and human behavior; and (b) the actual programming itself. The extraordinary stimulus complexity of a television program stands in the way of bridging the gap between principle and program. It is difficult to take a body of theoretical research and translate its general principles into new programming. The general principles may or may not operate as predicted, depending on how the translation into actual production is carried out. For the same reason, that is, stimulus complexity, it is similarly difficult to translate actual programming experience into a set of generalizable principles. That which appears to be general may instead be idiosyncratic and ultimately traceable to some unique feature of its execution in the production process.

The effort to provide research-based linkages between general principles and actual programming is nevertheless a worthy one, and the intent in this chapter is to make at least a modest contribution toward that end from the perspective of the production–project orientation of 3–2–1 CONTACT.

After an introduction to the formative research function on this project, discussion will turn to methods and findings that address appeal and comprehension issues, with a concluding hope that further work might be done to enhance the complementarity between theoretical and applied research in goal-directed children's television.

The Role of Formative Research

The discussion of appeal and comprehension issues will draw from part but not all of the formative research work conducted with 3–2–1

CONTACT. A "capsule history" of the research effort will highlight the range of activities.

The Children's Television Workshop maintained an in-house team of three to four researchers devoted exclusively to *3–2–1 CONTACT* for about 2½ years. The research agenda varied widely as project needs evolved. Early on, for example, researchers participated in the needs assessment and content seminars, exploring the feasibility of the series in the first place. They studied the target audience (children 8–12) and their media habits, and they evaluated a variety of materials produced externally. Later in the process, a group of test shows, designed as prototypes of the series, was evaluated extensively. When the series itself was in production, researchers represented the target audience in rather continuous meetings with producers, writers, and content specialists. Some of the early series shows were evaluated, and the research group disbanded when the major decisions for series production had been made.

This was the life cycle of the work encompassed under the label "formative research," that is, research devoted to in-house project needs while the product was still in its formative stages. When the needs evolved, so did the formative research. When the opportunities to modify series production drew to a close, so did the formative research function.

Formative research is project-driven and must operate within the discipline of the project schedule. Rather than setting out to conduct research on appeal and comprehension in television programming for young people, the objective with *3–2–1 CONTACT* was to produce an effective television series. Formative research is oriented to the decision-making needs of project management, not to the testing of hypotheses or the development of theory. Formative research typically refers to some specific set of stimulus materials, not to general theoretical categories for which the materials might be considered representative.

Formative research uses a variety of the tools and techniques of social science research but is not constrained by their traditions. It values hard data but is not data-bound; researchers' judgments and opinions are also valued and utilized. Formative researchers share traditional research values but are frequently required by their function to weigh the trade-offs between (a) reaching a judgment that goes beyond the data; and (b) having no research input into a decision at all. Formative research findings are only one of several forms of feedback employed. Because production must distill a variety of inputs into a course of action, and work within project constraints of time and budget, it is possible that a formative research recommendation may from time to time be overridden by demands of the project as a whole.

The zone of inquiry was rather sharply defined in the formative research for *3–2–1 CONTACT*. Imagine three large circles with a relatively small area of overlap, and you have a picture of the boundaries. One circle is the entire area of science and science education; the second is the medium of television; the third is children. The area of intersection among these three—science, television, and children—was the domain of *3–2–1 CONTACT*'s formative research. It was a rather specialized territory. Existing literature combining all three factors was virtually nonexistent. We worked extensively in that restricted domain, conducting over 50 formative research studies, and engaging the participation of more than 10,000 target-age children (Chen 1980–1981; Mielke & Chen, 1980, 1981; Myerson-Katz, 1980). What follows are some of the results of those efforts, originally intended for in-house use only.

Background Issues

The environment for *3–2–1 CONTACT*'s formative research has been characterized as falling within the intersection of children, television, and science. This area of intersection was not a vacuum or a blank slate awaiting new programming. Conditions that existed previously would obviously affect the reactions to later programming. Two such areas of research into this existing environment that are summarized here are insights (a) into the status of science education; and (b) into the nature of the target audience. Both areas influenced design strategy for the television series and helped set the stage for the measures of appeal and comprehension that comprised much of the formative research effort.

Science Education

There was substantial evidence of needs in science education at the elementary grades. As an extremely brief overview, the following points are illustrative. Half the states made no mention of science in their teacher certification requirements at the elementary level (Woellner, 1977). Science performance among 9-year-olds (and among older children as well) was declining (National Assessment of Educational Progress, 1977). Relative to other subject areas they taught, elementary teachers felt least qualified to teach science (Weiss, 1978). The increasing emphasis on "back to basics," which stressed such skills as reading and computation, frequently had the effect of lowering the priority given to science education (Stake & Easley, 1978). Relative to their proportion to the total population, women and minorities were significantly underrepresented in science and engineering fields (National Science Foundation, 1977).

The Target Audience (8–12s)

Inquiries into the nature of the target audience, through literature reviews and advisory groups, began before the proposal to produce the science series was written and continued thereafter. For example, through the work of cognitive psychologists (e.g., Bruner, Olver, & Greenfield, 1966; White, 1975; White & Siegel, 1976), as well as science educators (e.g., Karplus, 1973), science advisors to the project documented that children 8–12 years of age are beginning to think systematically about the world.

> These children are interested in organizing objects and events along the dimensions of time, space, and function. They are searching for patterns in their physical and social environments, examining their own beliefs and those of others. They are aware of cause and effect, reciprocal relationships, and the influence of variables upon each other. They are interested not only in phenomena, but in patterns among phenomena. Their asking "What if?" questions epitomizes their attempt to explore these questions [Children's Television Workshop, 1977, p. 5].

At the beginning of the 8–12 target-age range, children can perform numerous mental operations but are still mainly dependent on concrete, direct experience. Toward the older end of the target-age range, children are more able "to manipulate abstract relationships without constant reference to specific examples [Karplus, 1973, p. 1]."

Not only did the beginnings of systematic thought suggest the 8–12 age range as the target audience, but the formation of attitudes toward science at this time did so as well. Following a review of nine studies on this topic, Omerod and Duckworth (1975) concluded that "the critical ages at which pupils' attitudes toward science can be influenced extend from about eight years of age to about thirteen or fourteen [p. 42]". Johnson (1979), reviewing data from the 1976–1977 National Assessment of Educational Progress, found that at age 9:

1. Only 6% of the students were ranking science as their favorite subject.
2. Boys were already expressing more favorable attitudes toward science than girls were, with this sex difference becoming even more pronounced among older children.

3. Many pupils had already decided that a career in science would either be boring or too much work.

The *3–2–1 CONTACT* formative researchers investigated the images children had of a scientist's life-style. Insights were gained by having target-age children write essays, choosing one of two topics: "why I would (or would not) like to become a scientist" or "a typical day in the life of a scientist." Although there were many positive associations with a scientist's life, dealing, for example, with social contributions such as finding cures for diseases and inventing useful things, there were also negative and stereotypical associations. The image of the lengthy and rigorous training demanded and of super intelligence required to complete it was a turn-off for many. Scientists were viewed as rather narrow human beings who spend their lives in laboratories, having little fun or social interaction. Such images suggested a programming strategy of showing a variety of scientists—male and female, minority and nonminority—having social interaction and working in many different settings.

We also conducted inquiries into children's understanding of processes such as water cycles, their vocabulary of scientific terminology, and their conceptual approach, via hands-on exercises, to such issues as surface-to-volume ratios.

The Intervention of Television

Information about needs in science education and insights into the target audience members as they were relating to science were both important elements in defining the context into which responsive programming would later emerge. Formative researchers attempt to become informed about the environment into which programming will be introduced, and over which there is no direct control, so that recommendations can be made for message design and production, which *can* be controlled and manipulated. The most common target for these recommendations, as well as the most common request from producers, in whose service formative research is conducted, is in the area of appeal and comprehension.

Long-term effects (e.g., Will this child become a scientist?) are not accessible to formative research, but short-term effects of appeal and comprehension are presumed to be prerequisite conditions. Indeed, the attraction and retention of a voluntary audience for goal-directed programming in the first place is dependent upon appeal and comprehension. Making a television program appealing and comprehensible is a combination of art and science, of judgment and data, in which audience feedback through formative research plays an important but not an exclusive role.

The following sections review some of the methods, findings, and hunches in formative research measures of appeal and comprehension of materials produced both in-house and out-of-house.

Appeal

Behavioral Measures of Attention

Given the formative research purpose of providing feedback to the production staff while there was still time to alter the particular test program in question or future programs in the series, there were arguments in favor of both attention and appeal measures. Both have their pros and cons. The decision with *3–2–1 CONTACT* to focus primarily on measures of appeal rather than on attention per se was based on our analysis of the trade-offs in each.

A behavioral measure of attention, called the Distractor Method, had been developed and used successfully with *Sesame Street* and *The Electric Company* (Palmer, 1974, p. 318; Palmer, Crawford, Kielsmeier & Inglis, 1968). This method involved an observer continuously recording whether attention was or was not being paid to the television screen by a single child. A "distractor" placed near the television set consisted of a rear-screen projector with slides that changed every few seconds. By summing levels of actual attention across subjects and plotting this across time, the resulting attention profile was diagnostically useful in making recommendations to Production staff. We tried the Distractor Method with the *3–2–1 CONTACT* target audience, but it did not work. These older children were able to figure out what was going on, and devised clever strategies to view the distraction *and* the test program.

One methodological answer to the "divided attention" problem might be to adapt a procedure reported by Wakshlag, Day, and Zillmann (1981). A test program and one or more "distractor" programs could be fed simultaneously via cassettes to a single monitor, where actual channel selection behavior could be recorded electronically and/ or observed directly. Although this is very attractive in terms of methodological rigor, it still involves data collection from one child at a time. For formative researchers working on a production schedule, this presents special difficulties and trade-offs in regard to sample sizes. There is considerable incentive to use measures that can be group-administered.

Accordingly, we devised and experimented with a research apparatus we called the Program Selector, which allowed group administration as well as behavioral measures of viewer choice. Three monitors displayed different programs simultaneously, fed by three video cassette players. The audio was fed through individual earphones to test-audience members. Through push buttons, they selected the one audio channel of choice, and the audio-selection patterns were recorded as an index of viewing choice. The device was cumbersome, however, and not easily portable to schools, where most of the test audiences were recruited. Because the prototype device had other mechanical problems, such as having the audio-selection buttons visible to others in the group, thus introducing a potential group influence on individual responses, and because time was not available during production to revise and thoroughly test the apparatus, developmental work on the Program Selector was stopped.

In principle, it should be possible to construct a research apparatus featuring the strengths of the Wakshlag et al. (1981) procedure (actual simulation of program-selection behaviors via dial-switching) with those of the Program Selector (group administration). Such a device might feature, say, up to 10 private viewing booths with individual monitors, with audio coming through earphones only. It would be relatively simple to set this up on a semipermanent basis in a laboratory but more difficult to make it actually portable. In any case, there remain many opportunities for creative methodologies for behavioral measures of attention and/or selective exposure to test programming. In formative research applications, for example, it would be particularly useful to play a test program, before it goes on the air, against its actual competition in a particular timeslot.

Along these same lines, the increasing availability of interactive cable systems offers opportunities to the formative researcher to get out of the laboratory and into the home. One of our formative studies of 3–2–1 CONTACT test programs, for example, utilized the interactive QUBE system of cable television in Columbus, Ohio. Identifying and getting feedback from viewers were made possible through "touching in" on the home response units, with data automatically recorded via a central computer. This procedure was useful in determining such things as the proportion of those made aware of the special cablecasts who voluntarily tuned in, those above and below the target-age range also watching, and audience carry-over from one show to another.

Audience ratings, such as provided by the A. C. Nielsen company, although virtually indispensable for some purposes, are severely limited in their diagnostic potential in formative research. Most obviously, audience ratings come too late to serve a formative function. Even if that were not a problem, the home environment abounds in confounding variables and potential barriers, such as who has control over channel selection, what the viewing and nonviewing alternatives are at any given time, whether the audience is even aware of the presence of a particular program of interest, and whether the broadcast scheduling is convenient for viewing. Actual viewing must penetrate all these barriers. Interpretations of viewing records, for diagnostic formative research purposes, thus have many constraints.

Measures of *appeal* have considerable utility in formative research. A variety of designs are available that permit administration to groups of respondents. When coupled with follow-up interviews, appeal measures can be more readily diagnostic in nature than attention measures (i.e., the data can get at questions of "why" as well as "what").

One of the advantages of working with children at least 8–12 years of age is that various forms of asking questions are possible, including the use of simple questionnaires. The form of the response could and did vary, as in a gradated scale, a yes–no, a judgment in comparison to something else (e.g., forced-choice methods), or as a free-response answer to the question of what, if anything, was found appealing. Informal indices of appeal, such as facial expressions and posture, were routinely observed but not systematically recorded as quantified data.

Measures of appeal, as opposed to attention, can also be started well before production is underway, as in determining favorite programs, program types, and the relative appeal of various scientific topics. Some of these preproduction appeal measures are discussed next.

Early Indications of General Viewing Preferences

Formative research contributed to early series planning through studies on what the target audience already viewed and preferred on television. One major effort, well before production got underway, involved a survey of viewing interests in the spring of 1978 (Mielke, Chen, Clarke, & Myerson-Katz, 1978). To enable us to compare subgroups based on age, sex, ethnicity, and geographic region, a sample of over 4000 target-age children was enlisted, drawing from nine regions around the United States.

One portion of the questionnaire featured 20 programs that were of special interest because of their format (e.g., magazine, plotted drama) or content (e.g., science, science fiction). Response options, simple and reinforced with graphics for appeal and ease of reading, were (a) "I have never heard of this show"; (b) "I know about this show, but don't usually watch it"; and (c) "I watch this show whenever I can." Some of the things learned from this part of the survey were

1. Among sex, grade, and ethnic subgroups, five science-related shows (Wild Kingdom; Animals, Animals, Animals; In Search of; Jacques Cousteau; Nova) fell into the bottom half of awareness. The range for the total sample: 13% were unaware of Wild Kingdom; 75% were unaware of Nova. Less than 1% were unaware of Charlie's Angels or Happy Days.
2. All five of the science-related shows had substantially heavier regular viewing reported among boys than among girls. With the exception of Wild Kingdom, however, all five shows fell into the bottom half of the "regular viewing" rankings for both boys and girls.
3. Only two magazine–variety format shows (Donny and Marie; The Muppet Show) fell into the top half of the rankings of shows viewed regularly.

Another item that generated much interesting data asked the children to nominate their one favorite show on television. From the sample as a whole ($4000+), 166 different shows were nominated, but it was impressive that only 7 shows accounted for over one-half of all the nominations: Charlie's Angels, Happy Days, The Incredible Hulk, Hardy Boys, Baby I'm Back, Good Times, and Three's Company. Only 3 science or pseudoscience shows met our cutoff criterion of at least 10 nominations: Project UFO (18 nominations; 14 from boys); Wild Kingdom (13 nominations; 10 from boys), and In Search of (13 nominations; 11 from boys). Science programming was near the bottom of the list of favorite shows, and even there it was heavily male-dominated. Shows nominated substantially more frequently by girls than by boys (defined as a rank-order difference of 10 or more) tended to have themes of warm human relationships, often in family situations (e.g., Little House on the Prairie), and/or feature strong female leads (e.g., Wonder Woman). Shows nominated substantially more frequently by boys than by girls (same criterion) tended to feature competition (e.g., Sports programs), strong male leads in action–adventure formats (e.g., Black Sheep Squadron), or, as mentioned earlier, science or pseudoscience.

In the nominations of one favorite program, the Television Interest Survey generated several titles that would sequentially increase or decrease in rank order across the 4 years of age in the target audience. For example, *Brady Bunch* and *Donny and Marie* were popular among third graders, but decreasingly so among fourth, fifth, and sixth graders. Conversely, *Three's Company* and *CHIPS* were popular among sixth graders, but popularity declined among the younger viewers.

Additional indications of the appeal of shows with a plotted dramatic element—the central feature being the telling of an engaging story—came from two preproduction studies in which typical viewing was marked on a questionnaire resembling a *TV Guide*. Four timeslots were chosen in which popular entertainment shows in a magazine–variety format were playing against their real-world competition. Respondents (250+ in each sample) were asked to indicate the one show they "usually" watched at that time. If they typically were not watching television at that time, they were instructed not to mark anything. In no case were the shows in the magazine–variety format the most heavily viewed, according to the self-reports. However, in six of eight comparisons (four timeslots in each of two studies) there was higher reported viewing of the magazine format shows among 8–9-year-olds than among 10–11-year-olds. Through other studies, we confirmed that older viewers in the target-age range were better able to follow plotlines and to comprehend the information contained in dramatic stories.

Early Indications of Topic Preferences

Formative research made early contributions to the scientific content staff by getting insights into the types of topics appealing to the target audience. One method involved judgments of interest in response to photographs that were accompanied by brief and evaluatively neutral introductions. The phenomena or objects displayed (e.g., various animals, space colonies, supertankers, plants, insects) covered a wide range of subject matter, and responses were in the form of simple evaluative scales plus a forced-choice selection (best and worst) from subsets of the photos. Some of the highlights from two studies using this technique are

1. Photos that involved animals in some emotionally engaging way—such as beached whales—were very popular with both boys and girls.
2. Photos of insects tended to be low in appeal for both boys and girls.
3. Dramatic sex differences were found in both studies on one photo

about very young babies learning to copy the faces an adult makes. Girls placed this near the top of appeal, and boys placed it at or near the bottom.

4. Interest in the photo–concepts in general was higher among boys than among girls.
5. Some space colony photos appealed to both boys and girls, whereas some appealed only to boys. Photos with strong appeal to both sexes dealt not only with the technology of space colonies, but also with people, families, and social activities. Appeal to girls seemed to require this social component more so than for boys.

Another technique sought to elicit questions from target-age children that they were most curious about and most wanted the answers to. A mental set was established by requesting judgments of most and least interest in sets of prepared questions. This was then followed by the children writing down questions of their own that they had actually formulated previously. The child-generated questions could be categorized as follows:

1. Human body: How does your body know when it is time to grow? Why can't a man have a baby? Why do we go to sleep?
2. Animals: Why do zebras have stripes? How come animals have four legs? Do some animals have pouches?
3. Physical and natural phenomena: Where does snow come from? Who made mushrooms? How do clouds stay in the sky without falling?
4. Man-made phenomena: How do you make chalk? How does a television work? Is there gunpowder in blank bullets?
5. Miscellaneous–philosophy–human nature: Who created God? Is there a real Santa Claus? Why do I feel like I have no friends sometimes?

The most striking characteristic of the child-generated questions was their relative simplicity. The vast majority of questions were about objects, creatures, and phenomena familiar to children. Interestingly, sex differences were minimal in this question-asking form of inquiry.

Paper-and-Pencil Measures of Appeal
for Displayed Programs

Unlike the previous questionnaires directed toward general program and topic preferences, the paper-and-pencil measures here were designed to collect appeal reactions to displayed programming. Again, a major challenge was to make the questionnaires comprehensible and, if possible, fun to complete. Although the use of gradated scales was usually avoided due to the tendency of children to have positive response biases, there were occasions when their use was appropriate, as when they were used in combination with other cross-validating methods. When they were employed, it was typical to use figures of faces, smiling-to-frowning, to index the scale along with a verbal description. Photographs and drawings were used extensively, both for visual appeal and to aid comprehension.

Paper-and-pencil instruments were used in several design variations, such as:

1. Cast appeal (photos of the cast, with instructions to pick most and least liked)
2. Postviewing segment voting (selecting most- and least-liked segment from an entire program)
3. Topic preferences (A "triplet voting" design in which brief excerpts from programs on three different topics would be edited together. After all were shown, respondents picked the most and least liked. Then excerpts from three different programs on the same three topics, i.e., a second "triplet," would be shown and responded to, followed by a third.)
4. Program comparisons (overall judgments of preference between two complete programs or paired comparisons among a larger number of programs)

Quantified data from such paper-and-pencil measures were typically supplemented with small group interviews.

After the next major methodology for assessing appeal (the Program Analyzer) is discussed, additional findings on appeal will be presented.

Program Analyzer Method of Appeal Measurement for Displayed Programs

Program Analyzer methodology, which generates moment-by-moment measures of appeal, had been developed by Frank Stanton and Paul Lazarsfeld years ago, even prior to World War II (Lazarsfeld, 1963a,b) and was adapted for use with 8–12-year-olds in *3–2–1 CON-TACT*'s formative research (Mielke & Chen, 1981). A typical Program Analyzer application gives each respondent two push buttons; while viewing a program, one is pressed for positive reactions, the other for negative reactions. A recording device keeps track of each respondent's voting pattern over time, and this is reconstituted as a graph or appeal profile, indexed to the various programming content throughout the test program. Profiles are typically established for the total sample, with breakouts for relevant subgroups, such as by age and sex.

Working with an existing Program Analyzer at CTW, methodological tests were made to see if and under what conditions the procedure would work with children as young as 8–12. After determining that it could be used, CTW joined the Ontario Educational Communications Authority in developing a state-of-the-art apparatus that was portable, wireless, and computerized, called Program Evaluation Analysis Computer (PEAC). Conceptually, both versions are similar, but the PEAC system is far more convenient, flexible, and time-saving.

Through trial and error, we determined that the task of making both positive and negative reactions while viewing was a bit complex for young respondents. Also, the tendency of children to exhibit positive response biases was a problem in that mode. Therefore, we divided test groups in half, asking one group to press when material on the screen was "interesting or fun to watch" and asking the other group to press when the program was "boring or not fun to watch." These instructions, which also derived from field testing of alternatives, legitimized the negative response and provided a form of cross-validation from the independent subsamples. The PEAC system can be programmed to "read" the responses at various time intervals, and we found that 10-second intervals worked well for our purposes.

An advantage of Program Analyzer methodology is that appeal is measured constantly over time as the program is being viewed. Psychologically, this is different from a recollection of appeal after viewing, and it permits fine discriminations among portions of the program. When used as a Program Analyzer, the PEAC system records the exact time of a response along with the response itself. The PEAC system can also be programmed to convert to a multiple-choice mode, with different response options represented by different keys on the keyboard of the hand-held response unit; in this mode, the response is registered by question number and not by time. The multiple-choice mode of the PEAC system was used for cast appeal measures and, as will be discussed later, for measures of comprehension.

Sex Differences in Appeal Data

3–2–1 CONTACT formative research did not attempt to study sex differences as a theoretical issue but as part of a general series aim to make special appeal to girls and minorities because of their underrepresentation in the scientific and engineering workplace as adults. Confirming the needs assessment, we found consistent and sizable sex differences: Boys generally had more positive interests and attitudes in science.

No matter how sincerely one might have wished the findings to be different (i.e., to show fewer sex differences or at least less stereotypical differences), consistent findings from many different studies built up collectively to a persuasive picture that the audience would be bringing to the series substantial sex differences in scientific interests.

Although research could bring out these issues as general trends, one factor at a time (e.g., the appeal of mechanical themes to boys; the appeal of nurturant themes to girls), programming can rarely be completely explained by way of such single factors; nor can a "recipe" for production be inferred. It is not just the sex, age, or ethnicity of a television character that children evaluate, but also what he or she is doing, whether the character is perceived as attractive and competent, the programmatic context in which it is done, and the appeal and comprehensibility of the production treatment in general. If, for whatever reason, a segment is boring, it is doubtful that other factors (e.g., appeal of same-sex role models) will surface in measurable form. The production of and the reaction to complex television materials is inherently a holistic, multivariate process. That is why formative researchers must frequently go beyond hard data and single factors or single principles into "softer" impressions that take into account the actual complexity of particular programs. It is conceivable that in some complex blend of production factors an exception could be found or constructed for virtually any general correlate of sex differences or for any other single-factor principle.

Some of the sex differences were discussed earlier: favorite television shows, viewing of science-related programming, and topic preferences. Other formative studies add to the picture. For example, boys tended to prefer male cast members and girls tended to prefer female cast members. There was one male (Marc) and two females (Trini, Lisa) in the studio cast of *3-2-1 CONTACT*; 51% of the boys but only 5% of the girls preferred Marc. In the Bloodhound Gang cast, also on *3-2-1 CONTACT*, there was one female (Vikki) and two males (Ricardo, Cuff); 47% of the girls but only 10% of the boys preferred Vikki. Even dealing with characters on *The Muppet Show*, the majority of the boys preferred Kermit, whereas the majority of the girls preferred Miss Piggy. This trend of same-sex preferences was found repeatedly.

In general, animals, particularly mammals, were favorably perceived by both girls and boys, but more so by girls. In a forced-choice study (triplet voting), excerpts of animal themes were played against excerpts of space themes and insect–microorganism themes, with the selection of most- and least-liked segments being measured with three different triplets ($N = 200+$). Averaged across all three trials, 65% of the girls but only 31% of the boys chose the animal theme as most-liked. However, 57% of the boys but only 22% of the girls selected the space theme as most-liked. Programming about insects or snakes generally was preferred less by girls than by boys. The same relationship held generally for programming about mechanical and technical devices that did not have a strong social component.

Age Differences in Appeal Data

Shows differentially appealing to the upper end of the target audience appeared to contain more elements of verbal humor, satire, and male–female relationships. In Program Analyzer studies of the *Donny and Marie Show* and *The Muppet Show*, "boring" voting was generally higher among older than among younger children. In a different study, older target audience members were not attracted to cast members younger than they were, feeling that the show was more appropriate for younger children. There appears to be a strong sensitivity among 10- and 11-year-olds about any programming that might be considered "babyish."

Production–Format Features and Appeal

A considerable effort was devoted to developing the format for *3–2–1 CONTACT*. Several options were considered before the actual format was determined, which had these features:

1. Magazine format
2. Weekly themes, with five half-hour programs per theme
3. Three hosts, both in studio settings and in on-location documentary segments, visiting scientists and technologists
4. Inclusion of animation and graphics
5. An inserted mystery serial, "The Bloodhound Gang," featuring three young detectives who solve mysteries using scientific thinking
6. A "Summary Show" once a week designed especially for in-school use

Such a magazine format had the advantage of CTW's experience in working with a combination of forms and segments. Although there was considerable evidence of the appeal of plotted dramas to the target audience, a magazine format offered more flexibility in dropping pieces that did not meet expectations, whereas revisions to a dramatic program would be more costly and difficult. Also, the wide range of content envisioned for the series could be more readily addressed in a magazine format. Finally, a magazine show based in the real world of scientific phenomena promised to be more appropriate for our purposes than one that fictionalized the appeal of science.

In determining the "tone" of the magazine format, it was decided not to attempt to disguise the fact that *3–2–1 CONTACT* was a series about science and technology. As indicated in the Television Interest Survey, 8–12-year-olds do have an appetite for fictional dramatic programming. "The Bloodhound Gang" was designed to appeal to this preference among our viewers, and it was indeed very popular, no matter which methodology was employed. Through extensive formative research contact with the target audience, we also became convinced that viewers were sincerely interested in real-world phenomena. The viewpoint emerged that our target audience had a dual appetite: an eagerness to acquire information about the real world coexisted with an appreciation of dramatic conflict, fast-paced action, and comedy/escapism.

Some of the most successful documentary segments were able to combine both appeals. Documentaries dealing, for example, with life-and-death struggles of predator–prey relationships, or in the clash of interests between oil spills and the efficiency of supertankers, were frequently able to achieve high levels of both appeal and comprehension. Such documentaries engaged not only important scientific content, but significant social issues and/or human interest as well. The appeal of storyline, dramatic conflict, and human interest is no less in a segment of a magazine format than in a complete program.

Use of the audio track is very important, but, due to interactions with other variables, hard and fast generalizations are risky. In a descriptive mode ("show and tell"), as differentiated from dialogue in a dramatic setting, it was generally recommended to use the audio track sparingly and then only in support of a leading and motivating visual. Where an illustrated lecture might make the video slave to the audio, the best documentaries tested did the opposite. "Talking heads" would typically receive instant "boring votes" from children using the Program Analyzer.

Comprehension

Methods of Assessing Comprehension

The earlier section on appeal measures discussed how the PEAC system functioned as a Program Analyzer when the exact timing of the responses was recorded and how the device could also be programmed to go into a "multiple-choice" mode, in which timing was not recorded. Responses in this mode were recorded by question number. Whenever the desired response had been entered, an "advance" command on the individual hand-held units would register that response, indicate the number of the next multiple-choice question, and the unit would then await the next response.

The PEAC system in multiple-choice question mode was used in comprehension testing both for traditional tests of information gain in a quasi-experimental design, and, more typically, for postviewing comprehension tests of program structure (e.g., "Why did Vikki become suspicious about the weight card?"). Conceptually, this is no different from a paper-and-pencil form of multiple-choice testing, but the PEAC system automated the data collection and analysis process, which was much more efficient.

One of the most useful ways of testing both appeal and comprehension was the least automated of all methods: small group interviews. There is no good substitute for the ability of the interview to get children's interpretations of programming, expressed in their own words, with appropriate probes and follow-up questions generated on the spot. Interviews are more time-consuming, and data are typically less quantifiable, but the richness of detail made a useful complement to the quantified data and larger samples of other methods. Sometimes in a small group interview setting, a program would be "freeze-framed" at some point, and comprehension questions could therefore be asked in mid-program, using the "frozen" picture on the screen as a visual referent. Another technique, used less frequently, was to play a test program a second time with the audio turned off, with a target-audience child supplying the narration.

Age Differences in Comprehension

Older children (10–11) display greater comprehension of plot and content. For example, in a study of two plotted dramas, older children were better able to follow plot lines and to recall plot details. They paid closer attention and exhibited better comprehension of the problem, the motivations of the characters, and the resolution. In testing a documentary about an outward bound mission involving interpersonal relations among teenagers, older children not only understood the underlying themes (e.g., finding self-confidence, learning teamwork), but also indicated in postviewing interviews that they liked the film more than younger children did. Young children tended to see only the more concrete or visual aspects of the film, such as "how to hike safely" or "how to climb a mountain."

Multiple-choice comprehension questions were constructed for a series of four 3–2–1 CONTACT test shows, produced as test prototypes for the series itself. For almost every one of the items, higher percentages of older children gave the correct response. These data were interpreted to be based both on older children's greater background knowledge of scientific information (as in factual questions about supertankers) as well as their improved abilities to process information from a television program (as in plot comprehension of "The Bloodhound Gang" mystery stories).

Production Implications of Comprehension Data

Within the target audience, the predominance, in Piagetian terms, of "concrete operational thinking," with "formal operational thinking" yet undeveloped, had implications for production. As a general guideline, Research urged Production and Content not to assume prior knowledge on the part of the audience with most areas of science and technology. In those areas where some children, usually at the older end of the age range, did have some prior background, an elementary treatment of the scientific content did not generally detract from appeal for those viewers.

A clear example of concrete operational thinking came from a study of a visual paradox similar to an Escher drawing. The film involved a physically impossible four-sided staircase, with a ball appearing to bounce its way endlessly around the four sides, always bouncing up. Viewers tended to concentrate on the ball, not the paradox of the staircase. When asked what was unusual about the staircase, their responses included, "A ball just can't turn corners by itself. It would need walls or rails"; or "Balls can't bounce up." Only 2 of 24 children interviewed thought it unusual that the stairs appeared "to go up and up and up."

A comprehension study was made of a film called "Powers of Ten," which featured a rapid journey into both the macroscopic and microscopic universes. The field of vision was expanded 10-fold every 10 seconds, from a man on the ground out to entire galaxies, then back to the ground and into negative powers of 10, into the man's skin, blood cells, and the subatomic structure of the carbon atom. The children seemed to have a better conceptual background for the trip outward than the trip inward. Terminology that was familiar (e.g., Milky Way) tended to be recalled. Terminology that was new and not understood (e.g., neutron) tended not to be recalled, either voluntarily or through aided recall. When visual phenomena were recalled, but without their technical labels (e.g., carbon atoms), they were perceived and recalled in terms meaningful to children (e.g., "marbles," "balloons," "balls on strings, spinning fast").

Another recommendation was to present information visually. One study, for example, tested a program about a chimpanzee trained to learn sign language. Features presented visually (e.g., the chimp brushing his teeth, eating pancakes at the breakfast table, learning signs for various objects) were appealing and were recalled. More abstract scientific ideas buried in the audio track (issues of intelligence and language in humans and animals) in "talking head" segments had very low appeal and were not comprehended or recalled. What came across to the children was the idea that a chimp had been trained to do tricks, not the significance of symbolic language.

In voiceovers, when the verbal narration would go on to higher levels of abstraction while holding on a constant, static visual, that verbal information tended never to be recalled. In one example, a paleontologist stood next to a dinosaur bone, giving extensive verbal explanations on why it could not have belonged to a hippo or elephant, but the children, seeing the dinosaur bone throughout, did not follow the argument.

One interesting case of a need for more verbal audio was with a 3–2–1 CONTACT animated segment that originally had none. With a musical background only, the animation showed that by doubling the outside dimensions of a cube its internal volume would be increased eight times. Earlier formative research on surface-to-volume ratios, involving hands-on exercises with modeling clay and sugar cubes, had indicated some of the conceptual problems faced by children in relating surface to volume. Comprehension of the animated piece was low. Research recommended that a simple narration track be added. This was done, and comprehension was improved.

Another production implication, alluded to earlier, is the power of storyline, whether used in a complete program or in a segment of a magazine format. Stories can be a source of motivation to find out what will happen next, providing momentum that can carry the viewer through brief periods of less exciting material. The viewer makes an "investment" in a story, and this can justify delayed gratification, whereas nonstories will have a higher need to be gratifying continuously. Stories are also an effective cognitive organizer. The development of a story provides a logical sequence that can function as a mnemonic for recall of information. Particularly in settings of an engaging story, we found length of attention span not to be a problem among 8–12-year-olds.

Concluding Comment

Retrieving an introductory statement here, the enormous complexity of a television program makes it difficult for formative research to infer generalizations from possibly idiosyncratic programming or to pull out detailed guidance from general principles. A seemingly endless supply of variables can be imposed on programming and its relationship to the audience and still fall far short of a predictive recipe for a new program. It is always easier to "explain" an old program in detail than it is to prescribe in detail a new program. Even the traditional "production–feedback–revision" cycle of formative research is difficult to implement completely in television, relative, say, to print or computer programs, because of the expense involved. Formative researchers can always join the classical litany of their theoretical brethren: "More research is needed."

A very substantial amount of formative research was conducted for *3–2–1 CONTACT*, some of which has been highlighted here in the belief that it might be of interest beyond its original in-house function and readership and in the hope that better bridges can be built between theoretical and applied research in children's television. Formative research is more attuned to generating hypotheses than to testing them, but its basis in the real world—that is, real television programs and real test audiences—provides an external validity that should not be ignored by those who test hypotheses and construct or modify theory. Conversely, the considerable insight into the target audience from theoretical work in developmental psychology, as well as strategic approaches from science educators and philsophers of science indicate the value of theory at the project level. The challenge of complementarity is to keep building the bridges between theoretical and applied research, not only because both can benefit from the experience, but also primarily because children will benefit from better programming as a result.

References

Bruner, J. S., Olver, R. R., & Greenfield, P. M. (Eds). *Studies in cognitive growth.* New York: Wiley, 1966.

Chen, M. Television, science and children: Formative evaluation for *3–2–1 CONTACT. Journal of Educational Technology Systems*, 1980–1981, 9, 261–276.

Children's Television Workshop. *A children's television series about science and technology* (Proposal). New York: Children's Television Workshop, October 1977.

Johnson, R. T. Nine-year-olds' attitudes toward science: An interpretation of the National Assessment data. In *Attitudes toward science.* Denver, Colo.: National Assessment of Educational Progress, 1979.

Karplus, R. The science curriculum—one approach. In D. Bramwell & J. Fishleder (Eds.), *SCIS Omnibus.* Berkley, Calif.: Lawrence Hall of Science, 1973.

Lazarsfeld, P. F. Some reflections on past and future research on broadcasting (Afterword). In G. A. Steiner, *The people look at television.* New York: Knopf, 1963. (a)

Lazarsfeld, P. F. Trends in broadcasting research (Theoretical Research Center of the Radio and TV Culture Institute, the Nippon Hoso Kyokai, Toyko, Japan). *Studies of Broadcasting*, 1963, 1, 49–64. (b)

Mielke, K., & Chen, M. Making Contact: Formative research in touch with children. In *CTW International Research Notes*, No. 3, Spring, 1980. New York: Children's Television Workshop, 1980.

Mielke, K., & Chen, M. *Children, television, and science: An overview of the formative research for 3–2–1 CONTACT.* New York: Children's Television Workshop, 1981.

Mielke, K., Chen, M., Clarke, H., & Myerson-Katz, B. *Survey of television viewing interests among eight–to–twelve-year-olds.* New York: Children's Television Workshop, 1978.

Myerson-Katz, B. CTW's new science series: The role of formative research. *Televisions*, 1980, 7, 24–31.

National Assessment of Educational Progress. *Science technical report: Summary volume.* Denver, Colo.: Education Commission of the States, 1977.

National Science Foundation. *Women and Minorities in science and engineering.* Washington, D.C.: U.S. Government Printing Office, 1977.

Omerod, M. B., & Duckworth, D. *Pupils' attitudes to science: A review of research.* Windsor, England: National Foundation for Educational Research, 1975.

Palmer, E. L. Formative research in the production of television for children. In D. E. Olson (Ed.), *Media and symbols: The forms of expression, communication, and education* (Seventy-Third Yearbook of the National Society for the Study of Education). Chicago: University of Chicago Press, 1974.

Palmer, E. L., Crawford, J. J., Kielsmeier, C. J., & Inglis, L. *A comparative study of current educational television programs for preschool children.* Monmouth: Oregon State System of Higher Education, 1968. (ERIC Document Reproduction Service No. ED 032 123)

Stake, R., & Easley, J. *Case studies in science education* (Vol. 1). Champaign: Center for Instructional Research and Curriculum Evaluation, University of Illinois, 1978.

Wakshlag, J. L., Day, K. D., & Zillmann, D. Selective exposure to educational television programs as a function of differently paced humorous inserts. *Journal of Educational Psychology*, 1981, 73(1), 27–32.

Weiss, I. R. *1977 national survey of science, mathematics, and social studies education.* Research Triangle Park, N.C.: Research Triangle Institute, 1978.

White, S. H. Evidence for a hierarchical arrangement of learning processes. In L. P.

Lipsett & C. C. Spiker (Eds.), *Advances in child behavior and development* (Vol. 2). New York: Academic Press, 1975.

White, S. H., & Siegel, A. W. Cognitive development: The new inquiry. *Young Children,* 1976, *31,* 425–435.

Woellner, E. H. *Requirements for certification, 1977–1978* (42nd ed.). Chicago: University of Chicago Press, 1977.

chapter 11

Implications of Childhood Television Viewing for Cognition, Imagination, and Emotion[1]

JEROME L. SINGER
DOROTHY G. SINGER

Growing Up in a Television Environment

Research approaches to television since the late 1970s have increasingly reflected the role of this medium in relation to the natural cognitive and affective development of the growing child. Children are already attentive to the television medium as early as 6–9 months of age (Hollenbeck & Slaby, 1979). It therefore is no longer useful to talk of the television set as an extraneous and occasional intruder into the life of a child. Children are growing up in an environment in which they must learn to organize experiences and emotional responses not only in relationship to the physical and social environment of the home, but also in relation to the omnipresent screen on which miniature people and animals talk, sing, dance, and encourage the purchase of toys, candies, and breakfast foods.

As they grow up children must learn not only to decode the verbal utterances of parents and friends or to establish schemata for the mean-

[1]Some of the authors' research reported herein was sponsored by grants from the National Science Foundation, the American Broadcasting Company, the Teleprompter Corporation, and the Spencer Foundation. Portions of this manuscript were presented at meetings of the Society for Research in Child Development, Boston, 1981, and the American Psychological Association, Los Angeles, 1981.

CHILDREN'S UNDERSTANDING
OF TELEVISION

ings of the smiles and frowns of adults around them, but they must also learn the special conventions of the television medium, its smaller-than-life frame, its appearances and disappearances of characters, intrusions of irrelevant commercials to otherwise engrossing story material, the meanings of zooms, fade-outs, miraculous superhero leaps, and flashbacks. Children may be spending more time watching television than they spend engaged in conversation with adults or siblings, and certainly more time before the set than they spend in school. What impact does this new form of continuous input have upon the nature of their own cognitive growth? Is it possible that the structural properties of the television medium with its visual predominance, rapid shifts of sequence, and musical background may be influencing the very way new information from other nontelevision environments is now being processed? Is perhaps the very nature of thinking itself modified by the much heavier component of visual stimulation that characterizes regular television viewing in comparison with acquiring information through reading? What influence does television with its heavy load of fictional content and extremes of emotion have upon the affective development of the heavy viewer? Do heavy viewers come to rely on the medium for imagination and escape and neglect personal skill practice? We are just beginning to see research addressing some of these issues.

Some Implications of New Developments in Cognitive and Affective Research for Television Study

Cognition and Developmental Levels

Before considering some of the specific implications of recent research on television, it may be useful to look at the television medium from the standpoint of the major paradigm shift in psychology that has characterized the decades since the 1960s. It was in this period that the stimulus–response models of learning and memory began to give way to the cognitive orientation which predominates today.

Modern psychology regards the human being as playing an active and selective role in approaching each new environment. Cognitive theorists place much greater emphasis on the fact that individuals bring to each environment preestablished schemata or what might be called "preparatory plans," based, of course, on previous experience as well as fantasized anticipations about what may be expected in a situation.

These schemata have been built up over dozens of previous interactions with the environment as well as upon further reflections upon these experiences during mental rehearsal. Some of our schemata are more complex, more integrated or organized and differentiated than others.

The various schemata we have stored and organized in our brain also are in part dependent on the developmental stage we are at in life. Children in general have been exposed to far less information than adults. In addition, they lack certain kinds of organizing and interpretive skills. When they are very young, it takes them longer to grasp particular concepts. Indeed, there are some types of cognitive operations such as conservation of number that they cannot perform at all before they have reached certain age levels. Much of the impressive career of Jean Piaget was devoted to explicating the developmental stages of the cognitive capacities of children and to showing how notions of time, space, or morality are beyond their grasp before they have attained appropriate levels of development. Research on reading or on television viewing, as we shall see, makes it clear that it is not only limitations in vocabulary that impede children of preschool age from grasping materials that may be presented. They simply lack the fundamental integrative capacity to organize information into meaningful concepts, a task that may seem obvious to older children or adults.

Each person, as we have indicated, brings to a new situation a complex set of plans, private images, and anticipations. Indeed, this is one of the major ways in which we manage to avoid being completely bombarded by the tremendous range of stimulation available in any new environment we enter. These plans or anticipatory schemata are not only specific to situations but involve strategies of search and selection related to the kind of information to be processed or to the kind of social setting one anticipates (Blumenthal, 1977).

Here is where we see a close tie between emotional development and information processing. When our strategies for processing new materials and our specific anticipations match well with the information we actually confront in a new setting, we generally experience positive affect, joy, and a smiling response or a general sense of well-being. If, however, our anticipatory images or plans for processing information are inadequate, we may experience negative emotions (Izard, 1977; J. Singer, 1974; Tomkins, 1962, 1963). The average child probably develops the schema that a major difference between the adults on the television set and his parents or other grown ups is that the people on the television set do not answer the children's questions. Television also presents material generally unrelated to the child's immediate environment. Imagine the surprise of a child if one of the characters on television were suddenly to call out the viewer's name or address the child directly!

Some Characteristics of How Television Presents Information

In American television, the attempt is made to build up the viewers' anticipations through excitement, violence, and chases so that the viewer will be looking forward to the next event or outcome of some action or comedy sequence. At this point, one is generally interrupted with the presentation of a commercial. Presumably since anticipation has led one to be glued to the television set, the attention will be maintained for whatever commercial then appears, and the message of the commercial should come across effectively to at least some segment of the audience. This assumption of the television industry flies in the face of the cognitive research findings on the importance of reflection for storage of information in long-term memory. Indeed, Bryant and Comisky (1978) found that when commercials were sandwiched between highly exciting or absorbing action sequences of a detective show they were much *less* likely to be recalled.

The producers' approach also presupposes that viewers will not have developed an alternative private strategy for television viewing based on their years of experience of being interrupted. Actually, many people simply get up and go to the toilet or get some food or look down at some reading material they have in their lap whenever the commercials come on. Adults have often learned simply to tune out the commercials mentally. The advertisers, of course, count on the fact that not everyone will have developed such strategies, and therefore they will get at least some fraction of the vast audience who will carefully attend to the commercial message presented. Children, especially in the preschool and early elementary school ages, often do not have such commercial "tune-out" strategies; they may respond with even greater attention to commercial interruptions particularly since many advertisements are carefully produced, using language, sound effects, and music to which children's listening strategies are especially attuned.

Reflective Thought and Television Presentations

Another characteristic of the ongoing cognitive process is the significance of reflection. It is very likely that we experience relatively few really "blank" periods in ongoing thought. Even as we process new information from the environment we tend quickly to reverberate it briefly in short-term memory. In the course of such "instant replay" we may initiate a process of labeling events for later recall or of assigning events to particular verbal or imagery categories for encoding. Our ongoing thought, and indeed even our daydreams, may play a rather important role in how we organize information and how we begin to set up new plans and anticipations for our future behaviors. In the course of such continuous mental activity, we are clearly also laying the groundwork for carrying forward the actions designed to implement our major motives and values. We are creating intentions that have decision-making and action implications.

Some Problems Posed by the Structural Characteristics of Television

To what extent does the sheer proliferation of information provided on the television set interfere with the reflective thought which is necessary for the development of longer term intentions and action sequences? This issue needs to be more extensively addressed than it has been as yet, even in the literature to be presented here. The younger child who has not yet developed strategies for "tuning out" irrelevancies may be especially vulnerable in this respect. Even programs such as Sesame Street that seek to be informative as well as entertaining may often miss the mark because they allow the preschool viewer little time for reflection. The data brought together by Collins (1982), Rice, Huston, and Wright (1982) and D. Singer (1982) all provide some indications that the pacing of television programming geared for children may require more serious attention from producers interested in informing as well as entertaining children.

The question of pacing and of structural properties of the medium go beyond information processing. As suggested earlier, the close tie between cognition and emotion has been increasingly recognized by research investigators. Extremely rapidly paced material that presents much novelty along with higher levels of sound, fast movement, intercutting, etc., may generate surprise and indeed confusion in a viewer whose anticipatory strategies or well-established schemata are not yet prepared for coping with this material. Foreigners accustomed to a much slower pace of television have often told us that they become almost physically pained when they first observe American commercial television. In the case of children, there are indications in the studies cited by Rice et al. (1982), Zillmann (1982), and Dorr (1982) that hyperactive and aggressive behavior by children may be a reflection not only of imitation of specific aggressive responses but also of the sheer arousal produced by certain types of programming or commercial presentation. Natural field studies carried out by D. Singer and J. Singer (1980) and by J. Singer and D. Singer (1981) have yielded indications that children who were consistently heavy viewers of the more frenetic types of programming such as the Gong Show, and (for younger children) even the rapid-paced Sesame Street, three months or more later showed more tendencies toward overt aggressive behavior in a day-care setting.

It is also increasingly clear that there is a highly differentiated set of emotions that characterize the human being; these range from startle and surprise, fear and terror, through anger, sadness, distress, and shame, as well as joy and excitement (Izard, 1977; Tomkins, 1962, 1963). To what extent are children being socialized by constant viewing of television toward experiencing a full range of emotions and for identifying appropriate settings for the experience of emotions? Or, can it be argued that in a sense such extensive exposure, especially to events such as violence, may be neutralizing through habituation or satiation—the appropriate negative emotion at an early age? We have as yet unsatisfactory answers to some of these questions.

Television Viewing and Consciousness

So far emphasis has been placed on the most basic aspects of the cognitive and affective development of the child, questions of attention, sequencing, arousal, and reflection. There may be at a more molar level other important issues to be addressed with respect to the medium. To what extent is more general consciousness and imaginative capacity influenced by the fact that television is predominantly a visual medium? For young children recognizable speech or music and sound-effects cues may serve to direct their attention back to the screen after their attention has lapsed during less familiar content (Anderson & Levin, 1976). For adults or older children, television, in contrast to radio and reading, emphasizes our most significant modality, the visual. We also know that there are at least two major kinds of coding systems through which the brain operates. One is a verbal–linguistic and perhaps more action-oriented processing system linked especially to the left hemisphere of the brain. The other coding system involves a more receptive, global, spatially oriented or imagery-focused process linked to the right half of the brain. Is television maximizing reliance on one as against the other as a habitual form of thinking?

So far no adequate evidence has been adduced to support this view, despite the appearance of much passionate commentary in popular literature. It is possible that, by providing extensively prepackaged visual "fantasy" material, the television medium is precluding sufficient opportunities for practicing of imaginative skills by young children. The lively visual quality of television may make it more difficult for children to shift from such a medium to making sense of purely verbal presentations such as teachers' lectures. The visual factor in television may also contrast with the more complicated decoding and encoding processes involved in reading. It is clear that children who watch television 3–4 hours a night are simply less likely to be practicing the necessary skills required to master reading in their early school years. On the other hand, it might be argued that, for a sizable segment of the population (representing the socially and educationally disadvantaged groups), travel and reading experience prior to the era of television might have been so restricted that they suffered from limited awareness of the range of information outside their families or neighborhoods. The availability of world knowledge through television may actually enhance general information capacities for the poor or culturally limited children. Perhaps it may even stimulate interest in reading and education. As we shall see, some of these issues are only beginning to be addressed (Morgan & Gross, 1982).

Finally, as part of a child's experience of growing up in our culture, some investigators have called attention to the desirability that children learn something about *how to watch* television and *how to understand* the medium. Much as we teach them to appreciate literature or to read the newspaper carefully, we need to prepare them to understand the television in their home. The emergence of the field of critical television-viewing skills is essentially in its infancy, but it reflects a trend towards incorporating learning about the medium as a part of cognitive and emotional development.

Specific Cognitive Issues and Research Findings

Format, Attention, Reflection, and Adult Mediation

An analysis by J. Singer (1980) has proposed that United States television is a remarkably "cluttered" stimulus field, which holds viewer attention by piling up novelty through shifts of scene, content, mixtures of visual movement, music, sound effects, and speech. It maximizes the orienting reflex by its very rapidity, minimizes opportunities for reflection and thus for efficient encoding, storage and retrieval of information. Because viewers watch so much and because advertisements are repeated so often, the medium has been effective commercially, chiefly by reliance on the more passive recognition memory rather than by reliance on the more active process of retrieval of stored information. Would television advertising that ran much longer, but less frequently, and was positioned against a more neutral pre- and postpresentation background yield more effective reflective responses and storage in memory? Would such clustered, nonintrusive advertising be more conducive to later retrieval with buying intentions?

It can be hypothesized that the "busyness" of United State television serves to minimize self-awareness and reflective thought. Television's special appeal to many viewers may lie in the fact that it preempts attention to one's own ongoing stream of consciousness and thus avoids preoccupation with the many unfinished acts and "current concerns" that might otherwise come to focal awareness (Klinger, 1978; J. Singer, 1978).

This proposal also reflects the widely held view (at least among intellectuals or some critical groups of parents and educators) (Mander, 1978; Winn, 1977) that television viewing is an extremely passive, almost addicting experience. Although such a generalization seems too broad for a medium used in many different ways by adults at various life stages and children at different phases of their cognitive development, it does have implications that merit closer attention. If we are concerned with how and what children learn from television, then we must examine more carefully the interaction between the special properties of the medium and how it is watched.

A small controversy has grown up about the educational and emotional implications of *Sesame Street*, by far the most internationally successful children's program designed to educate preschoolers while entertaining them. *Sesame Street* was constructed on the model of United States commercial television with short unrelated sequences (usually no longer than 3 minutes until quite recently) and at times as many as 35 such segments in a 60-minute show. The principle was to hold preschool children's attention so that they would be watching when (instead of commercials) lessons about the names of alphabet letters or of numbers appeared on the screen (Lesser, 1974).

There can be no doubt from experimental evidence that *Sesame Street* is effective in attracting children's attention to the screen in contrast to other nonmeaningful distractors (Lesser, 1974), or to more slowly paced children's shows like *Mister Rogers' Neighborhood*, or the British–Australian *Playschool* (Noble, 1979–1980; D. Singer & J. Singer, 1976; Tower, Singer, Singer, & Biggs, 1979). What is less certain is whether the format of the program is genuinely conducive to effective learning or development of reading readiness. It may be that attracting attention to the screen in the way it does, *Sesame Street* may be maximizing an unreflective viewing stance. Indeed, its generally high levels of arousing material and pixillation may actually develop an expectation about how the world is, as teachers often complain, and may also lead to jumpiness or hyper-activity. Although the careful laboratory studies by Anderson and Levin (1976) and Anderson, Lorch, Field, and Sanders (1981) have demonstrated that preschool children already show signs of attentional "strategies" and look away from the set when adults talk or when very unfamiliar material is presented even in a lively format, their work does not address the impact of daily viewing under more natural circumstances or the issues of genuine comprehension or emotional response. Children may not be passive viewers in a mechanical sense, but it is possible that they may still not be adequately processing material from *Sesame Street*. Noble (1979–1980) has reviewed the research literature on the learning effect of *Sesame Street* from a perspective similar to the one just presented and has argued that, from available data as well as from a theoretical point of view, the educational effectiveness of the format can be seriously questioned.

A critical issue in how television can be effective in producing an active learning orientation by child viewers relates to the role of adult mediation and teaching. It can be argued that, because of their limited development of schemata, preschoolers are especially dependent for learning on the mediation of adults. Parents suggest features to which the children can attend, restructure complex environmental stimuli into miniature playlike components, or describe ongoing processes in vocabulary easily accessible to children, thus creating manageable information-chunks for the children (Feuerstein, 1977; J. Singer, 1973). Such adult mediation is rarely an on-screen part of *Sesame Street*; indeed the evidence from the extensive analyses by Cook, Appleton, Connor, Shaffer, Tomkin, and Weber (1975) has suggested the possibility that parental encouragement of viewing seems to have led to a widening of the gap between middle and lower socioeconomic child viewers. Their findings imply that adult mediation may be a crucial determinant of how much children take away from *Sesame Street*, but we lack further definitive evidence on this score. It is clear, however, that a conscious decision was made early in the development of *Sesame Street* by researchers to minimize adult teaching or adult voiceovers for fear that these might lead to less attention to the screen (Lesser, 1974).

A contrasting approach has been adoped by Fred Rogers in his development of the *Mister Rogers' Neighborhood* programs for preschoolers. He appears on the screen frequently, talks slowly, avoids sudden "magical" effects, asks children to reflect about issues and encourages them to talk back to the screen. Although children do not seem as enthusiastic or attentive while watching the show as they are to *Sesame Street* or cartoons, research on *Mister Rogers' Neighborhood* does yield consistent evidence of later spontaneous positive behaviors (Coates, Pusser, & Goodman, 1976; D. Singer & J. Singer, 1976; Stein & Friedrich, 1975; Tower *et al.*, 1979). Observations of children watching the program suggest that, even when children are not actually looking at the screen, they seem to benefit from listening to *Mister Rogers' Neighborhood* (Tower *et al.*, 1979). A very similar result is reported by Noble (1979–1980) in his studies of the British–Australian *Playschool* where adult voiceovers and modeling or mediation are especially emphasized. A study by Sturm and Jörg (1981) in Germany indicated that adults as part of a television show with clearly presented visual action sequences proved more effective in producing learning in children than did the identical sequences with minimal verbal commentary. The general thrust of research findings suggest, then, that "real" adult mediation is most effective in producing increases in prosocial or imaginative behavior in children (Ahammer & Murray, 1979; J. Singer & D. Singer, 1976). The availability of adult "parent-figures" on television or of mediating voiceovers by adults for visual action sequences, paced at easily comprehensible levels, may also be effective in producing learning in preschoolers.

Causal Sequences, Codes, and Comprehension

The recent review by Collins (1982) moves from predominantly experimental studies on the factors of attention and segment comprehensibility to broader comprehension of programs and attention to relevant material through deeper grasp of causality and inference. Some of the ingenious work of Anderson and his group cited earlier confirms the fact that children at early ages already demonstrate some attentional strategies. Increasingly sophisticated methodological procedures are available for studying sequences of viewing by children in relation to developing emphasis on visual versus auditory cues, different degrees of familiarity, and potential comprehensibility.

Collins has called special attention to the important issue of whether children are beginning to learn "scripts," that is, details derived from experience on how to fill in the missing "terms" in materials that are rendered pictorially with many gaps in sequence. They must also learn certain conventions or codes in the storytelling that take place on television. Indeed, here is where developmental differences are especially striking. Further research is especially urgent, particularly if one hopes eventually to see television not only as entertainment, but also as a potential source of significant learning for children.

Collins also raises some serious questions for the industry, not only by pointing out the necessity for attention to age-specific capacities of the child, but also in noticing that the pattern of American commercial television, characterized by interruption, often leads younger viewers to focus only on acts of aggression without being able to be aware of possible cause–effect sequences. Young children miss the implications of the aggression within the story line, recalling only the acts themselves. Collins' own research and the other work he summarized has emphasized that programming for children should pay special attention to the cognitive limitations of children in grasping cause–effect sequences from films.

Media Conventions and Behavioral Effects

Rice et al. (1982) have focused even more specifically on the special structure of properties of the medium, camera and production techniques of pacing, zooming, cluttering, and loudness. The child must learn to decode some of these conventions (e.g., the meaning of fades from one locale to another; of closeups versus long shots; of flashbacks presumed to represent memories and thinking). An increasing area of research in child development has been on what is called metacognition. We are more aware that children have to learn that people think and to identify their own thoughts much as they learn about the external environment. In this sense, children at earlier ages have a problem in decoding intended suggestions that characters on television are "lost" in thought or memory.

Rice et al. (1982) have proposed interesting and suggestive models for studying the relationship between familiarization, novelty, and complexity of material. These models can serve as a basis for examining the likelihood that children will be capable at various ages of decoding television conventions, maintaining interest in a plot, and ultimately showing adequate comprehension of increasingly inferential material. Their work also calls attention to the specific effect that television may have on children when it provides material that is comprehensible only in certain of its elements, such as the aggresson or liveliness of activity, and not in some of its other features. The possible arousal effect of rapid and loud material and the implications of this arousal for the child's subsequent behavior is identified. Children may over-focus on violent content, which is relatively easily comprehended. They can become sufficiently aroused by loud noise and music and translate such arousal into one of the few obvious responses available to a child, an aggressive act. Thus, some of the attention-getting devices widely used on television put children at risk of increased hyperactivity or aggression even when specific violent content is not represented on the screen.

In general, the review by Rice *et al.* again suggests that producers of television shows, whether for educational or entertainment purposes, are going to have to pay much more careful attention to the decoding capacity of the children and to the pacing of messages. For example, their review brings out rather clearly the fact that certain of the programs on Public Television, *Mister Rogers' Neighborhood* and *The Electric Company*, for example, are characterized by more moderate pacing, more mutual reinforcement of verbal and auditory material presented at a pace allowing for some degree of reflective attention by the child. Future research should include more work on optimal patterns of constructing television formats for children at various ages to maximize decoding or code learning and comprehension.

Implications of Television Viewing for Imagination and Emotion

We have called attention so far to the specific implications of television format for cognitive functions and comprehension, especially in early childhood. We shall next examine some relationships between viewing patterns and the development of imagination or the emergence of reality–fantasy distinctions. In carrying forward this review we will, of necessity, also note some findings linking the viewing of television content to overt emotional reactions or behavioral patterns.

It can be hypothesized that television viewing might have important advantages in providing children with a rich source of content on which to base their imaginative play and their emerging capacities for fantasy and creative thought. In this sense television might play the mediating role once provided for children by parental or family figures, teachers or professional storytellers and (for older children) by storybooks and, more recently, radio and the movies. It is possible, however, that, both in its format and its attractiveness as an alternative to self-awareness and reflective thought, television, particularly when viewed extensively and regularly, may come to substitute for self-generated imaginative activity. It may interfere with the necessary practice of the cognitive skills that are needed for imagination and creativity.

Using Television as a Substitute for Active Thought

Suggestions that television viewing may be less stimulating for memory retrieval and imaginative thought have come from experimental studies by Meringoff (1980) and Greenfield, Geber, Beagles-Roos, Farrar, and Gat (1981), which indicate that listening to story material on radio yields better recall and more imaginative responses than watching comparable material on television. These studies do not consider some possible individual differences in imaginative predisposition, television viewing experience, or other possible mediating variables. They do point towards the possibility that television-viewing may create a less alert, less active orientation toward dealing with the material presented.

Again we confront some indications that the general orientation adopted towards television is one of using it to substitute for one's own active thought and self-reflection. A remarkable study with adults by Csikszentmihalyi and Kubey (1981) examined patterns of cognition and emotion during television viewing as well as at other times during the day using random signal generators which "beeped" and required the participants to record what they were doing at the time. They also rated their levels of cognition, skill, challenge, emotion, and sense of "potency" or vitality at that moment. The data clearly suggested that "television viewing was consistently and closely tied to relaxation, to weaker cognitive investments and to lower feelings of potency when compared to other activities [p. 312]." A large scale study by McIlwraith (1981) has pointed to consistent correlations for children and adults between a pattern of unpleasant private fantasy and heavy television viewing. Careful statistical analyses ruling out other factors consistently indicated that heavy television-viewing children or adults also reported daydream patterns on J. Singer and Antrobus' (1972) Imaginal Processes Inventory which reflected a guilty–dysphoric dimension of inner life rather than a pattern of positive–constructive fantasy. It seems likely that, living in an uncomfortable "inner space," such persons seek out television to "replace" their own thoughts (a uses and gratification model). It is also possible, however, that heavy viewing with exposure to the considerable quantity of hostile and violent content that characterizes television may feed into consciousness further unpleasant fantasy material (an influence or social reality hypothesis). As yet we do not have truly adequate data to choose between these models (Lindlof, 1980), but it remains possible that either (a) a third undetermined variable mediates these correlations between television viewing and an unpleasant inner life; or (b) there may actually be a cyclical pattern in which reliance on heavy viewing to relieve unpleasant hostile or guilty thought also has further negative consequences on consciousness. Watching violent or frightening television may stimulate even more experiences of guilt, anger, or social distrust.

Imagination and Television Viewing in Preschoolers

In a longitudinal study with a sample of 141 male and female preschoolers, J. Singer & D. Singer (1981) attempted to determine which combination of variables (demographic background and television-viewing patterns) best predicted the degree of imaginativeness of play shown by the children across the year. The six variables that yielded a multiple correlation of .45 in estimating imaginativeness of play with F $(6,99) = 4.21$, $p < .01$ included sex (male); age; scores on the Imaginative Play Predisposition Interview (Singer, 1973); the weekly average number of hours of situation comedy viewing; the proportion of hours spent watching action–adventure television shows (negative loading); and IQ. In effects, brighter older boys who score higher on an Imaginative Play Predisposition Interview, who watch more hours of situation comedies but relatively fewer hours of action–adventure shows are more likely to be the most imaginative children in observed play. Is it possible that these children are being socialized away from watching the more grossly active violent programming towards a more "androgynous" nonaggressive viewing pattern? These data do not lend themselves to a clear determination of causality but are suggestive in this regard. A study at the Yale University Family Television Research and Consultation Center following up some of these same children indicated that sex stereotyping of toys and occupations by both boys and girls was related to parents' attitudes. Those children with more stereotyping were more likely to have parents who adopted strong traditional male or female attitudes in questionnaire responses. The viewing of less stereotyped public television programming rather than typical commercial fare was also characteristic of children who showed less traditional or sex-role stereotyped toy choices (Repetti, 1980). In general, data from our laboratory suggest that watching less violent or arousing programming is linked to less sex stereotyping and also to more imaginative and less overtly aggressive behavior.

If a child is watching considerable amounts of television, will he or she generate imaginary companions? It is conceivable that the development of an inner fantasy life and self-generation of a fantasy companion may play a counteracting role to the direct imitation of violent material observed either in the home or on television. The child with an extensive resource of fantasy may translate stimulating content from the television medium into make-believe play form, hurting no one, whereas the child who lacks such a play capacity as part of her or his repertory may imitate aggressive television by a direct assault on another child. In a study with 111 middle-class children, results indicated that 65% of the preschool children reported they had some form of make-believe friend (J. Singer & D. Singer, 1981). A parent's report that a child had an imaginary playmate proved to be a powerful predictor of the likelihood that the child would play happily in nursery school, behave cooperatively with friends and adults, use somewhat more enriched language in free play, and prove less likely to have been watching a good deal of television. Boys who had imaginary playmates at home and who watched few action–adventure shows were much less likely to turn out to be aggressive in overt behavior in the nursery school. Results were less clear-cut for girls.

Imagination, Creativity, and School Attitudes in Elementary Schoolchildren

Harrison and Williams (1977) analyzed data in 137 subjects in three Canadian towns: Notel (no television), Unitel (one channel) and Multitel (four channels). The study incorporated fairly careful controls to insure comparability of culture. They had administered the vocabularly subtest of the Wechsler Intelligence Scale for Children (WISC), a measure of spatial ability (the Block Design subtest of the WISC) and ideational fluency tasks from Wallach and Kogan's work on creativity. Children were tested in grades 4 and 7 in all three towns; following introduction of television, tests were given to children again in grades 6 and 9 after the Notel group had 2 year's exposure to television. When Notel children were divided at the median according to verbal associative fluency scores obtained before Notel was introduced to television, the authors found no difference in the mean hours of viewing reported after 2 years exposure to television. This would argue against a differential viewing preference for high and low creatives. The Notel children's verbal fluency scores decreased significantly from the first to second phase of the study. It appeared that television exposure is negatively related to children's performance on verbal fluency tasks. There was no town differences for the figural fluency scores in either phase of the project in the cross-sectional comparisons, but Unitel scores increased significantly from the first to second phases. Television apparently did not affect the vocabulary or the performance on Block Design but did seem to have an impact on the creativity scores. Harrison and Williams' observations suggested that displacement effects could explain these results; they noted that creative behaviors often reflected self-generated play activities that did not include television content.

Examining the correlation of television with the reading habits and imagination of 185 third-, fourth-, and fifth-graders, Zuckerman, Singer, & Singer (1980) found that imaginative behavior as rated by teachers was predicted by higher IQ and recorded home viewing of fewer fantasy–violence television programs. The amount of time children spent reading was inversely related to the amount of time they spent watching fantasy–violence programs. One explanation may be that fantasy–violence programs offer the same kinds of excitement as adventure books, fairy tales, or other popular children's books and therefore satisfy the need for escapism and fantasy. This study also found that those children who were heavy viewers of cartoons were rated as low in enthusiasm in schoolwork by classroom teachers. These data may argue also for a displacement effect. Watching fantasy–violence television may possibly replace reading or other self-generated activities that are known to stimulate imagination and "world knowledge."

In a study using 120 sixth- and seventh-grade children randomly assigned to print, audiotape, or videotape conditions, Meline (1976) found that there were differences in the capacities of each medium to stimulate or inhibit creative thinking. Children in the video condition gave fewer solutions that departed from given facts and concepts. Children in the audiotape or print conditions gave more stimulus-free and transformational ideas.

Using fantasy scales based on J. Singer and Antrobus (1972) Imaginal Processes Inventory, Rosenfeld, Huesmann, Eron, and Torney-Purta (1982) examined the major styles of fantasizing among 748 children. Three styles of fantasizing were found: *fanciful*, in which children daydream about fairy tales and implausible events; *active*, in which youngsters dream about heroes, intellectual pursuits, and achievement; and *aggressive negative*, in which daydreams concern killing, fighting, and being hurt. Results suggest that for both boys and girls, the viewing of violence, fantasy behavior, and sex-role preference are independently related to peer-rated evidence of aggression. Girls rarely engage in negative aggressive fantasy. Those girls who tend to fantasize about vigorous, action—daydreams where heroes and heroines win games or struggle to achieve—are the most aggressive of the gender. On the other hand, the most aggressive boys are those who fantasize chiefly about aggression—harmful acts to other persons. Children who watch a great deal of action-oriented or violent television seem likely to reflect this in their fantasies and to carry this out in overt behavior. In data reported by J. Singer and D. Singer (1981) preschool children whose play themes reflect specific television references to cartoons, superheroes and action-detective characters are also more likely to be aggressive.

A striking example of the interrelations of imagination, television viewing, and overt aggression emerged from a multiple regression analysis carried out during a year's study by J. Singer and D. Singer (1981). They looked at what combinations of variables best predicted the likelihood of overt aggression by children in nursery schools. Boys who showed the *least* inner imagination as measured by inkblot responses or as estimated from parental observations and who also watched programming in which there was considerable depiction of violence were the most likely to be overtly aggressive at school.

Results of a study with 200 lower socioeconomic status (SES) preschoolers indicated a persisting link between aggressive behavior or expression of anger at school and the viewing of *Sesame Street* as well as specifically action–adventure programming or news broadcasts (J. Singer & D. Singer, 1980). In general, this linkage of action shows to overt aggression confirms results obtained earlier in the work with middle-class preschoolers. In the lower SES sample these findings were especially characteristic of lower IQ, minority boys. The data do suggest that children who get into more difficulties at school and show less mature group behavior are among the heavier viewers; they watch more violent action–adventure programming and are less likely to be watching specially designed prosocial programs on public television such as *Mister Rogers' Neighborhood* (D. Singer & J. Singer, 1980).

The very recent studies by Eron (1982) and his group and McIlwraith (1981) indicate that, for middle childhood, imagination is differentiated into at least two dimensions, a positive–constructive, or playful, fantasy life or one characterized by negative emotions, fearful and violent fantasies. Heavy television viewers are more likely to be characterized by the latter type of fantasy life and also (at least in the Eron study) by greater proneness to overt aggressive behavior. Heavy viewers, particularly those oriented to action–adventure shows, are often also less able to separate reality from fantasy and are also more prone to negative affective reactions in school. In an as yet unpublished study we have also found that 7-year-old children identified as heavy television viewers also demonstrate poor integration of their use of materials and express more negative affect in a block play test. They are also reported by parents as having more school adjustment problems. It should be stressed that these results are not simply explained on the basis of intelligence scores.

Generally speaking, results for heavy viewing are mirrored by findings specifically for watching action–adventure shows. Although some television industry representatives have distinguished fantasy action from realistic action programs, our own data clearly indicate that children watching fantasy–action shows such as *The Incredible Hulk*, *Bionic Woman*, and *Wonder Woman* are more likely to be reported by teachers at school as uncooperative with peers, unsuccessful in interpersonal relationships, and generally unhappy. In general, the thrust of the research points consistently to an association between maladaptive social behavior and viewing of violent realistic or fantasy action shows as well as of violent cartoons (for the younger children). These results have also been reported for a study of white middle-class preschoolers in South Africa where television has only recently been introduced and where total viewing possibilities are far less than in the United States (Shmukler, 1981).

Separating Reality and Fantasy

We are very far from a solid understanding of the significance of cartoons and animation or of the relative value of realistic figures or settings versus cartoons in stimulating imagination or in mediating fear or aggression. Considering how much time children spend watching cartoons, we know very little about their impact on consciousness (e.g., whether they influence thinking styles). One wonders if the attraction of cartoons for children involves primarily their clarity of presentation (e.g., fighting, running, chasing), rather than any other intrinsic qualities. It does seem clear, however, that children do not seem to be stimulated in imaginative play by heavy viewing of cartoon or other television fare.

Intrigued by the effects of the formal features of television on a child's behavior, Rice et al. (1982) have been systematically studying which features gain and hold a child's attention and what effects these features have on a child's developmental changes relating to attention. These researchers suggest that form and content can influence arousal, as well as serve as models for behavior. Of particular importance is the strong support they found for the notion that arousing forms such as high levels of action and pace led to increases of aggression. It would be interesting to see which formal features lead to gains in imagination. For example, would music, sound effects, peculiar voices, nonspeech vocalizations, visual effects (such as zooms, pans, and split screens) enhance imaginative play? What effects would scenery, costumes, themes, or auditory events have on a child's imagination? The work on attention would be fruitful if carried a step further, then, to examine the effects of these formal properties on a child's capacity to engage in symbolic play.

Studies by Stein and Friedrich (1975) and D. Singer and J. Singer (1976) suggest that the slow-paced, gentle quality of *Mister Rogers' Neighborhood* may be one factor leading to changes in children's cooperation observed after several weeks of viewing. In addition, Tower et al. (1979) also found gains in children's imaginations as a result of viewing this show. One can speculate that the emphasis on careful camera work, especially the intelligent use of the zoom shot to slowly focus in on an object, helps a child to understand how the enlarged object fits into its contextual setting. The clear distinction Mr. Rogers also makes between reality and fantasy on his program through the device of the "trolley" gradually entering a magical kingdom also may help children understand the notion of "make-believe." These results suggest that a television show that uses moderate pacing and sequencing, an adult host, a clear delineation of fantasy settings from realistic ones *can* enhance children's imaginative tendencies. Such programming for children is, alas, rare.

Grant Noble has carried out numerous studies examining effects of television on children (1970a, b, 1973, 1975). He found that children played significantly less constructively after seeing realistic violence than stylistically filmed aggression. They played more constructively after seeing stylistic aggression filmed at a distance from the victim. Noble also suggested that 5-year-olds have more difficulty in determining what is true or real than do 6-, 7-, and 8-year-olds. He found too that in retelling stories they had seen on films, the 5-year-olds added people and objects that were not in the film. The 5-year-olds were also unable to comprehend when a story ended. They embellished film stories with their own imaginative people or ideas.

Noble (1975) also reported that in a study of 30 children exposed to either *This Is Your Life* or *Sports Day*, 14 thought a person had spoken directly to them, and 6 of the children answered back. The reality of the set for these children involved them in "conversation" with the television characters.

Snow (1974) asked 50 preadolescent children to tell what their favorite program was and if they thought the program was "real" or "make-believe." All of the children could identify cartoons as make-believe and news as real, but there was a split of opinion about shows like the *Brady Bunch*. Children were also asked if they recognized a difference between their own make-believe play and real situations. All were able to do this. It was found that the children preferred make-believe television and related it to their own play.

In contrast to Snow's subjects who could for the most part differentiate between what is real and what is make-believe on television, Garry (1967) reported that preschool and primary grade children accepted what they saw on television as real, actual events, not just fictional dramatization, but considered it as part of their play life—a form of entertainment. Westerns were less disturbing to them than crime and detective stories which seemed closer to real life.

Work with older children (Chaney, 1970) suggests that a television program has stronger effects on 12-year-olds if the viewer blurs the distinction between different characteristics such as between degrees of realism. Some boys in the sample who were highly involved in the aggressive aspects of program content were more likely to believe that the programs that contained the most violence were also the most realistic. Eron (1982) has reported that children who strongly identified with television characters were also most prone to aggressive behavior, perhaps because the characters they emphasized engaged in much violence (e.g., *Batman*).

Quarfoth (1979), using Piaget's theory of animism in relation to the television viewing experience, presented four tasks ranging from concrete picture-sorting to abstract interview questions to 34 kindergartners, 23 first graders, 20 second graders, 21 third graders, and 20 fourth graders. Children were asked to sort a set of television characters into human, animated, and puppet categories. They were also asked to explain how each differed from the other. Questionnaires were designed to determine the child's knowledge of the nature of cartoons and puppets. Results indicate that kindergartners had difficulty in discriminating among the three types of characters. They also seemed uncertain about the mechanics of television, and this affected their perceptions about the reality of television. These children did not seem to understand how characters "got inside of television," believing that "people are made smaller than us. . . . They're lowered down by a rope." Older children, about one-fourth of the second and third graders, were also confused about how cartoon characters were made. Although these children had difficulty understanding animation, they could discriminate among three groups. Hirshman (1977), reported in her thesis with 20 5–7-year-olds that many of them were having difficulty understanding how "characters got into the television set." Some thought they entered through the plug in the wall.

D. Singer, Zuckerman, and J. Singer (1980) also found that third-, fourth-, and fifth-grade children had difficulty with the notion of "realistic" characters, such as "Fonz" and Mary Richards, confusing their real names with those of the television characters they portrayed. Work by Lyle and Hoffman (1972) and Leifer, Gordon, and Graves (1974) also suggested that younger children have difficulty discriminating what is real on television.

Blatt, Spencer, and Ward (1972), using commercials, found that fourth- and sixth-grade children understand the reality or nonreality of characters and situations, but kindergartners and second graders had difficulty with the distinction. Camera effects such as zooms, split screen, wipes, use of chromakey; and special effects such as slow motion, fast motion, and ripple effects may confuse children and interfere with their understanding of reality versus fantasy. Susman (1978) investigated the effects of camera zooms and verbal labels on 80 preschoolchildren's visual attention to a television program of a prosocial nature. The zoom shots interfered with processing part–whole relationships in these preschoolers. Auditory features distracted children from competing stimuli and focused their attention on visual images. Thus attention was higher when camera zooms were absent and attention was lower in the camera zoom alone condition than in other groups.

Studies by Forbes and Lonner (1980) with Alaskan Eskimo and Caucasian children, by Gerbner, Gross, Eleey, Jackson-Beeck, Jeffries-Fox, and Signorielli (1977a,b) with urban elementary schoolers, and by Faulkner (1975) with Asian–English children all attest to the development of gross distortions of specific details of outside reality—of so-called world knowledge as a consequence of television viewing. Collins, Wellman, Keniston, and Westby (1978) identify specific patterns of misunderstanding that characterize elementary schoolchildren's comprehension of plot material as they watch action–adventure fictional programming. Our own as yet uncompleted studies support the Gerbner et al. findings that heavy viewing, especially of action shows, is associated with greater tendency to view the world as "scary."

There seems to be ample evidence that preschoolers and early elementary school-age children are confused by certain features of television and that their failures of comprehension are reflected not only in response to specific plots, but also in more general misrepresentations of the nature of reality and fantasy or in distortions of facts about the "outside world." These findings and those summarized in the next section provide good reasons for fostering more extensive and active mediation by parents or teachers to help children in growing up with television.

Television and School Achievement or Adjustment

Dorr (1982) has pointed to an issue that merits much further exploration in future research. In discussing the uses and gratifications hypothesis, which suggests that lonely youth might watch more television for "company," she also notes the possibility that such heavy viewing may further preclude the young person's acquisition of appropriate social skills. There are data that third, fourth, and fifth graders who were heavy viewers and who watched a good deal of fantasy–aggressive program content also were reported by their teachers as more unhappy and troubled in behavior at school (Zuckerman, Singer, & Singer, 1980). Further recent data from our laboratory concerning 7-year-olds also indicate evidence of poor school adjustment and aggression in heavy viewers. The possibility of a complex interaction, a mutually reinforcing system in which viewing preferences may further reinforce styles of emotionality and social experience, beckons for more sophisticated research than is currently available.

If we turn next to the cumulative effects of the special properties of television formats, do we find evidence of relationships to educational attitudes and school learnings? Morgan and Gross (1982) have systematically examined these issues and their review and research contribute much new information not hitherto available. It seems likely that heavy viewing may also limit intellectual growth in a number of ways by reinforcing poor habits of reading and homework so necessary for effective learning. Studies outside the United States have examined communities that have had minimal prior exposure. They indicate possible displacement effects leading to lowered reading or other general school performances scores (Morgan & Gross, 1982). There are reasons to believe that growing up in a television-oriented society may lead to some displacement of active home studying in favor of watching television entertainment or to variations in educational aspirations.

Morgan and Gross have pointed to the necessity for much more careful analysis of possible curvilinearity in the IQ–television or reading and school learning–television correlations. On the whole, studies report that heavy viewing is inversely related to reading or school achievement (California State Department of Education, Annual Report 1980), but this effect may mask an influence of television towards a middle-range performance. Heavy television viewers from low IQ groups may actually be somewhat stimulated and may improve in world knowledge and readiness for school achievement. Brighter children, however, who watch a great deal of television may indeed be reading less, generating less differentiated vocabularies, and may move to lower levels of school achievement than might be expected from their initial capacities. Television may be producing a homogenization effect around a lower central tendency, a result certainly in keeping with reductions in Scholastic Aptitude Test (SAT) scores over the last decades. The Morgan and Gross review has cautiously avoided strong statements but indicates that statistical analyses of large samples, taking into account IQ groupings, social class, sex differences, and differential educational aspirations may be able to yield some more precise conclusions soon. Our own data indicate that children from higher SES levels or those who showed higher IQs but who were heavy television viewers in the preschool years are now scoring significantly lower in reading readiness and comprehension at age 7 than comparable SES or IQ groups who watched relatively little television at age 4. It should be noted, however, that almost all these studies reflect total television viewing. It remains to be seen whether specialized programming may have differential influences on later reading or educational aspirations.

Adult Mediation: Using Television and Teaching about Television

Attempts to Train Parents and Children to Control or Reduce Television Viewing

We have already discussed the important role of adult mediation for effective learning by children and have pointed to some specific studies demonstrating that adult intervention along with exposure to television can lead to increased imaginative behavior or other prosocial actions (J. Singer & D. Singer, 1976; Stein & Friedrich, 1975). At the Yale University Family Television Research and Consultation Center, several projects were devoted to assess intervention techniques associated with television used by teachers and parents to enhance imagination. In one study (J. Singer & D. Singer, 1981), parents of 141 middle-class preschool children were randomly assigned to one of four conditions, *Imaginative Training*, *Cognitive Training*, *Television Information*, and *No Treatment*. They attended four sessions and received supplementary materials over 1 year's time pertaining to their specific training method. Parents were trained to stimulate imagination using television or play materials, to stimulate cognition and language, or to limit or reduce children's television viewing. Parents kept records of their children's television viewing for 2-week periods four times throughout the year. Children were observed during free play eight times over the year and rated on 14 variables. Results indicated that, by the year's end, those children whose parents had engaged in training them for imagination and for cognitive skills showed gains in these areas in their spontaneous play, as well as reductions in television viewing relative to their baselines and to the other groups. The training of parents for limitation of children's television viewing was generally ineffective, however, suggesting that the parents continued to rely heavily on the medium as a "baby-sitter."

The following year, a similar study was carried out with 200 lower SES preschoolers. Lesson plans derived from television programs were designed to increase a child's cognitive, social, and imagination functioning. Preselected television segments of 2 or 3 minutes, along with the teacher's lessons, were used in the classroom over 1 year's time to determine the efficacy of such a curriculum.

Children were randomly assigned to one of the following conditions: (a) television exposure plus teacher reinforcement of the television concept; (b) teacher reinforcement of the concept without television; and (c) the ordinary nursery school curriculum. There were 30 lessons employed; these dealt with imaginative, cognitive, and prosocial material such as sharing or taking turns. Teachers were trained before the experiment began in the use of the lesson plans and had ongoing inservice training and feedback sessions during the experiment. The results at the end of the year, by no means very powerful, do indicate that children whose teachers used the lessons along with television demonstrations showed gains when rated on imaginativeness, on interaction and cooperation with other children, and in leadership, and they showed a reduction in aggression. The important issue of whether children could generalize from the teacher's use of television to the home use of television for further learning was not addressed, however.

Still another study in this series demonstrated that teacher elaboration on fictional material from television as presented in the classroom could yield gains in children's constructive attitudes about friendship patterns and social or familial attitudes (D. Singer, J. Singer, & Dodsworth-Rugani, 1979). Children seemed to enjoy the limited use of exemplary but entertaining television segments along with teacher-led discussions and reenactments.

Development of a School Curriculum
for Understanding Television

Given the combination of extreme interest in television, the problem of children's confusion of reality and fiction on television, and the apparent advantages of adult intervention, it has seemed increasingly desirable to introduce training for critical viewing of television into the school system. At Yale we developed a curriculum to teach third-, fourth-, and fifth-grade children information about television. Approximately 230 children were involved in this study in two Connecticut schools. The children were middle-class with an average IQ of 110.

Lessons were designed to teach the children the different types of programs, to understand the difference between reality and fantasy on television, to understand special effects, to learn about commercials, to learn how television works, to understand how television influences our ideas and feelings, to understand how television presents violence, and to encourage children to control their viewing habits. Teachers were provided training in the use of the written materials. In addition television tapes were produced that highlighted points made in each lesson. The lessons were designed to utilize language arts skills such as reading, punctuation, analogies, critical thinking, and summary skills. Parents also attended four workshops where we explained the lessons to them and gave them material related to television (D. Singer, Zuckerman, & J. Singer, 1980).

In this experiment we had two opportunities to field test the curriculum. First, teachers presented the lessons to the experimental school, while the control school followed its usual practice. Pre- and post-test data on television knowledge and attitudes were collected. Then we taught the lessons about 3 months later to the control school after pretesting these children again. We were also able to test the children's knowledge 2 months after the experiment ended in each school to determine any lasting effects of the curriculum.

Results indicated that children in the experimental school showed a significantly greater increase in knowledge than children in the control school *before* the control school received the curriculum. Differences were most impressive in the measures of knowledge and understanding of special effects, commericals, and advertising. They understood how television characters could "disappear," what advertising techniques were used to enhance products, who pays for television programs, and where to write letters regarding programs or commercials. They also learned vocabulary words related to television and could identify camera techniques and effects such as dissolve, edit, zoom, and cuts (D. Singer, Zuckerman, & J. Singer, 1980). Children learned how to distinguish between real people, realistic people, and fantasy figures. The lessons were successful too in helping children understand that violence on television programs is not real. Samples of written work demonstrated that children could write imaginative scripts for programs and for commercials.

A further study with the same curriculum in still another school system has yielded very similar results. In addition the curriculum has been modified for use by kindergarten through second grade, and pre- and posttests have shown comparable gains in learning (Rapaczynski, Singer, & Singer, 1982). The same curriculum with more professionally produced videotape segments as supplements for the teacher-presented lessons have now been tested after use in school systems in another 10 school districts in the United States. Again the evidence suggests considerable learning and clarification for the children of the reality–fantasy elements of the television medium. The broader question of generalization to home television viewing or to increased critical attitudes outside the classroom remains unanswered, although anecdotal accounts from parents are encouraging.

Conclusions and Implications

Television, by its very nature, is a medium that emphasizes those elements that are generally found in imagination: visual fluidity, time and space flexibility, and make-believe. One might expect it to stimulate children's imaginations and also to serve a constructive role in socialization. Unfortunately very little systematic attention has been paid to the constructive potential of the medium in contrast to the extensive work on aggression or sex roles and stereotyping. What data emerge for very young children suggests that television viewing seems to preempt playtime and may impede creativity. Yet there are indications that with adult intervention the medium can be used to stimulate spontaneous imaginative play in children, as well as other prosocial behavior. There are few attempts on the part of producers or educators to develop age-specific programming designed carefully to enhance an interactive, self-generating playfulness in children. The *Mister Rogers' Neighborhood* show is one of the few programs for preschoolers that consciously strives for such an effect with them. Available data suggest that special materials designed to enhance adult intervention at home or school lessons can help children develop imaginative and language skills in relation to television and can also be useful in clarifying reality–fantasy distinctions with relation to the medium. Television viewing of broadcast or of videotape and videodisc materials will continue to be a major form of activity for the growing child. It is evident that more research for the development of programming and adult mediation is urgently needed.

A major conclusion that can be drawn from the various literature reviews that constitute the recent National Institute of Mental Health effort to update the 1972 Surgeon General's Committee on Television and Social Behavior is that of a *general learning effect*. Children can learn all kinds of things from television, but much of that learning, without adult mediation or without specially designed, age-specific, child-oriented programming turns out to be incidental and potentially harmful. Our review of the cognitive and affective literature suggests that adults are crucial for children's learning. Children seem to want the emotional attachment to parental figures who reshape a complex environment through simplified vocabulary, modeling, and play into components that are managable for children and that create an atmosphere in which children can themselves replay mentally this material through self-generated activities. Without adult help at home or in the classroom, television as it is presently constituted can become a hazard to children's cognitive development. If we are to see even more involvement of children with that medium in the next decade, then we will need not only more parent and teacher intervention, but also more responsibility by industry in producing adult-mediated programs, in providing age-specific content, and in paying more attention to structural properties of how programs are presented for children.

References

Ahammer, I. M., & Murray, J. P. Kindness in the kindergarten: The relative influence of role playing and prosocial television in facilitating altruism. *International Journal of Behavioral Development*, 1979, *2*, 133–157.

Anderson, D. R., & Levin, S. R. Young children's attention to *Sesame Street*. *Child Development*, 1976, *47*, 806–811.

Anderson, D. R., Lorch, E. P., Field, D. E., & Sanders, J. The effect of TV program comprehensibility on preschool children's visual attention to television. *Child Development*, 1981, *52*, 151–157.

Blatt, J., Spencer, L., & Ward, S. A cognitive developmental study of children's reactions to television advertising. In E. A. Rubinstein, G. A. Comstock, & J. P. Murray (Eds.), *Television and social behavior* (Vol. 4), *Television in day-to-day life: Patterns of use*. Washington, D.C.: U.S. Government Printing Office, 1972.

Blumenthal, A. *The process of cognition*. Englewood Cliffs, N.J.: Prentice-Hall, 1977.

Bryant, J., & Comisky, P. W. The effect of positioning a message within differentially cognitively involving portions of a television segment on recall of the message. *Human Communication Research*, 1978, 5(1), 63–75.

California State Department of Education. *Student Achievement in California Schools: 1979–80 Annual Report*. Sacramento, Calif.: Author, 1980.

Chaney, D. C. Involvement, realism, and the perception of aggression in television programmes. *Human Relations*, 1970, 23, 373–381.

Coates, B., Pusser, H. E., & Goodman, I. The influence of *Sesame Street* and *Mister Rogers' Neighborhood* on children's social behavior in the preschool. *Child Development*, 1976, 47, 138–144.

Collins, W. A. Cognitive processing aspects of television viewing. In D. Pearl, L. Bouthilet, & J. Lazar (Eds.), *Television and behavior: Ten years of scientific progress and implications for the eighties*. Washington, D.C.: U.S. Government Printing Office, 1982.

Collins, W. A., Wellman, H., Keniston, A., & Westby, S. Age-related aspects of comprehension and inference from a televised dramatic narrative. *Child Development*, 1978, 49(2), 389–399.

Cook, T. D., Appleton, H., Conner, R. F., Shaffer, A., Tomkin, G., & Weber, S. J. *Sesame Street revisited*. New York: Russell Sage Foundation, 1975.

Csikszentmihalyi, M., & Kubey, R. Television and the rest of life: A systematic comparison of subjective experience. *Public Opinion Quarterly*, 1981, 45(3), 302–315.

Dorr, A. L. Television and affective development and functioning. In D. Pearl, L. Bouthilet, & J. Lazar (Eds.), *Television and behavior: Ten years of scientific progress and implications for the eighties*. Washington, D.C.: U.S. Government Printing Office, 1982.

Eron, L. D. Parent-child interaction, television violence and aggression of children. *American Psychologist*, 1982, 37(2), 197–211.

Faulkner, G. Media and identity: The Asian adolescent's dilemma. In C. Husbard (Ed.), *White media and black Britain*. London: Arrow, 1975.

Feuerstein, R. Mediated learning experience: A theoretical basis for cognitive modifiability during adolescence. In P. Mittler (Ed.), *Research to practice in mental retardation. Education and training* (Vol. II). Baltimore: University Park Press, 1977.

Forbes, N. E., & Lonner, W. J. *The coming of television to rural Alaska: Attitudes, expectations and effects*. Paper presented at the Television in the Developing World conference, Winnipeg, March 1980.

Garry, R. Television's impact on the child. In *Children on TV: Television's impact on the child*. Washington, D.C.: Association for Childhood International, 1967.

Gerbner, G., Gross, L., Eleey, M., Jackson-Beeck, M., Jeffries-Fox, S., & Signorielli, N. TV violence profile No. 8. *Journal of Communication*, 1977, 27, 171–180. (a)

Gerbner, G., Gross, L., Eleey, M., Jackson-Beeck, M., Jeffries-Fox, S., & Signorielli, N. *Violence profile No. 8: Trends in network television drama and viewer conceptions of social reality 1967–1976*. Philadelphia: The Annenberg School of Communications, The University of Pennsylvannia, 1977. (b)

Greenfield, P., Geber, B., Beagles-Roos, J., Farrar, D., & Gat, I. *Television and radio experimentally compared: Effects of the medium on imagination and transmission of content*. Paper presented at the Society for Research in Child Development Bienniel Meeting, Boston, April 1981.

Harrison, L. F., & Williams, T. M. Television and cognitive development. In T. M. Williams (Chair), *The impact of television: A natural experiment involving three communities*. Symposium presented at the meeting of the Canadian Psychological Association, Vancouver, June 1977.

Hirshman, R. *Video-training: A means of modifying the mediated effects of television on the social behavior of young children.* Unpublished Master's thesis, Ohio State University, 1977.

Hollenbeck, A. R., & Slaby, R. G. Infant visual and vocal responses to television. *Child Development*, 1979, *50*, 41–45.

Izard, C. *Human emotions.* New York: Plenum, 1977.

Klinger, E. Modes of normal conscious flow. In K. S. Pope & J. L. Singer (Eds.), *The stream of consciousness.* New York: Plenum, 1978.

Leifer, A. D., Gordon, N. J., & Graves, S. B. Children and television: More than mere entertainment. *Harvard Educational Review*, 1974, *44*, 213–245.

Lesser, G. S. *Children and television: Lessons from Sesame Street.* New York: Vintage Books, 1974.

Lindlof, T. R. Fantasy activity and the televiewing event: Considerations for an information processing construct of involvement. *Communication Yearbook*, *IV*, 1980, 277–291.

Lyle, J., & Hoffman, H. R. Children's use of television and other media. In E. A. Rubinstein, G. A. Comstock, & J. P. Murray (Eds.), *Television and social behavior* (Vol. 4), *Television in day-to-day life: Patterns of use.* Washington, D.C.: U.S. Government Printing Office, 1972.

McIlwraith, R. D. *Fantasy life and media use patterns of adults and children.* Unpublished doctoral dissertation, University of Manitoba, June 1981.

Mander, J. *Four arguments for the elimination of television.* New York: Morrow, 1978.

Meline, C. W. Does the medium matter? *Journal of Communication*, 1976, *26*(3), 81–89.

Meringoff, L. K. Influence of the medium on children's story apprehension. *Journal of Educational Psychology*, 1980, *72*(2), 240–249.

Morgan, M., & Gross, L. Television and educational achievement and aspirations. In D. Pearl, L. Bouthilet, & J. Lazar (Eds.), *Television and behavior: Ten years of scientific progress and implications for the eighties.* Washington, D.C.: U.S. Government Printing Office, 1982.

Noble, G. Concepts of order and balance in a children's TV program. *Journalism Quarterly*, 1970, *47*, 101–108. (a)

Noble, G. Film-mediated creative and aggressive play. *British Journal of Social and Clinical Psychology*, 1970, *9*, 1–7. (b)

Noble, G. Effects of different forms of filmed aggression on children's constructive and destructive play. *Journal of Personality and Social Psychology*, 1973, *26*, 54–59.

Noble, G. *Children in front of the small screen.* London: Constable, 1975.

Noble, G. How children "use" Sesame Street and Playschool. *National Association of Australian University Colleges Review*, 1979–1980, 18–23.

Quarfoth, J. M. Children's understanding of the nature of television characters. *Journal of Communication*, 1979, *29*(3), 210–218.

Rapaczynski, W., Singer, D., & Singer, J. Teaching television: A curriculum for young children. *Journal of Communications*, 1982, *32*, 47–55.

Repetti, R. *Determinants of children's sex stereotyping: Parental attitudes, television viewing and imaginary play.* Unpublished Master's thesis, Yale University, 1980.

Rice, M. L., Huston, A. C., & Wright, J. C. The forms and codes of television: Effects on children's attention, comprehension and social behavior. In D. Pearl, L. Bouthilet, & J. Lazar (Eds.), *Television and behavior: Ten years of scientific progress and implications for the eighties.* Washington, D.C.: U.S. Government Printing Office, 1982.

Rosenfeld, E., Heusmann, L. R., Eron, L. D., & Torney-Purta, J. V. Measuring patterns of fantasy behavior in children. *Journal of Personality and Social Psychology*, 1982, *42*, 347–366.

Shmukler, D. A descriptive analysis of television viewing in South African preschoolers and its relationship to their spontaneous play. *South African Journal of Psychology*, 1981, *11*(3), 106–110.

Singer, D. G. Television and the developing imagination of the child. In D. Pearl, L. Bouthilet, & J. Lazar (Eds.), *Television and behavior: Ten years of scientific progress and implications for the eighties*. Washington, D.C.: U.S. Government Printing Office, 1982.

Singer, D. G., & Singer, J. L. Family television viewing habits and the spontaneous play of preschool children. *American Journal of Orthopsychiatry*, 1976, *46*(3), 496–502.

Singer, D. G., & Singer, J. L. Television viewing and aggressive behavior in preschool children: A field study. In F. Wright, C. Bahn, & R. W. Rieber, *Forensic Psychology and Psychiatry* (Vol. 347). New York: New York Academy of Sciences, 1980.

Singer, D. G., Singer, J. L., & Dodsworth-Rugani, K. J. Fables of the Green Forest *and* Swiss Family Robinson: *An experimental evaluation of their educational and prosocial potential*. Unpublished manuscript, Yale University, 1979.

Singer, D. G., Zuckerman, D. M., & Singer, J. L. Helping elementary children learn about TV. *Journal of Communication*, 1980, *30*(3), 84–93.

Singer, J. L. *The child's world of make-believe: Experimental studies of imaginative play*. New York: Academic Press, 1973.

Singer, J. L. *Imagery and daydream methods in psychotherapy and behavior modification*. New York: Academic Press, 1974.

Singer, J. L. Experimental studies of daydreaming and the stream of thought. In K. S. Pope & J. L. Singer (Eds.), *The stream of consciousness*. New York: Plenum, 1978.

Singer, J. L. The power and limitations of television: A cognitive–affective analysis. In P. H. Tannenbaum (Ed.), *The entertainment function of television*. Hillsdale, N.J.: Erlbaum, 1980.

Singer, J. L., & Antrobus, J. S. Dimensions of daydreaming: A factor analysis of imaginal process and personality scales. In P. Sheehan (Ed.), *The function and nature of imagery*. New York: Academic Press, 1972.

Singer, J. L., & Singer, D. G. Can TV stimulate imaginative play? *Journal of Communication*, 1976, *26*, 74–80.

Singer, J. L., & Singer, D. G. Television viewing, family style and aggressive behavior in preschool children. In M. R. Green (Ed.), *Violence and the family*. Boulder, Colo.: Westview Press, 1980.

Singer, J. L., & Singer, D. G. *Television, imagination and aggression: A study of preschoolers*. Hillsdale, N.J.: Erlbaum, 1981.

Snow, R. P. How children interpret TV violence in play contexts. *Journalism Quarterly*, 1974, *51*, 13–21.

Stein, A. H., & Friedrich, L. K. The effects of television content on young children. In A. Pick (Ed.), *Minnesota symposium on child psychology* (Vol. 9). Minneapolis: University of Minnesota Press, 1975.

Sturm, H., & Jörg, S. *Information processing by young children: Piaget's theory of intellectual development applied to radio and television*: Munich: K. G. Saur, 1981.

Susman, E. J. Visual and verbal attributes of television and selective attention in preschool children. *Developmental Psychology*, 1978, *14*, 575–566.

Tomkins, S. S. *Affect, imagery, consciousness* (Vol. 1). New York: Springer, 1962.

Tomkins, S. S. *Affect, imagery, consciousness* (Vol. 2). New York: Springer, 1963.

Tower, R. B., Singer, D. G., Singer, J. L., & Biggs, A. Differential effects of television programming on preschoolers' cognition, imagination, and social play. *American Journal of Orthopsychiatry*, 1979, *49*, 265–281.

Winn, M. *The plug-in drug*. New York: Viking, 1977.

Zillmann, D. Cognitive and affective influences: Television viewing and arousal. In D. Pearl, L. Bouthilet, & J. Lazar (Eds.), *Television and behavior: Ten years of scientific progress and implications for the eighties*. Washington, D.C.: U.S. Government Printing Office, 1982.

Zuckerman, D. M., Singer, D. G., & Singer, J. L. Television viewing and children's reading and related classroom behavior. *Journal of Communication*, 1980, *30*(1), 166–174.

chapter **12**

Television Literacy and the Critical Viewer

JAMES A. ANDERSON

Introduction

This chapter examines the theoretical foundations, rhetorical justifications, and classroom practices of instruction at the elementary and secondary levels dealing with the initiation or improvement of television literacy. Television literacy, variously called critical viewing skills, critical televiewing, or television receivership skills, is one member of the family of media literacy. Media literacy has been defined as the "skillful collection, interpretation, testing and application of information regardless of medium or presentation for some purposeful action [J. Anderson, 1981, p. 22]." The patriarch of this family is obviously reading. Reading so dominates this field that nonprint literacies in most elementary and secondary educational environments receive little more than a passing nod. Consequently the forms of nonprint literacy are in a continual struggle for recognition and serious treatment. As a result, classroom instruction in television literacy is an idea whose time has come and come again. As early as 1948, when television was a medium and not yet a message, Lewis (1948) called for instruction, not in technical skills, but in the "interpretation of the present as well as future potentialities [and] sociological as well as

297

CHILDREN'S UNDERSTANDING
OF TELEVISION

commercial implications [p. 157]" for students at all levels. As television gained international prominence, the 1962 International Conference on Screen Education (UNESCO, 1964) concluded: "Because television is already a major channel of communication, and will increase in scope and power, we believe it is the responsibility of educators to teach our young people to use this medium in a constructive way [p. 78]." Then, in 1975, the Ford Foundation-sponsored Conference on Children and Television rediscovered that

> there was an important need for widened and improved instruction about the mass media in the public schools. We decided that literacy of young persons in regard to the mass media is the proper concern for educational institutions analogous to their concern about language literacy [Ford Foundation, 1975, p. 31].

Finally, Ruth (1980) wrote:

> We must not close our eyes—literally or figuratively—to the powerful role the visual media already play and will continue to play in the lives of our students and in their future lives as adults. In this context it is imperative that we include nonprint media in our teaching, because they are truly basic to the education of today's students [p. 9].

These repeated calls are of interest in and of themselves, for it is not as if things were not being done in media and specifically television literacy. In fact, there has been widespread activity. The development of literacy curricula has been conducted in relative independence by several disciplines. Art education is the earliest predecessor by a few centuries, but film criticism and audiovisual instruction in the classroom was sufficient to promote commercial ventures by 1919, less than two decades after *The Great Train Robbery*. The work in visual perception has been organized into courses of visual literacy, and, finally, communication scholars have turned from perceptual and developmental questions to offer the unique contribution of the communication disciplines.

Television Literacy: A Brief History

Many of the concepts and classroom approaches basic to television literacy instruction were well-developed by the 1940s by teachers using films and radio. Wilke and Eschenauer (1981) in their survey of media education in Germany comment that instruction in the mass media "date[s] back almost as far as the media themselves [p. 11]."

When the television set made its appearance in the classroom as a delivery system for the presentation of instructional materials during the mid-1950s, teachers quickly realized that that same set could present all the commercial fare as well. The educational journals of the period are replete with "how-to-do-it" articles on the use of television news, entertainment programming, and even commercials.

What was missing during this period was a curriculum—an organized, systematic approach to a set of objectives supported by instructional routines and devices. The construction of marketable curricular packages in television literacy does not seem to have begun until the late 1960s. By 1972 there had been but one federally funded project and two supported efforts at the development of a multilevel integrated curriculum. These latter two are generally noted as the first disseminated projects.

The Milford Project was the first of the two to publish (Fransecky & Ferguson, 1973a, 1973b, 1973c). The project was a five-phase curriculum which progressed from kindergarten through grade 12. Skills directly related to television were introduced in grade 6, beginning with the technical skills of production. By the twelfth grade, students were involved with comparative analyses of the capacity and biases of all mass media. As a result of their 7-year involvement with television, students were to "understand the theory and operation of media hardware"; avoid being "intimidated" by the media; be able to "more effectively communicate with others" through television; "discern and appreciate the unique manner" in which television communicates meaning; discover the potential and limitations of television, and "to exercise critical judgment in relation to various media [Fransecky & Ferguson, 1973a, p. 47]."

The Critical Receivership Skills project funded by a consortium of school systems who were members of the Ohio University Cooperative Center for Social Studies was the second of the curricula to appear in print. The project was initiated in 1969 at the request of member school system administrators and continues to the present. The Receivership Skills project is a comprehensive program of media literacy based on the suppositions that

> 1) Children can utilize certain viewing, listening and reading skills and analytical procedures to modify source, message and medium effects toward pro-social consequences and 2) these skills and procedures can be taught in the ordinary classroom using curricular materials and instructional approaches specially designed for that purpose [J. Anderson & Ploghoft, 1974, p. 2].

The approach used by the project has been quite different from those which followed, as the intent has been to develop media objectives within the standard language arts and social studies curriculum rather than as an add-on or drop-in design. To date, its published materials have focused almost exclusively on television and have been aimed at the middle grades (4–8).

In the 1977–1978 school year, the Receivership Skills project was adapted as an Idaho Title IV-C Elementary and Secondary Education Act (ESEA) innovative education project in the Idaho Falls School District. Following intensive support from the Cooperative Center, the Idaho Falls system now independently supplies a 4-year, vertically integrated curriculum package for grades 3–6.

Prime Time School Television was organized in 1970 as a subscription service supplying program guides and program analyses for member schools and teachers. By the mid-1970s they were also supplying curricular materials for specific objectives within other content areas (e.g., *Television and Economics*, 1978). Their most extensive curricular efforts have been directed toward junior and senior high levels. It is expected they will provide more materials for elementary grades, as that is the direction television literacy programs are now moving.

The spring of 1978 marked the funding of several projects designed to develop curriculum materials expressly for children and television. ABC Television announced a grant to produce eight lesson plans about television for use with grades 3–5.

At the same time the Office of Education published a request for proposals for four critical viewing projects to cover the range of grade levels from lower elementary to postsecondary. The projects were awarded to four independent institutions, each of which developed their own definitions, objectives, and instructional approaches (C. Collins & Moles, 1980). The lower elementary project (up to grade 5) adopted a module approach ranging from a desk file of individual activities to short texts which might span 1 or 2 weeks of intermittent activity. The middle grade project (grades 6–8) developed a 10-week course of study. The high school project was designed for a 1-semester course with seven independent units. Individual units could be independently taught or integrated into other curricular areas. The postsecondary materials were organized as a college course.

As of this writing there is still considerable activity in the development of curricular materials and approaches to instruction in television literacy. New texts are appearing from the Office of Education, ABC, and Receivership Skills projects. Nevertheless we would anticipate further calls for media literacy curricula, because the relative standing of nonprint literacy programs has not substantively changed. Print literacy still dominates the classroom. What is clearly missing is the acceptance by school districts of *media* literacy curricula as basic components of their educational charge. Failing that, the concomitant development of preservice instructional programs by major teacher education institutions has had no motivation. Until the notion of media literacy replaces the more limited concept of reading education as a basic skill, media receivership skills programs will be considered as perhaps a useful, but not necessary, appendage to the fundamentals of schooling. In a similar vein until teacher education institutions change their own curriculum, the ordinary training of teachers will not prepare them to be responsive to the media literacy requirements of their students.

The Nature of Television Literacy Curricula

Because television literacy has had little history in the larger educational establishment, it shows a low order of organization as a course of study. Curriculum specialists and instructional staff have not, in sufficient numbers, had adequate experience with a course of work to arrive at a consensus as to what should be taught at what grade levels and with what student outcomes. The following sections consider the theoretical foundations from which the curriculum specialists appear to derive instruction and the instructional objectives which direct classroom activity.

Theoretical Lineages

To begin with, television literacy curricula come from four rather different theoretical stances—impact mediation, goal attainment, cultural understanding, and visual skills.[1] Each of these theoretical perspectives and their consequences for a television literacy curriculum is briefly explored in the next four sections.

IMPACT MEDIATION

The impact mediation model derives from the experimental research that has characterized most of the study of the effects of mass communication. This research assumes that content can be classified as types that have predictive utility for subsequent viewer behavior. The "vio-

---

[1]Most of this discussion appeared in Anderson, J. A. The theoretical lineage of critical viewing curricula. *Journal of Communication* 1980b, *30*, 64–70. Adapted with permission.

lent-television-leads-to-subsequent-aggression" research is, of course, the premier example, but any researcher who looks at the nature of content as the starting point of analysis belongs in this category.

In looking at the relationship between content and behavioral effects, this research has shown, among other things that the effects of content are not absolute. Respondent variables are likely to intervene in the process, and these variables can, in fact, be manipulated to modify subsequent effects. The mediation model, then, assumes that one can precondition viewers in order to heighten the likelihood of prosocial consequences of viewing. Doolittle (1977) provides a good example of the reasoning by arguing:

> Since television has been identified as a source of antisocial learning it is suggested that schools might consider developing methods of counteracting television's negative influence. [The] . . . approach would be to interfere with the broader television learning process so as to reduce children's acquiring of antisocial influences [p. 2].

Curricula developed on the mediation model are organized around problem areas—violent content, commercials, time spent with television, and the like—and provide strategies for the management of the problem. For example, this excerpt is taken from materials developed by the lower elementary Office of Education project (Southwest Education Developmental Laboratory, 1979a):

> Television often exposes children to adult actions and relationships on television for which they are unprepared. They are thrown into an adult world long before they have the information and maturity to cope with it. How television affects a child will depend on how the child interprets what is viewed and the use the child makes of that information. Parents and other adults can be the determining factor in making television a positive learning experience [p. 1].

The quotation highlights the two configuring elements of this perspective: (a) that television does things to the viewer; and (b) that intervention can change the consequences. This perspective is essentially protectionistic in its approach and therapeutic in its outcomes.

GOAL ATTAINMENT

The goal attainment model has been the dominant paradigm in the development of curricula at the secondary and higher elementary levels. The model draws its support from uses and gratifications research and theory. Uses and gratification theory can be briefly summarized as: Individual interpretations of basic human needs result in different

combinations of problems and solutions that in turn constitute individual motives for behavior which result in different patterns of actual
media use and consequences thereof (see Rosengren & Wendahl, 1978).
An individual's media behavior and the resultant consequences, therefore, can be interpreted and evaluated only insofar as that individual's
goal agenda is known.

Adopting the notion that media use is purposeful rather than passive
substantially changes the nature of instruction about the media. The
focus is no longer on the nature of the media but on the purposes the
individual holds. Curricula of the goal attainment lineage, first, direct
individuals toward an analysis of the motives they have for attending to
a medium; second, helps them develop standards by which that use
can be evaluated as a solution of or a gratification for those motives;
and, third, provides practice in the process of decision making that
involves media use. As the WNET/Thirteen Education Department
(1979) project puts it, "This . . . curriculum will provide your students
with the inner resources for making their own decisions about the
television programs they watch [p. ii]." The Far West Laboratory's
(1979) project states: "In seeking to teach students to become more
critical consumers of television, this course recognizes the central role
the student plays in this effort. It is not television itself that is under the
microscope; it is the student's relationship to television [p. 2]."

CULTURAL UNDERSTANDING MODEL

In the cultural understanding model, one studies television (or any
popular art) as an index of the culture from which it springs. It pre-
sumes that the members of a culture are in a continual process of
negotiating that culture. That negotiation gets done in the meeting
rooms of the clubs, in the halls of churches, in the living rooms of
homes, and in the expressions of the media. The contemporary content
of the media provides the panoply of issues, conflicts, offers and coun-
teroffers that the current negotiations involve. The content of the media, then, is not trivial but composed of the shared values, ideas, and
symbols by which individuals are joined as a people. In contemplating
this model Newcomb (1979) writes, "The cultural context, then, forces
us to look at television as used by people in history. More specifically
we will have to understand the role of entertainment in culture and
society and become more aware of the history of entertainment forms
and content [p. 4]."

One of the more complete curriculum efforts from this approach is in
the work of Deming (1979). In her work, television is not an adversary
but simply one more element of the culture. Educationally, television is

a particularly useful element to study because it contains expressions from the entire spectrum of the culture in which it appears. The critical examination of its content, then, is rich in insight into the ways that culture functions. Instructional approaches from this theoretical perspective are those of exegesis and criticism of media "text." Evaluation relates to the understanding and use of the tools and processes of analysis. Proximate outcomes are difficult to identify; the final outcome, as argued from this perspective, is the liberally educated individual.

VISUAL LITERACY MODEL

The visual literacy model is perhaps the converse of the cultural understanding model. Its focus is on technique as content. The message is dependent on its method of presentation. One understands messages and controls their consequences by being sophisticated about techniques. Undoubtedly a singular work in aesthetic pragmatics is that of Zettl (1973). He encapsulates this model in writing: "There are, of course, subtle aesthetic variables that we can use to produce a specific aesthetic response in the recipient, even if he is not consciously aware of these variables. In short, we can manipulate a person's perception, and ultimately his behavior, by a precise, calculated application of aesthetic variables and variable complexes [pp. 1–2]." More than any other, instruction from this approach is in the doing. Students are taught how to produce news programs, commercials, and entertainment. The methods of special effects comes in for particular attention as in the PTA module demystifying or perhaps detoxifying television monsters. Evaluation, of course, is cued to the ability to describe and/or produce technique.

Instructional Objectives

Given the diversity of starting points, it is not surprising that there is no necessary consensus on what instructional objectives should be pursued and at what level they should be presented. This section presents the findings of a review of eight major television literacy curricula.[2] The projects vary widely in scope, grade level, and documenta-

2The eight are The Milford Project; the Receivership Skills Project in East Syracuse/ Minoa; the Southwest Educational Development Laboratory Office of Education Project; the WNET Office of Education Project; the Far West Laboratory Office of Education Project; The Idaho Falls Elementary and Secondary Education Act, Title IV-C Project; The ABC Project; and The Anderson–Ploghoft curriculum. The author's sources and contact with each are as follows:

tion.[3] Nevertheless, the patterns of choices of instructional objectives give us good insight into what these curricular specialists have in mind concerning the notion of television literacy. Interestingly, objectives split into two sets, one supported by five or more projects and one promoted by just one or two projects. The following reports the objectives of the first set in order of number of appearances with the most popular presented first.

THE GRAMMAR AND SYNTAX OF TELEVISION

All eight projects consider aural and visual elements and their relationships within programs to be within the purview of television literacy. This objective entails the identification of visual and aural images; the analysis of their denotative, connotative, and affective meanings; the rules by which these images are interconnected; the limits of form imposed by program type, time, commercial requirements, and production methods; and the conventions of camera and sound. The objective appears to stand on the assumptions that images are discrete elements that can be lifted out of a flow of images; an image can have a literal or "dictionary" meaning to which all would agree; and there are standard forms by which television programs get constructed. These assumptions are, of course, those of traditional literary criticism.

1. Milford Project; Fransecky and Ferguson, 1973a, 1973b, 1973c; Shorr, 1978; personal contact (1974–1975) with Shorr.
2. East Syracuse/Minoa Receivership Skills Project: Tentative objectives, 1977; author served as consultant to the project, 1975–1980.
3. Southwest Educational Development Laboratory Office of Education Project: Southwest Educational Development Laboratory, 1979a, 1970b; ancillary teacher, student, and parent materials; personal contact with project director, manager, and consultants from 1978 to present.
4. WNET Office of Education Project: WNET Project, 1980a, 1980b; WNET/Thirteen Education Department, 1979; personal contact with project manager and chief writer.
5. Far West Laboratory Office of Education Project: White, 1980; ancillary classroom materials; Far West Laboratory for Educational Research and Development, 1979; author served as consultant for the project.
6. Idaho Falls ESEA IV-C Project: Idaho Falls School District 91, 1979; author wrote the substance of the proposal and was consultant and prime contractor.
7. The ABC Project: Singer, Zuckerman, and Singer, 1980; Singer and Singer, 1981; personal contact with D. Singer, 1978–1979.
8. The Anderson–Ploghoft curriculum: J. Anderson, 1981; J. Anderson, 1980b; Anderson and Ploghoft, 1974, 1978, 1980.

[3]Scope varies from the eight lessons of ABC to the 40-hour per year 4-year curriculum of Idaho Falls; grade level varies across kindergarten–grade 12; documentation varies from an 8-line statement from Southwest Educational Development Laboratory to a document of more than 30 pages "outlining" the objectives of the Receivership Skills project.

MANAGEMENT OF VIEWING

All projects support objectives dealing with the management of viewing time and program selection. The concept of the objective shows a distinct split into camps. One set of projects adopts a "judicious-use" approach which carries explicit or implied criteria concerning the amount of time spent in viewing and the content of programs selected. The other set presents a personal management strategy based on the individual's analysis of his or her goal for time spent viewing and for content selection.

The judicious-use approach tends to explain the consequences of too much viewing or of viewing the wrong things (e.g., violence). Alternatives are presented for making better use of time and for better program choices. Educationally this objective is structured like an innoculation or a preventative.

About an equal number of the projects present strategies for surfacing the motives for individual choice. Some then go on to present an evaluation of those choices implying that some motives are better than others. Two projects remain steadfastly nonjudgmental. They provide *methods* by which the efficiency of the solutions to the problems of how much and what to view can be evaluated.

The basic split here derives from the opposing views of "television does things to people" versus "people do things with television." The more fundamental of the judicious-use camp espouse the first position; those of personal management the latter. The larger number of projects adopt either position at different points in their presentations. Those dealing with younger children present more prescriptive material; those working with older students more analytical.

It is difficult to see the relationship of the management of time and program choices as developed by these curricula to the notion of television literacy. Literacy would not seem to be dependent on restricting one's exposure or one's content choices. One would not be considered musically literate if she or he were competent only with eighteenth century western composers. Rather, the objectives appear to be directive, a socialization in value. Even those projects that do not explicitly attach worth to specific choices promote values such as success, efficiency, and the like. Management of viewing, then, as an objective, would appear to reside outside of the rubric of television literacy and in notions like self-actualization or perhaps citizenship.

TECHNICAL KNOWLEDGE OF TELEVISION

The only other unanimous objective was that concerning how television works. Within this objective there was considerable variation in content and emphasis. All of the projects discuss in some way the process by which television programs are received in the home. Other technical subject matter includes program development, writing of scripts, shot blocking, stunts, sound, and lighting. This material is typically presented in expository writing—a "here's-how-it's-done" sort of approach. Three of the projects emphasize acquisition of technical skills as the route to understanding technical subjects. These projects encourage "hands-on" experiences in producing television programs, commercials, and news presentations.

There are several undercurrents in the presentations of this objective. One appears to be that an understanding of the technical process will debunk or lessen the impact of televised content. In the same vein, technical knowledge is thought to decrease the likelihood of making "reality" errors in assessing behaviors presented in television content. A third implication seems to be that the technical skills gained will increase the capacity of the individual to communicate within that medium and all others. Finally, there appears to be the presumption that technical understanding is inherent in the process of criticism. Just as the individual who has had some training in a musical instrument can better appreciate the quality of play, so, too, an individual can better judge a television program with an understanding of the techniques involved.

ADVERTISING TECHNIQUES AND CONSEQUENCES

Seven of the projects specifically state objectives concerning advertising, although all of them deal with it in their instruction. As with the objectives in the management of viewing choices, the projects approach advertising in different ways. Four of the seven treat advertising as a necessary evil. Acknowledged as a requirement of commercial media, nevertheless, advertising's potential for deception and trickery casts it as a message source to react against. The objective of these projects is in two parts: First is the identification and analysis of techniques of production and persuasion; second is the development of strategies of protection against "undue influence." Both objectives are heavily value-laden. Advertising is approached as a somewhat disreputable profession and certainly a suspect information source. Message forms are farcically characterized. Warnings against succumbing to "wants" rather than "needs" are offered. While never specifically expressed, the overall tenor is that advertising is inherently flawed, and those who would be unduly influenced are weak.

The remaining three projects, at least in their documentation, take a more objective view. Advertising is presented as a part of the competitive marketplace without which the free enterprise system of marketing could not operate. Advertising is described as an information source, the intent of which is "to persuade, not fully inform." Models for using advertising information in decision making are described, as are persuasion and production techniques. Verification of claims, however, shifts from an appeal to some external reality ("Can toothpaste really bring you friends?") to the perceptions and judgments of the individual purchaser.

The direction of both of these sets of objectives is clearly toward a larger realm of personal behavior. The end of instruction is not only the competent understanding of a message type, but also "right" decision making. The consequence of the character of this objective, the previous one, and a few yet to be introduced, is that they force value-laden content into instruction without justifying the values chosen in supporting arguments They also complicate just what the product of the instruction should be, as we will see.

COMPARATIVE STRENGTHS AND WEAKNESSES OF THE MEDIA

Seven of the projects seek to instruct their students in the relative values of presentations in different media. In general, this objective is met in the arena of news and information. The comparison revolves around the relative veracity of reports about events or in information stereotypes and images. The Receivership Skills project also provides considerable instruction in the relative structures of dramatic forms as presented in different media.

The identification of similarities and differences is, of course, a classic educational device. What separates the projects is their perspective on whether or not there are coherent information stereotypes and images presented in the media (as opposed to individual presentations or programs) that can be compared. For example, a majority of the curricula project the belief that coherent media images (such as the image of women), which permeate the general content of a medium, exist, and they can be compared with the image of the same subject in other media (e.g., the image of women in films as compared with the image of women in television). Others adopt a case-by-case analysis and argue the comparisons over individual programs and specific news events.

THE TELEVISION INDUSTRY AND SOCIETY

This objective also appears in seven of the projects and is revealed in essentially expository instruction on the institutional elements which compose the industry, the contractual agreements of both law and practice which bind them together, sources of income for various forms of television, and larger societal notions such as television's place in the mass media and mass media's role in society. The variety of the exposition is sociological and economic rather than anthropological and cultural. For example, the appearance of program types is usually described only in economic terms (ratings) rather than an expression of cultural forces. It is a fair characterization of all the projects that the "softer" naturalistic explanations of cultural criticism are neglected in favor of the "harder" construct explanations of sociopsychology.

VALUE ANALYSIS

Objectives in value analysis vary among six projects from the recognition of differing points of view to proficiency in value identification, clarification, and evaluation. The valuation process is explored in the affective language of commercial messages, in the identification of opinion in news and information, and in the characterization and problem solutions of dramatic programs. The extended projects develop value analysis to the point of comparison between television characterizations and solutions and common behaviors in the student's social settings. When considering actions, values are defined pragmatically as the reasons why characters or persons behave in certain ways.

CONSEQUENCES

For two of the five projects that state objectives dealing with the consequences of television viewing, the evidence on effects is already in. Television produces subtle and explicit messages that are commonly understood by viewers and evoke common effects. Television is dangerous, or, at least, it is not a "harmless toy." Television must be "used properly," and its present character changed by us, the audience, through political and economic pressure.

The other three projects call for a reflective analysis of the consequences the individual perceives occurring for him or her. Instruction centers on the techniques of documenting consequences both positive and negative, and evaluating them in terms of the initial purposes for viewing. Two of these projects also instruct on the methods of developing explanations for one's own personal preferences in programs, characters, personalities, and the like.

Curriculum developers in the first two cases are obviously responding to the direct, negative effect evidence supplied by a good portion of the violence studies. Instructional materials paint a very dark picture, indeed, for those who would be "heavy viewers." There is little escape for them from the consequences of violence, stereotypes, and so on. Our hope is in those who practice continence and limit their viewing.

The remaining three are only slightly less directive although more subtle in their approach in suggesting that the student is free to make certain choices. All choices are not equal, of course, and only certain areas of choice-making come in for scrutiny.

Traditional literary criticism appears as the main instructional mode to achieve this objective. Students are directed to describe and analyze story lines, characters, characterization, motivating elements, plots, themes, formats, and production values. This critical analysis is usually composed of two parts—first a description of what is there and then an assessment of worth.

All five of the projects approach criticism as an explication of the meaning residing in the presentation. They show little or no recognition of other critical approaches such as hermaneutics or "reader's criticism." The first omission is appropriate to the general neglect of cultural analysis, but the second is interesting in light of the uses and gratifications perspective of some of the projects. On the other hand, content criticism is indeed traditional in the elementary and secondary classroom.

Ratings studies have consistently indicated that young people of the age group covered by these projects make little or no use of television news. Despite their lack of attendance, or perhaps because of it, five of the eight projects provide extensive instruction on news programming. The outcome sought appears to be an understanding of the processes by which news stories are developed and an evaluation of the potential biases of the information presented. Between the lines one can easily read, however, the larger educational objective of an informed citizenry.

The objectives in fantasy–reality seem to derive from protectionistic concerns. At the lower levels, instruction is aimed at demystifying television by showing where programs come from, that characters are actors, that jumping off the roof of a garage in a cape does not permit one to fly, and the like. At the secondary levels, instruction considers the probability of plots and actions, the validity of images and stereotypes, and the utility of social information. The instruction is aimed at preventing errors resulting from what might be seen in television entertainment programming. The concept of reality that is promoted is an objective, external one, not an interactive, socially constructed one. Consequently for the developers, *a* reality of police work can be posited and compared with *the* reality of police work presented on television. With one exception, the five projects that work with this objective abandon the uses and gratifications perspective by considering only the predictiveness of dramatic information for "actual" events rather than remaining within the system of utilities for individual purposes.

OTHER OBJECTIVES

There remain a large number of other objectives championed by one or two of the projects. Most of these objectives come from those projects that integrate television literacy into existing language arts, English, and/or social studies programs. An objective of this kind might be "the student will increase skills in critical writing." Two of the more interesting ones are an objective in using formal communication theory and an objective to develop skills in public opinion polling to determine viewing trends among the individual's social group. Many of these objectives, while certainly of value in their own right, appear to be outside the arena of television literacy per se.

Summary: Toward a Definition of Television Literacy

Taken as a group the television literacy projects appear to support the following objectives:

1. The student will have an understanding of the grammar and syntax of television as expressed in different program forms.
2. The student will have available strategies for the management of duration of viewing and program choices.
3. The student will be able to describe the technical processes of television, including those dealing with electronics and production.
4. The student will be able to analyze the persuasive appeals used in television advertising and to relate those appeals to his or her own consumer behavior.
5. The student will be able to compare similar presentations or those with similar purposes but produced in different media.
6. The student will be able to describe the television industry and its operation and to provide an explanation of that industry's role in society.
7. The student will be able to identify values in language, characterization, conflict resolution, and sound and visual images and

to compare those values with ones held by the community and self.

8. The student will be aware of certain research findings concerning the effects of television content and be able to identify the effects of viewing in his or her own behavior.

9. The student will be able to identify the elements in dramatic presentations associated with the concepts of plot, story line, theme, characters, characterization, motivations, program formats, and production values.

10. The student will be able to describe common sources of news stories and to evaluate the worth of stories for his or her own purposes and the purposes of others.

11. The student will be able to distinguish and evaluate information from dramatic television programs for its value as an indicant of reality.

An analysis of these 11 objectives suggests that four different activities make up the nucleus of the notion of television literacy. They are exposition or description, identification, analysis, and attribution or decision making. The specific activities in *exposition–description* that support television literacy are the ability to describe the rules that govern the grammar and syntax of television program forms; the technical processes involved in production and television electronics; the parts of the television industry; the role of television in society; certain research findings and a catalogue of behavioral consequences of viewing. *Identification* activities are directed toward the application of various category schemes that extract and classify program elements, persuasive appeals, and value constructs from television content. The forms of *analysis* are surfacing personal purposes for viewing; selecting working elements into categories; comparing value constructs; attaching news sources to news stories; and distinguishing fantasy from reality. Finally, the activities of *attribution or decision making* are those related to duration of viewing and program choices, consumer choices, consequences of viewing, and the utility of information for some prior purpose.

Examination of the instructional support texts indicates that most of the instruction time is spent in the processes of categorical description. That is, the largest share of classroom activities is involved with the development and explication of classification schemes and the identification of content to fit those schemes. Less than a third of the print space is spent on analysis, attribution, and decision making.

Although we may be concerned at the relative balance of description

to analysis, actual instruction appears to well meet the following theoretical conceptualization developed in the initial stages of the Receivership Skills project (Receivership Skills, 1973, as adapted by J. Anderson, 1981, with permission of Charles C Thomas).

> [Television literacy] skills begin with those skills needed to identify
> and understand one's own motives and purposes for attendance. They
> include the ability to interpret the influence of those motives and pur-
> poses in the way we make sense of the messages we receive. That those
> motives, for example, may facilitate the acceptance of certain statements
> and the rejection of others.
>   They provide the ability to grasp the meaning of the message; to com-
> prehend language and visual and aural images discriminately; to in-
> terpret "hidden" meanings; to specify the working elements of the mes-
> sage; to identify to whom the message is directed and its intent.
>   They foster the observation of details [sic] their sequence and relation-
> ships; the understanding of themes, values, motivating elements, plot
> lines, characters and characterizations.
>   They direct the evaluation of fact, opinion, logical and affective ap-
> peals. They identify fanciful writing and images.
>   Receivership skills include an understanding of the sources of bias
> inherent in the medium of presentation, and a comprehension of the
> grammar, syntax and meanings contained in the methods chosen to pro-
> duce the message.
>   Finally, the individual trained in receivership skills can recognize
> intended affective reactions and motives; can relegate personal value to
> the message; identify emotional satisfaction and their sources in the mes-
> sages; relate the message to other experiences and information; can make
> inferences, draw conclusions and establish predictions or other criteria
> for evaluation [p. 23].

Television Literacy and the Critical Viewer

In the rhetoric that surrounds the press for the introduction of television literacy curricula, one finds the notion of the critical viewer. Identified as a national need by the Office of Education (Department of
Health, Education and Welfare, 1978), the critical viewer is seen as the
outcome of the television literacy curricula. *Critical Television Viewing*, the text of the WNET (1980a) project, defines a critical viewer as
one who plans television viewing in advance and who evaluates the
programs while watching. Certainly there is nothing in the curricula of
television literacy that would prevent these two actions, and there
seems to be considerable material to support them. The notion of the
critical viewer as one choosing wisely and well, however, is not much

help in the justification of television literacy without an understanding of the criteria by which those choices would be evaluated. Furthermore, based on our knowledge of the pragmatics of television viewing, we must wonder whether the combination of advanced planning and ongoing evaluation is not antithetical to most television-use structures. Consider, at least, that most critical viewing arguments look to the skeptical viewer, forewarned and forearmed, as the desirable viewer. Yet the traditional contract between playwright and audience is the latter's willing suspension of disbelief, to suffer the author's deceits in search of a play. Coupling immersion and acceptance with active reflection seems difficult at best. Is the critical viewer to watch but not enjoy?

The next several sections consider the idea of the critical viewer and its relationship to classroom instruction in television literacy. The first section reports the findings of research as to the effectiveness of television literacy curricula in establishing the skill of the critical viewer, and, then, in order, follow sections on models of the critical viewer, the pragmatics of television viewing, and finally some thoughts for the future.

Research Status and Findings

The entire field of research on television literacy and the effect of television literacy instruction on critical viewing has less than a dozen entries. The research reported to date is usually one of three types: findings concerning the effectiveness of instruction in terms of student knowledge outcomes; findings concerning the comparative effectiveness of instructional methods; and findings concerning projected changes in viewing behavior subsequent to television literacy instruction.

Doolittle (1977) in an early preliminary study found that students participating in two different immunization efforts showed reduced rates of verbal aggression and lower scores on paper and pencil aggression measures. Convenience samples were small and no statistical values were reported in this pilot study.

J. Anderson and Ploghoft (1980), working as evaluators of the Idaho Falls project, developed a television literacy test analogous to critical reading measures. The Television Information Game calls for the student to analyze short segments of television content in an increasing hierarchy of cognitive skills ranging from identification, to analysis of syntax, to drawing conclusions about implications and consequences. Using a pre- and posttest design, they found that third-grade students

showed rapid gains in cognitive skills vis à vis television and performed nearly at sixth-grade levels. Fourth-, fifth-, and sixth-grade students also showed significant posttest increases, but those increases
were better explained by maturation than by the instructional intervention. Subsequent evaluation (Research Design, 1981) on fourth, fifth,
and sixth grades showed fifth- and sixth-grade students who received
instruction posting greater gains than control students at the same
grade levels not receiving instruction. Fourth-grade findings remained
equivocal.

Singer, Zuckerman, and Singer (1980) report that third-, fourth-, and
fifth-grade students scored higher on tests of knowledge about television
and television-based vocabulary following instruction than students at
those grade levels who did not participate in instruction. Control students were as competent as experimental students in distinguishing
fantasy from reality, however. The authors further comment that it was
not possible to "assess how close we came to achieving our ultimate goal
of creating more discriminating TV viewers [p. 92]."

Dorr, Graves, and Phelps (1980) provided instruction for separate
groups of kindergarten, second-, and third-grade students in facts about
television production and economics; in reasoning about fantasy and
reality; or in social-process reasoning (as a control). Their results did
not clearly support the effectiveness of instruction, as the control group
often showed no significant differences from either one or the other of
the experimental groups. They were most successful in instructing students about the facts of television and least successful in showing gains
in "selectivity and reasoned judgments."

Desmond and Jeffries-Fox (1981) compared three modes of instruction on receivership skills emphasizing commercial messages, a traditional lecture approach, a mediated approach, and role playing. Significant gain scores were recorded in all factual areas across all modes; role
playing was the most successful mode of instruction particularly in
promoting awareness of commercials and their purposes.

The effectiveness of role playing as an instructional method was also
found by Triplett (1981) who compared the traditional lecture method,
a mediated lecture, creative dramatics (role playing), and a combination of the three with a noninstructional control group. All instructional methods showed significant increases over the control in commerical literacy with children aged 6–11. The creative dramatics
approach scored the highest absolute gain but not significantly so. The
mediated lecture was significantly less successful than all other
methods.

Wolfe, Ableman, and Hexamer (1981) made use of the question-asking Taba model of instruction (cf. Eggen, Kauchak, & Harder, 1979) to help children between the ages of 5 and 12 develop "generalizations, explanations and predictive inferences" concerning the broad spectrum of television literacy skills. They claim substantial success from this nontraditional method based on analysis of audiotapes of student responses.

Research to date provides us little more than the answer to the question of whether elements of television literacy can be taught in the classroom. (We asked 25 years ago whether the classroom could be presented on television; both questions are rather trivial.) The answer is "yes," of course. Whether learning about television literacy has any effect on critical viewing remains largely unanswered. There is some evidence from J. Anderson and Ploghoft (1980), Dorr et al. (1980), and Wolfe et al. (1981) that children can approximate more adult reasoning models following training. The value of accelerating the adoption of adult reasoning models is unquestioned by these studies; it is also untested—a point to which we shall return.

The assumption that it is better to reason as an adult rather than as a child is one of several notions that are used to develop the concept of the critical viewer. Typically these notions are implicit in the research, objectives, and instruction relation to television literacy. The next selection attempts to make manifest these notions and models.

Models of the Critical Viewer

It seems obvious that the circumstances that are appropriate to critical viewing are dependent upon the purposes the individual has for viewing and the criterion skills that are used to model the concept of the critical viewer. Except for a line here and phrase there, no systematic attempt has been made to define the critical viewer (J. Anderson, 1980b). The best that can be done is to extract models from 10 years of experience in working with teachers, school administrators, and researchers entering into the study of television, literacy, and critical viewing. The models that are presented are my interpretation of the organizing notions that seem to guide individuals at different times in their pursuit of curricula, classroom instruction, and research hypotheses.

The models divide nicely into two types: those whose major emphasis is on the classification and analysis of content, and those that emphasize the character of the cognitive processes used by the viewer. The content models are presented first.

CONTENT MODELS: RECTO RATIO; RECTO ACTIO

The belief that right thoughts will lead to right deeds is the covering notion for two disparate groups of practitioners in media education: those who pursue value education and those who pursue reality constructs. Value education in its most egregious form is the moral majority, but it appears less virulently in the idea of the critical viewer (see, for example, the publications of the National Coalition on Television Violence or the Media Action Research Center). Value education provides answers, whose justifications lie outside the individual viewer's purposes, for such questions as: How much television should one watch? What program should be selected? What to do about violence, and "adult programming" (also known as sex)? What is the right way to buy products? What is the responsibility of the good citizen to attend to the news?

Those who approach the critical viewer from concepts like fantasy, reality, and perceived reality are similarly inclined to establish the criteria for a critical viewer in a manner independent of the viewer per se (see Singer & Singer, 1981). The realists posit external realities for such concepts as "the image of" women, minorities, and working man, which can then be compared with "the image of" women, minorities, and working man, as constructed from media presentations. Errors by respondents occur when "media" image characteristics are selected instead of "real" image characteristics. Realists also concern themselves about proper media behavior and explanations. Responding to a question posed by a television persona is not proper; thinking Lou Grant is a real person is incorrect; believing in the power of shampoo to gain one social acceptance is unfortunate.

Whether generated from values or realities the model begins with a set of independent characteristics of how things ought to be, including critical viewing. In the end, this model requires critical viewers to arm themselves with effective mechanisms governing viewing and consumer choices and with acceptable explanations for the world around them.

CONTENT MODELS:
AURAL AND VISUAL COMPREHENSION AND ANALYSIS

The term *critical viewer* (a misnomer of some magnitude as the audio track carries much of the information of plot and product) is simply an extension of previous pedagogical terms—*critical reader, critical thinker*. *Critical thinking*, which most now accept as the overarching term, has been defined as the determination of the meaning of statements and their acceptability (Ennis, 1962). Comprehension, or the extraction of meaning, then, is the first step in critically analyzing any presentation regardless of medium. The critical viewer, reader, or listener is one who can first grasp the central meaning of a statement, recognize its ambiguities, establish its relationship with other statements, and the like. Most of the work on audio visual comprehension has emphasized the visual—a likely consequence of the visual emphasis in work on perception. Visual comprehension studies have focused on the conditions under which individuals make errors in the interpretation of what they see (cf. Davidoff, 1975; Gregory, 1972) as opposed to what actually is. Protocols using the trapezoidal window or lines with deceptive characteristics are examples. Television-based visual comprehension studies have studied the effect of lens and lens changes on judgments of size and speed (Acker, 1981; Acker & Tiemens, 1979). The move from these perceptual studies to instruction on comprehension of meaning (Dondis, 1973; Pickering, 1971) has carried forward the supposition of a literal meaning embedded in the visualization. There is, therefore, a "central meaning" to which we can all retire and to which we should all react in similar ways.

The second step of critical thinking, the determination of the acceptability of statements, is also conducted from a realist perspective. That is, the criteria for the tests of acceptability reside in the formal characteristics of the statement and/or independent standards of analysis. Students consequently are taught to recognize *improper* forms, *faulty* arguments, *false* appeals, *weak* evidence, and the like. This approach is, of course, in the mainstream of educational tradition. The comprehension and analysis model has been most effective in garnering support for classroom instruction concerning television from school boards, parents, and teachers. It appeals to an already existing educational objective and uses instructional methods familiar to teachers, parents, and students.

The model has its critics, however (Newcomb, 1981). It would appear to have little to do with the way people actually use television. It ignores individually constructed meanings, purposes for, uses of, and gratifications from attendance to television. Questions concerning the transfer of training from the classroom to the viewing room appear justified.

CONTENT MODELS: THE VIEWER AS CRITIC

The current batch of television literacy curricula and concepts of the critical viewer have generally sprung from psychological sources rather than artistic or critical sources. The discipline of criticism has been underrepresented both as a guiding perspective and as an instructional strategy. Nevertheless there continues well-established activity in media criticism. There is also some portent of a redirection of current efforts as television literacy curricula become assimilated in existing language arts and English programs. Activities in criticism at the elementary and secondary levels are typically an extension of literary criticism (Brown, 1972). At the college level, criticism as an approach to television literacy has sought to explicate cultural meanings residing in entertainment programming (Deming, 1979).

Instruction derived from this model aims at an appreciation of the forms of television. It is generally benign in its attitude toward television content seeking its worth rather than its errors.[4] The critical viewer, then, is one who can distill the qualities of, say, a situation comedy, evaluate the fineness of form and execution, and consider the program as one more negotiation of one's culture.

PROCESS MODELS: CRITICAL VIEWING AS EFFICIENCY

As noted, a dominant strain through television literacy curricula has been the combination of uses and gratification theory with decision making. The critical viewer that presumably results is one who can identify his or her purposes for viewing and evaluate the consequences of viewing in relation to the satisfaction of those purposes. The critical viewer is efficient in the pursuit of gratifications from the media. Instruction does not stop here, of course, for, in the essentially conservative nature of American education, there are purposes both good and bad. The evaluation of purposes, although often skirted in text, is certainly dealt with in the classroom. One does not offer "to get stoked on violence" as an acceptable reason for viewing to the average classroom teacher.

PROCESS MODELS: COGNITIVE DEVELOPMENT, THE CRITICAL VIEWER
AS THE ADULT THINKER

A fairly well-developed area of research has been the application of cognitive development models to the manner in which children of different ages assimilate and utilize information from television (e.g., D. Anderson, Lorch, Field, & Sanders, 1981; W. Collins, 1975, 1979). In

---

[4]Not always, however; the University of Kansas children and television research group has recommended the development of television literacy curriculum based on the forms and syntax of television from a very protectionistic perspective (Wright and Huston, 1981).

many of these studies the expressed or implied criterion of understanding is the adult explanation or, at least, the formal, literate meaning of a message that fully assimilated members of a society would acknowledge.

Drawing on this literature, curriculum developers (Dorr, 1981) have argued, if indirectly, for a critical viewer model for children as an approximation of adult reasoning. As noted, the efficacy of children imitating adult reasoning remains untested. It is, of course, possible that children should no more participate in adult reasoning processes than they should participate in physical activities requiring higher levels of development. (For opposing views on this subject see Bruner, Olver,& Greenfield, 1966; Sinclair 1975.) It is, of course, the theoretical perspective of invariant cognitive stages that leads one to the determination that the adult stage is the termination of normal development and that it is at that stage that one has full capacity. A different model of cognitive stages—call it a cultural socialization model—might argue that performance at later cognitive stages may or may not be at greater overall capacity than earlier stages. For example, there is some evidence that "normal" eidetic memory capacity may be suppressed (Haber, 1969) and visual reasoning weakened (McKim, 1980) in favor of later acquired verbal skills. In addition, most of that television that is the subject of greatest concern is directed toward the modification of adult behaviors. Normal, untrained adult reasoning may not be an adequate standard to identify the critical viewer. Certainly there is no evidence, for example, that adult consumer behavior is less directed by commercial media messages than children's. The value of having children approximate adult reasoning in order to improve purchase decision making through the analysis of commercial messages, therefore, is unknown.

PROCESS MODELS:
THE ECOLOGICAL APPROACH TO CRITICAL VIEWING

Interactionism continues its spread even into mass communication (see Meyer, 1980). In its fully developed form, interactionism leads to an ecological approach. Such an approach is holistic, contextually bound in the time, space, and social actors of the event. The consequent position of this approach is that normal media use occurs within its own ecology, which is self-contained and includes methods, standards, and satisfactions of performance. Given an ecological approach one can no longer maintain a single model of the critical viewer. Rather the notion of the critical viewer must be reinterpreted within the given ecology of the social actors. Common instruction becomes less useful, and the emphasis is placed on individual diagnoses and educational prescriptions.

The ecological perspective, despite its exciting explanatory potential, has limited utility to direct instruction in present classrooms. The initial, required task of revealing the media ethnomethods of each student appears insurmountable. Nevertheless, one cannot dismiss the ecological perspective out of hand. If human communication behavior demands an ecological explanation, then, in practical fact, what must be known by the individual viewer resides within that ecological system and not in constructed edifices of television literacy (see Rice & Wartella, 1981).

The Critical Viewer and the Pragmatics of Television Viewing

The absence of research evidence either for or against the relationship between television literacy and critical viewing increases the importance of the analysis of the environment in which critical viewing is to occur. The concept of the critical viewer is not limited to a classroom performer. It seeks a nation of "more knowledgeable viewers" (Dorr et al., 1980) analyzing what they watch in the ordinary concourse of their daily lives. Analysis of the pragmatics of television attendance—the ordinary methods by which televiewing gets done—holds at least one key to the likelihood of critical viewing.

Since 1978, the University of Utah has been part of a consortium of universities conducting observational studies using the methods of naturalistic inquiry in the analysis of individuals using television in family settings. (For a discussion of the nature of these studies, see Traudt, 1979.) These studies have generated a small collection of case histories of the way television is used in ordinary homes. One of the premises of these studies is that television viewing occurs in structures—more or less organized behavioral skeins—that regularly appear and that account for most of the viewing that gets done. These structures may be complex or fairly simple, but it is within these structures that television viewing is interpreted and understood. This section will present four cases that range in complexity of structure. No argument is made that these cases are representative of all viewing or even of other structures. Such claims, of course, are not appropriate to ontological research. Finally, the cases have been presented in an interpreted rather than evidentiary form to present the character of the case as quickly as possible.

OBSERVATIONS FROM A FAMILY OF FOUR: SET CONTROL

Little Davey aged 5 came deliberately into the room. This was his time of the day; he knew it, and he was about to exercise his rights. His brother, 14, was flopped on a bean bag in the center of the long, narrow, rather awkward room. The theme song for *Hogan's Heroes* was just announcing yet another rerun of the syndicated comedy. Davey went to the television set and changed the channel to *Sesame Street*. His brother sighed but said nothing. In the opposite corner of the room their mother was completing a grocery list at the game table. John knew Davey had been given control of the television set from 4 to 6 by decision of a family council. John also knew that Davey usually tired of *Sesame Street* within a few moments; he bided his time; he knew how he would play this game. A Bert and Ernie scene finished, and Davey pulled out some of his match book cars and began to play on the floor. "Davey," John said, using an obviously solicitious tone, "would you like to watch something else? *Hogan's Heroes* is on, you know you really like that." "Uh, I dunno," replied Davey. John glanced at his mother and siged again. After a few more minutes of playing Davey left the room. John waited what might be considered a decent interval and turned the channel. He had hardly settled into the story when Davey returned and as before immediately turned the channel without comment. John protested, "Come on, Davey, you don't wanna watch *Sesame Street*." His mother said in an even tone, "John. . . ." John rearranged his bean bag and prepared for a siege.

OBSERVATIONS FROM A FAMILY OF THREE: WATCHING THE NEWS

The father signaled a stop in the play of the three-handed competitive solitaire game. The weather forecast had finally come on. "OK, no rain tomorrow," he said. "Let's go." Play resumed. For the past several weeks, the family had gathered at the table by the television set to play cards during the late evening news. Play was usually continuous during the "hard news" section, although occasional discussion or questions by the adults concerning a story indicated at least a sampling of aural attendance. To be competitive in three-handed solitaire one must continually attend to the display in the center and that of the opponents. Competition was serious; victories were celebrated and defeats bemoaned. After about 20 minutes of play Melissa, 11 years of age, had had enough of the competition; she had won her share, and she was tired from the long day of summer activities. She propped her head with a pillow as she lay on the floor. " 'Bout time to hang it up, isn't it?" said her dad. Quick in defense, Melissa replied firmly, "No, I wanta watch M*A*S*H. It's next." "Well, you'll have to get on a schedule next week for school," said her mother. "That's why I want to watch M*A*S*H; I won't get to then." Seemingly satisfied the parents returned to their play which continued through much of the next half hour.

OBSERVATIONS FROM A FAMILY OF FOUR: NEIGHBORHOOD PLAY

Each weekday afternoon at 5:00 the doorbell rang, followed immediately by an impatient knock. "That's got to be Eric; right on time." She said to herself as she got up to answer the door. "Come on in; Amy and Eden are already downstairs with Angela." Eric, the 4-year-old, next-door neighbor, was dressed as always, with an apron around his shoulders for a cape, vinyl cowboy boots, and his gun belt wrapped twice around his shorts. He was dressed as his favorite superhero; it was time to watch the show.

Eric joined the three children downstairs. After watching for a few minutes they began to act out part of the scene they were watching, which quickly evolved into one of the regular fantasy games they played. The television became a back drop for this play activity. When a particularly exciting scene was signaled by the audio, they would stop to watch and then go back to play. The television show was over long before the playing stopped.

OBSERVATIONS FROM A FAMILY OF THREE: WATCHING TOGETHER

Each weekday the mother left early in the morning before Ellen and John were off to school. She depended on Ellen to clean up the breakfast dishes and to see that she and John made it to elementary school on time. This morning the two children had gotten up late. In their rush to make it to school on time, Ellen had left a mess on the table. Dinner was over about 7 each workday evening. The children would get up from the table and go into the living room to sit on the long couch and watch television. Their mother would join them after she had finished the dishes. They were a close family. The children would snuggle up on each side of their mother and watch until their bedtime. They rarely spoke during this time together but seemed to enjoy the closeness of one another. Tonight the mother came into the living room and said: "Ellen, I left those cereal bowls for you to finish. You go on in there now and get them done. I can't be doing those things for you." Ellen began to cry. "Go on, girl," her mother commanded. Ellen cleaned the two bowls in the kitchen but, still feeling the sting of rejection, spent the evening in her bedroom.

CASE STUDIES: IMPLICATIONS

The point of these four cases is that they are, first, well within the common understanding of how television viewing gets done in our families. They present no surprises even to persons who have made no observations. Second, the structures described could not exist if the individuals functioning within them were practicing critical viewing, assuming one considers critical viewing as alert, attentive, and actively reflective. Stating that does not suggest, of course, that structures which do involve critical viewing cannot develop. What it does suggest is that there are many circumstances involving television where critical viewing would not be appropriate and may, in fact, be detrimental to the purposes held for the viewing in the first place.

To fully appreciate the evidence presented in these case studies, it is necessary to return to a fundamental tenet of ethnological studies—that behavioral structures formalize behavior, define the action, and establish the contextual constraints of its performance (Geertz, 1973). Although the notion of contextual constraints residing in structures has not been adequately explored in media studies, the tenet does suggest, however, that the ethnomethods of "doing" something will limit the expressions that will appear. These limits are not positivistic determinants but a persistent resistance to change. Hence, when we say that television viewing appears in structures, we are saying (a) that what it means to view television is defined within these structures and not in others; (b) that these structures are likely to continue; and (c) that they will function to prevent other behavioral skeins, such as those that might support critical viewing behaviors, from appearing. It is, therefore, a statement of no mean magnitude to say that this collection of ordinary viewing structures does not admit to the performance of the critical viewing skills espoused in the six models. It is not to say that critical viewing *cannot* occur in these mundane cases of viewing; it is to say that it *will not*. It has not because critical viewing behaviors are simply not part of what here defines the ordinary, everyday act of watching television.

It is also true that the structures described in these cases (as with most) are not permanent. In fact, the television play and card-game viewing structures both broke up during the observation period with the start of the new school year. Little Davey will not forever be interested in playing his *Sesame Street* game, and Ellen and John may find themselves too old to snuggle. At the point of change, what structures will replace those passing? If Ellen, John, Davey, Eric, and the rest had participated in a television literacy course, would one expect the change to be one in which the critical viewer role is central? Our library of cases suggests not. None of the observations surfaced a structure that reflected one of the models of critical viewing, although at least one family had children who had participated in a television literacy course of study. We can speculate that the relationship among medium, content, and viewer is not fertile ground for the discipline of criticism. At least, television content does not appear to be such that it can stand continuous, systematic scrutiny. Perhaps its content cannot support the critical viewer who would simply turn away. Certainly, it is clear that one cannot merely change the performance of the audience without fundamentally affecting the nature of the total communication system involved.

What remains is to consider the condition under which one of the six models might appear within the pragmatic realm of actual viewing. In my opinion the content-based models of the critical viewer are restricted to the relatively few instances where individuals are viewing intentionally—to accommodate some expressed criterion of performance. That is, the individual is viewing as a function of one's job, one's opinion leadership role, formal decision making, and the like. As a consequence the critical viewer, as defined in the content models, rarely appears, but performance as a critical viewer can be improved by instruction in television literacy.

The process models on the other hand do not require a particular method of analytical viewing but rather are concerned with the outcomes of viewing in relation to some initial purpose or subsequent decision. Consequently, these models can be applied to any condition of viewing, which permits the ready appearance of the critical viewer. What slips is the relationship between instruction in television literacy and successful goal seeking–decision making. It would seem that the current content of television literacy is neither necessary nor sufficient to accomplish either of the latter two.

Thoughts for the Future

This chapter has been seeking the underlying assumptions of television literacy curricula and the idea of the critical viewer. It focused on the strengths and weakness of those assumptions and the consequences of holding them. The investigation of the foundations had indicated a less than satisfactory state; weaknesses were more easily found than strengths.

Nevertheless, I would expect the good continuation of the development of television literacy curricula. Many of the weaknesses are endemic to all curricula efforts that attempt to influence everyday living through classroom instruction. For example, I do not expect that a satisfactory definition of the critical viewer will ever be achieved, just as we have failed to define the critical reader or critical thinker. These notions are too burdened with competing values and goals of accomplishment. They are much more political concepts than pedagogical ones.

Television literacy as a course of instruction may best be served if practitioners would follow these four recommendations:

1. Stop trying to save children from television.
2. Value the child for being a child.
3. Justify the content of instruction in the conditions of everyday viewing.
4. Be knowledgeable about the educational establishment.

The following paragraphs offer a brief defense for each of these recommendations.

Stop Trying to Save Children from Television

It has been argued that television is no longer a free choice selection in American society, but rather it is a standard (although not required) part of normal membership in this culture (Pacanowsky & Anderson, 1981). The adversarial approach taken by many texts and teachers must be confusing to the child who is faced with a massive array of cultural inducements to attend to this medium. The focus of instruction should be strategies of satisfaction, not guilt inducement. Children enjoy television. Let them.

Value the Child for Being a Child

Children do not attend, assimilate, process, or use television content as an adult. We prejudice our understanding of the instructional needs of children when we approach television and children from adult models. It would seem appropriate to work from child-based models of behavior if we are to help the child approach the problems he or she faces. An understanding of the satisfactions and solutions gained by children from television should guide the selection of course material, not the content of the medium as interpreted by adults or adult concepts of productivity and return.

Justify the Content of Instruction in the Conditions of Everyday Viewing

Much of what is presently taught under the rubric of television literacy seems to have little relationship to how people view. That is, what is easiest to teach, such as vocabulary or facts about things, often has the least utility for the viewer. For example, a large proportion of viewing has little to do with content or its analysis (J. Anderson, 1980a). The decision for that viewing is a decision to participate in an activity called "watching television," which can serve a host of non-content-bound purposes. As a result, some television literacy curricula make demands that cannot be justified in the normal concourse of media behavior. It is not always useful to consciously select programs to watch, and superficial attention may be precisely what is called for in given circumstances.

Be Knowledgeable of the Educational Establishment

Certain instructional packages will never gain acceptance, because they ignore the realities of school boards, superintendents, teachers, students, and parents. The installation of curriculum within a district or a school is essentially a political process, and it is a process that, at some level, is renegotiated each year. New objectives vie with established ones for time and resources. Not all can be served. The history of programs of media literacy have an all too common pattern. They are introduced with the help of outside "consultants", are briefly championed by administrators within the school district, and then fade as teachers move to simplify their responsibilities under the pressure of student and parental demands. Successful curriculum innovations are ones that can be assimilated into established objectives to achieve traditional goals. Curriculum developers would do well to house television literacy objectives within existing programs of study.

References

Acker, S. R. Lens focal length and viewers' perception of velocity; A developmental study. Unpublished doctoral dissertation, University of Utah, 1981.
Acker, S. R., & Tiemens, R. K. Conservation of televised images: A developmental study.

Paper presented at the Society of Research and Child Development Convention, San Francisco, Calif., 1979.

Anderson, D. R., Lorch, E. P., Field, D. E., & Sanders, J. The effects of TV program comprehensibility on preschool children's visual attention to television. *Child Development*, 1981, *52*, 151–157.

Anderson, J. A. Methodological assessment of existing evaluative ratings systems. *Proceedings of the 1980 technical conference* (C1-121). Washington, D.C.: Corporation for Public Broadcasting, 1980. (a)

Anderson, J. A. The theoretical lineage of critical viewing curricula. *Journal of Communication*, 1980, *30*, 64–71. (b)

Anderson, J. A. Receivership skills: An educational response. In M. Ploghoft & J. A. Anderson (Eds.), *Education for the television age*. Springfield, Ill.: Charles C Thomas, 1981.

Anderson, J. A., & Ploghoft, M. *Curricular approaches to the development of receivership skills appropriate to televised messages.* Paper presented at the Speech Communication Association Convention, Chicago, Ill., 1974.

Anderson, J. A., & Ploghoft, M. *The way we see it.* Salt Lake City, Utah: Media Research Center, 1978.

Anderson, J. A., & Ploghoft M. Receivership skills: The television experience. In D. Nimmo (Ed.), *Communication yearbook 4*. New Brunswick, N.J.: Transaction Books, 1980.

Brown, R. G. *A bookless curriculum*, Dayton, Ohio: Pflaum/Standard, 1972.

Bruner, J. S., Olver, R. R., & Greenfield, P. M. (Eds). *Studies in cognitive growth.* New York: Wiley, 1966.

Collins, C., & Moles, O. *The family and television: An overview of federal programs.* Paper prepared for the National Workshop on Television and Children, National Institute of Education, Washington, D.C., 1980.

Collins, W. A. The developing child as viewer. *Journal of Communication*, 1975, *25*(4), 35–44.

Collins, W. A. Children's comprehension of television content. In E. Wartella (Ed.), *Children communicating: Media and development of thought, speech, understanding*, Beverly Hills, Calif.: Sage, 1979.

Davidoff, J. B. *Differences in visual perception.* London: Crosby, Lockwood, and Staples, 1975.

Deming, C. *Watch less—see more: Enriching the English curriculum through television.* Paper presented at the National Council of Teachers of English Convention, San Francisco, Calif., 1979.

Department of Health, Education and Welfare, Office of Education. *Development of critical television viewing skills in students* (RFP 78-94). Washington, D.C.: Author, June 26, 1978.

Desmond, R. J., & Jefferies-Fox, S. *Elevating children's awareness of television advertising: The effects of a critical viewing program.* Paper presented at the International Communication Association Convention, Minneapolis, Minn., 1981.

Dondis, D. A. *A primer of visual literacy.* Cambridge, Mass.: MIT Press, 1973.

Doolittle, J. *A proposed school intervention curriculum designed to help children cope with the effects of television.* Paper presented at the International Communication Association Convention, West Berlin, Germany, 1977.

Dorr, A. Television and affective development and functioning: Maybe this decade. *Journal of Broadcasting*, 1981, *25*(4), 335–345.

Dorr, A., Graves, S. B., & Phelps, E. Television literacy for young children. *Journal of Communication*, 1980, *30*(3), 71–83.

Eggen, P. D., Kauchak, D. P., & Harder, R. J. *Strategies for teachers: Information processing models in the classroom.* Englewood Cliffs, N.J.: Prentice-Hall, 1979.

Ennis, R. H. A concept of critical thinking. *Harvard Educational Review*, 1962, *32*, 81–111.

Far West Laboratory for Educational Research and Development. *Critical television viewing skills curriculum for high school.* San Francisco: Author, 1979.

Ford Foundation. *Television and children: Priorities for research.* Reston, Va.: Author, 1975.

Fransecky, R. B., & Ferguson, R. New ways of seeing: The Milford visual communications project. *Audiovisual Instruction*, April 1973, *18*, 44–49. (a)

Fransecky, R. B., & Ferguson, R. New ways of seeing: The Milford visual communications project. *Audiovisual Instruction*, May 1973, *18*, 47–49. (b)

Fransecky, R. B., & Ferguson, R. New ways of seeing: The Milford visual communications project. *Audiovisual Instruction*, June–July 1973, *18*, 56–65. (c)

Geertz, C. *The interpretation of cultures.* New York: Basic Books, 1973.

Gregory, R. L. *Eye and brain: The psychology of seeing.* London: Weidenfeld and Nicolson, 1972.

Haber, R. N. Eidetic images. *Scientific American*, 1969, *220*, 36–55.

Idaho Falls School District 91. *The way we see it handbook.* Idaho Falls, Idaho: Author, 1979.

Lewis, P. The future of television in education. *Pi Delta Kappan*, 1948, *30*, 157–160.

McKim, R. H. *Experience in visual thinking.* Monterey, Calif.: Brooks/Cole, 1980.

Meyer, T. *Mass communication: A symbolic interaction perspective.* Unpublished manuscript, University of Texas at Austin, 1980. (Available from T. Meyer, University of Wisconsin at Green Bay, Green Bay, Wisconsin.)

Newcomb, H. *Television as popular culture: Towards a critically based curriculum.* Paper presented at the Children and Television: Implications for Education conference, Philadelphia, 1979.

Newcomb, H. Television as popular culture. In M. Ploghoft & J. Anderson (Eds.) *Education for the television age*, Springfield, Ill.: Charles C Thomas, 1981.

Pacanowsky, M., & Anderson, J. *Cop talk and media use.* Paper presented at the International Communication Association Convention, Minneapolis, Minn., 1981.

Pickering, J. M. *Visual education in the primary school.* London: B. T. Batsford, 1971.

Prime Time School Television. *Television and economics: From medium to the marketplace.* Chicago: Author, 1978.

Receivership skills: Restructuring our principal justifications. Athens, Ohio: Ohio University Broadcast Research Center, 1973.

Research design and statistical assessment of the Idaho Falls T.V. project. Pocatello, Idaho: Idaho State University Bureau of Educational Research, 1981.

Rice, M., & Wartella, E. *Television as a medium of communication: Implications for how to regard the child viewer.* Paper presented at the Society for Research in Child Development Convention, Boston, Mass., 1981.

Rosengren, K. E., & Wendahl, S. *Media panel: A presentation of a program (Media Panel Report #4).* Lund, Sweden, 1978.

Ruth, D. D. Expanded literacy: The new basic skill. *AFI Education*, 1980, *4*, 8–9.

Shorr, J. Basic skills of TV viewing. *Today's Education*, April–May 1978, pp. 72–75.

Sinclair, H. H. The role of cognitive structures in language acquisition. In E. H. Lenneberg

& E. Lenneberg (Eds.), *Foundations of language development: A multidisciplinary approach* (Vol. I). New York: Academic Press, 1975.

Singer, D. G., & Singer, J. L. Television and the developing imagination of the child. *Journal of Broadcasting*, 1981, 25(4), 373–387.

Singer, D. G., Zuckerman, D. M., & Singer, J. L. Helping elementary school children learn about TV. *Journal of Communication*, 1980, 30(3), 84–93.

Southwest Educational Developmental Laboratory. *Television: A family focus.* Austin, Tex.: Author, 1979. (a)

Southwest Educational Developmental Laboratory. *Training manual for teaching critical TV viewing skills.* Austin, Tex.: Author, 1979. (b)

Tentative objectives for teaching television viewing skills in language arts and social studies classes at some grade levels. East Syracuse, N.Y.: East Syracuse/Minoa School District, 1977.

Traudt, P. J. *Television and family viewing: An ethnography.* Unpublished Master's thesis, University of Utah, 1979.

Triplett, J. *How to teach children about the "commerce" of commercials.* Paper presented at the International Communication Association Convention, Minneapolis, Minn., 1981.

UNESCO. *Screen education: Teaching a critical approach to cinema and television.* Paris: UNESCO Workshop, 1964.

White, N. *Inside television.* Palo Alto, Calif.: Science and Behavior Books, 1980.

Wilke, J., & Eschenauer, B. *Mass media use by children and media education in Germany.* Paper presented at the International Communication Association Convention, Minneapolis, Minn., 1981.

WNET Project. *Critical television viewing.* New York: Cambridge Publishers, 1980. (a)

WNET Project. *Critical television viewing* (Teacher Edition). New York: Cambridge Publishers, 1980. (b)

WNET/Thirteen Education Department. *The television criti-kit: Teacher's guide.* New York: Author, 1979.

Wolfe, M., Ableman, R., & Hexamer, A. *Children's understanding of television: Some methodological considerations and a question-asking model for receivership skills.* Paper presented at the International Communication Association Convention, Minneapolis, Minn., 1981.

Wright, J. C., & Huston, A. C. The forms of television: Nature and development of television literacy in children. In H. Gardner & H. Kelly (Eds.), *Children and the worlds of television.* San Francisco: Jossey-Bass, 1981.

Zettl, H. *Sight–sound–motion.* Belmont, Calif.: Wadsworth, 1973.

chapter 13

Research on Children's Television Viewing: The State of the Art

DANIEL R. ANDERSON
JENNINGS BRYANT

Introduction

From one perspective, television viewing is a reasonably straightforward behavior that can be observed directly and measured rather easily. From another perspective, it is part of a complex system that defies such simple scrutiny or analysis. We have come to believe that optimal progress can be made only by employing and then integrating both perspectives. As reflected by many of the contributions to the present volume, new knowledge has been gained by careful observation and experimental analyses of the details of television viewing, but, at the same time, there is a very real awareness of the need to relate these findings and this process to the structure and dynamics of the system as a whole. In this final chapter we will provide a representation of the greater system, describe in more detail the part of the system that is the focus of this volume, and discuss how the various research programs and approaches represented in this volume contribute to understanding the system. We will then present our view of the points of central agreement and disagreement revealed in this volume and other contemporary literature, provide a critique, and make some suggestions for future approaches.

CHILDREN'S UNDERSTANDING
OF TELEVISION

The Larger System

Television viewing cannot be fully understood apart from its relationship to the viewer's immediate sociological context (family and neighborhood characteristics, socioeconomic status, ethnic background, and the like), or from the viewer's behavior and experiences outside of the television-viewing situation. Also, from a larger perspective, these things influence and are influenced by the television industry from which the programming originates, and they affect and are affected by the larger society as a whole. This larger system is schematically outlined in Figure 13.1 (which bears some resemblance to similar notions outlined by Himmelweit, 1980). The arrows in the schematic indicate possible directions of influence. A long-range part of the research task is to specify the strengths of such influences and to detail the processes underlying them. Clearly some of the influences, as between the family and the larger society, are beyond the purview of television research, but they must also be considered, particularly when examining media influence from a historical perspective. Such a perspective must be maintained when, for example, one considers the relationship between the decline of Scholastic Aptitude Test (SAT) scores and amount of television viewing, as cited in Chapter 11 by Singer and Singer.

Considerations of the larger system arise explicitly and implicitly in a number of the present contributions. Mielke's description of the development of 3–2–1 CONTACT outlined not only his concern with the child viewers' interest in and comprehension of certain science topics, but also his concern with the larger societal need to interest children in science and especially to get girls interested and involved in scientific pursuits. It is apparent from his chapter that each element of Figure 13.1 and its interrelationships had to be explicitly considered in the development of 3–2–1 CONTACT. Ultimately, the needs of the larger society, available technology, considerations of family structure, and sociology, and of course the preferences of viewers themselves, all influence the nature of the television medium, the breadth of available programming, and the structure and content of any particular program.

Concerns of the larger society about the effects of television on children have led to, among other things, the development of intervention programs aimed at teaching "critical viewing" skills. As discussed by J. Anderson and also by Singer and Singer and by Dorr, one type of intervention strategy can involve teaching children about the economic nature of the television industry as well as about the technical nature of television production itself. Dorr presents evidence that without such

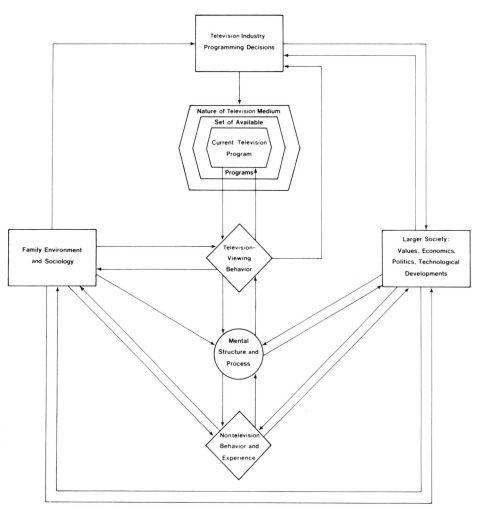

Figure 13.1. *A schematic diagram of elements of the larger social system that influence behavior in the television-viewing situation. The diamonds represent observed behavior; circles represent mental entities; rectangles are potentially observable aspects of the environment; and items in the ovals represent "television."*

intervention, children's judgments of the reality of television presentations are rarely based on such concerns. J. Anderson, however, suggests that the evidence is not yet available to determine whether such intervention is particularly effective and that to some extent the determination may rest on a debate within the larger society as to what constitutes the proper goals of such intervention.

Even the seemingly more individualistic matter of comprehension of a television narrative is not independent of family sociology and of the larger culture. Salomon argues that what is gained from television depends on the amount of "mental effort" invested in the cognitive processing of the program, and he notes that to some extent this investment is related to the values and experiences of the larger culture. Thus, Israeli children may pay closer attention and gain more from a television program than their American counterparts. Collins describes several findings that indicate that young children's comprehension of television drama is related to their socioeconomic background and family value system. These inputs to the child's general knowledge structure are some of the basis for the child's assimilation of the television program and account for differences in comprehension between young children. Interestingly, the lack of such differences in interpretations of programs by older children may indicate the importance of television in contributing to a common knowledge base among American children of varying social classes. Thus, television may itself act to influence the larger society, in part through the homogenization of cultural experience.

A Closer Look at Part of the System

Most of the research and theory presented in this volume attempts to clarify and specify the factors of the child, television medium, and viewing environment that determine attention and comprehension. Figure 13.2, a schematic expansion of the central portion of Figure 13.1, illustrates the behaviors, mental structures, and cognitive processes that have been the focuses of this research. Each contributor to this volume has emphasized a different aspect of television viewing, and, as such, the contributions contain different units of analysis, methodologies, and theoretical approaches. Nevertheless, viewed as a system, each of the programs of research has helped clarify the structure of television viewing and the interrelationships of each of its components.

The television viewing system, from this closer perspective, consists of the television stimulus, observable viewing behaviors, the local viewing environment, and the various inferred mental structures and processes that control, and are controlled by, the observable components. The television stimulus, depending on the level of analysis, consists of general characteristics of the medium, general classes of programming (e.g., commercials, news, cartoons), and particular programs that can be analyzed into formal features and units of content.

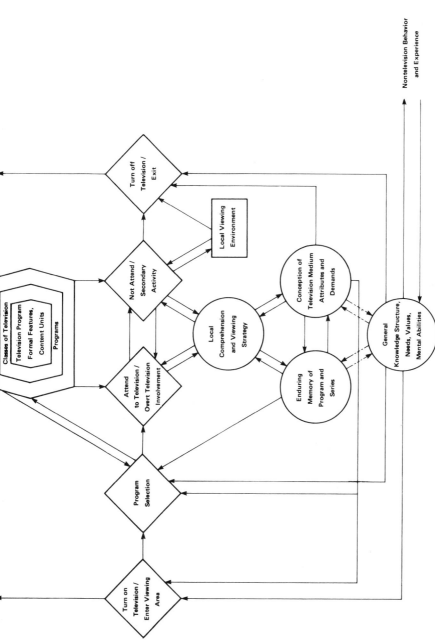

Figure 13.2 A schematic diagram of the central processes of television viewing. The diamonds represent observed behavior; circles represent mental entities; rectangles are potentially observable aspects of the environment; and items in ovals represent "television."

Observable viewing behaviors include entering the viewing area and/or turning on the television, program selection, attention to the television, and/or overt television-involved behavior such as talking about the program; inattention and involvement in secondary nontelevision-viewing activities; and turning off the television and/or leaving the viewing area. Much of the effort in the present volume is directed at clarifying the mental processes that control and are affected by television viewing. These include attention, memory, comprehension, reality judgment, and imagination. Depending on the level of analysis, each of these mental structures and processes is closely tied to television (e.g., memory for a particular television program) or is more generally part of a person's psychological repertoire (e.g., general imaginative abilities that may, over a long period of time, be influenced by television). With the perspective on television viewing illustrated by Figure 13.2 in mind, we will now examine the state of the art in empirical knowledge, research methodology, and theory.

The State of the Art of Television-Viewing Research

Research Questions

Since behavioral research on children's television viewing (as distinct from research on the effects of television viewing) for the most part began in the 1970s, considerable effort has been expended by the various research groups on defining questions and developing methodologies appropriate to answering those questions. Formulation of a research question implies the adoption of a unit of analysis. Much of the difference between the various research programs can be seen as differences not only in research questions, but also in the unit of analysis chosen to approach the answers.

THE TELEVISION STIMULUS

Each research program. according to its goals, has chosen somewhat different ways of characterizing television. Levels of analysis include television as an entire medium of communication to be compared with other media (Meringoff, Vibbert, Char, Fernie, Banker, & Gardner, Chapter 6; Salomon, Chapter 7); classes of programs based on formal and/or content characteristics (Huston & Wright, Chapter 2; Singer & Singer, Chapter 11); individual programs or series compared to other programs or series (Singer & Singer, Chapter 11; Watt & Welch, Chapter 3); content and plot structure within programs (Collins, Chapter 5);

characters and events within programs (Dorr, Chapter 8); and formal features and individual content units within programs (Anderson & Lorch, Chapter 1; Bryant, Zillmann, & Brown, Chapter 9; Huston & Wright, Chapter 2; Krull, Chapter 4; Watt & Welch, Chapter 3). Some of the real progress in research on television viewing, we believe, has been in methodologies for characterizing, presenting, and examining the stimulus; but also, some of the logical inconsistencies, controversies, and replication difficulties may be due to inconsistent or even inadequate methodologies—a point which will be discussed more fully later.

Medium Comparisons. There has been a long history of research that attempts to demonstrate the advantages and disadvantages of one medium of communication over another. Many studies of the 1950s, for example, compared television instruction to classroom teaching, with the general conclusion being that difference between setting-conditions were minimal (e.g., O'Bryan, 1980). In our opinion (with inspiration by Dorr), this is an area of research easily providing the researcher with dangerous preconceptions that point the way to logical pitfalls. One potential pitfall is the notion that a medium of communication can be treated as a unitary entity.

The notion of a communication medium as a unitary entity is probably largely due to McLuhan's (e.g., 1964) creative musings about media, technology, and society. We were told of media that had temperatures (e.g., hot versus cool) and that could be examined without any specific reference to content. Although McLuhan's ideas are often intuitively appealing, they rarely lend themselves to logical analysis or scientific verification. Present day researchers rarely attribute their comparisons of media to McLuhanesque ideas, but they nevertheless frequently treat a medium as a unitary entity. We have serious concerns about such treatments in the absence of rigorous definitions of what is meant by a medium. Television, for example, is constantly evolving both in technology and content. Is television of 1950 the *same* medium as television of 1960, 1970, and 1980? Are comparisons of other media with 525 raster-line, four-network broadcast television of today likely to yield the same results as future comparisons with television having high-definition screens, interactive cable, and multiple programming sources? Without clear definitional constraints as to what constitutes the media being compared, we believe that media comparison research is problematic. An example of such a definitional problem is alluded to in the chapter by Meringoff et al.: A picture storybook read to children by a real person produces different comprehension results than the test of the same book played to children on a tape recorder. The replication failure is a consequence of an unclear idea of whether the receiving context appropriately constitutes part of the storybook medium. The definitional problem is exacerbated when reception of any given content is compared. As noted by Meringoff *et al.*, attempts to make content nearly equivalent may lead to decidedly atypical presentations on one or both media being compared, whereas making presentations of content media-typical usually introduces numerous differences such that observed differences in reception may not be due to the media, but to the differing contents.

A separate problem, but one that at times is apparent in comparisons between media, is the bias that one medium may be inexorably superior to another. This bias can lead to research that, rather than exploring the *differences* between media, attempts to show the weakness of one medium relative to another. This problem is mentioned in relation to television by Singer and Singer insofar as most television research has been designed to reveal potential harmful effects rather than beneficial qualities. This bias is not very apparent in the present contributions but is often clear in other work.

Despite these and many other problems in media-comparison research, there has been some advance in knowledge from this work. Salomon, for example, avoids some of the medium-definition problems by asking his subjects *their* conceptions of medium differences in terms of mental effort required to process information. He shows that these conceptions are reflected in differences in comprehension. He demonstrates, furthermore, that these conceptions of processing requirements are context-bound: The subject changes his or her conception of processing requirements as a function of the demands of the media-consumption setting. Meringoff *et al.* have made substantial progress in preparing stimulus materials which avoid the pitfalls discussed earlier, and in addressing head-on some of the more critical issues in the area.

Comparisons of Classes of Television Programs. It has long been a research strategy to classify television programs into loose groupings based on intended audience, time or day of the week presented, general content, or producer intentions. Various studies have thus used classifications such as children's programs, news, Saturday-morning programs, or educational programs. Content analyses of these groupings have been based on characters and events (e.g., Gerbner & Gross, 1976) or, as discussed by Huston and Wright, on occurrence of various formal features. Such content analyses require heroic labor and also considerable methodological attention to technologies to aid measurement, definition of variables, and interobserver reliability. The research by Huston, Wright, Wartella, Rice, Watkins, Campbell, and Potts (1981), reviewed by Huston and Wright, compares Saturday-morning, educational daytime, and prime-time television programs on a variety of formal features. This work represents a major step in characterizing the nature of the television stimulus. Speculations about the pace and tempo of various program types, for example, can be supported or refuted by referring to their findings. There nevertheless remains a great deal to be done in reporting the methodological, statistical, and definitional details of such content analyses in referred journals, as well as eventually relating the analyses to behavior.

Comparisons between Programs. Any conclusions about the source of relative effects of different television programs is vulnerable to many of the pitfalls of media comparisons. The many statements in the popular and professional literature about the merits of *Mister Rogers' Neighborhood* versus *Sesame Street*, for example, must be tempered by consideration of the many differences in content, production technique, and producer intent. An example of such a comparison comes from assertions by Singer and Singer to the effect that observed differences in the effects of these programs are likely due to differences in "pacing" (Tower, Singer, Singer, & Biggs, 1979; as well as numerous newspaper and magazine articles). At a minimum, before such conclusions are reached, concepts such as pacing must be operationally defined, and program differences in pacing documented. Relationships between these program differences and effects (such as comprehension) should then be carefully explored, attempting to hold other program factors constant or at least to account for them. Watt and Welch in Chapter 3, also interested in pacing differences between *Mister Rogers' Neighborhood* and *Sesame Street,* approach this difficult problem with several strikingly innovative technical approaches to measuring auditory and visual static and dynamic complexity. Their findings do not, however, lead to simple conclusions about pacing differences between the two programs nor about the relationship between pacing and attention or comprehension. It is clear that the Singers have raised an important issue regarding program differences in pacing, and their potential effects, and that Watt and Welch have provided a possibly significant new approach to the problem. A problem remaining to be resolved, however, is the operational correspondence between program pacing as it has been measured by Watt and Welch for *Mister Rogers' Neighborhood* and *Sesame Street;* by Anderson, Levin, and Lorch (1977) for different versions of *Sesame Street;* by Bryant *et al.* for specially created programs; or by Huston *et al.* (1981) for different classes of programming. Until operational descriptions of programs are systematically and clearly applied and the broad range of possible differences between programs experimentally or statistically controlled, conclusions about differences between programs should be entertained most cautiously.

Characters, Events, and Program Structure. A major question that has been repeatedly raised is children's conception of the reality of the things that occur on television. Indeed, as J. Anderson comments, many of the intervention programs designed to produce "critical viewing" include as an objective the comparison of characters and events with "objective" reality. From Singer and Singer's review of research on children's judgments of reality, it is apparent that many investigators have concluded that younger children are less likely than older children to identify what is true or real from an adult perspective. Fernie (1981b), as reviewed by Meringoff *et al.*, reported that younger and older boys tended to wish they were like television characters with super powers, but that older boys were more likely to identify themselves as actually being like real people rather than television characters. Again, the argument is that younger children are less likely to comprehend "objective" reality.

Dorr argues that the concept of "reality" on television must be examined in terms other than the adult experimenter's judgment of what is real. Her analysis of the various ways that a child might interpret the notion of reality led her to examine what in fact a child *means* when he or she says a television event or character is "real." When viewed from this perspective, a child's judgments may not necessarily be seen as "wrong," but they are often based on different criteria than those employed by many adults. Dorr suggests that young children tend not to relate contextual cues to the evaluation of individual characters and events, but that the tendency to do so increases with age and is reflected in reality judgments. Dorr thus has moved the level of discourse on children's understanding of television reality from repeated demonstrations that young children make different reality judgments than adults, to an analysis of why. Such a perspective might lead to a closer examination of the reasons for children's reality judgments reported in earlier studies. Fernie's (1981a) dissertation, for example, reveals that, although younger children are more likely than older children to say they are like a superhero, their reasons indicate a better sense of their judgments of reality. The boys see similarities insofar as they are behaviorally active, because they play superhero games, and the like. These young boys explicitly deny, however, that they themselves have super-hero capabilities.

Dorr's hypothesis that the young child represents television as a set of characters and events somewhat unrelated to larger contexts corresponds to Collins's conclusions based on analyses of school-age children's comprehension of adult action television programs. A decade of Collins's research has revealed, among many other findings, that while young children may remember many individual actions and events from an adult television show, they "often fail to grasp the interscene relations [Collins, p. 129]." Insofar as a connected understanding of the individual events and scenes of a television program is essential to an adult level of comprehension, it is implicit that such comprehension is essential to adult-like judgments of the reality of a television program.

Collins's work has contributed to our knowledge of children's comprehension of television in several regards. Not only are younger children less likely to make relevant scene-relating inferences, they are also more likely to provide idiosyncratic interpretations of television programs based on the limited supply of world knowledge with which they interpret the programs. This knowledge, as mentioned earlier, is likely to be closely related to family socioeconomic status and presumably other characteristics and values. An important insight into children's comprehension processes also comes from Collins's observation that younger children stereotypically apply their knowledge of common event sequences in interpreting a program. They are less likely than older children to notice program-specific deviations from these event sequences.

Collins's research goes far beyond demonstrating that younger children understand less of a television program than older children: He has provided numerous insights as to why and how their understanding is different. Collins has also provided examples of useful methodology in analyzing the content of a television program and using the product of those analyses in developing comprehension questions.

Much, however, remains to be done. Collins has emphasized the importance of a child's general world knowledge as well as inferencing in comprehending an adult television show, but he has only touched on the possible interaction between world knowledge and inference. Trabasso's research on inference provides strong indications that young children are capable of engaging in a variety of inference processes when encountering simple stories (cf. Stein & Trabasso, in press), and this finding has very recently been extended to pre-schoolers' understanding of simple edited television sequences (Smith, Anderson, & Fischer, unpublished data). It may be that young children fail to engage in appropriate inference processes only when their small repository of world knowledge is heavily challenged, as in the complex adult action dramas used by Collins.

D. Anderson and Lorch, as well as Collins, have commented on the relevance of recent research on text analysis for television research. Event chains, scripts, story grammars, and propositional coherence are all concepts recently developed in cognitive science research that are yet to be fully applied to television. We expect that these approaches may have a significant influence on television research in future years.

Formal Features. Huston and Wright, more than any other research group, have drawn attention to the possible importance of the formal features of television in influencing attention, comprehension, and arousal. Their theoretical position has developed on similar lines to that of Anderson and Lorch: Both have moved away from simple "formal features attract attention with ensuing memory" models to more complex formulations such that formal features play important signaling functions for attentional and comprehension strategies. Huston and Wright further emphasize the possible roles that formal features may have in determining comprehension, citing possible functions such as helping the viewer mark and parse content as well as signaling conceptually important content.

Huston and Wright as well as Singer and Singer have differed from Anderson and Lorch on the attention-drawing power of formal features. Anderson and Lorch remark that there have been no demonstrations that formal features attract attention independently of associated content. Bryant, Zillmann, and Brown, however, do provide such a demonstration. In an as yet unpublished study, they determined that experimental insertions of audiovisual "fireworks" unrelated to content enhanced visual attention and information acquisition. This result suggests that formal features indeed can act on attention and information acquisition independently of their relationship to ongoing meaningful content.

Huston and Wright note repeatedly that formal features may have multiple organizing functions for attention, information acquisition, and affective aspects of television viewing. Future research should be directed at demonstrating and clarifying these possible functions, and conceptual work needs to be done on the development of a useful taxonomy of formal features. Additionally, further research is needed on children's comprehension of cinematic conventions as used to convey implied concepts of time, space, action, and psychological perspective. The existing literature (for example, Tada, 1969, as discussed by

Collins) indicates that children have difficulty comprehending the interrelationships between scenes as conveyed by standard cinematic practice. Unpublished research by Smith, Anderson, and Fischer, however, indicates substantial comprehension of content conveyed through cinematic techniques utilizing cuts, fades, pans, and zooms in children 4 years of age. Since television producers apparently introduce formal features to convey content, this aspect of television's form must be thoroughly explored.

TELEVISION-VIEWING BEHAVIORS

Some aspects of observable television-viewing behavior have been studied considerably more than others.

Entering the Viewing Area, Turning on the Television. This element of television viewing has received scant attention, although some insight can be garnered from research in the Uses and Gratifications tradition of media audience analysis. The methods have largely been unstructured observation (e.g., Lull, 1980) or questionnaire procedures (e.g., Greenberg, 1974). The findings clearly indicate that children, like adults, initiate television viewing for a wide variety of reasons and under a range of conditions (e.g., Rubin, 1979).

Contributors to the present volume have not examined this important behavior, but we believe that future research efforts would do well to formally observe the circumstances surrounding children's decisions to watch television.

Program Selection. Given that a viewer decides to watch television, he or she must choose a program. The viewer may have a particular program in mind; may consult a viewer guide; or may run through all the channels, stopping at one, then another, until the selection is made. As the new technologies produce larger and larger numbers of programs from which to choose, identifying the basis for program choice becomes increasingly important. Zillmann and his colleagues are to our knowledge the only researchers to directly study this behavior. In the present volume Bryant, Zillmann, and Brown, Chapter 9 report that features that in general enhance attention also lead to selective exposure. This is a finding with considerable implications for program design and for understanding program appeal and thus needs verification and elaboration.

Attention and Overt Television-Viewing Behaviors. Virtually nothing was known 10 years ago about attention to television except that different programming received different levels of visual attention from children (Bechtel, Achelpohl, & Akers, 1972; Lesser, 1972). Since then a number of laboratories have studied children's attention to television, as reflected in several of the chapters in this volume (Anderson & Lorch, Chapter 1; Bryant et al., Chapter 9; Huston & Wright, Chapter 2; Krull, Chapter 4; Watt & Welch, Chapter 3). This work has led to numerous empirical findings, useful methodological developments, and, recently, the beginnings of serious theoretical development.

One major class of empirical findings is that visual attention is related to the occurrence of various formal features including both visual and auditory features. A substantial part of this relationship is due to the eliciting of visual attention from otherwise inattentive viewers. Hypotheses explaining these relationships include elicitation of the orienting response, enhanced vigilance, learned association of formal features with comprehensible content, and strategic use of formal features to conceptually parse content. At this time there is no basis to firmly exclude any of these hypotheses; instead there is evidence (ranging from meager to substantial) in support of each of them.

Another class of findings concerns the relationship of visual attention to different kinds of content. Anderson and Lorch argue that, at least for young children, there is an important relationship between the comprehensibility of the content and visual attention. Zillmann, Bryant, and their colleagues have examined visual attention to more specific content designations. Their work using humor, for example, shows positive relationships with visual attention regardless of whether the humor is related to the major content of the program.

A much smaller set of findings relates visual attention to aspects of the viewing environment. Several studies have demonstrated that visual attention is modified by the presence of coviewers and by the availability of alternative activities. It is quite apparent that future research or application utilizing visual attention measures must carefully consider the context in which the measures are taken.

Anderson and Lorch (Chapter 1) and Krull (Chapter 4) have observed an attentional phenomenon that they have labeled "attentional inertia." This phenomenon, which serves to maintain visual attention across wide variations in content, has not been described in the attentional literature outside of television viewing. It is apparent that future research should apply multiple convergent operations to explore the dimensions of attentional inertia including its generality beyond television viewing. Bryant et al. (Chapter 9) comment on an analogous phenomenon in program selection: The longer a viewer leaves a particular program on, the less likely he or she is to change the channel. This notion of audience carryover is widespread in television programming strategy (e.g., Wakshlag & Greenberg, 1979) but has yet to be explored through formal experimentation.

Finally, there has been little integration of the scattered few studies that examine television-related behaviors while attending to television. Children comment on programs, respond to questions posed by characters, ask questions about content, display emotional responses to television fare, dance to television music, and the like. Documentation of these phenomena has ranged from anecdotal to formal research, but there is presently little information on the frequency of occurrence of such behavior outside the laboratory, its causes, the content of the behaviors, or consequences of such active involvement with television. It is often popularly noted that television viewing is an apparently "passive" activity, but the frequency and importance of "active" viewing remains to be determined.

Inattention and Secondary Activities. A television "viewer" may spend substantial portions of time in front of a television set, looking at it only infrequently, often engaged in a secondary activity. There is a distinct paucity of research on the nature of this apparently inattentive behavior. The issues that need to be considered include the degree to which an apparently inattentive viewer is attending auditorily and the frequency and nature of involvement in secondary activities.

Auditory attention to television has yet to be intensively examined. Conflicting inferences about auditory attention have been made based on comprehension and visual attention findings, but a few studies by Friedlander and his colleagues (e.g., Friedlander, 1975) stand as the only direct effort. They report that young children are oddly insensitive to the meaningfulness of television dialogue—a notion with substantial implications but also one which requires substantial inquiry and verification.

Secondary activities in front of the television set have frequently been commented on but not substantially assessed. If secondary activities occupy a substantial portion of viewing time, then the notion of television having effects through "displacement" of other activities has to be reconsidered. The frequently cited but unpublished study by Williams (Chapter 11 by Singer & Singer), for example, includes as a major explanatory concept that X hours of watching television displaces X hours of some other activity. Before such a concept can be fully accepted, we need descriptive information on the kinds and frequency of secondary activities and subsequently detailed studies of their nature. It may be that play in front of television is desultory and unimaginative relative to play without television, that social interactions are superficial, and that work accomplished is merely rote. Before such conclusions are reached, however, serious descriptive and experimental research is required.

Turning Off the Television, Leaving the Viewing Area. Why do people stop watching television? This straightforward but important question has received little attention from behavioral researchers. Likely reasons for turning off the television include: end of the program, time for bed, time for meals, time to engage in another prearranged activity, lack of interest in the programs available, unexpected distraction, parent or other demanding the set be turned off, and the like. It is striking that while many books and articles have been written bemoaning the amount of television viewing and that, while numerous intervention programs have been developed to inoculate the child viewer against the potential evils of television viewing (see J. Anderson, Chapter 12), we know virtually nothing about why viewing stops.

Related to this question is temporary leave-taking from the viewing area. There is no systematic descriptive information available as to how frequently viewers leave, for how long, for what reasons, or how leave-taking relates to ongoing content. From D. Anderson's time-lapse videotapes of family home television viewing, it is apparent that leave-taking is frequent, but the data have not at this writing been coded and analyzed.

THE TELEVISION-VIEWING ENVIRONMENT

Television viewing occurs in a context: physical *and* social. An area of little research is the description of the physical context of television viewing and the relationship of context to television-viewing behavior and its consequences. The availability of a television in a child's bedroom, for example, may produce different viewing behaviors and consequences as compared to availability of a television in the kitchen. The physical location and surroundings of a television are obviously part of the determinants of social interaction around television. For example, a set in an area of high family activity is likely to provide a considerably more active social context for television viewing than a more isolated set. Although accounting for such ecological determinants of television viewing has not been an area of research interest, it has obvious implications for understanding individual differences in amounts of viewing and is an area for possible intervention strategies (cf. Howe & Solomon, 1979)

Lesser's (1972) characterization of the "zombie" and other styles of television viewing has been often quoted and qualified (e.g., Bryant et al. Chapter 9). In fact, individual differences in style of viewing have only been considered anecdotally. In spite of this we have gained some useful, albeit incomplete, information about individual differences. There is now good evidence that attention to television increases throughout the preschool years (see Anderson & Lorch, Chapter 1), although information about school-age and older television viewing is sketchy at best. Sex differences in television viewing in the preschool years are not apparent, but by the school-age years dramatic differences in program and topic preferences emerge (see Mielke, Chapter 10). It is not clear whether these preferences are also reflected in attention. Collins's chapter shows that in younger children comprehension differences are related to family background and sex-role attitudes, but that these individual differences tend to disappear in older children. Salomon not only notes possible cultural differences in television comprehension, but also provides evidence that these differences are related to the perceived difficulty of processing the information.

It is apparent that much more work can be done on individual differences in viewing style, comprehension, and what viewers find entertaining. The research on the effects of televised violence has often emphasized individual differences in susceptibility. Many other areas of television research could benefit from such an emphasis.

Methodology

To some extent the history of scientific progress is also the history of progress in scientific methodology. Research on children's television is replete with difficult problems requiring methodological innovation. Although many of the problems of methodology are problems faced by other areas of behavioral science, many are unique to television research. A number of the present contributors have touched on these issues. Watt and Welch describe novel and highly innovative techniques for measuring static and dynamic stimulus complexity via physical measurement and analytic devices more usually found in the physical sciences. Although it remains to be seen how generally useful their novel approach will be, it represents one direction of potential advance in measurement of the stimulus.

Another essential methodological advance over earlier approaches is found in the ability of a number of laboratories to systematically modify and/or create video stimuli for expermental purposes. Experiments using such "prepared" stimuli were discussed in this volume by Anderson and Lorch, Chapter 1; Bryant et al., Chapter 9; Collins, Chapter 5; and Huston and Wright, Chapter 2; and Meringoff et al., Chapter 6. The growing sophistication of behavioral researchers in controlling the video stimulus should result in considerably clearer future understanding of the effects of particular aspects of the television medium.

When working with children, methodologies for testing and observation are critical. Meringoff et et al. (Chapter 6) discuss the importance of using a variety of testing approaches, and we believe Collins's (Chapter 5) work reflects special care and innovation in developing comprehension questions and analyzing answers.

One important addition to research methodologies on children's television viewing has been provided by Singer and Singer: longitudinal assessment. A recent study with adults employed longitudinal treatment and assessment in determining the effects of massive exposure to pornography. The findings indicate that the results from longitudinal treatment differ dramatically from those of "one shot" studies (Zillmann & Bryant, in press). Studies of individual differences, the viewing environment, medium differences, and the like require long-term assessment in order to provide accurate, useful, and comprehensive findings.

Another area in which we have been somewhat remiss is in integrating with other developing areas of clearly related research, such as basic research on what types of programming children find to be entertaining (e.g., Zillmann, Hay, & Bryant, 1975). Formative research for Sesame Street, The Electric Company, and the like has typically included appeal as a critical factor for assessment. Our research programs have typically deemphasized this construct and other elements relating to developmental aesthetics. At another level, the relationship between autonomic and cortical arousal and children's attention to and comprehension of television has seldom been given ample attention in our models and protocols (cf. Zillmann, in press; Krull, Chapter 4).

Much more remains to be done. We have already commented on the need for better characterizations of television program content. In addition, methods for assessing auditory attention need to be developed, a variety of techniques should be worked on for field observations, and methods for testing very young children should be improved. Obviously methodologies must evolve to fit the questions that emerge from our growing knowledge and theoretical sophistication. We are optimistic they will do so.

Theory

There is no general theory of television viewing that can satisfactorily deal with all the elements of Figures 13.1 and 13.2; nor is there likely to be for some time. As evidenced in many of the chapters in this volume, however, there is active theoretical and pretheoretical development on some of the subsystems of television viewing. D. Anderson and Lorch develop a set of theoretical premises that attempt to link comprehension processes, formal features, attentional inertia, and secondary activities in order to account for visual attention to television. Huston and Wright develop a set of theoretical principles that they apply to ongoing attention, comprehension, and motivational processes. Watt and Welch develop statistical models of the interrelationship between formal features, attention, and comprehension, to which they apply some theoretical interpretation. Collins presents a wealth of hypotheses and theoretical possibilities that very nearly amount to a theory of comprehension. Dorr provides hypotheses on the nature of children's reality judgments which would have to be seriously considered as part of a theory of comprehension. Singer and Singer speculate on a large set of possible mediating factors that may account for television's long-term effects on behavior. It is apparent that the field is rich with theoretical hypotheses and even has some small theories on restricted aspects of television viewing. Eventually, as our data base grows, the empirical anchor points will be available for theoretical development of a larger sort. Given our lack of knowledge about many basic issues of television viewing, however, we suggest that, at the present time, such a theory would likely be premature.

Applications

Meringoff et al. (Chapter 6) end their chapter with the assertion that research of the type contained in this volume has application both for television production and for informing parents about television's effects on their children. Indeed, many of the contributors to this volume consult with educational and commercial television producers, speak to parents' groups, grant press interviews on television effects, and write popular magazine articles about children and television. It remains to be seen, however, the degree to which research proves to be useful for television production and/or parental understanding. In his chapter on the production of *3–2–1 CONTACT*, for example, Mielke gave no indication that academic research had proven to be particularly relevant for the program (except for some general non-television-related developmental research). Rather, the research which apparently proved to be most useful was done in-house, was highly specific to the needs of the program, and, due to practical limitations of such formative research, is probably of limited generality. Granted, Mielke did not have the benefit of access to most of the research reported here at the time *3–2–1 CONTACT* was developed, but it is not clear that he or another producer would find this research useful in the ways it has been presented. Documentation of the practical use and misuse of basic research on television viewing would be of considerable interest. Most discussions of research in educational television extol the virtue of in-house formative research but remain silent about the usefulness of research that attempts to establish general "truths."

A similar issue exists concerning advice given parents. Our reading of much of the popular literature on television is that research is often oversimplified and distorted. In medical research, a result must be replicated in several laboratories before it is ordinarily translated into medical practice. Behavioral researchers should be no less subject to such restrictions. It is highly tempting in a newspaper interview or magazine article to apply the unreplicated results of an as yet unpublished study to parental practice at home, but it is our view that in the long run such premature advice will dilute the impact that truly solid, replicated, integrated findings could have.

It may be that efforts by the society to grapple with the impact of television will in any case ignore relevant research findings. For example, J. Anderson's (Chapter 12) review of the critical viewer intervention projects shows no evidence that basic research on the nature of television viewing entered into the formulation of those projects. Rather, the projects appear to have been based on a set of goals developed from implicit value systems reflecting the intervenor's philosophical perspectives on the nature of childhood. If relevant research had been available in the development of these intervention programs, it is not clear that it would have been utilized. The public presentation and practical use of research findings constitute a difficult set of issues. We guess that they will be a matter of debate for some time.

The Future

Only one thing appears to be certain about the future of research on television viewing: It will be different. Two major problems will have to be faced, and progress to some extent will depend on how they are dealt with. One problem is straightforward: Television research is more expensive than a good deal of other behavioral science research. A well-functioning research program has to have access to a variety of expensive video technologies, requires access to computers, and presents labor requirements that are often substantial. At this time it is not clear that, with United States government cutbacks in social science research, more than a few research groups will be able to operate in a substantial manner. Given the many issues that remain to be explored, the problem of funding has to be overcome if any rapid progress is to be made.

The second problem is how to confront the explosive changes in television technology. The television medium in the United States is changing from a system of limited choice of programs to cable or direct satellite broadcasting of dozens to perhaps hundreds of programs. Already these changes are reflected in not only more of what went before, but also new television content: esoteric sports, new kinds of religious programs, first-run movies, pornography, and high culture. It is likely that these changes in content will by themselves rapidly change our stereotyped conceptions of the medium of television, but more and different content is only a part of the change. There are enormous economic incentives for business to underwrite interactive text and information services since these services can form the technological and information base for commercial transactions directly from homes. With interactive systems in place, interactive entertainment and educational television will also emerge. Experimental interactive children's programs such as *Ready, Set, Go* on the QUBE system already appear to be drawing strong audience enthusiasm and program loyalty, despite low production budgets. Insofar as technical developments allow interactive programs to proliferate, television may become a different medium in relation to its impact on children. Already, the new medium of the video game is drawing enormous participation from children followed by many of the same public alarms directed at form, content, and time displacement that we have heard so often directed at television. As home computers proliferate and as programmable interactive videodisc systems begin to appear in homes, highly sophisticated interactive television will become possible. When these developments are supplemented by high-definition color displays, new large screen formats, three-dimensional pictures, and high-quality stereo sound, the possible cumulative change in the medium over the next several decades is staggering.

If research on the impact of television is to have any future coherence, we are going to have to try to assess which factors of television viewing are relatively timeless and universal and which are relatively time-bound and context-dependent. Certainly we must be careful about our generalizations based on the medium as it is now to the medium as it will be. Even as we try to understand basic processes underlying present media usage, we must at the same time struggle to assess the impact of the new technologies. In a historical sense, we have a unique opportunity. Rather than reacting years later to developments already in place, we can attempt to understand their impact as they occur. The future decades present us with challenging but exciting times.

References

Anderson, D. R., Levin, S. R., & Lorch, E. P. The effects of TV program pacing on the behavior of preschool children. *AV Communication Review*, 1977, *25*, 159–166.
Bechtel, R. B., Achelpohl, C., & Akers, R. Correlates between observed behavior and questionnaire responses on television viewing. In E. A. Rubinstein, G. A. Comstock, & J. P. Murray (Eds.), *Television and social behavior, (Vol. 4): Television in day-to-day life: Patterns of use.* Washington, D.C.: U.S. Government Printing Office, 1972.
Fernie, D. E. *Boys' understanding of television and real-life models.* Unpublished doctoral dissertation, University of Massachusetts, 1981. (a)
Fernie, D. E. Ordinary and extraordinary people: Children's understanding of television and real-life models. In H. Kelly & H. Gardner (Eds.), *New directions for child development.* San Francisco: Jossey-Bass 1981. (b)
Friedlander, B. Z. Automated evaluation of selective listening in language-impaired and normal infants and young children. In B. F. Friedlander, G. M. Starrett, & G. E. Kirk (Eds.), *Exceptional infant* (Vol. 3). New York: Brunner–Mazel, 1975.
Gerbner, G., & Gross, L. Living with television: The violence profile. *Journal of Communication*, 1976, *26*(2), 173–199.
Greenberg, B. S. Gratifications of television viewing and their correlates for British children. In J. G. Blumler & E. Katz (Eds.), *The uses of mass communication: Current perspectives on gratifications research.* Beverly Hills, Calif.: Sage, 1974.
Himmelweit, H. T. Social influence in television. In S. B. Withey & R. P. Ables (Eds.), *Television and social behavior: Beyond violence and children.* Hillsdale, N.J.: Erlbaum, 1980.
Howe, L. W., & Solomon, B. *How to raise children in a TV world.* New York: Hart, 1979.
Huston, A. C., Wright, J. C., Wartella, E., Rice, M. L., Watkins, B. A., Campbell, T., & Potts, R. Communicating more than content: Formal features of children's television programs. *Journal of Communication*, 1981, *31*(3), 32–48.
Lesser, G. S. Assumptions behind the production and writing methods in *Sesame Street.* In W. Schramm (Ed.), *Quality in instructional television.* Honolulu: University Press of Hawaii, 1972.
Lull, J. The social uses of television. *Human Communication Research*, 1980, *6*, 197–209.
McLuhan, M. *Understanding media: The extensions of man.* New York: McGraw-Hill, 1964.
O'Bryan, K. G. The teaching face: A historical perspective. In E. L. Palmer & A. Dorr (Eds.), *Children and the faces of television: Teaching, violence, selling.* New York: Academic Press, 1980.

Rubin, A. M. Television use by children and adolescents. *Human Communication Research*, 1979, 5, 109–120.

Smith, R., Anderson, D. R., & Fischer, C. *Children's comprehension of television montage*. Unpublished data, University of Massachusetts.

Stein, N. L., & Trabasso, T. What's in a story: Critical issues in comprehension and instruction. In R. Glaser (Ed.), *Advances in the psychology of instruction* (Vol. 2). Hillsdale, N.J.: Erlbaum, in press.

Tada, T. Image-cognition: A developmental approach. In *Studies of Broadcasting*. Tokyo: Nippon Hoso Kyokai, 1969.

Tower, R. B., Singer, D. G., Singer, J. L., & Biggs, A. Differential effects of television programming on preschoolers' cognition, imagination, and social play. *American Journal of Orthopsychiatry*, 1979, 49, 265–281.

Wakshlag, J. J., & Greenberg, B. S. Programming strategies and the popularity of television programming for children. *Human Communication Research*, 1979, 6, 58–68.

Zillmann, D. Cognitive and affective influence: Television viewing and arousal. In D. Pearl, L. Bouthilet, & J. Lazar (Eds.), *Television and behavior: Ten years of scientific progress and implications for the eighties*. Washington, D.C.: U.S. Government Printing Office, in press.

Zillmann, D., & Bryant, J. Effects of massive exposure to pornography. In N. M. Malamuth & E. Donnerstein (Eds.), *Pornography and sexual aggression*. New York: Academic Press, in press.

Zillmann, D., Hay, T. A., & Bryant, J. The effect of suspense and its resolution on the appreciation of dramatic presentations. *Journal of Research in Personality*, 1975, 9, 307–323.

Author Index

Subject Index